AMERICAN DAWN

AMERICAN DAWN

A New Model of American Prehistory

by LOUIS A. BRENNAN

The Macmillan Company

Collier-Macmillan Ltd., London

ACKNOWLEDGMENTS

For permission to reprint copyrighted material the following acknowledgments are gratefully made to:

Douglas D. Anderson for excerpts from "A Stone Age Campsite at the Gateway to America," copyright © 1968 by Scientific American, Inc. All rights reserved.

J. L. Coe for excerpts from "The Formative Cultures of the Carolina Piedmont" in *Transactions*, American Philosophical Society, 1964.

Carleton S. Coon for excerpts from *The Origin of Races*, copyright © 1962. Reprinted by permission of Alfred A. Knopf, Inc.

Calvin J. Huesser for excerpts from *Late-Pleistocene Environments*. Reprinted by permission of the American Geographical Society.

David M. Hopkins for excerpts from "The Cenozoic History of Beringia—A Synthesis" in *The Bering Land Bridge*. Reprinted by permission of Stanford University Press.

The Macmillan Company
866 Third Avenue, New York, N.Y. 10022
Collier-Macmillan Canada Ltd., Toronto, Ontario

Library of Congress Catalog Card Number: 71-93718

FIRST PRINTING

Printed in the United States of America

FOR
Mauck AND *Sig*
AND THE MANY YEARS
WE DUG TOGETHER

Contents

AMERICAN DAWN

1

The Subject Is Models

THE FIRST ACCOUNT of contact between prehistoric America
and the rest of the world is that written in A.D. 1127 by Ari the
Learned in the *Islandinga Bok*, which reads, in the translation
by my friend Sigfus Olafson (all four of whose grandparents
were immigrants from Iceland to Minnesota), as follows:

> The land that is called Greenland was discovered and settled out
> of Iceland. It was a man named Eric the Red who went out from
> here to there and occupied that land which has since been called
> Ericsfiord. He gave the land a name, and called it Greenland, and
> said that men would more readily go there if it had a fair name.
> They found there the works of men, both in the eastern and western
> settlements, and boat fragments [Olafson explains that *keipl*, "small
> boat," is a deprecatory term, implying that the seagoing Norse did
> not think highly of the wrecks of what were probably kayaks] and
> tools of stone. From this it may be understood that these were the
> kind of people who occupied Vinland and whom Greenlanders call
> Skraelings. It was then that Eric undertook settlement of the land
> [Greenland] fourteen or fifteen winters before Christianity came
> here to the island [Iceland] as this was told to Thorkell Gellison
> who himself followed Eric the Red out [to Greenland].

Christianity came to Iceland in A.D. 1000, the date given by
oral tradition for the settlement of Vinland by Eric's son Leif

the Lucky, which would put Eric's settlement of Greenland at
A.D. 985 or 986. Thus Ari the Learned was writing over a century after the traditional settlement of Greenland and Vinland;
but there is no good reason for doubting the historical truth of
his note, since the existence of both colonies has been verified.

One wonders whether there was not, in Eric's company or
among the Vinland colonists who confronted these Skraelings
more personally and violently, a speculative mind to ask, "Who
are these people, that they do not have metal and do not farm
or herd stock or build cities, when all the rest of the world
does?" If there was such, he did not speak up, and we must
assume that the Norse thought of the Skraelings only as the
people who had always been in Greenland and Vinland, as the
Norse had always been in Norway. You took the whale-path
west-over-sea and there they were, with their backwoods stone
tools and their funny little boats.

The subject did not come up again until Columbus had made
the acquaintance of the inhabitants of the New World and,
thinking them Asiatics, mistakenly dubbed them Indians. Probably this misconception was in the mind of Father Acosta, the
Spaniard who first suggested, shortly after Magellan's circum-
navigation of the earth, that Asia must approach the Western
Hemisphere rather closely somewhere to its northeast. Very
probably the first expression of the hypothesis that America had
actually been populated from Asia by Mongols, Tartars in the
terminology of the day, was that of the Englishman Thomas
Gage in his "English-American, a New Survey of the West
Indies" (1648). He called attention to the similarities between
the Tartars and their American neighbors across the water,
particularly in their barbarous and uncivil temperaments, and
made what seems to have been the inspired guess that Tartar-
land and some part of western America, if not actually joined,
were "disjoynted by but a small strait."

This small strait appears as the Strait of Anian on a world
map by Adam Aigneler in 1664, but it was not explored and
established by longitude and latitude until the 1776–77 Pacific
voyage of Captain James Cook, who sailed through it searching
for the presumptive Northwest Passage between the Pacific and

the Atlantic. This confirmation of the existence of the strait, "only about thirteen hours [sailing time] in width," came to the attention of the Jesuit Father Ignaz Pfefferkorn, a German, as he was writing his *Description of the Province of Sonora* (1794–95, translated in 1949 by T. E. Treutlein). He had intended to begin his treatise, said Father Pfefferkorn, with the conjecture of such a strait across which "people and animals might pass without difficulty from one continent to the other." The strait no longer being conjecture, he stated a premise—and seems to have been the first to state it—which, all Americanists agree, is the basis of American archaeology and prehistory: "To me, it is almost certain that the first inhabitants of America really came by way of this strait."

To the reader with a globe in his library this appears to be self-evident, an insight in no way remarkable; it seems no farther from Asia to Alaska than one could row a boat, if he particularly liked rowing boats. But the distance is some fifty-one miles, although there is a landfall on the Diomede Islands halfway across through very rough and dangerously chill water. And when you get down to the specifics of how and when man first crossed from the Eastern Hemisphere to the Western Hemisphere, you find that the fifty-one miles does not narrow down the problems at all; as a matter of fact it is not even relevant to them.

But by 1955, five years after the advent of dating by radioactive carbon (C_{14}) and the acceptance by most archaeologists of the validity of its results, American prehistorians were taking it for granted that they knew not only who the Asiatics were who transformed themselves into Americans during the progress of a day's journey, but how and when and why they did. All these answers they assembled into what used to be called an hypothesis, but is now being called a model, of the American genesis. We shall call this the standard model, since it is what most American archaeologists would describe if called on to make such a presentation.

On October 4, 1956, however, Soviet Russia projected Sputnik into orbit, and it scared scientific America out of its complacency like a firecracker at a picnic. Catch-up-with-Russia money, from the government, foundations, and business, began to flow into research—all kinds of research—so that at the end of the first post-Sputnik decade, *The New York Times*, in its issue of January 7, 1967, was able to say that more than half the research ever done in the world in pursuit of knowledge had been done in the previous ten years.

Although it contributes nothing to the pursuit of the cold war, the hot war, the war on poverty, or the war between the sexes, American archaeology has shared in the new affluence of research in general. The result is a replacement model of American prehistory that makes the standard model look its years. The comparison of the two, in the light of recent investigations, will occupy us for the next few hundred pages.

2

Up the Down Corridor

THE STANDARD MODEL of American prehistory has the mythic simplicity and instant plausibility of the story of Adam and Eve. The Western Hemisphere was a magnificent Garden of Eden and a roving band of men and women found it and their descendants possessed it and filled it, in time, from the Arctic Circle to Land's End in South America.

The anthropological details that you will hear in the classrooms are that this band was of racially Mongoloid hunters who crossed, about fifteen to twenty thousand years ago, from eastern Siberia to Alaska, by a then-existent isthmus or land bridge. These hunters are called the Clovis people, after a locality in New Mexico where the distinctive stone spearpoints that are their mark of identity have been found scattered among the bones of the mammoths they had killed; it was on this big, all-purpose game animal that they relied for food and hides, as the Plains Indians of historic times depended on the buffalo.

Those whose file of *National Geographic* magazines reaches back to December, 1955, have seen what they are thought to have looked like. In his illustrations for an article entitled "Ice Age Man, the First American," written under the eye of the late Frank H. H. Roberts, in his day a specialist on the First

Americans, artist Andre Durenceau conceived them as being squat and sturdy of build, with skins the color of weathered copper, manes of crow-black hair, and flat, stolid Mongoloid-Eskimoid faces. One double-page spread, in color, shows a statuesquely arranged, three-generation grouping of them, babe-in-arms to dotard, huddled together calf-deep in snow, clad in loose wraps of hide, and facing into a rising blizzard against a background of blasted heath and imperturbable woolly mammoths. The picture caption reads, "America's Pioneer Family Crosses an Ancient Land Bridge Out of Asia."

The only detail of "Ice Age Man, the First American" that the licensed lecturer would change to bring it up to date in 1970 is the date of the crossing. It was given there as twenty thousand years ago. But the oldest date on a Clovis site that has since been proved by C14 is about 11,700 B.P. (before present), or some eight thousand years later, and the discrepancy has reversed the mild liberal trend of the 1950's toward thinking of the arrival of the Earliest Americans as earlier and earlier into a conviction that it was later and later. This was a bit of a comeback for the conservatives who had once laid down the laws of Americanist studies and who had fallen from power when C14 dating, on sites like Clovis, had at first seemed to make a mockery of their canon that man had been in America for no more than six thousand years.

The present view about the Earliest Americans has been summed up by Edward P. Lanning and Thomas C. Patterson in the November, 1967, issue of *Scientific American*, in their account of discoveries in South America called "Early Man in South America": "The interpretation of American prehistory that is most widely accepted at present holds that the Clovis complex represents the [North American] continent's earliest human occupation." (This is not the view of Lanning and Patterson, since it is controverted by their discoveries of non-Clovisian, pre-Clovisian, sites in Peru. Obviously, if there was a pre-Clovisian man in Peru, there must have been a pre-Clovisian man in North America, since the only humanly traversible route to South America lies across North America. The discoveries of Lanning and Patterson will be discussed later in their proper place.)

The current consensus doctrine has it that after the crossing depicted by Durenceau, the Clovisians had to take up residence in Alaska for some centuries, perhaps millennia, because the Wisconsin glacier lay across Canada, from the Atlantic to the Pacific, to the south and cast of them. There were parts of Alaska where the precipitation was light enough to prevent the buildup of glacier-making snowfields, and in this open country the vegetation was sufficient to support large herds of the big-game animals: mammoth, bison, horse, and other browsers and grazers. Since these animals were the major source of food, it follows that the Clovisians were hunters, not vegetarians, or they would not have come to Alaska in the first place.

There could not have been many of them. The Durenceau painting is certainly accurate by this much: the community unit was the family-sized band. (There was, indeed, a First Family of America, no matter what view is taken of the peopling of the hemisphere.) During the generations when the Wisconsin ice mass barred any further roving, the First Family would have been joined by other bands whose livelihood depended on big game; and the New World can be said to have finally been claimed by the human race some two million years after its birth in Africa.

So slow was the increase in population among hunters—two or three per band every hundred years—and so dismal was the region in which they lived, that it is doubtful if more than two hundred or so Clovisians would ever have made Wisconsin-period Alaska their home. The record, however, does not corroborate even this, for there are no Clovis kill or hearth sites in Alaska for this or any other time. The few scattered spear-points of Clovis design found in Alaska are much better explained as having been dropped by Clovis spearmen wandering *northward* from the area of the present United States, where there are plenty of Clovis sites, than by hunters out of Siberia, where there are no Clovis sites at all.

The persistent failure, throughout four decades, to find Clovis sites in Alaska or Siberia, despite the diligent search, has cramped the standard view painfully. It must now be postulated that it was not the Clovisians who crossed the Bering bridge, but their so-far unidentified ancestors, who were like the

Clovisians in every way except that they had not yet invented
the Clovis spearpoint. This innovation came, it is said, either
just before or just after the Wisconsin ice opened up, like the
Red Sea for the Israelites, and let the Clovisians through to the
promised southland.

According to standard-model reckoning, this opening came
about fifteen thousand years ago, when a corridor split open
between the eastern and western ice masses as they began to
melt apart. The eastern mass had formed at two centers: one in
Labrador, called the Laurentian or Laurentide, and the other on
the shore of Hudson Bay, called the Keewatin. The Laurentide
and Keewatin masses had quickly joined, and this combined
mass had moved westward to meet what is called the Cordilleran glacier, which had formed in the region called the Cordillera that includes the Pacific coastal ranges on the west and
the Rocky Mountains in the interior. The hiatus between the
Cordilleran and the Keewatin-Laurentide masses, which had
gradually disappeared as they spread toward each other, thus
ran north and south, a long, narrowing, isthmus-like corridor
of ice-free land connecting Alaska and the non-glaciated south.
Since it had been the last bare earth to be covered by ice, it
was the first ground to be bared when the ice masses began to
recede. The recession was a reversal of the advance, the masses
melting at the edges back toward the centers from which they
had come, enormous lakes shrinking back into the basins from
which they had overflowed.

But it should not be inferred that the corridor closed or
opened its whole length simultaneously, like the lid of a box.
The southern end, being in a warmer latitude, would have been
the last segment to close and the first to open. The joining and
disjoining can be imagined as a zipper on a coat of ice, the
tab being pulled from north to south to close, and vice versa to
open. The result was more an up corridor than a down one.
This being so, the thought naturally occurs that if there were
men living south of the ice, they had probably followed the
rupture of the ice front north as the warmth zipped it open and
were leaning on their spears watching when the last ice block
went up in smog and liberated the Alaskan Clovisians.

But the proponents of the standard model will have none of this. How, they say, could there have been any men south of the ice before the corridor opened? They mean, of course, the corridor of fifteen thousand years ago, not the one that was open from about twenty-seven to twenty-five thousand years ago —too early, they say, to have allowed for the remotest chance of human migration. It was too early because stone spearheads were not being used in this part of the world twenty-five thousand years ago and the Clovisians, who the standard model says are the Earliest Americans, most certainly did make stone spearheads. This kind of argument, called begging the question, would not be acceptable in debating circles; but it has been frequently made plain by its board of governors that archaeology is not debatable—it is only decretory.

There is another way to answer this argument, and any third-string quarterback knows it: when you can't go through the opposition, go around. Archaeological scholars have done very little with this stratagem, but we shall, at the first opportunity. Meanwhile we must continue with our exposition of the standard model.

This model supposes that the Clovisians or ancestral Clovisians, once the ice barrier was lowered, came pell-mell down the corridor, all two hundred, or three hundred or four hundred, of them, and, by a miracle of propagation on the fly, had spread themselves within less than two thousand years all across the present United States—there is a site in Florida with a C14 date of 10,000 B.P.—and to the farthest tip of South America, where there is a cave site with a date of about 10,500 B.P.

Even more remarkable than their fertility was their gift of tongues. The late Morris Swadesh, probably the foremost authority of his day on American aboriginal linguistics, estimated that 2,200 languages were being spoken here when the white man first walked on the stage in a speaking part.

And that is all there is to the standard model: a long walk by a single tribe—we must call them a tribe because they were all makers of the same distinctive type of spearpoint, which must have been a tradition handed down through blood-kinship lines—and everything aboriginally American follows. It was once thought that other Asians in similar population movements had taken the Clovisian track somewhat later, about six thousand years ago, and had brought with them a hunting-gathering way of life called, not too descriptively, Archaic; but the diligent post-Sputnik decade disposed of that notion. People were following the Archaic pattern of subsistence in caves all over North America by ten thousand years ago, and if they brought that pattern from Asia, they were traveling the corridor at the same time as the Clovisians. But the corridor, after all these years, has yielded no more evidence of their passage than of the Clovisians'.

And this, dialectic aside, is the fatal weakness of the standard model. Plain archaeology—finding sites, digging them up, and recording and dating what has been dug—does not sustain it. Projectile points of the Clovis pattern found within the precincts of the erstwhile corridor are later by a millennium or more than the typical Clovis sites in New Mexico and Arizona and by nearly two millennia than the oldest fluted point in America

Clovis Fluted.

(found in Orange County, New York), for which the startling age of 12,530 ± 370 years was established in June, 1969. No Clovisians ever came down the corridor; when they got as far north as Canada they were going up the corridor, and it was somebody else who was coming down.

It is neither necessary nor desirable to take a hard line about

this corridor. If there were men in Alaska when it opened, they certainly used it; and we would have them use it, because the polyglot, widely settled world of aboriginal America needs all the adits we can find to explain it. They were certainly hunters, since there was almost no other way to make a living in glacial-period Alaska, and they would have followed their familiar prey: mammoth, bison, and horse, which roamed the southern sward in even greater numbers than in Alaska. There is evidence of these hunters, superior craftsmen who handled flint like the gemstone it is, in the projectile points they made, with beautifully controlled flaking—known as the Eden, the Scottsbluff, and the Angostura or Long—that are as fine as any work in flint anywhere in the world. But these were not Clovisians.

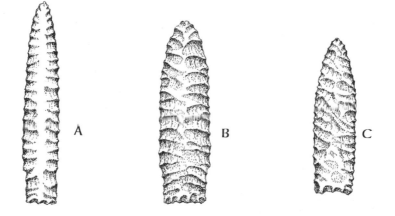

(*a*) Eden. (*b*) Scottsbluff. (*c*) Angostura.

The objection to the standard-model corridor of fifteen thousand years ago is not as passageway but as Fallopian tube. It did not bring into the unglaciated south its firstborn, nor did it guide there the Clovisians, who were *not*, by many generations, America's firstborn (nor immigrants either). It was a secondary road, not a turnpike, an overflow pipe, not a flume. It was used only by trade-union hunters, not by the Archaic-pattern foragers and gatherers óf the humbler produce of the

earth, who probably never tasted loin of mammoth or brisket of
horse in their lives. It may not even have existed in 15,000 B.P.
And, not least of all, if it did exist in 15,000 B.P., to bring the
Clovisians down it is to do them an injustice. Their fore-
fathers were already here. The evidence is in the Clovis fluted
point.

Readers of this or any literature on New World prehistory,
if they are also generally familiar with Old World archaeology,
will notice, sooner or later, that little attention is paid in Old
World studies to the form and attributes of stone projectile
points, while there is scarcely a page of the literature of Early
Man in America without its mention of Clovis or Folsom,
Sandia or Lerma points. In America the stone point is the
single most helpful hint to the identity of its maker and his

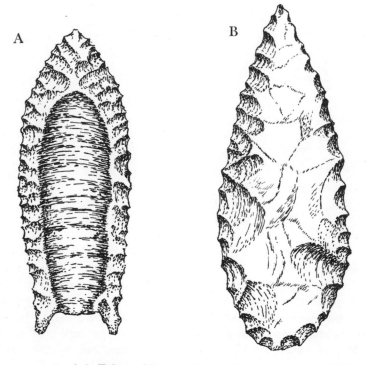

(a) Folsom Fluted. (b) Lerma.

other concerns from the beginning of stone-point manufacture until ceramic pottery began to be made forty-five hundred to three thousand years ago. In Europe and elsewhere, the total stone industry, much more uniform in technique and richer in tool types, provides the clues to cultural and chronological placement. But America can boast no such succession of differentiated working methods and tool production as the Clactonian, Abbevillian, Acheulean, Mousterian, Aurignacian, Solutrean, Magdalenian, Azilian, Tardenoisian, and the others of Europe, Africa, and Asia. Although Amerind flint knappers used all the chipping techniques known in the Old World, there is a certain journeyman look about much American workmanship, as though the workman belonged to no particular school of practice, or to all. Projectile points turned out by the millions are by far the most common artifacts made in aboriginal America that show variability of design as well as of method and skill in handling stone, and the styles run into the hundreds. At least a dozen catalogues have been compiled of these styles, and the end of cataloguing is not yet in sight. To know all the styles would be like knowing all the makes and yearly models of automobiles produced in the United States since the motorization of wheels, including the Edsel and the Stanley Steamer.

The Clovis industry is one of the exceptions to the Amerind rule of generalized stone working; it is distinguishable usually by two characteristic tools, the snub-nosed-end or end-and-side scraper, often with an incising or perforating spur at one or both corners of the broad end, thought to be a hide-working tool; and the Clovis fluted point, the most prized find in American archaeology. It is the point that gives the Clovisians their star quality. It has a pleasing, classic simplicity of outline, being lanceolate, with parallel or gently arcuate blade edges and no stem or extrusion at the base. Its blaze of distinction is the fluting or channel, formed by a deftly removed chip, which runs longitudinally from the base up one or both faces. The channeling thinned the point and is supposed to have made a groove for the split end of the shaft of javelin or spear to lie in when point and shaft were joined, although one is inclined to doubt this, in view of the narrowness and frequently indifferent formation of the flute. But nobody has ever seen a Clovis spearshaft and attached point, and the channeling may have had a purpose of which we are not clever enough to have thought.

The Clovis fluted point is almost exclusive to the United States, with a peripheral provenience in southern Canada and a few specimens reported from below the Mexican border. (There is a site in Ecuador that produces fluted points apparently related to Clovis only by the occurrence of fluting.) With the find of a Clovis point in Utah in 1966, they are now known from all the forty-nine continental states, although I am not as sure as I should be about Rhode Island. They have shown up in greatest numbers, not in the Southwest, where the best-authenticated sites are located, but in Alabama. Where they are really concentrated, however, is in the attics of old houses and the basements of local historical societies. I know a man who moved into a house and found in the junk left behind a box of "arrowheads," jargon for Amerind stone work, with two Clovis points in mint condition, one of them the finest I have ever seen. The only two fluted points in my own collection of thousands of points came into my hands from donors who were getting rid of things under domestic pressure.

The Clovis fluted point is conventionally estimated to have been first made in America perhaps a millennium before the earliest example so far to be dated, at 12,530 B.P. Since fluting is a uniquely American feature, 13,500 B.P. would be the earliest acceptable date for what would be typologically Clovis. Although primitive craftsmen were quite conservative about the design of their tools, the three thousand years between 13,500 B.P. and 10,500 B.P., when Clovis ceases in the West, seems to be about as long as it is humanly possible to reproduce a design without alteration or degeneration or innovation into something descriptively different. The famous Folsom fluted point, the first of the fluteds to be recognized as a weapon point used on now-extinct big game and a localized development from Clovis in the direction of finer workmanship, is dated at about 10,700 B.P., but it may have been made for another few hundred years. Following it is the final fluted-point type, called

Meserve in the West and Dalton in the East, which is no longer lanceolate in form nor very well made. These date to about 9,000 B.P.; and one may even question whether the Daltons are in the Clovis tradition at all, or simply imitations of the fluting by another people entirely.

If the corridor had opened by 15,000 B.P. and had not closed again by 13,500 B.P. (and it did close again, at a date subject to various interpretations), the Clovisians, it would seem, could have trickled down it. But, while the Clovis lanceolate fluted point is thirteen thousand years old, at the oldest, the practice of fluting is decidedly older. It occurs in a style of point called the Sandia.

In 1939–40, archaeologist Frank Hibben directed the excavation of Sandia Cave, in the mountains of that name within sight of Albuquerque, New Mexico, where Sandia points were first revealed to the world. The lanceolate symmetry of the

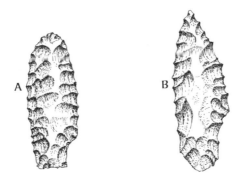

(*a*) Sandia I. (*b*) Sandia II.

blade of the Sandia point is broken at about a quarter to a third of its length by a shoulder indentation of one blade edge to form a stem; this shoulder not being matched by one on the opposite edge, we may call the point demi- or semi-stemmed or mono-shouldered. Sandia Cave was stratified, the strata being formed of hard material caused by water dripping during interludes of wet climate. The Sandia points were at the bottom, in two layers; in the next higher stratum were two fluted Folsoms and a Clovis; in the next, unfluted lanceolates called Plainviews, usually found with the bones of extinct bison.

The lower-level Sandias were the cruder; they were thicker in cross section and blunt at the base. The upper-level Sandias had progressed in workmanship to a flatter, thinner cross section and a firmer outline, with thinning flakes taken out of the base that look, now that fluted Sandias have been found, like incipient fluting. It was established by the Sandia Cave excavation that there was a projectile-point style older than Clovis; when that style was found elsewhere with fluting, it was clear that fluting is a practice older than the Clovis point. But fluting

Sandia Fluted.

of projectile points is found nowhere else in the world. The Clovisians had learned fluting from a people who were in America before them, probably their own ancestors. When were these Sandian ancestors here?

The Folsom-Clovis deposits in the Sandia Cave have been related to the so-called Two Creeks interstadial, an interglacial warm period which ended, by C_{14} dating, in about 12,000 B.P., and to the subsequent period of glacial readvance, called the Valders. A period of snowy precipitation in the glaciated regions, the Valders advance was a pluvial or rainy period in the Southwest. The dampness of the limestone cave during the

Valders caused the deposits that consolidated over the floor
where the Folsom and Clovis points had been dropped during
the preceding warm Two Creeks period. Since the Sandia
points were beneath these deposits, they fell into a time range
between 25,000 B.P. and 13,000 B.P., or the time of onset of
the third great resurgence of the Wisconsin glacier. Their age
would seem to have been pinned down by a C14 test on a piece
of mammoth-tusk ivory, which gave a result of about twenty
thousand years, but archaeologists are chary of accepting it; the
association is not as indisputable as they would like, and they
question an age of twenty thousand years for any kind of stone
projectile point.

One wonders at their scruples. Elephants are neither troglo-
dytes nor have they powers of levitation. Tusk ivory in Sandia
Cave is most easily explained as a trophy brought home by
hunters, or as material saved to work on over a shut-in day. The
Sandians might have brought home some fossil ivory already
several thousand years old, but they hardly needed it if they
were killing their own tuskers. Still, even if the archaeologists
are right, the C14 date of 20,000 B.P. does create a disposition
to believe that the Sandia-point makers date at least as far
back as 17,000 B.P. to 15,000 B.P.

The fluted Sandia points came from the Estancia Valley of
Central New Mexico, at a railroad siding called Lucy, dug by
William B. Roosa under Hibben's direction. The collection from
the site, dug in 1966 and not stratigraphically satisfactory, was
very similar to the combined assemblage at Sandia Cave: bones
of extinct big-game animals and Folsom, Clovis, and Sandia
points. Of the six Sandias found, two were fluted on both faces.
The fluting is unquestionable, technologically; and the probability that two points accidentally fluted on both faces in the
normal process of chipping would be found within a few feet
of each other is statistically negligible, about one to the square
of the distance between Sandia Cave and Siberia. But the way
the flute flakes were taken out eliminates even the single
chance: it was by the Clovis technique—and so the Sandians,
not the Clovisians, must have invented fluting, that feature as
telltale as the Hapsburg underlip.

Sandia points are not at all ubiquitous, though you may have a mono-shouldered point in your collection that looks Sandian; I have one, picked up in Depew Park, Peekskill, New York, which could be, but is not. The test of a true one is the dulling of the edges of the stem by grinding, a precaution taken by the makers presumably to prevent cutting the lashings securing the point to the shaft. Seemingly true Sandias have been reported from Alberta, Canada, and Geauga County, Ohio, the latter from a surface collection made about 1910. Doubtless there are more that might be recorded; for the Clovisian habit of wandering all over the map was likely a Sandia habit as well, since they were both in the same line of work. Yet, although Clovis sites or workshops have been excavated as far away from Clovis, New Mexico, as the Debert site in Nova Scotia, the only two sites accepted as Sandian are Sandia Cave and Lucy.

The Ecuadorian fluted-point site mentioned earlier, the Hacienda El Inga site near Quito, is a surface spread, the collec-

El Inga.

tion from which was reported by Robert Bell in 1960. The points, none of which were complete, are neither Clovis nor Sandia, but are much nearer Sandia in line of descent, in that they show a full, bilaterally developed stem or tang. It is plausible that this formal stem evolved out of the demi-stemmed Sandia, while the Clovis evolved in the other direction, into no stem at all. The only vestige of a stem is a slight constriction in the outline in many Clovis specimens that gives them a feminine sinuousness rather than a workaday masculine rectilinearity.

Of such clues as this note of fluting is prehistory made. It tells us that from 17,000 B.P., plus or minus a millennium, at which time the corridor was frozen as solid as the North Pole on Christmas Eve, there was abroad on the American landscape a consanguinity, or at least a freemasonry, of Paleo-hunters who would not perish from the earth for another six to eight thousand years. The abundance of game everywhere eventually lured them, like the famous fur-trapping mountain men, across the breadth of the unglaciated North American continent and to the extremest tip of South America; and they made their kills with a weapon of their own invention, the stone projectile point. It was this invention that made them what they were, self-reliant nomads who could go wherever the game was afoot and make a living. With his weapon in hand—it probably never left his hand except for sleep—the spearman was as much a hunter by instinct as any carnivore alive.

The authoritative Dr. James B. Griffin of the University of Michigan and the equally authoritative Dr. Douglas S. Byers of the Peabody Museum, excavator of the Clovisian Debert site in Nova Scotia, have argued that hunting has been overemphasized as the way of life of the Sandia-Clovis-Folsom spearmen and that they must have been as omnivorous as are, for instance, we eaters of spinach and rutabagas. The fact would appear to be self-evident: hunters have their good days and their bad; there are seasons when game is plentiful and seasons when it is scarce; some men are lucky and some are unlucky. That the genealogy of big-game hunters runs through thirteen thousand years on the archaeological record, and by observation to the 1880's, when the last buffalo herd was killed off by the Sioux, is proof enough that they did not starve when there was no meat for the fire. But beyond the exigencies of hunger is another dietetic factor that can only be ascribed to fond appetite.

The *New York State Conservationist* for October-November, 1967, carries a short but lively discussion on the eating of fish by the white-tailed deer. It seems that the deer will not only eat a fish if it happens to swim into the deer's mouth while he is drinking or munching sedges, but will follow fishermen throwing trash fish up on the bank and snap up these rejects as tid-bits. This is not a leg-pulling tall story; it is on film. There is no limit to what an animal, man included, will eat as long as he can swallow it.

In *The Story of Man and His Food* (1937) by C. C. and S. M. Furnas, one of the most entertaining books I have ever read on the subject and now undeservedly out of print, appears the following, one of many pertinent passages:

Almost everything that can be pulverized between the teeth has been tried and in some cases found good. The Sandy Lake Indians boiled the excrement of rabbits with their rice to season it. Before they were contaminated by civilization, the greatest delicacy of the South American Coroados was roasted entrails with original contents. The Pomo Indians of California once included barnacles in their diet—probably wholesome but undoubtedly rather abrasive to the stomach. In the pre-white days it took only a mild case of vegetable hunger to set the Coronation Gulf Eskimos to gathering deer droppings from the snow for sustenance. Caribou droppings were used to thicken blood soup, which they did very effectively.

This testimony supports the Griffin-Byers premise without winning the argument. When there was no game on the horizon, the pastures frequented by the grazers were certainly dotted with mammoth plops and other road-apples, as useful for internal as for external fuel (for which the Plains Indians used buffalo chips). The convenient plenty of this item of diet must have made chasing mammoths much less of a gamble with starvation than it appears to us.

Too much should not be made of this one entree, however. Before recourse to it, if recourse it was, became necessary, there was a list of comestibles to be had for the snatching within the big-game environment: turtles, tortoises, raccoons, rabbits, lizards, snakes, birds, fish, skunks, moles, frogs, prairie dogs, mice, nuts, berries, and seeds, the remains of which have been found on Paleo-hunter sites and all of which could have been, and probably were, contributed to the commissary by the women and half-grown children while the men were squatting in ambush at some waterhole waiting for the big bag.

A second dig of the original Clovis site, reported by James Warnicka in 1966, turned up bones of turtles, rodents, and birds, but the bulk of this could have amounted to no more than canapes compared with the meat from the four complete and one partial mammoth skeletons that were unearthed, surrounded by the bones of bison, horse, camel, antelope, deer, wolf, and peccary. Few Paleo-hunter kill-camp sites are without mammoth bones, of course, because where this behemoth fell, there was home for a while, until the cupboard was bare. But this tells us what we are trying to divine: what was on the minds of the Paleo-hunters, what was the central objective that determined the pace, rhythm, and direction of their lives. It was not merely killing to eat; it was hunting and killing the biggest game of all. It is true that no mammoth or mastodon bones have been found on fluted-point sites in the East. But then no bones at all, except slight evidence of caribou, itself big game, at the Holcombe Beach site in Michigan and the Dutchess Quarry Cave site in Orange County, where the 12,530-year-old fluted point was found, survive in the acid forest soils; and since mammoths roamed all that territory, who will gainsay that it was this prize prey that lured the Clovisians there?

The tool kit of the Clovisians spells out what they were, as certainly as the saw and hammer denote the carpenter. The hide scraper, the flint knives, the chopper (a heavy, edged stone like a hand ax), the cutting-edged flakes: these are the implements of flesh eaters. But most of all, there are the stone projectile points. A simple wooden shaft with fire-hardened point or a javelin tipped with bone or antler or ivory—and all these have been used by man at one time or another—will bring down the smaller, thinner-skinned game or wound it sufficiently for it to bleed to death. Yet such weapons would be no more than rocks thrown against the hides of the larger beasts. It takes something as hard as steel and as sharp as glass to puncture

A   B

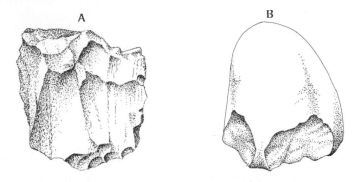

(*a*) End Chopper. (*b*) Pebble Chopper.

living leather, and high-quality flints, chalcedonies, jaspers, and rocks of similar structure have these qualities.

The Paleo-hunters used the best flints; they knew most of the outcrops, and they traveled hundreds of miles to mine them. Deepkill (a locale name, not a pun) flint from the Coxsackie flint mines in the mid-Hudson Valley was the material used for the fluted points at Bull Brook, near Ipswich, Massachusetts, at least three days' journey away. The source of the Onandaga chert used in fluted points found at Neversink Station in Pennsylvania is two hundred miles farther north, near Niagara Falls. At the Holcombe Beach site, in Michigan, as reported by Dr. James E. Fitting, nodules of Bayport chert from the glacial drift of the vicinity had sometimes to be used in point manufacture; but the preference was for the same Bayport chert selected for quality from an outcrop over one hundred miles away, and persons or parties went on missions to obtain it. The lengths to which the Paleo-spearman was willing to go for the highest-quality material for his points tell us plainly enough that he was professionally aware that his livelihood depended on the quality of the weapon with which he was armed.

In the first place, impure, cross-grained, or non-conchoidally-fracturing rocks will thwart the removal of the flute flake, yet this consideration must have been secondary to the razor-edged cutting efficiency which could be flaked into good material. The propulsive power was the human arm only. Paleo-hunter sites have yielded no evidence of that simplest of propulsive auxiliaries, the atlatl, or spear-throwing stick, which has the effect of extending the length of the arm by eighteen inches or so, to give added momentum to the cast. You get the idea of the atlatl if you can visualize how hard a baseball pitcher could throw with an arm that hung down to his calf. Lacking even this aid to propulsion, the spearpoint itself had to be the keenest possible, because the success of a cast was measured by its penetration. The wound inflicted just might be to a vital organ, and of itself eventually mortal; but hunt-to-hunt success must have depended on setting two or three shafts deeply enough in the quarry to cause quick and heavy bleeding, after which, if he ran, one only had to follow him till he dropped.

In the case of the mammoth, this driving of a blood-letting point into the innards was a formidable task. Armored, when in good condition, by a four- to six-inch layer of fat and with bones like four-by-fours, the disruption of the physiology of the mammoth was a matter of the application of available thrust to precision incision. One would imagine that a good mammoth hunter was like a .300 hitter in baseball who can also reach the outfield fence.

Without an effectively designed projectile point of best-quality flints, there could have been no weapon hunting of big game, specifically the mammoth. The flip side of this statement would be that the stone projectile point was invented and refined by a people who aspired to become mammoth hunters and who, by means of this invention, fitted themselves to bring down all the lesser game that wandered within range. What they may have eaten between their sirloins of mammoth, horse, camel, and bison does not explain them; the bones of killed mammoth, and the specialized points used to do them in, do make this people live again. To kill the mammoth, these Paleo-hunters had to trail the herds in seasonal shiftings of pasture and migration to new grasslands; and wherever there were mammoths, there were the spearmen.

They are an epical people, these rovers of the plains, spear at the ready, competing by choice with the saber-toothed cat, the dire wolf, and the American lion for their meals and probably their shelters. They deserve a Homer or a Melville. It was a spectacular setting in which they played their strenuous roles. They lived in the last epoch of great and marvelous beasts this planet will ever know, unless ravenous man becomes extinct and leaves what is left of it to what is left of them. The stalwarts of the fluted point were the heroes, the men of action, but they were not the principal players; it was not through them or anything they bequeathed that aborigines reached climaxes of civilization in the Andes, Central America, and Mexico. And yet the vividness of their character and their trueness to themselves have deceived even archaeologists into exaggerating their importance in the drama of prehistory. It was Paleo-hunters on horses, using bows and arrows (or rifles when they could get them) who raided the westering wagon trains and wiped out Custer. There were no more mammoths, but in the buffalo there was the same gross weight and the same irresistible temptation to the wild, free life.

It has already been hinted that the fluted-point spearmen were not alone on the scene. Their contemporaries have only just begun to emerge from the background, where they had to be lurking somewhere. It is these inhabitants of the environments outside those of the big-game herds—the forests, mountain valleys, and seashores—who set the pattern of living that is much more typically Indian than herd hunting, and that led eventually to the cultural divide of cultivation of plants for food. Men living in this pattern discovered corn, beans, the gourd-squash family, and dozens of other vegetals the world would be poorer without, from peanuts and potatoes to chicle and chocolate; and on this base of horticulture and agriculture were founded the city-states of Mesoamerica, not inferior in cultural level to the city-states of the Fertile Crescent.

The contemporaneity was accepted by Ronald J. Mason, when he wrote, in what is still the most inclusive summary of Paleo-Indian prehistory, in the June, 1962, issue of *Current Anthropology:*

The Paleo-Indian, *Archaic* and *Desert* Cultures [italics mine] as presently known are most reasonably interpreted as indigenous American developments whose ultimate origins lie earlier in time and in a complex or complexes still unrecognized in both the New and the Old Worlds.

Unrecognized? No. Ignored? By some, perhaps the cautious many, by no means all. This primal "complex or complexes" is the pebble-tool tradition (on which much attention will be lavished later), as old as man the toolmaker himself, though it is not, by two million years (give or take a couple of hundred thousand) that old in America, as we shall see. Since the "complex or complexes" are unrecognized, we shall have to give them a name. Let it be the Chopper people, after the tool most typical of their industry. But let us not assume they were one people, for there were in America, we must remember, more diverse language groups than in all the rest of the world together.

One obstacle may be retarding recognition of the Chopper people: it imposes a whole new anthropology on investigators, since the industrial evidence for it (crude stone tools made of river pebbles), none too formal to begin with, has never been seriously analyzed, as well as a whole new model of American prehistory, with a more intricate plumbing system of population supply. But there are those who are facing up to the chore. One of these is Dr. Alan L. Bryan, in his 1965 monograph "Paleo-American Prehistory," who founds his study on much the same premises as have already been stated here: the multiplicity of languages, the "many physical sub-races in America and many highly diverse cultural assemblages." In short, a band or two of big-game hunters wandering down the glacial corridor could not have implanted all the polymorphic diversification of Amerind life.

In his approving review of the Bryan thesis, Dr. Robert L. Stephenson of the Smithsonian Institution delivers this pointed judgment: "The possibility that North America may have been populated by a single movement of people is good to bring up for theoretical discussion, perhaps, but it is so improbable as to be almost absurd."

Need anything further be said in summary of the affairs taken up in this chapter? Very little, I think. The peopling of the New World by a "single movement of people," that is, by the Clovis or proto-Clovis spearmen, is held by the most advanced students to be no longer a tenable proposition. Since the tradition of big-game hunting, however large it looms in archaeology so far, is not the only tradition discernible in American prehistory, the other movement or movements into this hemisphere must have been of that other tradition which we recognize latterly as the Archaic and which must have originated in the quite primitive pebble tool-chopper tradition. This way of life was so generalized—the exploitation of every usable resource within a restricted area, rather than the pursuit all over the landscape of one favorite four-legged article of food—it could easily have begotten the specialized big-game hunting through a slight modification. That modification was the invention of the stone projectile point with a concomitant talent for expertness in its use. Hence it is no longer imperative to explain the presence of the big-game hunters in Arizona or Nova Scotia by a trek from Alaska down an intraglacial corridor; they need only have been the descendants of pebble tool-chopper people who had developed what was then the ultimate weapon and committed their lives to their skill with it. The assembling of evidence that fluted Sandia points, which date before the opening of the corridor, were antecedent to fluted Clovis points, had as its purpose to support the logic of a pebble tool-chopper parentage for the big-game hunters with arguments from archaeology. Far from being the First Families of the standard model of American prehistory, the Clovis spearmen were very likely not immigrants at all.

What should now follow, in the orderly development of our theme, is a study of the people who made the pebble tool-chopper, of where they came from and when, and of how they settled themselves into the manifold environments of America, from the coastal lowlands to the grim, inhospitable deserts. We will meet them first in their descendants, the Archaic oyster eaters of the lower Hudson Valley, where I have spent twenty years digging them up; and we will follow them back to the very beginnings of man, in Olduvai Gorge, East Africa. But, as it happens, there is another matter that must be disposed of first: the adventures and misadventures of American archaeology's pocket watch, dating by the C14 or radioactive carbon method.

Frederick Johnson of the Peabody Foundation thus begins his article in *Science*, January, 1967, "Radiocarbon Dating in North America": "The development of radiocarbon dating by W. F. Libby revolutionized archaeological ideas concerning the chronology of human events during the last 40,000 yrs." Anything that happens to this chronometer happens to American prehistory, and it has undergone some interesting changes recently. They belong in this story.

3

The Accurate Atom

THE USE OF C14 tests to determine, within extremes of statistical error, the absolute age of archaeological materials was begun in the late 1940's; and the first list of test results was released, with a nice regard for the decimal system and clean beginnings, on January 1, 1950, which is the Year One of the C14 era. When test results are given as so many years before present (B.P.) the numerical value of "present" is A.D. 1950. A date of, for instance, 5650 B.P. becomes 3700 B.C. on the Christian calendar, by subtraction of the 1,950 years before the advent of the C14 era. If the age is less than 1,950 years, the calendar date is obtained by subtracting the age from 1,950; thus an age of 1,140 years is translated as a date of A.D. 810.

The principle of dating materials by the rate of "decay" of a radioactive substance which they contain was first used around 1920 in determining the age of the earth's oldest known rocks by means of their inherent uranium (abbreviated U) 238. Radioactive substances decay or transmogrify from radioactivity to nonradioactivity at a fixed rate not subject to acceleration or retardation by any kind of force or influence—heat, cold, pressure, or movement. But each radioactive substance has its own rate of decay, from millionths of a second to billions of years. U238, which is the isotope that constitutes about 99 percent of natural uranium and which breaks down or decays into lead 206, has a "half-life" of 4.5×10^9, or 4.5 billion years. What this half-life means is that half of any given quantity of U238 will decay into lead 206 over a period of 4.5 billion years; that is, an ounce of uranium will become a half-ounce in 4.5 billion years, but it will take another 4.5 billion years for that half-ounce to become a quarter-ounce. Thus U238 has the span to measure the age of any substance on earth with which it occurs, since the earth itself is now thought to be only about 4.5 billion years old.

Radioactive C14 is not in the U238 class. Its half-life, as first determined by Willard F. Libby, when he was working on the World War II atomic-bomb project at the University of Chicago, was $5,568 \pm 30$ years. Though this has since been redetermined by the United States Bureau of Standards to be $5,730 \pm 30$ years, the Libby half-life is used by C14 laboratories, for a variety of technical and statistical reasons and by formal agreement, in calculating age. The theoretical limit of C14 dating is 70,000 years, but its practical limit at this time seems to be about 40,000 years. However, 40,000 years is, for the most part, an ample enough span, because the only substances that contain C14, as far as archaeology is concerned, are organic and seldom last 40 millennia.

Libby's "invention" of C14 dating consisted of the scientific discovery or realization that radioactive C14 molecules, manufactured by cosmic rays (with an energy of five to ten million electron volts) from nitrogen, exist in apparently uniform distribution in the atmosphere at breathing level and are therefore breathed in, or taken in with food consumed, by all living organisms, vegetal and animal, including you and me. C14 intake continues while the organism lives, but stops on death, fixing in the tissues the C14 inherent at the time of death. It is as though a bullet that kills a victim also smashes his calendar watch at the exact second of death. The problem is to read the atomic dial.

The C14 atom is an isotope of carbon in which the nucleus contains fourteen neutrons, hence the designation. This nucleus

is unstable to the degree that it emits or discharges radio-
actively one of the neutrons at a random but statistically average rate, to become C_{13}. A C_{14} laboratory test consists of
counting the scintillations of emission from a prepared material
in a specially constructed Geiger counter for a period, for
standard runs, of forty-eight hours. Modern material averages
6.68 emissions per minute; the older the material, the fewer the
emissions. Since the counting falls within the rules of statistics,
the result is given as the mean between two extremes; the actual
report on the 5650 B.P. date referred to above was $5,650 \pm 200$
years, the extremes constituting the value of the standard deviation. Thus the probability is $66\frac{2}{3}$ percent that the age of the
tested material falls between 5,850 and 5,450 years.

The results in this manner are far from being the loose estimate they seem. One reason is the adoption of the Libby half-
life, which is 2.9 percent under the more accurate figure. Those
who like to doodle mathematically can do the calculation on
their thumbnails: for the 5,650-year age, this mean, increased
by 2.9 percent, becomes 5,814, or very near the older extreme
of 5,850. In effect the deviation is cut in half, and is actually
5,850–5,650.

It would be hard to overestimate the value to archaeology of
C_{14} dating, especially to American archaeology, where there
are no dates of record whatever that we can read (one problem
it has not resolved, though, is which of the two rival correla-
tions of the Mayan calendar with the Christian calendar is
correct)—until bookkeeping white men arrived on the scene,
and even they did not penetrate all parts of North America
until the middle of the nineteenth century. A handful of charcoal from a campfire, an oyster shell from the midden (the heap
of shells discarded by Amerind oyster snackers on a river
shore), a wooden house support or the shaft of a spear, a
section of antler used as a punch or a harpoon head, a burned
bone left in the ashes after a meal, the seeds or undigested pulp
of chewed plants that have passed through the alimentary canal
and are present in ancient feces, the strands of willow in
baskets, the fibers in cloth or twine—all these have been sent by
archaeologists from excavated sites to the university labora-

tories, Yale, Lamont at Columbia, the University of Michigan, the University of Chicago, to the commercial laboratories, Geochron or Isotopes, Inc. (there are now many others); and they have been returned date-tagged and meaningfully related to their times and ours. To receive such explicit information, as I have, from relict things disinterred from the burial vaults of time can prickle the back of the hand that holds the message; momentarily it seems to have been written by the hand of a ghost.

Dating by C_{14} did for archaeology what the Julian calendar did for history: it put numbers on the completions of the solar cycle, and the civilized world on a schedule. Before C_{14}, prehistoric dating was relative; this was older than that but younger than something else, by stratigraphy, that is, by where it appeared geologically. But the dit-dit transmission of C_{14} neutrons before the watchful eye of the Geiger counter was Morse code out of the misted past: one could read the numbers; here was the score, in carbon black.

By 1955, C_{14} dating was sweeping archaeological America like a new detergent. Anybody who had something to be dated was looking up old fraternity brothers who knew somebody who had an in with somebody who had influence at one of the few and overburdened laboratories, which steadfastly kept to a program of working only in materials from cardinal sites. An articulated chronological skeleton was assembled for American prehistory, and many controversies were arbitrated out of the field by the impersonal decisions of the Geiger counter. There were some embarrassing bloopers in the beginning, of course, as was to be expected, and some of these were traced to the gremlins in "solid" carbon. In the first few years of C_{14} dating, the court was taken on the dated material itself, a chunk of wood or a fold of cloth; but laboratory technicians soon devised a method of reducing the solid material to CO^2 gas, which corrected previous egregious errors and brought forth a beautiful consistency of dates, as though the Geiger counter were a time-vending machine. The gas-corrected ages were, in almost every case, greater than the solid-carbon results.

By and large, archaeologists were happy, and their reliance on C_{14} dating grew to the proportions of the modern cultural reliance on the automobile. But there were some portents of trouble. Not suddenly, but in one instance here and one there, like measles breaking out, discrepancies began to appear: not overt inconsistencies which would be attributable to contaminated charcoal or to faulty cleaning of materials (hair roots and the leaching of decayed modern materials into charcoal are constant contaminants that must be removed), but repetitive, constant nonconformity of C14 ages and dates of record. This kind of discrepancy, when laboratory procedures had been refined and tested, directed the glance of suspicion at the basic assumptions of C14, of which there are two major ones: that the distribution of atmospheric C14 is uniform all around the globe, and that its occurrence in the atmosphere has been constant through datable time, the last forty thousand years. If either of these was seriously wrong, then C14 dating might not be much more reliable than spinning a teetotum.

The validity of these premises had been examined by Libby and his colleagues (solar activity affects the production of cosmic rays, the agent of C14 production) within the framework of theoretical physics and found satisfactory, but in the early demands on C14 laboratories by archaeologists for site dating, there had been little opportunity for empirical comparisons of C14 ages and orderly columns of record dates. Some of the few opportunities had turned out well: a loaf of bread that had been buried in Pompeii in the lava of Vesuvius in A.D. 79 or 2029 B.P. (keep this in mind) gave a reading on the atmosphere of that year exactly similar to that of today's. But other instances had a premonitory air about them.

The first test result ever published, numbered C-1 (C for the University of Chicago laboratory), was on a piece of wood from the tomb of Zoser at Sakkara in Egypt, of a known age of 4,650 years. The C-1 result was 3,699 ± 770 years, and two rerun results were 4,234 ± 600 years and 3,991 ± 500 years, for an average of 3,979 ± 350 years. This was hardly encouraging; but when later tests on other materials came nearer the mark, the tomb of Zoser was forgotten, as a trial of inexperience. Test C-62, for instance, on wood from a tomb of the Ptolemaic period with a known age of 2,280 years, gave a result of 2,190 ± 450 years (keep this in mind in relation to the Pompeiian bread). But over the years from 1960 onward, there accumulated too many tombs of Zoser.

The construction of tables of comparative C14 ages and dates of record is, for some regions, a straightforward problem of finding the money to finance the laboratory time for C14 assays. Since in the Middle East inscription begins in some places at about 3500 B.C., while no intelligible records exist in western and northern Europe until Roman times and in America before Spanish times, with what chronology were C14 dates to be compared in America?

It happens that there is one, the natural calendar of the growth of trees, which, as all the world knows, expand by one discernible ring of wood each year, so that the age of a tree is the count of its annual rings. The idea of using annual tree rings as a chronometer in American prehistory first occurred to, or was at least first exploited by, Dr. A. E. Douglass, in the late 1920's. He called it dendrochronology, that is, wood timing.

Tree rings do not come, of course, stamped with the mint date. The expertise is in determining the sequence pattern of ring growth, since the weather during the season of growth directly controls the width of each ring; i.e., moist growing seasons make wide rings and dry ones, narrow rings. The exact succession of wide and narrow rings is therefore a graph of the climate of the years through which the tree has lived. When a house beam or post or a log of wood is discovered in an archaeological situation, its age can be determined by comparing its sequence of wide and narrow rings with a master chart or graph, for which the calendar dates have already been determined. No plus-or-minus statistical error has to be reckoned in. Each ring in the master chart indicates an exact year of growth, and once you have matched the pattern of ring growth of an unknown wood specimen with the master chart, you have its dendrobiography as clearly as though it had kept a diary.

Douglass began his master chart with what is still commonly thought of as the oldest of living beings, the majestic sequoias of California; and he kept at it, counting rings on the stumps of trees (probably until he had circles under his eyes) felled de-

cades before in timbering operations until he found one with a
sequence going back to 1307 B.C. (General Sherman, the patri-
arch tree of Sequoia National Park, placarded for tourists as the
oldest living individual of any race in the world, has been estimated to be 3,500 years old, but since dendrochronologists have
been forbidden to take a boring from it, they really don't know
how old it is; in any event, it is not what the placards claim.)
With Douglass's stump that was a stripling in 1307 B.C. and
died under a lumberman's saw in 1902, the sequoias had given
away their innermost secret and dendrochronology seemed to
have come to its living end. There were no more big trees to be
looked into, and wasn't size a consequence of age by the very
definition of tree-ring accretion?

Not necessarily. Dendrochronologists began to suspect that
the oldest trees might not be very conspicuous at all because
they would be growing where conditions were harshest, in dry
forests high up on mountains near the timberline, where growth
is annually infinitesimal and, for some reason, the secretion of
preservative resin is high. In pursuit of corroboration of this
notion, the late Edmund Schulman of the University of Arizona
went with a party on a tree hunt in Inyo National Forest ten
thousand feet high up in the White Mountains of California,
near the Nevada border, to investigate rumors that some of the
bristlecone pines in a stand there "looked old." Indeed they did;
they were gnarled and scrubby and senilely bent, only ten to
thirty feet tall, but the look was that of premature old age, a
kind of arboreal progeria, brought on by malnutrition and hard
times. Yet looks are not always deceiving; there was one specimen thirty-seven feet in circumference that was fifteen hundred
years old. Schulman and party kept going back and looking
around in this grove, and early in 1958 he was able to announce
that seventeen bristlecone pines had been bored and counted at
over four thousand years of growth. Nine of these were in one
grove, dubbed Methuselah's Walk, where reigned the oldest
known (until recently) resident of this hemisphere still transpir-
ing, an ancient of forty-six hundred years. He—or they—was of
a peculiar type called the pickaback, actually a succession of
four separate growths out of a common trunk, in an order

Schulman recognized as great-grandfather, grandfather, father, and junior—a family tree by any definition.

What more could the C14 laboratory technicians ask than this? The very material that they were to date itself bore the numeral of a calendar year. There was no intervening step of documentation, or necessity to prove association. The wood was precisely the word.

The laboratory went into production, notably the Yale C14 Laboratory and the Geochronology Laboratories of Arizona, and the results were reported by Minze Stuiver of the Yale Laboratory and Hans E. Suess of the University of California at San Diego in 1966 in the professional journal *Radiocarbon*. The wholly unexpected, the genuinely startling, discovery is well summarized in *American Antiquity*, July, 1966, as follows:

> Several laboratories have confirmed the existences of discrepancies between radiocarbon dates and true dates. The nature of the variations in the last 6000 years has been established by radiocarbon measurements of bristle-cone pine wood which has been dendrochronologically dated by the laboratory of Tree-Ring Research. These measurements indicate that radiocarbon dates are within about 200 years of the correct value for the last 2500 years, but radiocarbon dates before that time are too young. The deviation increases almost linearly up to about 6000 years ago, where radiocarbon dates are too young by about 1100 years. There is an indication that the discrepancy decreases beyond this point and that radiocarbon dates are once more near the true value by about 10,000 years ago.

To recapitulate: at ten thousand years ago C14 years and true solar years are in tolerable agreement; then, for some reason, probably a decrease in cosmic-ray production of C14, C14 years begin to "slow down" relative to solar years, lagging farther and farther behind until six thousand years ago. Then, more or less suddenly, cosmic-ray activity reverses itself and begins to accelerate; C14 years begin to catch up with solar years and by 2500 B.P. are approximately equal in duration. And they so remain.

Stuiver has calculated that the divergence begins at 2300 B.P., and he has proposed this formula for correction of C14 dates between 2300 B.P. and 6000 B.P. (but not beyond): T (*true time*) $= C$ *14 years* $\times$ *1.4* $-$ *900*.

At this juncture the reader should recall the Pompeiian bread at A.D. 79 or 1871 B.P. (before 1950), when the $C14$ content of the atmosphere was like that of modern times, and C-62, the test on the wood of a Ptolemaic tomb with a known age of 2,280 years which gave a satisfactory result of 2,190 $\pm$ 450 years. Both of these are prior to the beginning of divergence. But the tomb of Zoser, with a known age of 4,650 $\pm$ 75 years and the unsatisfactory average measurement of 3,979 $\pm$ 350 years, falls about midway in the period of divergence. So let us recalculate by the Stuiver formula: *3979* $\times$ *1.4* $-$ *900* $=$ *4670.6*.

Such accuracy inspires confidence in the new mathematics of $C14$ dating; obviously the laboratory technicians have found what was amiss and are taking a stitch in time. The effect is considerably more than to add a few gray hairs and wrinkles of age to Amerinds who lived between 3000 B.P. and 9000 B.P. (These limits are stated because, when Stuiver's formula for correction of the deviation is applied, the difference is still within the standard deviation; presumably the error at the other end of the curve is similarly trivial.) This stretch of six thousand years happens to coincide with the Archaic (the temporal-cultural period that follows the period of the Paleo-hunter of big game and terminates with the Woodland period in the eastern United States, when ceramic pottery first began to be made), and with its roughly contemporary periods in Middle America when village farming began to get underway, and in the Southwest when the Basketmaker-Pueblo tradition took root. The whole column of dates within the Archaic now moves backward, crowding against the fixed barrier at 9000–10,000 B.P. However, they do not all move backward at the same rate, so that their chronological, and therefore developmental, relationships jam up, particularly between 6000 B.P., where the maximum divergence occurs, and about 8000 B.P., where it is much less wide. Some cultures which were thought to have been of the grandson generation may turn out to be sons or even younger brothers of established elders.

It may be asked quite legitimately whether the degree of

deviation before six thousand years ago, and extending to nine thousand years ago, can ever be determined with empirical accuracy, since we certainly must have reached the limit of longevity of even the bristlecone pine. The fact is that we haven't. The death of Schulman on January 8, 1958, brought to a temporary halt the arboreal exploration of the White Mountains; but funds were eventually advanced for its resumption, and C. W. Ferguson of the Laboratory of Tree-Ring Research gave a summary of work in progress, in *Science*, January 23, 1969. Four trees took the record back successively to 6,436 years ago (4466 B.C.), to 6,485 years ago (4515 B.C.), to 6,702 years ago (4732 B.C.), and to 7,117 years ago (5147 B.C.). And then, Ferguson writes:

Radiocarbon analysis (in December, 1967) of a single small specimen [of bristlecone-pine wood] that contains a 400-year, high-quality ring series indicates that the specimen is approximately 9000 years old. This holds great promise for the extension of the tree-ring chronology farther back in time.

In the foregoing instance it is evident that C14 dating is being used as a rough check on the age of the bristlecone-pine specimen, after which the pattern of ring growth will be added to the master chart. This appears to be interdependence rather than corroboration, and leaves us hoping for a completely unrelated standard of checking on the behavior of C14 atoms in our atmosphere. Such a standard has been found in, of all places, Antarctica. The ice there is up to three miles thick, the accumulation of snowfalls turned to ice for at least fifty thousand years. It contains air, trapped at the time of each fall, which is C14-datable when enough can be obtained for laboratory purposes. It takes three to four tons of ice to provide a datable quantity, a fearsomely expensive matter when the ice you want is five thousand to ten thousand feet below the surface. Oh, for the days when Ben Franklin established a scientific principle with a boy's kite and a house key!

How the now scrambled alignment of Archaic cultures is to be reorganized is the work of the next decade, but what this scrambling did to one Archaic problem, with a key figure of

5,863 ± 200, at the peak of divergence, is the work of the next chapter.

Meanwhile all C14 ages given herein will be those originally issued by the laboratory. No calibration of C14 and solar-time dates has as yet been published, and to make the calculations freehand would be without authority; but the reader is warned.

4

Don't Raise the Bridge —
Lower the River

THE LOWER HUDSON VALLEY ("lower" signifying that part of
the valley where the Hudson is more marine than riverine) can
provide as many instantly recognizable historical and literary
references as any comparable area in the United States. Just beyond its northern limit is West Point, now the location of the
United States Military Academy but during the Revolutionary
War the stronghold that Benedict Arnold conspired to sell out
to the British. About halfway between West Point and the end
of the lower Hudson, which is Coney Island on lower New
York Bay, is Tarrytown, where Major John André, Arnold's
redcoat contact, was captured. Washington Irving, the creator
of Rip Van Winkle, lived at Tarrytown, as did another of his
creations, Ichabod Crane, the ectomorphic schoolmaster.

Westchester County, probably the principal or secondary setting of at least one novel a month for the past twenty years,
holds the eastern bank for a curving thirty or thirty-five miles,
then relinquishes it to the Bronx, after which come Manhattan
and Brooklyn, on the eastern tip of Long Island. The western
bank belongs to Rockland County, aptly named because it looks
down on the river from the world-famed Palisades, a sheer rock
escarpment about three hundred feet high, and New Jersey, also

palisaded until it flattens out into the plain where are located
Hoboken and Jersey City. There is probably not a name, person
or place in the foregoing introduction that would not be recognized instantly by 90 percent of the high-school graduates of the
United States. But for all of them the existence of the lower
Hudson undoubtedly begins with Peg-leg Peter Stuyvesant sing-
ing "September Song" and swindling the Indians.

What happened before that, considered as the beginning of
European occupation, has been my problem, and that of my
accessories after the artifact, for well over a decade. There is
little of the recent past that has not been permanently immured
under concrete and asphalt by the sprawl of the megalopolis,
but along the banks of the Hudson north of Ossining (my residence and the location of Sing Sing Prison) are the remnants
of innumerable oyster middens—aboriginal garbage dumps—
containing archaeological materials dating back to—but that is
the point of this tale of exhilaration and exasperation.

The lower Hudson Valley is indeed a region and an environ-
ment distinct, separate, and *sui generis*. It begins in the north,
at Bear Mountain Bridge, on the Westchester-Putnam County
line and at the southern tip of the United States Military
Academy Reservation. Here the Hudson leaves the region and
environment called the Hudson Highlands and splays out into
Haverstraw Bay, where one of the mothball fleets of World
War II cargo ships has its anchorage in Tompkins Cove.
Haverstraw Bay becomes the Tappan Zee, or bay, at Croton
Point, below which enters the Croton River, the Hudson's
largest tributary from the east—though very little water enters
the Hudson from it now, because it is dammed just east of the
village of Croton-on-Hudson to form a reservoir for the New
York City water system. The southern boundary of the Tappan
Zee is vague because the stretch of water south of the West-
chester-Bronx line, and passing Manhattan, has no name. At
the Battery, which is the land's end of Manhattan, the lower
Hudson becomes upper New York Bay, then lower New York
Bay, finally emptying into the Atlantic.

This roll of bays and coves and points gives the proper

impression of the maritime character of the lower Hudson, which does not flood fluvially, though it carries the drainage of the 306-mile-long Hudson with its tributary the Mohawk, but instead pulses twice daily with four-foot tides. And the answer to the next question is: No, you can't drink the water, not until you get to Poughkeepsie, about 80 miles upstream, where it is potable but makes execrable iced tea. Yet, despite all these pertinent facts, and its coastal picturesqueness, with ocean-going vessels plying the main past flashing navigational lights on channel rocks, and buoys marking the shoals, and an occasional lost blackfish (a member of the whale family) which took a wrong turn on its way to Newfoundland, the lower Hudson is not nearly so marine as it once was. That is the silent testimony given by the oyster middens that were long ago heaped up on its banks wherever there was a convenient camp site; for oysters do not grow in the Hudson now and have not grown there, certainly not of the size and in the quantity indicated by the still existing middens, for two thousand years.

Local folklore has various explanations for these middens: they mark the spot of clambakes of nonnative oysters by gourmandizing picnickers; they are native oysters left high and dry by a sudden drop in water level; they are white man's trash; they are Indian trash of late precolonial times; they are the flotsam remains, washed up by waves, of oysters that died in their beds. Archaeologists had noted their existence and their probable archaeological character but, influenced by their presumed similarity to oyster middens on the New England coast, regarded them as not worth the effort of digging.

I well remember the gloomy April day when I heard this judgment delivered by the doyen of archaeologists of the Northeast (who shall be nameless because he deserves his eminence) as we stood looking at the chalky exposure of weathered oyster strata at Croton Point, overlooking Haverstraw Bay. In the group were, in addition to the doyen, Dr. Rhodes W. Fairbridge of Columbia University, the geologist and authority on fluctuation of sea level during the Pleistocene; Parks Commissioner Charles E. Pound of Westchester County, which holds the five-hundred-acre Croton Point as a county park; my two archaeological accomplices, Sigfus Olafson and Mauck Brammer; and my anxious self.

This field conference had been called by Pound because of my request for permission to dig at Croton Point. What was to be decided was whether the past master, with an acknowledged prior right to dig, wanted to exercise that right.

He did not. "There is," he said of a locus that was to yield a C_{14} age older than anything then known in New York State, "nothing here worth bothering with."

By visual inspection he was right—the midden looked like the sweepings from a cannery, with nothing more archaeological in evidence than a couple of pre–flip-top beer cans—and he did know the literature. The books said that all oyster-shell middens in the Northeast were from ceramic-pottery times, which began about 1000 B.C., and he had already dug sites full of that kind of material. This dig would enhance his reputation only as a corroborator of somebody else's discoveries.

My opinion was not asked, and it was not volunteered. I wanted to dig the site, and my reason was personified in the presence of Fairbridge, who had recently published in *Scientific American* (May, 1960) a chronological scheme of the rise and fall, as he saw it, of sea level for the past twenty thousand years, or since the withdrawal of the Wisconsin ice sheet from the lower Hudson. Here was our chance to test the Fairbridge hypothesis; you don't often get a chance to work on something of this magnitude, where you play with the ups and downs of the world ocean as though it were a Yo-Yo.

For several years Brammer, Olafson, and I had been digging in and around shell middens on the banks of the Hudson and the Croton rivers and tossing the shells away like dirt—which is what they were, for all we knew about oysters. As reprehensible as this sounds, and is, I can only plead the example of our betters in archaeology who had also treated them as bulk fill, after having made certain obtuse observations about them *in situ*. One of these was that layers of shattered shell, which we now know to have been the result of disintegration by weathering, had been reduced to the size of hominy flakes by trampling feet. A child would know better; walking around barefoot or in moccasins on knife-edged oyster valves would be like playing shoeless hopscotch on the spoil pile at the bottle works.

But you cannot excavate oyster shell by the cubic yard without making some observations, if you keep your eyes on what your shovel is doing. It began to impress itself on us that the shell valves in the lower, hence older, layers, within which typologically older materials were found, were distinctly larger than later valves, and that the later the shell was, the smaller it was, until finally oyster shell disappeared from the record, as we saw it, surprisingly long ago, by about 1000 B.C.

The explanation for this apparent dwindling, we were cheerfully told when we mentioned it under the impression that it was an acute insight, was childishly simple: the Indian oyster gatherers plucked the big ones first and then went back for the leavings and scrapings; eventually beds were reaped out. Since this explanation was offered by those who had never dug a lower-Hudson shell midden, we were not as impressed with it as with another pronouncement: the reason there are no oysters in the lower Hudson now, and have been none, to all intents and purposes, in modern times (there was a period when spats were gathered for transplant), is pollution. Since the Hudson is one of the world's largest scenic open sewers, this seemed plausible, until Olafson, of our group, had the good fortune to fall in with a man who had to know about oysters because he made his living out of them. To bring it close to home, he was the holder of a federal license to grow oysters in the Tappan Zee. He had exercised his rights under this license once, laying down a bed of spats in a deep hole near the present Tappan Zee bridge in 1957. Within a matter of months they had been wiped out, not by detergents or coliform bacteria or the fouling of pumped bilges, but because the water was too fresh.

The tale was brief and somber. Water temperature, which we had considered a possible discouragement to oysters because the lower Hudson usually freezes over for longer or shorter periods during the winter, is no more than an inconvenience when it gets beyond the limits of tolerability. Oysters like a temperature of 72°F., but will grow within a range of 40°–

80°F. Beyond these limits they simply withdraw into their shells, as it were, and wait for better times.

The critical factor is salinity. Optimum salinity for *Crassostrea virginica*, the Virginia oyster, is twenty-two parts per thousand, .022 percent. The salinity of the open sea is normally thirty-five parts per thousand, wherefore *Crassostrea* grows in bays and inlets fed by freshwater streams. The tolerable minimum salinity is eleven parts per thousand, and this is the direction in which oysters will seek their environment, rather than toward the open-sea maximum. Below eleven parts salinity, *Crassostrea* "suffocates," as we would in a low-oxygen Martian atmosphere.

The silent tragedy of 1957 happened almost overnight. With a heavy snow on the ground, there came a pouring March rain; fresh water gushed into the Hudson through all its tributaries, and the spate dispatched the spats.

The oyster is an unusual animal, in one respect like a tree. As the tree enlarges by its annual growth of rings, the oyster adds annually another plate or layer of shell. It is this kind of enlargement, incidentally, that makes the shell so vulnerable to weathering; the plates are not well cemented together, and acidic groundwater can infiltrate the plates and dissolve them apart. In the shell heap we were looking at that day at Croton Point were many *Crassostrea* valves six to eight inches long, composed of up to thirty-five plates, that is, about thirty-five years old. In their lifetimes there had been no "poisoning" of their environment by fresh water that had lowered the salinity to a lethal level. The Hudson had been, on this evidence, more consistently saline, more of a sea bay, in their era than it is now. Why?

The only source of salinity for the lower Hudson was the ocean. There had been more of it in the valley during the period of the big oysters than now, for a reason that had to be geologic, and geologist Fairbridge seemed to have the answer as to how it got there.

He had just published in several journals, the most available of which is the *Scientific American* of May, 1960, his hypothesis and scheme of the recovery of world sea level from its nadir of 400 feet below present level at the climax of the last glacier about nineteen thousand years ago. The ocean, being the ultimate reservoir of terrestrial waters, is the source of the water impounded in glacial ice; glaciers are simply immobilized, landlocked, piled-up seas. The consensus is that the last glacial period, consisting of the Wisconsin ice mass in America and the Würm ice mass in Europe, drew on the reservoir for enough water to lower it by about 400 feet, according to some authorities as much as 450 feet. The shape of continents was much different in glacial days. In our immediate area of interest, the Wisconsin's farthest front was across Long Island; dry land then extended eastward about 125 miles almost to the continental shelf, the "shoulder" of the continent beyond which are the pelagic deeps, the true ocean. The continental shelf was a vast landscape of coastal plain, covered with forests and appropriate vegetation and roamed by the animals then current, including the mammoth and mastodon. Teeth of these two kinds of elephants have been hauled up during dredging and trawling operations from over forty localities on the continental shelf, some of them now under 380 feet of water.

About nineteen thousand years ago the long succession of hard winters halted, for reasons about which there is no agreement, and summer returned, climatically, all over the world. The ice masses began to sweat, and the perspiration off their mountainous brows returned to and replenished the shrunken ocean. Filling like a free-form bathtub, the sea advanced across the continental shelf, and up the shelf's river valleys, including the Hudson "canyon" or trench east of Long Island. It was a good bargain. The territorial expanse eventually freed of its icy overload, from Long Island to the Arctic Circle and from the Atlantic to the Pacific, and returned to occupancy by flora and fauna, was many times in area that lost at the continental fringe along both the Atlantic coast and the Pacific coast, where the shelf is much narrower.

It was Fairbridge's C14-data-based conclusion that the sea had reached its present level about six thousand years ago, as the Wisconsin-Würm ice fields vanished completely, and that it had then continued upward for another ten to twelve feet, as the warming trend made inroads into what are now considered permanent polar ice caps. (If, by the way, all present permanent ice were to melt, the sea would rise, relative to the present basin, about two hundred feet, solving the municipal problems of New York City and other near-sea-level cities by a dramatic change of administration: the Coast Guard would take over.) The upsurge that took sea level ten feet above present was, Fairbridge thought, quite precipitate, amounting to about forty feet in two hundred years or so, and was the kernel of fact embedded in worldwide traditions about a great flood, the deluge of Noah. During such a rise, any people living along seacoasts or even far up tidal rivers would have been able to observe the inundation as they were forced to move farther and farther back to higher ground.

But, having reached a height of present level plus ten feet, sea level subsided to present level minus ten feet, only to begin a resurgence to present level plus six to eight feet, then, rhythmically, to subside again, rise again, and subside again—but in decreasing oscillations, like a wave running out. Fairbridge's opponents have called this scheme an "exercise in curvesmanship," and there can be no doubt that the turn of his mind favors cycles and rhythms; but then, is not the whole Pleistocene geologic period, the great Ice Age, one of the cyclic formation of a continental glacier, followed by melting, followed by another glacier?

Fairbridge is Australian by birth, English by education (Cambridge University), and American by residence and place of occupation for the last ten years or so; the data for his hypothesis was gathered in Australia, the Bahamas, and other far-flung places. But it seemed to us to fit our guesses about the oyster ecology of the Hudson River as though he had been born in Westchester, the son of a Yonkers ferryboat captain. When we called on him, he responded immediately and keenly to what we had to show and nerved us to our digging with the encouragement that it was certainly important in what it would reveal about sea-level rise, no matter what that revelation was.

What it revealed at the Kettle Rock locus on Croton Point was an almost exact reflection of the Fairbridge scheme done in

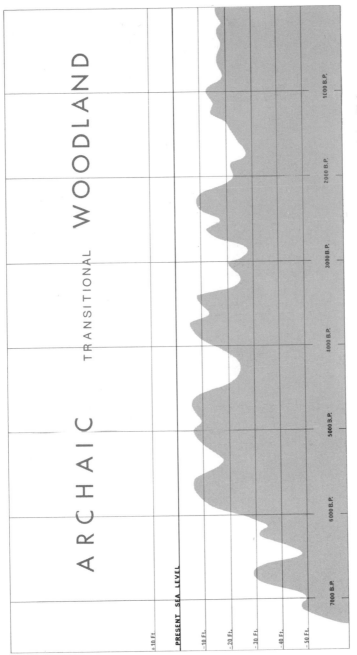

The scheme of sea level fluctuation for the past 7,000 years, as proposed by Fairbridge. The peaks do not represent the actual heights reached by sea level, but the peak periods are probably periods of rapid rate of rise.

oyster shell, a demonstration *in situ* of the Fairbridge ups and downs, not only in their cyclic sequence but in the properly decreasing magnitude of swing. At the bottom of the heap, in the soil that had been covered by humus only when the first shells were dumped there, was a layer of what were, on the average, the biggest valves occurring anywhere in the vast accumulation of shell along the shores of Croton Point. We called this the G-O, for "giant oysters," horizon, though the valves were not, strictly speaking, giants, except by comparison with later oysters. This G-O layer was topped off by a thin stratum of weather-shattered shell admixed with humus, indicative of a period when there were no oysters in the waters nearby. This would be the time when, after the initial rise at 6000 B.P., reaching a climax of ten feet above present level at 5800 B.P., sea level receded to ten feet below present level. The next shell layer was of smaller valves, matching the second high rise, which was not as high as the first; it was demarcated by a weathered-shell and soil zone, which was topped with a layer of lesser shells. Probing around in other shell accumulations on Croton Point, and coordinating our findings with such previous, less alert, digging as we had done, we came to the conclusion that the last time there had been enough oysters around Croton Point to throw up a respectable shell heap was about 3500–3000 B.P., at about the advent of ceramic pottery in the Northeast. Thereafter, oysters in the lower Hudson were very much a sometime thing and not much more stomach-filling in bulk than fat snails.

If we had never dug in shell heaps, never moved upwards of fifty tons of midden material, we could have arrived at the same deductions by reading the Fairbridge graph as an oyster chart. Whatever else it was good for, it registered oysters as a thermometer registers fever. Whenever it showed water above present level, there were oysters as though it were September; whenever it showed water at or below its present level, they were out of season. Although we were the first to apply the Fairbridge rhythm theory to the elucidation of shell middens, the archaeologist Wesley Hurt found that it worked with the same uncanny precision on the coastal *sambaqui,* or shell mounds, of southern Brazil. In his work Hurt correlated the dates of the shell mounds with their distance from the present shoreline, the older mounds being those farther inland. Reporting on his Brazilian work in 1964, Hurt wrote: "Correlation of these dates [as given for a period back to about 10,000 B.P.] with geologic context of the sites indicate close agreement with the theoretical climatic fluctuation and changes of sea level proposed by Fairbridge."

We were ready, we thought, to put in our claim to the title and perquisites of office of doyen of Northeastern archaeology, in the new department of oyster middens. But there was resistance all along the line. Where was the C14 date on the lowest shell that synchronized it with the Fairbridge highest rise of 5800 B.P., we were asked. And where was the proof that there had been such a rise, beyond the curves Fairbridge had been throwing? The first objection was the stickler—in those days C14 tests cost six hundred dollars, and we were working on our own. But wasn't our self-confidence as good as a C14 date? And wasn't the second objection a mere restatement of the first in non-financial terms? Kettle Rock was the proof that Fairbridge was right.

And then I fell into temptation. Asked to write a piece on the lower Hudson by a leading regional journal, the *Pennsylvania Archaeologist,* I wrote (with the recklessness of that ancestor of mine and notorious road agent, Bold Brennan o' the Moor, the so-called Irish Robin Hood) that I followed cyclist Fairbridge, and that the G-O horizon at Kettle Rock was 5,800 years old. For six hundred dollars, who was going to contradict me?

But this was that decade when research became the pop art of the university crowd. Dr. Ralph Solecki of Columbia, who kept hearing about the lower Hudson from us, made a suggestion. Minze Stuiver of the Yale C14 Laboratory was engaged in a dating project on the rise of sea level; since our site, along with our proclamations about it, was relevant material, why not submit it to Stuiver? With a good word having been added by noted archaeologist Dr. Irving Rouse of Yale, Stuiver accepted a sample of charcoal collected by one of Solecki's doctoral candidates at about one-twentieth of the commercial cost. That we could afford to pay. My bluff had been called.

The gestation period of archaeological publications and C_{14} assays is roughly equivalent, and on the order of the gestation of elephants. So we forgot about my piece and the sample—whatever came of these, our job was to establish the archaeological character of the Kettle Rock midden—and went on digging. Through the shell, itself garbage, were plentifully scattered, since shell is a good preservative matrix, the bones of game animals—mostly deer, as the common occurrence of deer teeth and astragali attested. The long bones had been shattered into fragments for the extraction of marrow, and perhaps for boiling since bone itself contains nutriments that can be got at this way. The crude choppers, or edged sections of approximately softball-sized pebbles, to which there will be many references in this volume, were undoubtedly used to dismember joints of meat and to hack wood, while the small sharp-edged stone flakes were oyster knives. The hammerstones came in various sizes of pebbles, suggesting the matching of weight to the job. Larger pebbles were also used as manos, that is, hand stones, to grist seeds for meal and to pulp roots and other fibrous matter for cooking. What cooking? There were only two or three sherds of ceramic pottery on the site, and these were on the surface and probably from much later times than the midden. But prepottery Amerinds cooked by the boiling-stone method. They could make watertight baskets into which went the liquid contents of stew or gruel. The heating, or cooking, of the contents was done by dropping in hot pebbles; these, some cracked open from too many dunkings in the pot, were found in appropriate numbers—appropriate, that is, to the amount of charcoal that had been filtered through the shell by seeping groundwater.

It was alimentary, Dr. Watson, entirely alimentary, this site. It consisted of the leavings of countless pickup meals and the rudimentary implements with which they had been prepared. By the surviving signs, no other activity but ingestion-digestion had taken place there. There were all those deer bones, even one elk astragalus; but where were the stone projectile points with which they must have been killed?

Stone projectile points—spearheads, dart tips, javelin points (the bow and arrow is believed not to have been used in this area until well into the first millennium of the Christian era)— have time-fixing utility because they are style-variable, like cars, though modifications took place over the centuries and not every fall. Hundreds of styles and varieties have been described as to attributes and time of occurrence, and a known style can be as time-telling as a buffalo nickel. Had we been lucky enough to find points in each of the layers, we should have had a neat little index that could have been cross-referenced with dated point types elsewhere in the archaeological vicinity for a chronological sequence that would support my headlong thesis.

There was one point, not too typical because of the grainy quartzite of which it was made, high up in the midden that might have been related to an upriver station fixed with some plausibility at about 3900 B.P. Very suddenly I was not sure of anything. That four-foot height of midden—couldn't it have been accumulated in a century, or less, maybe ten years, or even one? Maybe the dark humus layers between the shell horizons were nothing more than pigments of my imagination. It was no time for the galley proofs of the piece for the *Pennsylvania Archaeologist* to descend on my bemused head. They did, and I was horrified: the typography was, as usual, impeccable; my text was impossible. There wasn't a scientific subjunctive or a stylistic qualm anywhere in it. I had said, unequivocally, that the G-O horizon was 5,800 years old, and I had built a whole ten- or twelve-page article on that assertion; the only way to cool it was to burn it. And the editor, a friend who trusted me, wasn't going to like that.

I was actually staring at the proofs of my folly when there came a midnight telephone call, from Olafson.

"I just got the date on Kettle Rock," he said. "Guess."

"Yesterday," I said, low in spirit.

"Maybe we don't need to spend money on C14 tests," he said. "The age is 5,863 ± 200."

No, I didn't rewrite the article. I had learned my lesson.

Under my 5800 B.P. guess I put a modest little footnote that my thesis had been confirmed by C14 assay Y-1315, which means Yale's 1,315th C14 test.

So Kettle Rock was as old as creation—as calculated in 1650 by that pious churchman and biblical scholar, Bishop Ussher of Ireland, who had analyzed the Old Testament and put his finger on October 4, 4004 B.C., at 2:00 P.M. as the date when Adam opened his eyes on the delights of Eden. So I did know an old oyster when I saw one.

Never was so head-in-the-clouds a triumph afflicted so immediately with acute fallen arches. It lasted three months. In the normal course of archaeological discovery, a coup such as this would have been good for at least five years' honorable mention and respectful allusion. I know one man who got fifteen years' worth of distinction out of a site with an early C14 date that had been run on solid carbon and that proved to be a thousand years too old when the gas method was finally used on it. The loss of a thousand years took all the glamor out of the site, but it will still be in the books fifty years from now.

In *Science*, November 15, 1963, appeared the results of the study of rise in sea level on which Stuiver and his colleague, Joseph Daddario, had been working. They had been date-testing shoreline peat, a compaction of vegetable matter that forms at the high-tide line and remains fixed there after submersion. The localities tested were along the Atlantic coast, from about Atlantic City to Massachusetts. Croton Point was not mentioned. The column of tests, with interpolations, showed this:

6,000 years ago	sea level 40 feet *below* present level
5,000 " "	" " 30 feet *below* " "
4,000 " "	" " 25 feet *below* " "
3,000 " "	" " 20 feet *below* " "
2,000 " "	" " 10 feet *below* " "
1,000 " "	" " 2 feet *below* " "

To be brisk about it, there had not been at any time before the present any rise of sea level higher than or even as high as the present level. Instead of the graceful swell and slack of Fairbridge's theory of the undulant oscillation of a truly bounding main, there had been only a trite, pedestrian, straight-line creeping up, with the only fluctuation in the rate of rise. Fairbridge was wrong about sea-level rise, but he must have been right about something. He was wrong, for the right reason, whatever it was; and I was right, for the wrong reason.

Shortly after this unnecessarily prompt rebuke of a poetic fallacy, I was back at Croton Point, this time with Dr. Walter Newman of the Queens College geology department, one of the investigators who had supplied data for the Yale project. He had wanted to see for himself where I had gone wrong. He studied his graph of sea-level rise and a geological survey chart of Haverstraw Bay showing its pond-like shallowness, and then he turned his back on the layered mess of shell.

"There's no problem at all," he said with a grin. "All you have to do is to ignore the midden. Obviously it doesn't exist, and never did, because it couldn't have."

What he meant was that Haverstraw Bay is so shallow (from three to twelve feet deep, except in the channel) that if the level of water were to be suddenly dropped by forty feet, to where data said it had been 5,800 years ago, the Croton Point shell midden would not be within a mile and a half of salt water and oyster beds. And why would anybody carry oysters a mile and a half before extracting the meat?

"And what's more," I said, "I can show you another midden just like it if you can stand the shock."

This duplicate is about three and a half miles directly up the shore, on Montrose Point, and the specifications are exactly the same. It is the top four feet of a bank, and its base is about ten feet above present water level, just about where it would be expected to be if Haverstraw Bay had been at its present level when the shells were dumped there. The bottom layer, resting on an old humus, contains numerous very big shells with a sparse intermingling of the fragile ribbed mussel; and the upper, later, shells fall off in size. Newman took a valve from the bottom layer for dating, and in due time the result came back from Columbia University's Lamont Laboratory. All suspicion that Croton Point was an illusion created by Fairbridge's fondness for symmetry, my weakness for the unorthodox, and

an errant C14 date instantly vanished. The age was 5,560 ±
200 years.

Two different laboratories, testing two different materials,
charcoal and shell, a couple of years apart had been in agreement that Croton Point and Montrose Point had been living sites
of oyster collectors when, to the extent of geologic knowledge,
both stations were at least a mile from oyster-producing waters.
There had to be something missing from geologic knowledge.

One variable in physiographic conditions following the retreat of the Wisconsin has not been mentioned up to now. During our Fairbridge period it would only have been a distraction,
and a factor, moreover, that we could not measure. This variable, but certainly not imponderable, is the rebound or recovery
of height of the surface of the earth when it was relieved of the
mountainous weight of the ice mass. Perhaps mountainous is
the wrong word, for mountains are built into and are integral
with the crustal structure; but the ice mass was extraneous to
this structure and an immense burden on it, and the effect was
depressing. Most of the area glacially weighted down is still
uplifting, and, curiously enough, Croton Point is at the hinge,
or bend point, between upwarp of all the land to the north of it,
even on to the Arctic Circle, and the sinking of land to the south
and eastward. This southerly sinking is a bending down of the
edge of the crust, the continental shelf, which now has to support the tremendous tonnage of seawater and the lesser tonnage
of sediments that bury it. The land north of Croton Point has
been freed of its burden; the continental shelf has taken on a
load.

What we now had to consider was this possibility: at about
6000 B.P. the sea, though forty feet lower in absolute level than
at present, and the crust of the earth in the lower Hudson, still
depressed by the glacier, *were in the same relationship to each
other as they now are;* that is, Haverstraw Bay was as wide,
shore to shore, as it is now. From that level of conformation,
sea and crust continue to rise together, in synchronization. But
not quite in exact synchronization: when the sea has a spell of
quick rising, it forges somewhat ahead of the land, the lower
Hudson becomes deeper and more saline, and oysters move into

this favorable environment. Then the rebounding land begins to catch up, the lower Hudson shallows out, the ratio of salt water to fresh water drops, and—no oysters. Any discrepancy between the elevation of Haverstraw Bay and the Atlantic coast, according to the shoreline-peat age depths, could be very easily explained: the continental shelf did not rebound very much because it was sustaining the effect of the rising, encroaching ocean.

Arrival at this ingenious solution, which explained everything we knew and made no assumptions about anything we didn't know, made new men of us. We changed our digging location to a new midden, about fourteen miles downriver and on the western shore, in a search for diagnostic artifacts; and Newman turned his attention toward more peat dates, this time in Haverstraw Bay itself, almost directly across the river from Montrose Point.

Salisbury Meadow and Ring Meadow, about a mile south of Bear Mountain Bridge, are peat accumulations of considerable depth, with enough fuel in them to cook all the oatmeal in Ireland during any given winter. The peat had built up as the level of water rose postglacially, so that it was the perfect gauge for dating of rise. Cores were drilled all the way to the bottom, which was ninety-three feet down. A piece of wood that had been lying on a sandy beach at that level was turned over to Lamont, along with peat samples from the twenty-foot level, the twenty-one foot level, and the nine-foot level. The ages were: ninety-three-foot level, 12,500 ± 600 years; twenty-seven-foot level, 4,630 ± 470 years; twenty-one-foot level, 4,080 ± 220 years; 9-foot level, 2,500 ± 250 years. This was the Atlantic-shore column all over again, and it takes no aptness with figures to interpolate for 6000 B.P. The high-water mark at Croton Point and Montrose Point was forty feet below what it is now. Furthermore, it is plain that postglacial rebound was negligible after that time. Newman had figured that 75 percent of it had already taken place by 12,500 B.P.

I was beginning to feel persecuted. If the Fairbridge scheme of ups and downs did not hold water, and the rebound play did not stand up, what other gimmick was topographically possible? And then there came to me in a dream that gem of engineering advice once expostulated by that misanthropic master of the reverse twist, the late W. C. Fields, "Don't raise the bridge, folks—lower the river." Would it work vice versa? The lower Hudson could be raised without budging the earth's crust by so much as an inch. It could be raised to keep pace with the rise in sea level very simply—by silting.

Now our theory, more in the nature of a confession of past errors and oversights, was this: the lower Hudson, fjord-banked on both sides when the water was lower, had always been as wide as it is now, and its present shallowness is due entirely to sedimentation, of which thirty to thirty-eight feet had been deposited in the last six thousand years. Very little has been published on the sedimentation of the lower Hudson, but tests made early in the century seem to show that the bottom is mud to depths of up to four hundred feet. The question is how much of this mud has been silted in and how much is glacial till dropped by the Wisconsin when it melted. A thirty-foot deposit of sediment in six thousand years means a rate of only six inches a century, hardly unthinkable for an estuary that has no means of cleaning itself, since it has no gradient and the incoming tides run counter to its current. Now all we had to believe was that the Croton Point and Montrose Point middens were located on promontories some fifty feet above the shoreline, but no more than an easy slope away from it, say a hundred feet. Surely we could postulate that much walking on the part of people who used their feet even when they rested, as something to sit on.

We had by then moved our digging downriver to the opposite shore at a site called Twombly Landing, where the placement of the midden is even less self-explanatory than at Croton and Montrose. A fifty-foot-long ridge of shell yielding hundreds of artifacts, it is located on a narrow terrace or bench a hundred feet (the height of a twelve-story building) above the level of the Tappan Zee. The only access to this penthouse of a site is by a rill that borders it to the north, the bouldered bed of which provides a stairway with a forty-five-degree slope, rough going but humanly possible. To look up now at this site from the

beach, which is nonexistent at high tide, is to know that there
must have been an exploitable oyster bed in the vicinity and no
dry camping spot nearer than that elevated perch in which to
shuck and eat them; it is to know, therefore, that the midden
makers had taken to the hills here only when the lower Hudson
had reached its present width.

Twombly Landing is only fourteen miles south of Croton
Point, but the content of its midden is surprisingly different.
The bulk of the shell is oyster, and there is the same ribbed
mussel, but there is in addition enough bay scallop, hard clam
or quahog, and whelk to show that these species grew in
nearby waters along with the oysters and were gathered for
eating. This amounts to a fully coastal inventory of mollusks,
what you would find along the shores of the open sea where
salinity is about thirty-five parts per thousand. Comparison was
ineluctable: this high-salinity period that produced a whole sea-
food menu downriver must have been the same high-salinity
period that produced the biggest oysters upriver. And if it was,
then the Hudson was as wide six thousand years ago as it is
now, and the explanation is mud, the sedimentation of millennia.

In our enthusiasm for the high old Twombly midden and its
array of open-sea mollusks, we thought it might antedate Croton Point; and on this assumption the Ottinger Foundation gave
us a grant to pay for C_{14} dating and similar luxuries when,
working now out of Briarcliff College, Briarcliff Manor, we
found a hearth in association with the lowest shell. There was
about a quart of charcoal in the hearth, two samples of which
we sent out: one to a commercial laboratory, Geochron, and one
to Yale as a double check.

In due time we had the results: the Geochron assay was
4,725 years; Yale's, 4,750 years. (The assay costs and financial
help in digging the site were provided through the good offices
of our Congressman, Richard L. Ottinger, a noted conservationist, by his family's Ottinger Foundation.) The Twombly
midden was almost exactly 1,000 years younger than the big
shell layers at Croton and Montrose points; and if this proved
anything at all, it proved that the Hudson was not as wide
5,860 years ago, when it was forty feet below present level, as

it was 1,000 years later, when it was twenty-seven feet below present level, by Newman's Salisbury Meadow peat.

It was now apparent that we had exhausted all the easy, one-explanation-covers-everything answers to the lower-Hudson problem, and it seemed that we were back to where we had started: We knew that there had been two heavy-salinity periods, and they were, in time, where the Fairbridge scheme placed them; probably if we dug another ten years, we would be able to interpolate for the rest of his ups and downs. And then came the new count on C_{14}, and it was like the mod era enveloping us.

Croton Point becomes 7,100 years old and Twombly 5,700 years old, and the difference between them becomes 1,400 years. As they are retrodated, they move backward against a fixed barrier: the 10,000 B.P. limit when C_{14} time and solar time are equivalent. Now when we interpolate for a 7,100-year-old Croton Point, using Newman's Salisbury Meadow peat column with its bottom date of 12,500 B.P. for 94 feet, we get a value of 65 feet below present instead of 40 feet. It was all too clear that after seven years of work, we had only succeeded in digging ourselves in deeper, by about 25 feet. The Twombly midden was a skyscraper site 140 feet above the oyster beds, and where Croton Point and Montrose Point were in relation to salt water we were now too intimidated to venture a guess.

And then it dawned on us: it didn't really matter. The geological answer was not yet found, but the archaeological answer lay at our feet. We knew who these shell-midden makers were and whence they had come. *They had always lived in the lower Hudson, as previously defined, that terminal stretch of the river on the margin of fresh water and water salty enough to support marine mollusks; what we had been overlooking was that the lower Hudson had not always been where it is now.* In the millennia before oysters reached as far north as Haverstraw Bay, it had been out somewhere on the continental shelf, in what is now called the Hudson Canyon, the undersea trench that was once the ancient Hudson Valley through the broad coastal plain that stretched, at its maximum, 120 miles east of New York City. When the lower Hudson was out there, the midden makers lived out there, where were the oysters that meant more in their lives than mere food.

There is no way now of knowing whether there were Amerinds living on the continental shelf when the sea began its glacier-melt rise from eighteen to nineteen thousand years ago. Those who deny any American population before about fifteen thousand years ago will say, "Positively not," quite confident that no evidence is ever likely to rise from the bottom, four hundred feet down, to contradict them. But there is a C_{14} date of approximately 10,000 B.P. on a site in a limestone cave in Florida now about thirty-five feet under water (a skull was found at this site with parts of the brain still preserved inside) that does establish population near the seaboard when a considerable portion of the continental shelf was still dry and habitable land. There certainly is no reason why we should not assume that the lower Hudson, well east of Long Island, had its permanent, oyster-eating residents at the same time.

Foot by foot, year by year, the rising sea invaded the Hudson Valley, salinizing the water farther and farther upstream, even unto the narrows of the riverbed now spanned by Bear Mountain Bridge. The oyster eaters were not aware of these subtle changes in geography taking place over generations, for, to them, where they lived was where they had always lived, along a stretch of the river that produced oysters. This was the habitat to which their way of life was adjusted; they were the lower-Hudson riverine people.

But that is not what the archaeology of the midden sites tells about them; they were not even riparian, much less riverine. The midden sites are mere camping stopovers, hardly more than bivouacs, certainly not villages or even seasonal settlements. The only evidence that anything at all was taken from the Hudson is the shells; these are antacidic and preserve bone very well, but among the thousands of bone fragments we have collected over the years there is only a small sample of fish remains. Nor is any fishing gear to be found: no notched-pebble net sinkers such as lie strewn by the hundreds around fishing-camp sites; no fish hooks or gorges for line fishing; none of the specialized kind of projectile heads used in spear fishing—the harpoon, leister, or gig. There are a few fragments but no convincing provenience of adzes and other kinds of woodworking tools for the manufacture of dugouts or other water craft; if the oyster gatherers used some sort of float in gathering shellfish in water over their heads, it must have been a stray log or a raft of lashed driftwood. When these people paid their visits to the riverbank, it was as though they made no special preparation for a visit to a waterfront at all.

It is unthinkable that they would have spurned fish entirely, since during the spring spawning season the waters must have teemed with shad and other species. We have to suppose that fish bones seldom got thrown in with the shell and that fish were taken by unspecialized tools. Stone projectile points— spear, dart, or javelin heads—are the most numerous class of artifacts found in lower-Hudson shell middens, but they are of conventional hunting types, without the barbs one would expect in a weapon head that must snag in flesh for retrieval. One is forced to believe either that these simple penetrating points served well enough for the short period during which the midden makers remained at the river, or that some wholly perishable, expedient kind of spear was used, a plain wooden shaft cut off near a branch so that it had a pronged or hooked end. In any case, the equipment is not that of fishermen by trade.

Everything bespeaks the brevity yet the periodicity of sojourn at these stations. Fireplaces are rarely found, because the fires were at ground surface, never in pits or stone-enclosed hearths. The overall shell midden consists of innumerable small mound-like dumps, the contents of which could be measured in bushels —the garbage of a small band for perhaps no more than a week. The amount of deer bone, especially at Twombly and Croton Point, neither of which could have been deer-hunting environs, strongly suggests that the midden makers came to the riverbank lugging a haunch or two of deer with them to fill in the menu in case oysters were in short supply or in case the water was too cold for collecting them. And finally in this list of evidence, so much of it negative, of the special character of the midden sites, is the absence of burials. It is not likely that there were many deaths, considering the brevity of stay, while a band encamped on the riverbank, yet over the centuries there must have been some. Perhaps the bodies were consigned to the river, but it is just as possible that they were borne away for funeral rites and disposal to a traditional place elsewhere, a place that was "home," or the seat of the band or clan or tribe.

What is the special character that all this suggests for these shell-midden camps? We know pretty much what kind of life our midden makers had to lead from the nature of their food-getting routine. They were usufructians: that is, they were users of the fruits of the earth as nature provided them. They were harvesters only, not sowers. They hunted and foraged, with skill and exact knowledge of the food resources of the district they considered their own by hereditary right, going from berry patch to nut grove, from swampy haunts of turtles and plantations of edible roots to fishing brooks and deer runs. They could not settle down very long in one place, as could crop raisers; and whenever they did settle down for a short time, it had to be in small bands. The forest supplied a wide variety of food for omnivorous man, but he had to roam constantly to be where it was when it was ready for plucking, and there was never enough in any one place to feed a community of mouths for a year, or even for a full season.

Now we have to imagine one of these bands, perhaps ten to fifteen persons, ranging in age from grandparents to infants, at the end of a hard Northeastern winter. This band has spent the previous three or four months of closed-in weather in a camp in a sheltered cove in the hills, isolated and lonely. Now the game has been hunted out, the supply of preserved foods—dried meat, fish, and nut and seed meal—is down to crumbs, and animals and men have scoured the earth of everything edible left over from the year before. Half-starved, with eyes mattering and lungs congested from the heating and cooking fires in the wickiups, which have grown sour and fetid with too intimate living and insanitation, the band moves out as soon as the ice begins to break up and the snow season is past. It heads for the only wide-open space in the region, Haverstraw Bay or the Tappan Zee, those prairies of water across which blow the still chill but eye-cleaning, lung-clearing winds. It is here that spring comes first. There is a variation from year to year, depending on the number of hours of clear sunshine, but green-up time in the marshes and thickets along the Hudson shores is never less than a week and often two weeks ahead of the stirring of roots and the rising of sap inland. (This is true today, but when the inland region was heavily forested, with the trees, though leafless, shielding out the sun's rays, the difference may have been even greater. The cause of this climatic precocity is, of course, that the shores are at sea level and that they receive not only direct sunshine but the refraction of it off the water.)

This band may be the first to arrive at the river, but it will be joined within a day or so by all the bands which have their hunting grounds in the vicinity, each band occupying a spot that has been "in the family" for generations—rather like modern urbanites with their lakefront or seashore cottages to which they return summer after summer. With this convening begins a most crucial occasion in the life of the tribe, the people to whom the bands consider themselves to belong. It is a time of reunion and the renewal of the bonds of clan and consanguinity after the long separation, and after the deaths and births and other changes the winter has brought. It is a time of visitation, gossip, and exchange of information; of romantic dalliance among the nubile; of conferring among the elders; of ceremony, ritual, and "medicine"; and of festival and feast, to the extent that there is something to be happy about and something to feast on.

It was with considerable satisfaction, then, that after reaching these conclusions about our midden makers, we came on this passage from an essay by Verne F. Ray, "The Life Cycle of the Plateau Sanpoil," reprinted in *The North American Indians: A Source Book* (see the Bibliography of this volume), on one of the more typical cultural groups of the Plateau region of northwest Washington State:

Life began anew for the Sanpoil with the coming of each Spring. After the enforced extreme inactivity of the winter months the first signs of spring were occasion for rejoicing. Moreover, fresh food would soon again be available to replace the winter diet of dried products broken only by an occasional meal of venison. The underground houses were deserted at the first opportunity. Temporary camps were established nearby for the sake of a change in surroundings and fresher air. The transfer of residence was usually made during the month called "Time that the buttercups bloom," which corresponds roughly to March. The new quarters were occupied for two or three weeks during which time the men gathered shell fish and hunted fowl and rabbits. At the same time the women were digging the few early edible roots which had appeared on the warm sandy hillsides near the river, and were gathering prickly pears which were eagerly eaten after the spines had been burned off and they had been roasted. At this time those who had spent the winter away from home returned one by one to their own villages.

More than thirty-five hundred transcontinental miles separate our oyster eaters and the Sanpoil; and there are sixty centuries between them across the ages—actually more: we may reasonably fix their habitation out on the continental shelf at ten thousand years ago, for that is the C_{14} date ($10,000 \pm 200$) of a log recovered by diving archaeologists from a cave floor in Florida now forty feet under water. To object that Florida was occupied at this time because it was warm and the lower Hudson was not because of its hard winters is to ignore the fact that all over the present United States the same kind of people were living at the same cultural level at about the same time. At the Raddatz Rock Shelter in Sauk County, Wisconsin, with an average winter temperature below that of southern New York, and well below that of southern New York at sea level, there is occupation evidence in a stratum dated 11,000-10,000 B.P., and Warren L. Wittry, the excavator, suggests an age in excess of twelve thousand years. At the Modoc Rock Shelter in southwestern Illinois, in Danger Cave in Nevada, and in Fort Rock Cave in Oregon, there are dates on lowest occupation layers of 11,000 B.P., and these are certainly in foul-winter-weather zones.

Yet the thirty-five hundred miles and the hundred centuries are as nothing. For the seventy-one hundred years that we can document, by the corrected C_{14} date for Kettle Rock, and the ten thousand years that we have a right to deduce, from the Florida data, this way of life had successfully persisted in America, and it bears the stamp of having been developed out of something very like it thousands of years before 10,000 B.P. It is nothing like that of the Clovis big-game hunters, in pattern, in stone technology, or in the location of its sites. This usufructianism is the way of life that any thoughtful argument about American prehistory must account for, along with the Clovis spearmen. Yes, the Clovisians were everywhere within the present limits of the United States eleven to twelve thousand years ago, but so were the usufructians, and they were much the more numerous.

5

The Ups and Downs of Beringia

IN THE PREVIOUS CHAPTER was introduced, by the somewhat indirect and underhand method of personal experience, the proposition that the Wisconsin-Würm glacier was the great geopolitical tyrant of its time. Its protean changes in shape and size kept altering the shape of continents at a rate that would have driven a cartographer out of his mind. Nowhere were those alterations so rapidly extensive as in the Siberian-Alaskan region, where the Eastern and Western Hemispheres approach, at the Bering Strait, within fifty-six miles of each other—a day's journey in a umiak, as they figure overwater distance at that latitude. Here is where the game of "Earliest Americans" in which we are now engaged finds its field of play.

As in Monopoly or chess, a playing board is indispensable. This would be a map of the Pacific Ocean lying like God's own millpond between an eastern shore of what we Americans call our Far West and a western shore universally known as the Far East, the coast of Asia. There is no enclosure to the south, the Pacific becoming the Antarctic Ocean at the Antarctic Circle. But in the north the land masses of the Eastern and the Western Hemispheres arch toward that union with each other that has existed for long periods in the past and still lies not deep beneath the surface of the Bering Sea.

The gap between Alaska and the Siberian peninsula of Chukotka (also written Chukotsk, Chuckchi, and Chukchu) is not only the boundary that separates the present two greatest powers on earth, the United States of America and the Soviet Union; through it runs the international dateline that decides, for us, where today is and where tomorrow is, and for Asians, where today came from and where yesterday went. Merely to glance at this situation, with the ups and downs of the continental shelf during the Wisconsin-Würm now in mind, is to suspect that there once had to be a great deal more between the two continents than a land bridge; the final separation must have been preceded by a gamut of union and disunion.

The existence of even a causewaylike land bridge for one-way traffic has been generally conceded by Americanists for scarcely three decades. During the regime of speculative repression imposed on American studies by the late Ales Hrdlicka of the Smithsonian Institution and his cabinet of scientific colleagues, which lingered in some degree until the era of C14 dating began in 1950, a hands-across-the-sea connection would have been of only geologic, not archaeological, interest. The Hrdlickan ukase was that there had been no population movement into North America before man in Siberia had reached the Neolithic cultural stage, when he made and used seaworthy boats capable of crossing stretches of the open sea. Hrdlicka had no data at his command about either the era when men first began to make boats or about the lie of land or water at the Bering Strait, but fact was a requirement he laid upon his opponents, rarely himself. Since it was even then known that the British Isles had, in late Paleolithic and Mesolithic times, during a period of glacially lowered sea level, been a peninsular appendage of Europe, the failure to imagine a similar attachment during the same period for the similarly proximal Alaska and Chukotka strikes one as parochialism at the very least and at its very worst. If the waters of the Atlantic had been lower at that time, why not the waters of the Pacific?

The serious investigation of what underlay the Bering Strait began in the early 1950's and was largely the work of D. M. Hopkins, research geologist with the United States Geological Survey. Simple (as to theory, not as to execution) mensuration of the depth of offshore waters soon revealed that a lowering of sea level, or a combination of this and an upthrust of the sea bottom (and Alaska is certainly in a period of tectonic restlessness), of only 46 meters, or about 152 feet, would expose a causeway or land bridge between Chukotka and Alaska south of the strait, by way of St. Lawrence Island. A further subsidence and/or upthrust of about 13 feet would re-create a second causeway north of the strait. Since estimates were then being made—world-wide data not having yet been obtained—that sea level had dropped during the Wisconsin-Würm by from 300 to 400 feet, the Bering land bridge became a matter of when, not whether.

But depth plumbing and the mapping of the offshore bottom continued, and in 1956 Hopkins found, at 100 meters or about 312 feet, the Lost Atlantis of the Arctic, a vast undersea platform measuring a thousand miles along a north-south diameter running through the Bering Strait, which, if exposed, would add to the dry-land area of the earth a Canada-sized territory approaching that covered by the whole Wisconsin glacier.

The question of whether it had actually been exposed was answered during the 1960's by a series of C14-dating studies such as those that had caused our troubles in the lower Hudson: the sea had receded by at least 123 meters, or 400 feet—more probably, some believe, 420 to 450 feet. This Beringia was an enormous, low-lying plain, bleak and monotonous and as open as the sea itself to the winds and the weather off the polar ice cap; but it was unglaciated, and it was, for millennium after millennium, in some part or section, there.

The difference between the hitching together of the peninsulas of Chukotka and Alaska by a mere isthmus or a pair of land bridges and their incorporation in a territory so large that their peninsular identity was lost in it, imposes a whole new set of premises on how and when the New World became humanly populated. Neat little lines of dashes indicating routes of travel out of Asia, across a footbridge over the Bering Strait

and into the corridor, no longer suffice. As sensitive as its
expanse was to the slightest vacillation in sea level, the am-
phibious subcontinent of Beringia, more boundless beach than
mainland, was no dead end of the earth. Cold and drought
notwithstanding, it had its flora and fauna in an established
ecological pattern; that is, there was thriving life there, and
where there is life, for the omnivorous there is food.

The question that archaeology has now to ask is not, When
did man become American? but, When, in the course of his
quest for an adequate diet obtainable by the crafts of which he
was then master, did man become Beringian? He cannot be
thought of as a trekker, following a trail to a destination, so it
must be assumed that he came into Beringia because it afforded
what he needed to keep himself alive and content, and that he
did not, therefore, move on until he had to. But such were the
times, so incessant were the changes in his habitat, that there
could not have been many generations in succession that called
the same landscape home.

The Wisconsin-Würm began building up, it is estimated by
a consensus of most glaciologists and geologists, about 70,000
years ago. This recurrence of universal frigidity brought to an
end a long, mild, iceless period called the Sangamon interglacial, which had begun some 120,000 years ago, when the
Illinoian-Riss glacier petered out. This summer, climatically
speaking, of 50,000 years was a critical time in man's evolution.
He entered it at the *Homo erectus* level, that is, a Neanderthaloid, and at its close was an archaic *Homo sapiens*, or nearly
such. This does not mean that Neanderthals ceased to exist—in
western Europe classic Neanderthals survived into the first
phase of the Würm—but that the races of men were advancing
generally beyond *Homo erectus* to *sapiens*. Implicit in this
advance is their increasing success as a species of animal with
a culture, and their ability to spread, by reason of cultural
competence, into new environments. That cultural competence
was not, however, of a degree that would enable man to live in
large communities, which quickly exhaust available natural
foods, and the social unit was the small family band. As man
prospered, multiplying in numbers, new family bands had to

strike out farther and farther to find food-producing niches. Since *Sinanthropus*, of the pre–*Homo erectus* pithecanthropoids, capable of making fire and of living in a climate colder than today's, was resident in a cave near Peking, about the latitude of North Korea, some 360,000 years ago (during the Mindel-Kansan glaciation), it is no less than probable that family bands of human beings extended their range into a hospitable Siberia during the benign Sangamon.

A hospitable Siberia? With world-wide climate during the Sangamon warmer than today, it had to be. The pollen evidence is that the timberline, the limit of forestation, was much farther north than now. Whatever else this means in the expansion of the environment familiar to subtropical- and temperate-zone men, it does mean fuel for cooking and warming fires and poles for lodges, both of which would seem to be indispensable to winter survival in even Sangamon Siberia. A more northerly tree limit would mean a more northerly limit of the taiga, the scrub tree-bush zone which provides fodder for browsing animals; and the tundra zone, which has a low animal-supporting capacity, would have been reduced in favor of more vegetation-producing zones. Almost from the beginning, man, as a carnivore, has been a member of faunal assemblages centering on big game, and the faunal assemblage of Sangamon Siberia would have been a natural place to find these animals.

But he could have gotten no farther east than the Bering Strait; Beringia had ducked out of sight at the end of the Illinoian-Riss glaciation and was, barring a tectonic upheaval, more deeply submarine than it is now by a few meters during that long climatic optimum. The higher sea level during the Sangamon, resulting, possibly, from dehydration of continental bodies of water and melting down of alpine glaciers and polar ice caps, only made more certain that the Alaskan shores were attainable only by the winged, whether water or aerial.

Although it is something of an aside, the matter of human travel across the Beringia of the Illinoian-Riss falls reasonably into place here. Few authoritative voices have been raised in discussion of such a possibility. The noted geographer Dr. George Carter, formerly head of the Isaiah Bowman Institute

of Geography at Johns Hopkins University, has argued in favor
of it, from both geologic and archaeological evidence. But
geologists and archaeologists have given his evidence rough
treatment—rougher than valid speculation about ambiguous
data deserves. Beringia did have its animal population during
the Illinoian-Riss, even as it did during the Wisconsin, and the
mind might at least be kept open to the off chance that man
was among them. One might feel that at his developmental
stage at the time—he was emerging from the pithecanthropoid
stage and was not yet *Homo erectus*—he could not have coped
with the prevailing hyperborean conditions. But, remembering
Sinanthropus in his 360,000-year-old lair in Choukoutien Cave,
Peking, with the ashes of campfires and the bones of the beasts
he fed on strewn about, one hesitates to trust feeling too far
when one has no experience at being a *Pithecanthropus*.

The species or varieties of animals in Choukoutien Cave included an ancient elephant, two rhinoceroses, horses, an extinct
elk, an extinct buffalo, a wolf, bears, hyenas, a saber-toothed
cat, a giant beaver, and other cats and rodents we wouldn't
recognize if we saw them.

In his summary chapter in *The Bering Land Bridge*, which
he edited and which contains in its almost five hundred pages
every scrap of information known up to 1968 about Beringia,
Hopkins notes the "dramatic occurrence" there during the Illinoian-Riss and Wisconsin-Würm, of the saiga, or steppe antelope, and the yak-like *Bos poephagus*. He continues:

But even more impressive is the fact that the obligatory grazers—
horse, bison and mammoth—are by far the most common fossil land
mammals collected in late Pleistocene beds in Alaska; in fact, these
animals compose 85 to 95 percent of the total individuals in four
large fossil mammal faunas collected near Fairbanks. Feral horse
and bison can survive in present day Alaska only in a few restricted,
highly specialized and isolated environments. Grasslands must have
been far more widely distributed when large heads of bison, horse
and mammoth were present.

Man at either the *Pithecanthropus* or *Homo erectus* level
would not be an incongruity in this picture. But we are dealing
in the actual; and, in fact no cranium of a *Pithecanthropus* or

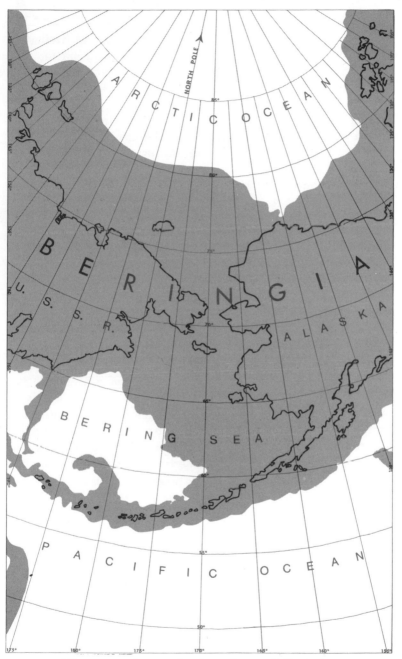

The now submerged subcontinent of Beringia.

a *Homo erectus* has ever been found in America, and Beringians during the Illinoian-Riss glacial or Chukotkans during the Sangamon interglacial would have had to be the former or the latter. But this is not too sweeping a statement: the crania ten thousand years old or older found so far—all of which belong to a narrow-headed, low-browed, sagittal-ridged archaic *Homo sapiens*—can be numbered on the fingers of a couple of catcher's mitts, with several being in dispute.

Illinoian-Riss followers of game into Alaska seem only a remote possibility, and both game and followers had to stop at the water's edge of the Bering Strait during the Sangamon. But shortly after seventy thousand years ago, when the Wisconsin-Würm began to reach its full growth, that barrier ceased to be, as sea level began to recede from Beringia's broad back. From that time, say sixty-five thousand years ago to be safe, until the last dike through the St. Lawrence went permanently under rising seas about 10,000 B.P., all or a traversible part of Beringia knew sunlight except for the period from about 30,000 B.P. to 25,000 B.P. Sometime, somewhere, in Beringia, archaeologists should come upon traces of human population sixty-five thousand years old. *They* will be the first Americans.

This is, perhaps, not the safest prediction ever made, but there is more behind it than a self-deluded sense of prophetic mission. If there were any human species resident in Beringia for the next twenty-five thousand years, that is, from 65,000 B.P. to the end of the Early Wisconsin about 40,000 B.P., they had most likely established themselves near there during the Sangamon. As climatic conditions worsened with the onsetting Wisconsin, they had perhaps five thousand years to adjust their lives to the imperceptible shortening and cooling of the summers and the lengthening of the winters. As long as the game did not disappear—and it did not—they could make out, in an area they had inhabited for thousands of generations. But, by the same token, the climatic deterioration would have repelled, not attracted, further settlement by those not adapted to the cold. The effect of the Wisconsin on population movement was to displace all life southward; but Beringia was a special case. Here new game-supporting land appeared, as the ice mass spread; and though the backside froze, the stomach could be filled.

This is the anomaly of Beringia: the bigger the land-consuming Wisconsin grew, the bigger Beringia grew; the less land there was elsewhere, as the ice mass trespassed on it, the more there was of the territory of Beringia. But the bigger it was, the more isolated, the more adamantly walled off from the rest of the world, it became. The conspiracy of circumstance was so ingeniously contrived to prevent Beringia from participating in any significant way, that we could write it off as a mere geophysical curiosity, a kind of trick played by nature just for the fun of it, except that here was the indisputable conduit by which some fifty biological species were transferred from the Eastern world to the Western world—and one of the species was man.

But a second set of complications is involved in the mechanics of Beringia and the Wisconsin glacier. Hopkins says, "The complex chronological sequence of openings and closings of a land bridge from Siberia to Alaska, and of closings and openings of a corridor from Alaska to Central North America has evidently operated increasingly as a set of one-way valves, allowing unrestricted flow of biota in one direction and extremely limited flow in the other."

That is, whenever the inlet valve, permitting the flow of living things to cross what is now the Bering Strait, was open, the outlet valve, the corridor between the Laurentide and Cordilleran ice masses along which Clovis man is supposed to have traveled south, was closed. We may well wonder, then, just how well this system operated, or whether it actually did, and our skepticism is going to lead us into considering alternatives. The Wisconsin waxed and waned, it is true, with what was, on the geologic time scale, a restless inconstancy, and there must have been short periods when man could have crossed the land bridge just as it was closing and made it to the corridor just as it was opening; but he would have had to have both a map and a schedule to do this, and how could he have had either? Only in the last few years have even we, the investigating generation, learned what actually took place.

Studies over the past decade of the Würm in Europe and the Wisconsin in America have confirmed the view that the two ice masses were synchronous in their behavior: there were three phases of advance separated by two phases of deep retreat, or interstadials. These were protracted periods of warmth within a glacial period, as interglacials like the Sangamon were protracted periods of warmth between glacial periods. But the two major interstadials, during which continental ice almost disappeared altogether, are not the whole story. The exact details of the story differ according to every student of the subject, but a composite version of Wisconsin events as understood in 1970 would include the following series of glacial substages or advances, separated by periods of shrinkage:

1. Early Wisconsin   70,000 B.P.
                    Port Talbot interstadial

2. Middle Wisconsin   50,000 B.P.
                    Peorian interstadial

3. Late Wisconsin
        Farmdale   25,000 B.P.
                    Interstadial
        Iowan   23,000 B.P.
                    Interstadial
        Tazewell   19,000 B.P.
                    Interstadial
        Cary   16,000 B.P.
                    Interstadial
        Mankato   14,000 B.P.
                    Two Creeks interstadial
        Valders   11,000 B.P.
                    Interstadial
        Cochrane   10,000 B.P.

4. Anathermal (meaning "return of heat"), the
    beginning of the climate we are living in
    now, though also having its cooler and
    warmer subdivisions   9,500 B.P.

It will be immediately noted that all the substages are attributed to the Late Wisconsin and none to the Early and

Middle Wisconsin. The explanation is simply that substages are known by the terminal moraines they left at their point of farthest advance. When the Late Wisconsin made its advance to Long Island, fronting thence westward across southern Ohio and angling up to southern Wisconsin (its terminal moraine there gives it its name), it erased the moraines of the substages of the Middle Wisconsin; and the Middle Wisconsin erased the moraines of Early Wisconsin substages. The substages given for the Late Wisconsin are obviously readvances during the Late Wisconsin's general retreat from its Long Island climax.

If we estimate for the Early and Middle Wisconsin the same number of substages (seven) that occurred during the Late Wisconsin, we arrive at a total of twenty-one readvances, set off, of course, by a similar number of ice recessions. To each of these, sea level responded commensurately, and whenever it rose or fell, so, inversely, did submersible Beringia. From at least seventy thousand years ago to fifteen hundred years ago there must not have been stable sea level—what geologists call a still-stand—for more than a century or two at a time. The listed substage-interstadial oscillations of sea level, for which Fairbridge's scheme would serve as an average illustration (it was only ill timed, not misconceived), were only undulations in general trends: down during Wisconsin-Würm I, II, and III to 350 or 400 feet below present level; up during the Port Talbot and the Peorian interstadials to near recovery of present level. Such recovery entails the entire submersion of Beringia, for perhaps two thousand years during each interval, but only minor interruptions in its bonding of East and West.

The one infringement on its territorial integrity that Beringia did not suffer was glaciation. It did not receive enough moisture for the accumulation of snowfields, for the same reason that the Great Basin of the United States receives little rain: the moisture-laden winds off the ocean drop their burden of dampness as rain or snow as they rise over the coastal ranges. In Alaska the coastal ranges curve out across the North Pacific toward Asia in a great arch; the Aleutians are the peaks of mountains in the coastal range isolated as islands. It was their southward, sea-facing slopes on which the sea-wind moisture was deposited; under Wisconsin-Würm climatic conditions it fell as snow,

which compacted into alpine or mountain glaciers. Alaskan glaciation was part of the Cordilleran, not the continental ice sheet.

Beringia, lying on the leeward side of the coastal ranges, was
a near-desert. Hopkins summarizes:

> Compelling paleontological evidence confirms the assumption that
> Alaska had a drier climate and supported Xeric [semidesert] vegeta-
> tion unlike any modern tundra, during parts of the Illinoisian and
> Wisconsin glaciations. Colinveaux reports high abundances of Arte-
> misia [the genus to which our Western sagebrush, *Artemisia triden-
> tata*, belongs] in many Alaskan pollen spectra of full glacial age.

Yet, as he goes on to explain, the abundance of the obligatory
grazers in the fossil fauna argues for a wider extension of
grasslands. I think we may assume that these must have been
nourished by the mists that were doubtless prevalent during the
short summers, seeping in off the Arctic Ocean's briefly melting
ice cover.

It is now possible to make an assessment of Beringia, considered as the dry region north of the coastal ranges and their
alpine glaciation, as habitable by men at the level of culture of
that time. The temptations of the flesh—mammoth, bison, horse,
saiga, and *Bos poephagus*—were there in abundance, for the
kind of consumers of animal protein who littered Choukoutien
Cave near Peking, China, with the bones of dismembered prey.
But there was little else: none of the easily caught creepers and
crawlers, tortoises, snakes, lizards; none of the freshwater fish
or mollusks, because there were no freshwater streams; none
of the nuts, fruits, berries, roots, or stalks to be had for the
picking—very little of the vegetable at all, except the previously
mentioned droppings of herbivores. In that unblemished plain
there were no coves or other natural shelters and no wood out
of which to build shelters. If we place men as living there, we
shall have to imagine a shelter for them: a pit dug in the
ground behind a sand dune stabilized by the frost, covered over
with a mammoth hide and heated by fires of dung (it must have
been a frequent matter for decision toward the end of a hard
winter whether to burn this precious material or eat it).

It might be concluded that any inhabitants of inland Beringia during any of the three phases of the Wisconsin could have survived only as herd followers, since these migratory meat markets were the only dependable and abundant food resource. Hunters in the Sandian-Clovisian tradition they would not, however, have been. Even twenty-five thousand years ago, when the Late Wisconsin bared Beringia after the Peorian interstadial and blocked the corridor, stone projectile points were not being made in any of the regions adjacent to Beringia. The Aterians of North Africa were making stone points about thirty-five thousand years ago, as were the Solutreans of France, who were big-game hunters, some twenty-five to thirty thousand years ago. But they are half a world away. Nor do we have to reach so far for an argument. None of the stone-point cultures now known in Alaska exceeds, by the most generous estimates, nine thousand years of age. Exactly one pre–Late Wisconsin discovery is in the record of Alaskan prehistory, and it has been bulletined only, not reported in detail. It is the Old Crow site, discovered by Richard Harrington and said to have been C14-dated at "more than 20,000 years." But its projectile points, and tool industry, are of bone, the effectiveness of which against big game has already been discussed.

The tactics of pre-stone-projectile-point stalkers after big game would need to have been those of the jackal, the hyena, and the vulture, with a few added tricks of luring and ambush learned in the school of do or die. The straying young, the laggard cripples, the faltering senile, the mangled corpses abandoned by those killer cats, the saber-toothed and the Alaskan lion—these must have been the height of big-game ambition for those who had no weapon with which to wound seriously the tough and the swift. The Beringians of full glacial times had to make a living in just this precarious way if they were to survive at all in this far from the best of all possible worlds.

One would think some did survive; after all it must have been to improve just such a hard lot as this that stone projectile points were invented. But there is not the slightest evidence that Beringians invented them, or even had them, during any of the major phases of the Wisconsin—which is to say, before the corridor opened. And when was that? Guesses of all kinds,

shaded by the view of the guesser about when the corridor had
to have been used if his model of early America were to stand
up, have been set forth in the minutes of various conventicles.
It is time, therefore, to repeat the opinion of Hopkins, Beringia's
paleogeographer in residence:

> Unfortunately, little attention has been given to the detailed gla-
> cial chronology of the remote regions in Yukon territory, northeast-
> ern British Columbia and northern Alberta, where a conjunction of
> the Laurentide [continental] ice sheet and the Cordilleran glacier
> system would have formed earliest and persisted longest. One can
> state only than an ice-free corridor must have existed there during
> the Mid-Wisconsin episode of mild climate that took place between
> 35,000 and 25,000 years ago [the Peorian interstadial]; that waxing
> glaciation probably closed the corridor again earlier than 20,000
> years ago; and that the corridor must have remained closed until at
> least 14,000 years ago and possibly until almost 10,000 years ago.

We must be realistic. However many bands of human beings
found themselves pinned down in Beringia after entering it
during the Sangamon, or the Port Talbot or Peorian interstadials, they did well to hold their own in that gelid, misanthropic
netherworld during full glacial times, when no accident or mis-
adventure was anything less than grave. Those were not the
times nor the conditions for prosperity and increase in numbers;
there could hardly have been any teeming tribes standing
around in Alaska waiting for the corridor to open, whenever it
opened, even had they known that it was a corridor or that it
led anywhere.

It must be said again, now that what must be called the
northern or inland route across Beringia has been cursorily
surveyed: there must have been a better way into southerly
America, a quicker way, a way open more often and longer, a
way that could be taken by less specialized itinerants than the
big-game stalkers, a way along which food could be plucked
rather than killed after arduous, wily, and all too frequently
dangerous pursuit.

I do not know to whom should go the credit for first per-
ceiving that a glacier-flanking route down the Pacific coastal
shelf was just such a course. Probably it occurred to many

alert minds after the studies of Fairbridge and others on glacial-period sea-level fluctuation began to appear in the journals. It may be, therefore, somewhat arbitrary to name as the two sponsors in respectable scientific society of the Pacific-shore road the archaeologist Dr. Chester A. Chard and the paleoecologist Dr. Calvin J. Huesser. First or not, their pronouncements make them pioneer spokesmen.

Chard, a translator and editor of Russian-language archaeological literature and editor for Soviet Asia for the Council for Old World Archaeology, was writing as early as 1959, in the English journal *Antiquity*, in an article called "New World Origins: A Reappraisal": "It is my own belief that most of the record of such [early migrant] movements has been obliterated by rising sea levels." That is, the most important "corridor" had been the Pacific coastal shelf. For American audiences Chard was more explicit in the October, 1960, issue of *American Antiquity:* "The southern route along the coastal shelf may have played a more significant role in the initial settlement of the New World than did the northern route along the Arctic shore. . . . Owing to the difficulties of the terrain under present conditions, it seems virtually certain that the use of the southern route was confined to periods of lowered sea level when the *level coastal shelf* [italics mine] was exposed."

We have been at some pains in this chapter to show that lowered sea level was prevalent during the Wisconsin epoch. The stressing of the exposure of the *level coastal shelf* is necessary because the "present conditions" Chard speaks of are a ruggedly mountainous coastline that places a thousand detours around cliffs and inlets in the path of the coastal pedestrian.

Huesser begins his 250-page monograph *The Late-Pleistocene Environments of North Pacific North America* with this description:

The North Pacific coast of North America is a bleak and gloomy edge of the continent where the forces of nature are dynamic and often violent. Low-pressure storms are frequent invaders from the ocean, tracking inland over the western Cordillera and bringing heavy rains and cloudiness during the greater part of the year. In winter, at high elevations in the northern mountains, blizzard conditions prevail and deep snows accumulate that persist through the summer. The cyclonic disturbances are commonly associated with squalls and atmospheric turbulence, causing floods over the low-lying areas and strong tide rips through the islands and fjord networks of southeastern Alaska and British Columbia. Where cold water wells up from the ocean depths, particularly along the California and Oregon coasts, off-shore fogs form in summer, move landward by night and retreat under diurnal temperature control. Along this sector, storm winds, mostly in winter, have pitched up massive sand dunes and sped their destructive migration along broad alleys many miles inland.

Not an excerpt from a travel brochure, this passage. Yet after 250 pages of microscopic examination (literally, since any study of paleoenvironment has to depend on analysis of pollen grains in ancient soils), Huesser, fully cognizant of the current popularity of the northern, or inland, route, writes, somewhat diffidently:

Some favor is attached here to early *coastal* [italics mine] migration in preference to the generally accepted belief of passage through the continental interior. The coastal-migration thesis is suggested by: (1) equable oceanic climate, (2) available marine food and (3) greater travel facility by water, particularly through coast archipelagoes. If early man worked his way southward along the coast after having crossed the Bering Strait or the Bering-Chuckchi platform during the opening of the pre-Wisconsin interglacial when the platform was still exposed he could have reached California as early as 30,000 B.P. as some findings suggest. However, the traces he may have left along the way have not come to light because of several reasons.

The reasons are submersion under a rising sea, as in Chard, and site destruction by glaciation and vulcanism.

The relevance of Huesser's ill-expressed advantage 3 escapes us. The southern shoreline of Beringia was the first to emerge from the sea and the last to go under, and the *level coastal shelf* would obviate the need for water craft; moreover, a technology that would produce boats is not what we would like to credit to these strandloopers. But reasons 1 and 2 are the left jab and the right cross of conviction: all the plagues of the elements that Huesser explained so thoroughly, yes, but an absence of the extreme of immobilizing cold of the interior, and the prodigality with which the sea cast up shore dinners along the tidal margin. This prodigality, memorialized by the folk saying along the Northwest coast, "When the tide is out the table is set," is, in fact, that of a smorgasbord, requiring no more in the getting than quick hands, sticks, and stones; for the nourishment to be had is not embodied in formidable beasts like the mammoth or bison, and it does not attract killers menacing to man, like the lethal cats and the dire wolves. Seabeach is the overlapping zone of two environments, where the terrestrial mingles with the marine and where the legged creatures resort to feed on the biological flotsam and jetsam. As rambling men faced east and then south along the Pacific littoral, on the right hand was the biota of the tide range and tidal flats, shellfish and crustaceans and the leavings swept in from the deeps, and on the left hand were the vegetals and tool materials of the earth.

Beyond doubt it was this conjunction of two food-producing worlds that addicted the appetites of most aboriginal Americans, like our lower-Hudson oyster eaters, habituating them to shoreline environments with their aquatic cafeterias, and set the metronome of their lives. Most early Americans must have taken this way, where they who ran might ruminate, chewing their way from hemisphere to hemisphere as though on a traipse through a berry patch.

That this is the way it was depends on the existence of a continental-shelf line of march. And about this, Hopkins, of all people, seems dubious. The glacier that certainly stood in crystalline cliffs at the water's edge during the three Wisconsin maxima did not melt there as fast as the sea rose when warming trends set in, according to Hopkins. He writes:

It seems probable that the waxing phases of a glaciation are tightly linked to reductions in sea level, since glaciers can increase in mass only at the expense of the reservoir of water in the sea. During waning phases, on the other hand, sea level evidently begins to rise long before appreciable shrinkage of glacier margins begins.

By this scheme of put and take, there would have been a continental-shelf land bridge during glacial buildup, and a minimal to nonexistent one during glacial retreats, when it seems most likely that a warming climate would have heated up men's blood again and set them adventuring, after the conservatism forced on them by frigidity. Warmth induces confidence that there may be something better, rather than worse, beyond the horizon. Hopkins's second, pessimistic posit draws our scrutiny, therefore.

It is self-evident that a glacier melts along its front, where the ice is thinnest, most recent, most exposed, and farthest advanced into the region of warmth. Hopkins seems to think that the edge that was exposed to the Pacific held hard against the rise in temperature, while that which faced southward across the continental interior and that which faced the Atlantic melted and supplied the runoff which raised sea level. This theory is not easy to accept, while the contrary is: the sea-verge glaciers had to be the first to melt, since they are the source which would most quickly return water to the sea; otherwise sea-level rise would have lagged far behind the diminishment of the ice mass. Nothing could be more obvious than that the water shed by a melting glacial front onto land takes its time about wending its way back to the ocean.

Nor does all of it find its way there through river drainage systems. The great periglacial bodies of water like Lake Agassiz, which covered most of Ontario, Manitoba, Minnesota, and North Dakota, Lake Albany, which covered the Mohawk Valley, and the Great Lakes themselves of glacial time, larger than they are now, stored up enormous amounts of water and so long delayed its return to the sea, by evaporation and by discharge through stream systems. It was the lesson learned in our dealings with sea level in the lower Hudson that though the last cube of Wisconsin ice disappeared about six thousand years ago, it was not until five hundred years ago that the sea came up to its present level. During those fifty-five hundred years the land was dehydrating from its glacial soaking to the extent of a forty-foot rise in sea level.

Not a great deal of bared land was necessary to put the continental-shelf route into being: a withdrawal of the ice cliffs by fifteen to twenty miles, or even less, would have left tenantable an elongate zone stretching forward in the direction in which the sun dropped in autumn. It did not have to be a primrose path; all that was necessary was that there be men committed by experience, by temperament, and by physical makeup and adjustment to the kind of life that it allowed.

Physical makeup, physiologically and metabolically different from us? Yes, different enough from us that they could endure naked what we could not endure for very long clothed and internally fortified. Such folk do not have to be invented or conjectured (one would not dare suppose so wildly about ancient physical constitutions), for there are men alive today who exist in an environment even harsher than a homeland between a distant glacier and a chill ocean under a murky sky—exactly the kind of life that the corridor travelers lived. They live it in Tierra del Fuego, at the tip of South America; but where they learned how to live it, and where they got the bodies to live it, must go up and back to the strands of Beringia. These people are the Canoe Indians; and Carleton S. Coon, who studied them firsthand, reports on them thus in *The Origin of Races* (1962):

A far more spectacular and much better known example of cold adaptation is that of the Canoe Indians of Tierra del Fuego and adjacent South American shores and islands. . . .

When first discovered by Magellan, these Indians were going about in canoes in freezing weather with no clothing except an occasional sea otter skin cape, and with their bodies smeared with sea-mammal fat and ocher. At night they usually slept in small, domed huts covered with skins and heated by fires of Nothofagus, an evergreen tree closely related to the beech. This wood throws off great heat and burns nearly all night.

Except for the early morning hours these Indians were as warm indoors as we are. Out of doors they exposed themselves unclothed to heavy winds and pelting sleet and snow. Furthermore, they walked and swam in the icy water and dived for shellfish. The work of Hammel and his associates [of whom Coon was one] shows that the Fuegians, taking the Alakaluf [the tribe specifically studied] as an example, were able to survive freezing temperatures without clothing by burning off a large quantity of calories, much more than the Alaskan Indians needed to keep them warm at night. The

Alakaluf live mostly on shellfish and the flesh of sea mammals, and they eat heartily. Their basal metabolism is 160 per cent higher than the norm for whites at the same weight and stature.

How does this transfer of food calories into surface body heat occur? Coon says:

The hands of Alaskan Indians respond in the same fashion [as the hands of Eskimos] producing twice as much blood flow as those of white men tested under the same conditions. The same response was obtained from the hands of Alakaluf women who collect shellfish by hand in cold water. In Manchuria four groups of Mongoloids were tested by the Japanese for this same phenomenon, and a gradation or cline was found which corresponds to the climates of the regions inhabited by the people studied.

This dermic blood flow is only one of the mechanisms of adaptation to inclement conditions; another is morphological, the shape of the body and of its individual features, nose, facial structure, and so forth. Coon also mentions the strange case of the Australian desert tribe of Pitjenderas, who endure naked the day's burning heat, followed by a cooling off in the night to freezing or below. Sleeping on the ground, the Pitjenderans maintain nearly normal body warmth, but the temperature of their feet will fall as low as 54°F. This temperature drop at the extremities prevents loss of body heat in feet and hands, which, at a temperature more nearly that of the air, don't feel the chill as unpleasantness any more than the body at its normal temperature of 98.6° shivers at 72°.

These are primitive adaptations, and they provide the clues to the originating environments where they were the basic pattern for survival. Fully aware of what his Alakalufs mean to American prehistory, Coon writes:

A third conclusion [the other two are that subspecies of men tend to sort themselves out on this basis and that the adaptations, genetic and linked to climate, may have been acquired by several subspecies at the *Homo erectus* grade] is suggested by the Alakaluf study. It indicates that ill-clad human beings carrying fire and the crudest of tools (the Alakaluf cutting tool was a quahog shell) could have entered North America over the Bering Strait at any time the sea level was low enough to permit passage. At such times, with the flow of Arctic water cut off [flowing, that is from the Arctic Ocean through the Bering Strait] and the Japanese current swinging along the southern shoreline [of Beringia] the climate could have been no colder than it is in modern Tierra del Fuego.

There were, we can now safely say, a "level sea level" route along the Pacific coast and men physically fitted and technologically equipped for it. What we now need are the archaeological sites denoting the passage. These we already know, from Chard and Huesser, we are not going to find. Sea level has risen four hundred feet twice and on the order of three hundred feet once over this glacier-skirting beach route. And the evidence is not only well out of reach but very likely dissipated by current and tidal action. It could not have been much to begin with—sticks and edged and battered stone, and shell middens. But the middens would be more than sufficient. And there are some, along the southern California coast, that date from an horizon about six to seven thousand years ago.

Perversely enough, California archaeological doctrine does not look out longingly to the submerged continental shelf for the ancestors of these midden makers, as we do in the Hudson Valley, despite the fact that there is a C14 date of about 30,000 B.P. on hearths on Santa Rosa Island, about thirty miles off the coast of Santa Barbara. These hearths are associated with bones of butchered dwarf mammoth, which stood about four to six feet at the shoulder and which would have been easily taken without stone projectile points. With these hearths were a stone flake or two and an abalone shell—see Coon's statement about the use of quahog by the Alakaluf. The shell-midden makers of the California coast, it is currently construed, were people from the interior who happened on the food resource of shellfish during a meat shortage in the interior, rather than people who had always dined at the shore and who, forced to retreat by a rising sea, became acquainted with the animal protein running loose back in the hills. But we have assumed that our first arrivals were beachcombers before they were hunters, and we'll stick to it.

The Aleutian authority W. S. McLaughlin, in his contribution to *The Bering Land Bridge*, "Human Migration and Permanent Occupation in the Bering Sea Area," writes:

> The Bering Land Bridge provided two distinct kinds of routes for migration into North America, and at the same time provided sites for permanent residence based on two distinctly different kinds of adaptation to the ecological resources of the bridge. It is in fact likely that movements across the land bridge were so slow that the people themselves were scarcely, if at all, aware that they were migrating. The idea that these people moved onto the bridge in order to accomplish a crossing—or perhaps even that they knew there *was* something to cross—is not tenable. The long term result was, of course, migrations, both along the coast and through the interior. From the point of view of those living on the bridge it was permanent occupation, and from the point of view of one who has investigated 8000 or more years of Aleut habitations, it continues to be permanent occupation.

McLaughlin's description of the slow drift of population along the coastal flat that "can command a large portion of the marine resources of the ocean in addition to those of the land" is a pregnant one. Would this drift have stopped just as it turned the great bend of jutting Alaska, with the way south lying ahead? If population had spread this far, why would not the spread have continued? In the Aleutians and in southern California we have two of the way stations along a path that stretched onward to Tierra del Fuego. But again we have that 8000 B.P. barrier, which may well prove to be the limit beyond which no earliest physical evidence can be found. It may, it *must*, betoken a sharp sea rise that altered the coastline as well as drowned its edge and drove some of the population well back to permanent high ground. If only we could go down through Alice's rabbit hole into the past, we would find, in all probability, a geography of this period as strange to us as her Wonderland.

Perhaps some remnant of a coastal site on the far side of 8000 B.P. exists by chance somewhere. Until it is found, the only thread to be followed is the living pattern and the tool-making tradition of these Chopper people. But this is a long story, inextricable from that of the beginnings of man himself, and will be reserved for the next chapter. But before we approach that, there is a stint of summarizing to be done about the use of the Bering land bridge, merely as a reference. (There is no way really to simplify the complexities to which Hopkins referred; and it must be remembered that the bridge grew in size and traversability during times of increasing cold, when people were least likely to be moving around, and decreased in size during warming trends.)

PERIOD	ONSET DATE	CURRENT TECHNOLOGY	BRIDGE	CORRIDOR
angamon interglacial	120,000 B.P.	Chopper	Closed	Wide open
Wisconsin I	70,000 "	"	Open	Closed
ort Talbot interstadial	55,000 "	"	Closed 50,000 to 45,000 B.P.	Open when bridge closed
Wisconsin II	45,000 "	"	Open	Closed
eorian interstadial	35,000 "	"	Closed 30,000 to 25,000 B.P.	Open when bridge closed
Wisconsin III	25,000 "	"	Open	Closed
ary-Mankato interstadial	14,500 "	"	Closed (briefly)	Possibly open
Mankato substage	14,000 "	"	Open	Closed
wo Creeks interstadial	12,000 "	"	Open	Probably open
alders substage	11,000 "	"	Possibly open	Possibly open
nathermal	10,000 "	Projectile point	Closed	Open for good

The current technology referred to is that of Alaska, as we now know it archaeologically, not the technology south of the ice, where Sandia points are older than the earliest opening of the corridor during the Late Wisconsin. The Chopper people are, quite evidently, the earliest Americans.

6

Rocks of Ages

ONE OF THE FEW articles of the faith of our archaeological fathers that has withstood the iconoclastic research of the 1960's is that man, in all the forms that we can classify as hominid, is a Pleistocene, or Great Ice Age, happening. His evolution from a physical-intellectual-cultural status not much in advance of the tropical chimpanzee to that of the engineer of space vehicles was accomplished, by coincidence it would seem, within the period of cyclic glaciations that sculptured the face of the earth—certainly in the north temperate zone, where man is most numerous today—into the lineaments with which geography has familiarized us.

The coincidence may not even yet have ended, though geologists officially consider the Pleistocene to have closed ten thousand years ago, with the Cochrane substage of the Wisconsin. It cannot be said with any confidence that we are not now in a mere interglacial, and a short one at that. The three centuries of the "Little Ice Age," 1550–1850, when it began to look ominously as though the Iceman Cometh again, is only about a century behind us, and world climate has by no means warmed to a Sangamon balminess.

But the letter of the article has been sustained only by

redefining its terms: what is hominid and how long was the Pleistocene? In 1960, when Fairbridge published his graphs of the fluctuations of sea level in *Scientific American*, he used the then popular time scale of a four-hundred-thousand-year span for the Great Ice Age. That this required man to have made his great leap forward from carefree animality to the psychiatrist's couch in less than half a million years evoked remarkably little questioning from the anthropologists, who, of all people, should have known better. To them most of all it should have appeared incredible that the brain, which, like any other organ or muscle, has to make itself by response to increasing demand, could have expanded from the 400–700-cubic-centimeter volume of the upright ape-man australopithecines of South Africa to the 1500–2350-cubic-centimeter volume (the latter figure the size of the poet Byron's brain) of modern man—*Homo sapiens sapiens*—in what was, for an evolutionary process, a trice. But they were at the time undecided about the australopithecines, both as to their placement in time and their relation to human heredity. The deposits in which their remains were found were regarded as early Middle Pleistocene, which would give them an age of about three hundred thousand years at most. But even by the most conservative estimate, some form of more advanced tool-making hominid must have by then been in existence somewhere, and the australopithecines, smarter than a chimpanzee but only as smart as a gorilla, could only have been a retarded collateral anthropoid ape.

Then, on July 17, 1959, Dr. L. S. B. Leakey of the Coryndon Museum, Nairobi, Kenya, found what he had been looking for during the past quarter of a century in the remote, fossil-rich Olduvai Gorge in Tanganyika (now Tanzania), East Africa: a hominid-looking skull in Bed I, the lowest geological stratum or horizon of that 328-foot-deep canyon. An authority on human paleontology, Dr. Leakey named the skull *Zinjanthropus*, "Man of East Africa," considering himself justified in calling it man rather than ape because tools had been found with it—pebble tools. But when the academy of paleoanthropological savants had finished with their analysis of *Zinjanthropus*, the consensus was that he was an australopithecine, a "Southern

Ape" (which is what *Australopithecus* means), and the first
ever found with undeniable evidence of human culture. The
official definition of *hominid* immediately became "australopithecines and men," and appears this way in Carleton S. Coon's
The Origin of Races.

Even as *Zinjanthropus* was undergoing his anatomical entrance exam, as it were, for hominid status, he was being tested
for age. The volcanic-rock matrix from which his bones had
been waiting to be born into the world of science had been
found to be datable by the new radioactive potassium 40-argon
40 method, the sophisticated apparatus for which had been set
up by Dr. Garniss Curtis and Dr. Jack Evernden of the University of California. The age they elicited for *Zinjanthropus*
from the tuff was an astounding 1,750,000 years.

Again the college of scientists had been caught being tight-
fisted with time, as though it were money and the money were
their own. Something had to give. If Bed I was Middle Pleistocene by reason of the geological events with which it was
correlated, then the Pleistocene was not, in October, 1961, when
Curtis published his K/A results in the *National Geographic*,
what Fairbridge, on other authority and data, had assumed it
to be when he wrote about changes in sea level in the *Scientific
American* for May, 1960. It had lengthened overnight from
four hundred thousand years to at least three million. There
was now more than enough time allowance for an australopithecine to have participated as an ancestor in hominid genealogy,
and the definition of man had to be changed to include him.
Everything had changed but nothing had changed, except size.
Bed I, no matter what its age, was geologically Middle Pleistocene, and the Pleistocene remained that period during which
had happened glaciers and men.

Leakey has emerged within the past decade as the most
successful discoverer of specimens of Adamic man in the history
of human paleontology. With his wife, Mary, who actually was
the spotter of the teeth of *Zinjanthropus* gleaming porcelainly
out of the drab rock, he has made the finds, not only at Olduvai
Gorge, but widely over East Africa, which give us the plot
points through the twenty million years during which anthro-

poids have been evolving in the direction of man. The common ancestor of the anthropoid apes, considered as a separate line, and of the hominine line now appears to be *Dryopithecus*, "Forest Ape," of the Miocene period of twenty-five to thirty million years ago. Several fossil apes of the Miocene and the following Pliocene period—*Propliopithecus* and *Pliopithecus*, of Egypt; *Oreopithecus*, found in coal deposits in Italy; *Sivapithecus* and *Ramapithecus*, of India—all attest to the broad distribution of varied and vigorous species of primates throughout the Old World during the Middle Cenozoic epoch (the last seventy million years). Of these, *Ramapithecus* seems in anatomy and aspect to prefigure man most unmistakably and to provide the most likely stock for hominids. Leakey made the first discovery of *Ramapithecus* in East Africa, on Rusinga Island in Lake Victoria, and he has found other ramapithecines since, one of which is reliably estimated to be twenty million years old. *Zinjanthropus* is at the other end of that string. But, within the slightly less than two-year period 1959–1960, Leakey found two other fossil hominids that not only have revolutionized concepts of Dawn Man but have complicated them disconcertingly.

Leakey has cheerfully admitted in print that the alliterative epithet "Lucky Leakey" is well deserved. But his luck is well beyond that of the winner of door prizes or the stumbler on archaeological trove. It is four-dimensional, in that it includes the element of timing. His finds at Olduvai came close together, so that they supplement each other; they came at a time when paleoanthropology was prepared to recognize their significance; and, finally, they came at just that moment when laboratory technology had the means to date them.

Had Leakey made his finds in 1931, when he first began pickaxing away at the Olduvai bluffs, he undoubtedly would have had ahead of him the sorrows of Galileo, and of Dart— Dr. Raymond S. Dart of Witwatersrand University, Johannesburg, South Africa. Dart is the father of the australopithecines, since not only did he name them, but the first one found, a four-year-old infant, was dubbed "Dart's child" by the derisive. This little fossil exemplification that the child is father of the man came out of a limestone quarry at Taungs, South Africa, in 1924, and was shipped off to Dart in two boxes of fossiliferous rock containing mostly calcified turtle and ostrich eggs. In his *Adventures with the Missing Link* (1959, and in press as Leakey was delving up *Zinjanthropus*), Dart describes how he first laid eyes on it while dressed in "London cut morning clothes" for his official duties as best man at the wedding of a university colleague, which was scheduled for within the hour in his own home. It was thus, standing under a pergola where draymen had deposited the boxes, the tools for opening them still in his hand, that he uncovered the face of a child that had last looked upon the world "nearly a million years ago." He confesses that he was utterly oblivious of the encompassing nuptial bustle and that, though he walked through his prescribed role, he "could scarcely wait for the ceremony to cease and the guests to leave, so that I could re-examine my treasures."

No wonder. In the brief examination he had been able to give it, Dart had seen in the limestone endocranial cast "the replica of a brain three times as large as that of a baboon and considerably bigger than that of any adult chimpanzee. The startling image of the convolutions and furrows of the brain and the blood vessels of the skull were plainly visible." So the first man to recognize it as such had made the first cognizant acquaintance with the first demi-man, who was his forefather by several hundred thousand generations, and had laid fingertips on the bone-turned-to-stone that had encased the brain where had been conceived, or was about to be, the human soul. This was the long-sought "missing link."

In his conclusions, published in February, 1925, Dart did not use the phrase that had, during the vituperative days of Darwinian controversy, become a kind of fundamentalist curse, the very uttering of which damned Darwinians to hellfire.

The phrase "missing link," already in disrepute, became such an acute pain in the ears to science as a result of the famous Scopes "monkey trial" that, instead of inventing a euphemism or a circumlocution for it, a stratagem at which scientists are usually adept, they abandoned the necessary concept altogether and turned with bared fangs on any of their fellows who saw it as necessary. To deny that there is, or was, a "missing link" —now, of course, no longer missing—is quite simply to deny linear evolution and indulge in a sophistical concept of special creation.

In his initial report on the Taungs brain cast, Dart, as I say, avoided the provocative term "missing link," though he has used it boldly enough since, in the title of his book about the affair. He used the more careful description of "ultra simian and pre-human," but he left no doubt that he found in the skull just those characteristics that would be expected in an anthropoid intermediate between small-brained, semiupright apes and expanding-brained, fully bipedal man. What followed was depressingly predictable. The establishment was outraged, for Dart was, after all, not of it.

The words that sent Dart and his child into that Limbo where, according to theology, go the souls of infants who die unbaptized, were those of Sir Arthur Keith, in that day the grand eminence of human paleontology, but they were actually the decision of a panel of hanging judges as rendered by the president. Sir Arthur wrote:

> An examination of the casts exhibited at Wembly [by Dart] will satisfy zoologists that this claim [that the Taungs australopithecine was intermediate between ape and man] is preposterous. . . . At most it represents a genus in the gorilla-chimpanzee group. . . . The Taungs ape is much too late in the scale of time to have any place in man's ancestry.

It is a wise child that knows its own father.

Dart, whose primary interest was neurology, dropped the subject entirely, without even a search for further australopithecines, though an adult specimen might well have provided a vindicating illustration of his thesis—as eventually adult australopithecines did.

They were found by an outspoken partisan of Dart, Dr. Robert Broom, a Scotsman indoctrinated with no humbleness before the Sassenach synod of science and with a position on the Witwatersrand faculty. Immediately on his appointment to the anthropology staff in 1934, Broom began looking around for another missing link, a phrase he was to use defiantly in his short book published in 1950, *Finding the Missing Link*. Success came instantly, considering the kind of needle in the kind of haystack for which Broom was probing. In 1936 a second australopithecine, recognized as a somewhat more advanced form and loyally designated by Broom *Australopithecus transvaalensis* was blasted out of the rock of another South African limestone quarry, this one at Sterkfontein. After publishing on *A. transvaalensis* in the English journal *Nature*, Broom came to the United States in the same year for a lecture on this first adult australopithecine before the International Congress of Anthropology in Philadelphia. One American verdict, delivered by Dr. W. K. Gregory of the American Museum of Natural History, can be summed up in these words of his: "It is the missing link no longer missing. It is the structural connecting link between ape and man."

But that was not the only comment. The once famous Harvard anthropologist Ernest A. Hooton, not now much referenced as an anthropologist but a very quotable homiletic scold, wrote in his book *Apes, Men and Morons*, in veiled allusion to Dart's temerity in doing his own anthropology of the Taungs braincase, "The tendency towards aggrandizement of a rare or unique specimen on the part of its finder or the person to whom its initial scientific description has been entrusted, springs naturally from human egoism and is almost ineradicable."

Dart, who had acceded to a request by Broom to do the endocranial interpretation of *A. transvaalensis*, confesses that he read this and dropped the project, turning the skull, with the Taungs material, over to Broom and another colleague. He had had enough of the *argumentum ad hominem*.

But australopithecines continued to turn up. In June, 1938, a schoolboy led Broom to another skull on Kromdraai Farm, near Sterkfontein, more nearly complete than the other two, and of a different and larger variety, which Broom named *Paranthropus robustus*. Three specimens of *Australopithecus* and three different types—this was no evolutionary-dead-end race.

Came World War II and it was the future, not the past, of mankind that was in doubt. That finally determined, for a generation anyway, Broom went at it again. Kromdraai seemed played out, but Sterkfontein was more promising. The face bones of a baby with some teeth, the face of a youth, and an adult tooth came out of the pits. Then, on April 18, 1948, "a lucky blast" disinterred from its sepulcher an almost complete female *Pleisanthropus* skull. The summer and fall that followed yielded a bumper crop of australopithecines: from Sterkfontein a male lower jaw, a female pelvis with a thighbone and vertebrae, then three more skulls; and from the new cave site of Makapansgat, the lower jaw of a youth, the side of a female face, the upper jaw of an adult, a partial skullcap of a young adult, and fragments of a pelvis and a hipbone.

Altogether there was soon enough of the anatomy of *Australopithecus* to make an accurate reconstruction. He was no crouching ape, scuttling about on feet and knuckles or swinging from bough to bough. His posture was as upright as a modern Bushman, and his locomotion was as pedestrian. His teeth were not fighting fangs, and his face was not the muzzle of a beast that goes headfirst into the fray. Then how did he fend for himself? With his hands, with tools and weapons in them. Lacking fangs and a substitute for claws, that is, edged and pointed tools, *Australopithecus* would most certainly have become extinct.

No tools of stone were found with the South African australopithecines, but Dart deduced a very probable industry for them. He called it osteodontokeratic, meaning that the australopithecines used the tools they saw in use in their daily experience and handled constantly—the bones, teeth, and horns or antlers of the beasts they killed and dismembered, already shaped by nature for piercing, cutting, and clubbing. He has even found such "tools" at australopithecine sites; but it will always be very difficult to prove they are tools and not simply the indigestible offal from feeding, or, it might even be said, from prepared meals. At the Makapansgat site, what looks to have been charcoal carbon was found in association with a skull which was thereupon named *Australopithecus prometheus*, for the Titan of Greek mythology who stole fire from Olympus and gave it to man.

A bipedally ambulant ape that had no way of making a living except by use of his forelimbs as arms ending in tool-using hands, that had nearly human teeth and a brain just under human size according to Keith's Law—was it not possible that he was no longer an ape? Sir Arthur, among his other contributions to anthropology, had set the standard for brain size: any under 750 cubic centimeters could not be human. It might be wondered how he could have arrived at such a precise figure without a Moses-like consultation with God on the mountain, but there is an argument for it from analogy. The gorilla has a brain volume of up to 700 cubic centimeters; what it lacks of rudimentary humanity is a spoken language. Sir Arthur therefore set 750 cubic centimers as the limit below which a brain would not be big enough for a developed speech center.

There is another way of looking at it, of course. The gorilla exemplifies the limit to which an anthropoid brain will develop without speech, whereas the australopithecines must have had speech in order to continue to develop beyond the 700-cubic-centimer size. Granted that brain size is a gross physical clue to intelligence, it is still what goes on inside that brain that determines whether it will stop at a given size or be enlarged by that activity to the human norm. There was something in the australopithecine brain, setting behavioral patterns, when it was at gorilla size that impelled it beyond the gorilla dead end. Most likely this was true spoken language, the verbalization of abstractions, even though the abstraction be no more than that of the difference between one and many, or a he-type and a she-type.

To some, this would amount to a begging of the question. We assume that the australopithecines became, in time, human, and we therefore impute to them the functional attributes that would make them human. But did they, in fact, become human? Since this question cannot be answered by observation or test, we must put our trust in the opinions of those whose studies most fully acquaint them with whether the australopithecines had the constitution and composition to make inevitable the step to humanity. Sir Arthur Keith bluntly did not think so in 1925. But nearly a quarter of a century later, in 1947, in a gentlemanly apology rare in science he made this handsome retraction in *Nature*, where he had published his original anathema:

When Professor Dart of the University of Witwatersrand, Johannesburg, announced in *Nature* the discovery of a juvenile Australopithecus and claimed for it human kinship, I was one of those who took the point of view that when the adult form was discovered it would prove to be nearer akin to the living African anthropoids— the gorilla and the chimpanzee. Like Professor Le Gros Clark [also a knight and equally eminent] I am now convinced on the evidence submitted by Dr. Robert Broom that Professor Dart was right and I was wrong. The Australopithecinae are in or near the line which culminated in the human form.

But Sir Arthur still had one objection: the designation Australopithecinae was too long for colloquial use. Why not, he proposed, call them Dartians, in honor of the man who had discovered them and "so rightly perceived their true nature." It was Sir Arthur's most valuable contribution to the study of missing links, and those of us who have had to write *Australopithecus* and its forms as often as though in punishment for misspelling can only wish that for once he had been heeded.

As of this writing, skeletal parts of some 65 individual australopithecines, including 536 teeth, have been collected from South and East Africa, with one specimen recently reported from Egypt. It is the best-represented fossil race of hominids in the repository of anthropology, Neanderthals not excepted. In the twenty years since Sir Arthur's reversal of his original cavalier opinion, australopithecines have been the subject of serious study, instead of the butt of deploring reference. It is now the consensus that they came in two sizes.

The smaller form, *Australopithecus africanus*, a fuzzy-faced manikin about four feet tall and weighing about a hundred pounds, is the earlier. It is to be regretted that one of the subvarieties of these did not dead-end at the gorilla brain level and survive, like the gorilla and chimpanzee, in modern fauna. This one would have been the premier attraction at any zoo, and he could have had all the roles in jungle pictures and television series now monopolized by the much less talented, much more

simianly crouch-postured chimpanzee. And he would have provided us centuries ago with such an obvious example of a
walking-around missing link that man's evolution would have
been self-evident to Aristotle. Through the Middle Ages *A.
africanus*, rather than dwarfs and hunchbacks, would have been
the pet of princes.

The larger, later variety, *Paranthropus robustus*, was about
five feet tall and weighed perhaps 125 pounds, and if he were
still extant, his cage at the zoo would be next to the gorilla's.

It was to the *Paranthropus* group that Leakey's *Zinjanthropus* was assigned, after due analysis, but with his own name.
Leakey had called him *Zinjanthropus boisei*, the subspecies
name being that of a friend who had helped and encouraged his
work. In Kenneth Oakley's *Frameworks for Dating Fossil Man*
(1964) he became what he probably will remain, *Paranthropus
boisei*. An artist's impression of *Zinjanthropus* approved by
Leakey, who had assembled the nearly complete skull, shows a
singular countenance, a very long face with so little forehead
that the eyebrows are a fringe at the scalp line, and a deep and
massive jaw with an unmistakable chin, all in a vertical plane,
like modern faces. It was simply not genetically possible for
this hominid to have been the ancestor of the pithecanthropines,
with their apelike prognathism, their foreheads and chins re-
ceding from the mouth-nose projection. Yet by all the signs of
priority—including a brain below the 750-cubic-centimeter dividing line, while that of the pithecanthropines was about 100
beyond it—he was the grade just below and preceding those
who, as *Homo erectus*, are the first to bear the family name of
Homo. The face of *Zinjanthropus* was headed in another direction entirely, yet there could be no doubt where he was heading
—the stone tools found with him were on a "living floor," the
camp site and working area of what he must have thought of
as "home," whether he had a word for it or not.

Many of the critical human fossils—*Pithecanthropus erectus*
is one—from which the genealogy of man has been deduced
have been found in the roiled context of river gravels or in
other imprecise circumstances. Not *Zinjanthropus*. When Mrs.
Leakey found him, he was still in his original locked box, a

matrix of volcanic tuff. He had died, probably of pneumonia or
some such fatal seizure, in camp on the shores of a lake, during
a rainy season that had filled the lake, causing it to rise over
his corpse and deposit around it a covering silt. Soon afterward
the grave was geologically fixed by the eruption of a nearby
volcano which had showered down over it a layer of ash. Thus
the cover over the tomb was put there by a single, short-term
event of an exact date in time. It was Leakey luck that this
cover of ash or tuff is rich in potassium 40.

Like $C14$, $U234$, and the spectrum of materials now being
used in dating, potassium 40 is radioactive. With a half-life of
1.3 billion years, it breaks down into "daughter products,"
calcium 40 and argon 40. The measurement of the rate of decay
is much more complicated than in $C14$, but the results are the
same—years of age—although, of course, of much greater magnitude because of the immensely longer half-life. Two tests were
run on the *Zinjanthropus* tuff; they yielded figures of 1,590,000
years and 1,890,000 years. This was averaged and rounded off,
and the birthday of *Zinjanthropus* became officially 1,750,000
years ago.

But Leakey had not finished. The 328 feet of deposits exposed on the face of Olduvai Gorge consist of five beds or
distinct geologic horizons. Bed I, the basal horizon and the
earliest, is 105 feet thick. *Zinjanthropus* was found 22 feet
below the top level. In 1960, 5 feet below *Zinjanthropus*, or
27 feet below the top of Bed I, Leakey found the remains of
another hominid species, cranial and other bones of an eleven-
year-old child and bones of one or more adults. The 60-inch
difference in the lie of these remains and those of *Zinjanthropus*
may represent only a few millennia or thousands of millennia;
but for the present, this new hominid, named by Leakey *Homo
habilis* ("Handy" or "Adept Man") is only "more than 1,750,000
years" old.

The circumstances of the find were almost identical with
that of *Zinjanthropus*, except that the child seems to have been
killed by a blow—Leakey suspects murder. The victim was
lying in the midst of a living floor on the shore of a lake that
had risen and drowned the site; and, again, it had been covered

by a fall of volcanic ash. Scattered about the floor were stone tools made of rudimentarily chipped pebbles, the industry called "Oldowan," and there was a circular arrangement of stones, some on top of others, suggesting that some sort of shelter or windbreak had covered the living area. The Plains Indians left all over the west "tipi rings" of stones arranged in this fashion, the stones having been used to weight down tipi skirts. A stone industry, artificial shelter, murder: man.

Of the "Olduvai child" enough fragments were collected to make him seem an individual: a broken mandible or lower jaw with the teeth, by which his age was known to be eleven or twelve years, two parietal bones or midsection parts of the cranium, a wristbone, and seven finger bones. One collarbone may or may not have belonged to the child, for odds and ends of other, adult, members of the tribe were collected during the more than a month of screening through the *Homo habilis* camp site. They consisted of another clavicle, six finger bones, some teeth, and twelve bones of a left foot. The hand bones are, Coon says, "well within the human range" and the foot "fully or almost fully adapted for walking rather than grasping." A cast of the child's skull, reconstructed by a committee of experts in 1965, made possible a braincase measurement of between 642.7 cubic centimers and 727.6 cubic centimers. *Homo habilis*, antecedent to *Zinjanthropus* by five feet of lithic accumulation, was his intellectual equal, as the tools showed them to be cultural equals. However, he was not *Zinjanthropus*'s ten- or hundred-times great-grandfather. *Zinjanthropus* was *Paranthropus*. But the teeth of *Homo habilis* were already reducing in size below those of *Zinjanthropus* and were, in many respects, fully human. He was, the anatomists decided, *Australopithecus africanus;* Oakley lists him as *A. habilis*.

It appears then, that there were two varieties of proto-man, of different aspect and different bearing, that must have been in passage under the lintel of manhood at the same time in that wild Garden of Eden in East Africa some one and three-quarters million years ago. Though *Homo habilis* is distinctly older than *Zinjanthropus*, from here and now they look to have been contemporaries. What was their relationship to each other?

Though pebble tools occur from the bottom of Bed I upward and thus suggest that both the *Zinjanthropus* and *Homo habilis* lines were culturally parallel, there is a view that they were not in a sort of footrace for the laurel of humanity, but that one of them, probably *Homo habilis*, was a predator on the other and probably eventually wiped him out. This is less a scientific view than the comment of a kibitzer trying to earn a footnote for himself. Let us turn, rather, to P. V. Tobias, to whom the *Zinjanthropus* skull was submitted for thorough analysis. In his *Olduvai Gorge*, volume 2, *The Cranium and Maxillary Dentition of* Australopithecus (Zinjanthropus) boisei (1967), he develops the thesis that the australopithecine stock "diversified into several lines." A megadontic ("big-tooth") line became *Zinjanthropus* (reduced in classification from a subgenus to a species), and another line divided into the *Homo habilis* line and a second line, *Meganthropus paleojavanicus*, which surfaces in Java. In short, nobody wiped anybody out. On the contrary, there was multiplication, not subtraction.

What may be thought of as a third view is one of those bizarre and, to his colleagues, infuriating "insights" of Coon, otherwise one of the most encyclopedic and first-hand-experienced of the students in physical anthropology. Coon writes, "That he [*Homo habilis*] could have descended from the Australopithecines so far seems unlikely, but some of them could have been descended from him." So *Homo habilis* was not of the australopithecines though he fathered them (and who was the mother?), and a hominid with the classification of *Homo* (though Coon does not accept this classification for *Homo habilis*, calling him only the Olduvai child) begot those not yet exalted to this status. These are neat tricks, but they have a place only in the field of entertainment.

Where, then, do we go from here? To the southern shore of Lake Rudolf, in the same Great Rift Valley of which Olduvai Gorge is a feature, where "one hot afternoon in August of 1965" Dr. Bryan Patterson of Harvard stooped over and picked up a fossil bone. That was why he was there—to collect fossils—so he popped the specimen into his pocket, his heat-struck eye registering it as "just another knuckle bone," and went on. But only for a few steps: the inner, professional eye had alertly registered something else, and demanded a recount. It was right. On second glance Patterson found in his palm not the foreleg knee joint of a quadruped but the well-preserved distal end of a humerus, that end of the upper arm bone which is, in a two-legged, two-armed animal—an advanced primate—the elbow joint. Languid no more, Patterson went back over the ground. That was all there was, the funny bone. The rest, he concluded, had been devoured not by time but in the original by a crocodile that had lost this one final morsel in the mud.

Frustrating, wasn't it, to have found this tantalizing leftover of the most coveted of fossils, proto-man, and to be denied the most toothsome, scientifically speaking, parts of him? Not to Patterson. Back to Harvard went the joint for some six months of study and "discriminate analysis," from which it emerged with a full-blown and specific personality, "hereafter to be known" (in accordance with the location of the find near a stream called the Kanapoi, which flows into Lake Rudolf) as Kanapoi Hominid 1.

The justification for this apotheosis of an elbow was summarized in a piece which appeared in *Science*, April 7, 1967, over the signatures of Patterson and Dr. W. W. Howells of the Peabody Museum of Archaeology and Ethnology. The heart of it was a table of seven comparative index measurements of the humeri of the chimpanzee, *Paranthropus*, man, and the Kanapoi fragment. The conclusions are as follows:

In these diagnostic measurements Kanapoi Hominid 1 is strikingly close to the means of the human sample. . . . The fragment can be distinguished on inspection from gorilla and orangutan; discriminate analysis of humeri of *Homo* and *Pan* [chimpanzee] assigns it as hominid. From other evidence we consider it more likely to represent *Australopithecus S. S.* than *Paranthropus*. . . .

Napier has presented evidence that *Australopithecus S. S.* and *Paranthropus* were widely different in the structure of the pelvis bones and the proximal ends of the femora [upper leg bones] to a degree indicating a difference in gait, with *Australopithecus* being much closer to modern man. This evidence supports the view of Robinson and others that *Australopithecus* was a hominine.

Considering that Kanapoi Hominid 1 and *Homo habilis* had been found in what, regionally, amounted to close proximity, could Coon's opinion that "some of them [the australopithecines] might have descended from him," meaning *Homo habilis*, have been a valid insight? It might have been at least tenable, and paleoanatomists might have been divided for years over the chicken-and-egg question of which came first, *Australopithecus africanus* or *Homo habilis*, had not Patterson and Howells come up with Kanapoi's birthday. Determined by Geochron Laboratories by K/A test of a "lava capping" over the fossil-bearing sediments at the site, the age was 2.5 million years, three-quarters of a million years older than *Homo habilis*. Kanapoi Hominid 1 is, in Patterson and Howell's words, "the earliest Pleistocene representative of the Hominidae yet found."

It will have caught the eye of the attentive reader of the foregoing that as late as 1967 hominids continued to be regarded as a glacial-period circumstance, the association now resting on a secure date of 2.5 million years; and curiosity must have set in about how the individual glaciations are being recalculated to fill in this elongation. Obviously our understanding of glaciation is going to have to be stretched into a new dimension, or the interglacials are going to have to be assigned durations of up to a half-million years, or other glacials are going to have to be added to the original four. Probably all these measures will have to be taken. As to the first two, a chronology that almost doubles the length of the Wisconsin has been very recently (March 1968) proposed, based on data secured from sea-bottom cores taken from the Indian Ocean. It hints that if the Wisconsin was thus miscalculated, so may have been the other three. As to the third measure, traces have now been confirmed of a pre-Gunz ice phase in Europe and in the Himalayas, named the Donau, and of what may be its counterpart in America, named the Deadman Pass glaciation.

An account of the radical revision of the Wisconsin period outlined by William E. Frerichs in *Science*, March 29, 1968, might seem to have been more appropriate to the previous chapter on Beringia. The fact is, however, that this revision

would not significantly change the order of events from the
assumed onset of the Wisconsin 70,000 years ago that was set
down in that chapter, even if it were fully confirmed tomorrow
by some new radiometric device. What is proposed is two
earlier substages of the Wisconsin, with one long and one short
interstadial and with ice beginning to build at 120,000 years
ago, or about the same millennium as the beginning of the Sangamon interglacial according to the conventional scheme. Frerichs's argument is founded on studies of the succession of
warm-water- and cold-water-dwelling microscopic fauna in sediments in the Andaman Sea and the Bay of Bengal. Such indices
are not precise, any more than twilight and dawn are precise,
but the warm- and cold-water phases, concurring with the
phases of terrestrial climate, are unmistakable and their span
can be calculated. They appear to confirm the order of events
during the Wisconsin—from about 54,000 years ago, rather
than 70,000—with which we are already familiar, and then
they go further, to add two prior ice advances and retreats that
make the Wisconsin a full-blown five- instead of three-act
drama, on the order of 120,000 years' duration.

Whenever anything new is learned about the Wisconsin, the
knowledge can be applied by analogy to its three predecessors,
the Gunz-Nebraskan, the Mindel-Kansan, and the Riss-Illinoian.
Since each erased most of the evidence of its predecessor, not
much is known about them—least of all, as is now clear, their
placement in time. No radioactive substance by which they can
be dated is associated with them, since they are at an awkward
age, too old for $C14$ and too young for K/A. Heretofore they
have each been known by a single terminal moraine or a single
till deposit, so that it appeared that each ice sheet made one
full advance, held for millennia (estimated only) and then
evaporated into the clouds. Wakefield Dort, Jr., of the University of Kansas reported in 1966 traces of two advances during
the Nebraskan and three for the Kansan and drew the long-
overdue conclusion that each of the pre-Wisconsin glaciers must
have been as complex as that vacillating mass. If the Wisconsin
has been undervalued, and was actually 65 percent longer than
supposed, we can apply this factor to the rest of the Pleistocene,

because it is absolutely the only arithmetic of estimation which
there is any observational excuse to apply. And when we do
apply it to a million-year Pleistocene, the value becomes 1.7
million years, about half the length now proved for that eventful
period.

Where did a figure like the four hundred thousand years
used by Fairbridge ever come from? The story is not too long
to tell. During the 1940's and 1950's there had been a growing
tendency among both human and feral paleontologists to be
more liberal about the span of the Pleistocene, because the un-
folding story of human and lower-animal evolution was becoming too difficult to fit into the five hundred thousand years of
the conventional allotment that was nothing more than a round-
number guess—it had seemed to early researchers to be the
convenient value to express "a very, very long time." But just
as acceptance of a million-year Pleistocene was becoming general, on the grounds of reason alone, there came the release of
a highly original marine-geology study by Cesare Emiliani of
the temperature changes of the Cenozoic as laid down in the
column of sediments in the Caribbean Sea. From the succession
of cold and warm sediments, as determined by color, texture,
and molluscan life, Emiliani constructed a temperature curve
which he then compared with the estimates of terrestrial geologists for the advance and retreat of ice.

The story goes that when he made the comparison, it
was with the outmoded five hundred-thousand-year chronology
handed him by an obtuse science librarian who was out of
touch with the latest literature in the field. The result was that
he adjusted his data to a time scheme that was even then becoming obsolete. The originality of his study, however, and the
thoroughness with which it was carried out were so convincing
that when he found a correlation between his marine-tempera-
ture curve and the temperature curve derived from the obsolete
timing of glaciation, the obsolete chronology seemed actually to
have been validated.

Discovery by Emiliani of the error and a return to the million-year Pleistocene came about 1959, just in time for Leakey
to guess that Zinjanthropus, geologically Middle Pleistocene,

was 600,000 years old. The Curtis-Evernden age by K/A of 1.75 million years followed on the heels of, and more than corroborated, the more liberal allowance for this period of man's rise from australopithecinedom.

But where does the three-million-year span of the Pleistocene get its sanction? Is it another prediction only, like previous "authoritative" consensus? No—the end of timorousness about the Great Ice Age came in 1966 with the announcement of Dr. Robert R. Corry of the University of California at Berkeley that he had found a glacial till at Deadman's Pass in the Sierra Nevada of California which he had been able to date by the K/A method. The till was sandwiched between a datable rock formation 2.7 million years old and another one 3.1 million years old, for a round-number average of 3 million years.

Thus the statement that Kanapoi Hominid 1, 2.5 million years old, is of Pleistocene age is confirmed by a glacial event that occured halfway round the world. The equation *Pleistocene = man + glaciers* has been demonstrated. But there is something more to it.

It has always been assumed that, generally speaking, glacial periods were periods of much heavier worldwide precipitation than we moderns have any experience of. In northern latitudes the moisture fell as snow, which heaped up into the enormous snow-piles-turned-to-ice that we know as glaciers. The coordinates of glacier periods in the subtropics and tropics, where water fell simply as rain, are called pluvials. Some, perhaps most, authorities consider that there were four great pluvials in Africa corresponding with European glaciers thus: Kageran equals Gunz; Kamasian equals Mindel; Kanjeran equals Riss; Gamblian equals Würm. It will be remembered that the living floors of both *Zinjanthropus* and *Homo habilis* had been on the shores of a lake, in what is now an arid land where there is surface water only during the rainy season. Not only had there been a standing lake there during the lifetime of these fossils, but it had risen under heavy rains, drowned the living floors, and interred the bodies in sediment. Though they need not have for the case to be proved, it appears certain that *Zinjanthropus* and *Homo habilis* lived during a pluvial-glacial; and

Kenneth Oakley, in his *Frameworks for Dating Fossil Man*, places the Oldowan pebble-tool industry associated with both in the Kageran-Gunz, now known by us from K/A dating of the tuff over the sediments to be 1.75 million years old. Curiously enough, this is the order of age (1.7 million years) we arrived at not too many paragraphs ago by noting that Frerichs's new Wisconsin chronology is 65 percent longer than the current one and that the same error factor might apply to the other three periods. It might not mean a thing, but if it does, what used to be called the Pleistocene is only the latter half of it, and during all of it a protohominid or hominid, including man, was making pebble tools.

Against this background of three million years of glaciation and the rising and falling of Beringia, it seems incredible that no hominid found his way to America before Wisconsin times. But what is even more incredible is that when a man did find his way there, it was an Asiatic man still at the pebble-tool-making stage of industrial development, though the men of Africa and Europe and a good part of Asia were making tools of a far more sophisticated design and had passed through innumerable evolutionary stages in lithic craftsmanship. But to understand this, we must return to Olduvai Gorge, to the two morphologically distinct hominids from Bed I there, and to Leakey.

That *Zinjanthropus* and *Homo habilis* are morphologically distinct subvarieties of hominids is not a proposition appearing here for the first time. It is favored by both Leakey and Coon, with the most succinct quotation this one from Alan H. Brodrick's *Man and His Ancestry:*

It seems clear, then, that at Olduvai, during the upper Villafranchian [this refers to the faunal assemblage and means the Early Pleistocene] and the lower part of the Mid-Pleistocene, two different branches of the family of man, the Hominidae, were evolving side by side.

In *The Science of Man*, Ashley Montagu uses almost the same words:

On present evidence, it appears that *Homo habilis* lived before, during and after the Zinjanthropines. It seems, then, that two very different forms of man, one apelike and one much more manlike were evolving side by side at Olduvai, and probably elsewhere, during the Upper Villafranchian and during the lower Middle Pleistocene.

So let us get on with it. What happened then? The more manlike *Homo habilis* exterminated *Zinjanthropus*, or *Zinjanthropus*, having gone as far as his apelike body would take him, died out. Isn't that what happened? Some day we may know, but now we don't. Here the record blanks out, and it does not pick up again at Olduvai, or anywhere else, for at least a million years.

In 1960, to complete a perfect triangle of luck, Leakey came upon another skull—actually a calvarium, the skullcap without the face—in Bed II, forty-three feet above the dividing line between Bed I and Bed II, or about sixty-five feet higher in the bluff than *Zinjanthropus*. Since the top of Bed II has been dated at about 500,000 years ago, this cranial fragment may be up to 750,000 years old, though one K/A date, which may or may not apply, is 360,000 years. Whatever the age, that is not what gives the find its primary importance. Under this skullcap was the brain that directed the making of the earliest phase, called the Chellean, of the most famous of Old Stone Age tools, the hand ax. It was the finding of this tool by Boucher de Perthes and the recognition that it was a tool of human manufacture that opened academic eyes to the existence of an "antediluvian" past, older than Noah's flood, older than the biblical Adam. At Olduvai the first Chellean hand ax makes its appearance at the top of Bed I; and the Chellean man of Bed II was well along in the tradition, turning out hand axes in what is called Chellean 3 style. But this Chellean 3 man is the first fossil of a Chellean hand-ax maker ever discovered with his product.

While it is tiresome to have to make such explanations, it has to be mentioned here, because there are readers who may be confused, that in Europe this first hand-ax phase is called Abbevillian. It had originally been named Chellean, but the later discovery that the hand axes found at Chelles, in France, were actually of a second and already named phase called Acheulean, and that hand axes of the first stage had been found at Abbeville, necessitated the change. But the terminology was never changed in African studies, and there Chellean continues to be synonymous with Abbevillian. It is one of those tolerated things, like a hole in the roof which, instead of being repaired, is solved, as a household problem, by putting a tin can under it to catch the drip when it rains.

The hand ax, it is plain from the technology, is an inevitable development of the pebble chopper. The earliest pebble tools, called the Kafuan industry, could not be technologically any simpler: they consist of knocking a chip or two off the corner or out of the curve of a pebble to make a scraping or scoring, rather than a cutting edge. In the next stage, called the Oldowan, which some authorities insist is the first stage that can be certainly recognized as of human workmanship, a real cutting edge is achieved by chipping both sides to a median edge. The hand ax is what results when chipping is continued all over the pebble or core until it is thinned down to a flattish cross section like an ax blade. Its shape is somewhat that of a conventional valentine heart, with the broad top being the hand grip and the sharp edges converging to a rounded point. Incorporated in it are the principles of nearly all the hand tools in the basement workshops of suburbia; you could hack, scrape, cut, ream, pound, and grub with it, and it might even have been used as a screwdriver if nature had put anything together with screws. It was made from the time that the top of Bed I was formed—which ought to be, considering the 1.75-million-year age of *Zinjanthropus*, very nearly a million years ago—up until 40,000 years ago, when those stereotype cavemen, the Neanderthals, vanish from fossildom. The long-headed, heavy-browridged skulls of Neanderthals, the last of the *Homo erectus* line, are consistently found with the industrial complex called Mousterian, in which the hand ax has become a relatively small tool about the size of the palm of the hand. The disappearance of the hand ax marks the end of the Lower and Middle Paleolithic, and coincides with the arrival on the scene of the Aurignacians, modern man, *Homo sapiens sapiens*, the maker of a whole new kit of specialized tools.

Of the skullcap that Leakey found with the Chellean 3 hand axes (that Leakey spells it *Chellean* and Coon *Chellian* gives one an idea of the free hand authorities allow themselves) Coon says: "It has very large brow ridges, a sloping forehead, a nuchal crest and small mastoids: the hallmarks of the *Homo erectus* grade." Coon then adds the braincase volume, between 1100 and 1200 cubic centimeters, which clinches the status of Chellean 3 man; he is well beyond the australopithecines and has crossed Keith's arbitrary boundary for humanity of 750 cubic centimeters of brain volume with cubic centimeters to spare. He must have been a language user, an utterer of words, not merely exclamations and signals, and he was well along in a progressive tradition of tool making. He is, in short, exactly what the taxonomists would have hoped to find with Chellean hand axes, a hominid sophomore.

In the scheme of progression from protohominids to modern man that is now generally in use, there are four grades, just as in high school or college. The australopithecines are the freshmen; the sophomores are the pithecanthropines or *Homo erectus;* the Neanderthals and their cultural and chronological peers like Fontechevade man are *Homo sapiens*, the juniors; and the seniors are modern man, *Homo sapiens sapiens*. The postgraduates? *Homo socius*, we hope.

But there is a catch. Anatomically and culturally a second classman, Chellean 3 man could not, as anatomists see it, have evolved from either *Zinjanthropus* or *Homo habilis;* in mien he is more noticeably apish than either. Coon says:

It is tempting to relate Chellian-3 man to its local predecessor, *Zinjanthropus*. But in at least two aspects Chellian-3 is more primitively hominid, or even pongid, than *Zinjanthropus*, or indeed any other known Australopithecine. . . . To derive Chellian-3 man from *Zinjanthropus* would be biologically impossible.

Hence Chellean 3 man is *sui generis*, with an as yet undisclosed ancestor lying entombed somewhere in Bed I in the midst of a living floor with pebble tools scattered about, bringing to three the number of distinct lines of human genealogy. This is more than most theorists of human evolution had bargained for. What happened to the promising *Zinjanthropus* and the even more promising *Homo habilis?* Extermination by the unknown ancestor of Chellean 3 man? Or species exhaustion? Or hybridization, with *Zinjanthropus* and *Homo habilis* males stealing one another's females to mix genes and found a whole new, single-lineage first man?

The only real thread of investigation we have, and may ever have, to guide us is that of culture-industry, since the chance of finding enough intergrades in either of the two australopithecine lines or the third line (which may or may not be hybrid) to test so that the matter can be clarified is near zero. Traditions in tool making are, in a limited sense, genes of culture; they must, by definition, be handed down from one generation to the next by teaching and example, and so they comprise a heritage that is genetically related. When we trace this thread, it leads to some interesting results.

The Asiatic counterpart and contemporary of Chellean 3 man, a pithecanthropine and of *Homo erectus* grade, with a braincase volume of about a thousand cubic centimeters, is *Sinanthropus pekinensis*, from the lowest level, called Locality I, at the already noted Choukoutien Cave, near Peking. Chinese man of Peking, considering his *Homo erectus* grade, should have been making hand axes, and it would have changed archaeology the way the discovery of the Straits of Magellan changed geography if he had been. Instead he was making implements, generally formless in the sense of standardized design, which today are recognized as being in the tradition of the chopper-chopping tool. Oakley writes:

The raw material of the industry comprised mainly pebbles of sandstone and quartz collected from the bed of a local stream, and blocks of vein quartz obtained from the outcrops in the nearby granite hills. . . . core implements in the sense of flaked pebble-tools formed an important element in the typical or Early Choukoutienian industry, including both choppers and chopping tools, which were mostly large and heavy. . . . Flake-tools are actually far more numerous than core tools in the Choukoutien industries, but the

impression gained from examining a total assemblage is that the
early Peking tool makers simply made considerable use of the waste
chips which resulted from the flaking of boulders or pebbles into
choppers or chopping-tools.

(This passage touches the live nerve of our subject, American archaeology, because it describes succinctly the basic pattern of most American lithic technology—the invariable use of
the chipping waste from core tools as casual knives and
scrapers, the common occurrence of choppers, and the customary use, except by the Paleohunters, of pebbles—even as the
repetition of the pebble-tool theme takes us back to Olduvai.)

What are pebble tools doing in eastern Asia at this stage of
the game? It has been firmly established by decades of investigation that the hand-ax tradition never reached eastern Asia.
Ubiquitous in Africa, Europe, and the Middle East, it peters
out in India, where it overlaps with the chopper tradition. (The
chopper is technically a split pebble with chips taken off the
pebble rind or cortex at the thin edge to sharpen the edge further, while the chopping tool is the whole pebble with an edge
chipped on it, but herein we shall use *chopper* to mean both
forms.) East of India, in all the areas from which resident
populations are likely to have migrated farther east to America,
the chopper industry, based on pebbles or the local or country
rock, prevails from the beginning to the end of the Paleolithic,
and in some places even into the historic era.

Anthropological literature is studded with red-letter warnings
against trying to correlate tool traditions with human lineages
or races; but in this case, if we have no key we will have to use
a lithic picklock. Either one of the lines of proto-men of East
Africa spread into East Asia while it was still in the pebble-tool-
making stage and so established the chopper tradition there, or
a hominid line totally distinct from the australopithecines developed in East Asia and spread to Africa, to account for strangely
nonaustralopithecine Chellean 3 man.

In all of Asia the fossil record has produced no hominid
older or more primitive than Dubois's *Pithecanthropus erectus*,
Java man, who, though probably a hundred thousand years

older than *Sinanthropus*, is the same *Homo erectus* grade. There is nothing hominid east of Egypt within a million years of the age of *Homo habilis*. Though strongly predisposing, this is negative evidence. Asia has certainly not been exhaustively explored, and there was a period in the late 1930's when it seemed possible that the ancestor of *Pithecanthropus erectus* was a great Chinese ape called *Gigantopithecus*, through a line that included one *Meganthropus*, identified from a jaw, whose kind had begotten a large relative of *Pithecanthropus erectus* called *Pithecanthropus robustus*. This is not a respectable hypothesis today, but there are enough variant fossil *Homines erecti* of Southeast Asia in museum inventories to keep the mind open, just a crack, to the possibility that Asia may have had its homegrown hominid fauna.

Meanwhile, the cultural clues of hand axes and choppers, the ideas that hominid lines were carrying in the pockets of their genes, give us something to work with. The evolution of the hand ax out of the chopper, just as has been outlined previously —a refinement of the chopper by continued dressing down of the pebble bulk until a total blade, a new tool, has been achieved— is illustrated, in all its intergrading stages up to the final Acheulean, in the artifacts recovered at Olduvai. There is nothing that hints at an intruder with an innovative, alien idea or technique. The least circuitous way to interpret this orderly progression is to conclude that a lineage of hominids passing their know-how from parent-teacher to child-pupil was the fabricator, and that improvement in tools followed closely the expansion of the brain, all within this very neighborhood.

It is possible that a pithecanthropine from Southeast Asia wandered into East Africa during the million years between *Zinjanthropus* and the first hand axes and drove out the local australopithecine population. It is not, however, plausible. He could have brought with him only the pebble tool-chopper tradition, which was all there ever was in his native land, so it would then become incumbent on us to explain why he was suddenly inspired to make hand axes, when his Asiatic kin were satisfied for the next several hundred thousand years to make choppers and when the hominids in the area into which he moved were making basically the same choppers he was making. Where would the stimulation to change have originated?

It is much more likely that some of the australopithecines, or members of that mysterious third line of hominids which evolved into Chellean 3 man, walked out of Africa eastward before hand-ax times, carrying their pebble tool-chopper tradition with them and never developing it further, since it met their equipment needs. But one essential they must have carried with them, the germ of humanity which we may legitimately associate with language; for the advancement of the Asiatics was at the same pace and in the same direction as that of the Africans and Europeans, passing upward through *Homo sapiens* neanderthalism, and thence to *Homo sapiens sapiens*, in parallel but independent courses.

Dare we speculate thus? It has already been done. In his *Olduvai Gorge*, volume 2, Tobias has advanced, and put down in figure form, what he believes happened to the Olduvai hominids. The *Zinjanthropus* hominids moved through the Lower Pleistocene into the Middle Pleistocene along a line that produced the Kromdraai australopithecines, whose descendants, if any, are still unknown. The Sterkfontein line of australopithecines led forward through the pithecanthropine *Atlanthropus mauritanicus* of Ternifine, Algeria, to Rabat man, a neanderthaloid of Northern Africa. The *Homo habilis* line Tobias traces to Choukoutien Cave; with him must have gone pebble tools. Of these roots, then, must have come the earliest Americans.

This scheme is going to be disputed—and has to be until its proponents are vindicated, as were Dart and Broom, or until the view is supplanted by a better-supported one. This much, however, we may say without attempting slyly to imply more than is asserted: wherever on the map of the Paleolithic world are found hand axes, there today are resident populations that are predominantly Caucasian and Negro; and wherever in the Paleolithic is found the chopper-chopping tool tradition, today the long-resident population is basically Mongoloid. But what is Mongoloid?

The racial Mongoloidism of American populations is, according to anthropologists, beyond question. Coon says, in the grand manner:

Both the American Indians and the Eskimo, which inhabit North and South America, are Mongoloid. All the skulls and bones of their ancestors which have been unearthed to date are also Mongoloid. There is not a real Australoid, Melanesian, Negroid or Caucasoid piece of bone in the lot.

W. S. Laughlin, the Eskimo-Aleut authority who has already been quoted on the occupation of the Aleutian Islands during the Beringia period, agrees, but with this exception:

Studies of the blood groups of living individuals show a basic similarity between the Aleuts and Greenlandic Eskimos, as distinguished from American Indians, *who are much less Mongoloid* [italics mine].

There are degrees of Mongoloidism, then, very substantial differences in, as Laughlin says, "morphology, dentition, growth, pathology, physiology and serology." American Indians could not agree more. The Indian opinion, as strongly expressed to me, is that they are not Mongoloid at all. While they do not have anthropological expertise, and their sentiments are purely that, they do know, as they put it, what they look like and what Chinese, Japanese, and Eskimos look like. And more than one anthropologist has agreed with them to the extent of conceding like W. W. Howells that "In many groups a Caucasoid [in addition to Mongoloid] element also appears to be present." But what it comes down to is, When do you start keeping score?

J. S. Birdsell has pointed out, in his *The Problem of the Early Peopling of the Americas As Seen from Asia*, that the Mongoloid race "was the last of the major groups to differentiate" and that "the available evidence suggests that the Mongoloid race has reached its present geographical limits by a very rapid, possibly by an explosive, expansion." This expansion he relates to the Neolithic infusion of farming and animal husbandry, at about eight thousand to nine thousand years ago. What he means here is what the layman means, the Sino-Japanese "slanty-eyed Oriental" of the epicanthic eye fold, the strawberry nose, the round head, the scanty body hair, and the flat, "inscrutable" face. His estimate of the date of the explosion of these Mongoloids, which have differentiated into the "yellow race," accords well with Laughlin's archaeology in the Aleutians, where the population is purely Mongoloid in Birdsell's sense, which begins at eight thousand to nine thousand years ago. When the term *Mongoloid* has Birdsell's meaning, the "red" Indian cannot be Mongoloid (compare an Aztec nose with that of a Chinese), but only of the same basic stock as that from which the Mongoloids derived the characteristics that are adaptations to a dry, cold climate, as we have already seen the Alakalufs were adapted to their sea-level environment. But if this basic stock is, by common consent, called Mongoloid, then he is Mongoloid, because he shares with Mongoloids, and the population of East Asia all the way back to *Sinanthropus*, one telltale dental trait, the shovel-shaped incisor tooth. About 90 percent or more of all Indians have the shovel-shaped incisor, compared with 94.2 percent for Chinese and 9 percent for whites. Albert A. Dahlberg of the University of Chicago defines it thus:

The term is applied to incisor teeth which, when viewed from the lingual [the tongue side] have the appearance of a shovel because of the prominent lateral borders on that surface. These prominent borders are not overgrowths of enamel, but rather a curving lingually of the enamel and the underlying dentine.

By the standard of the shovel-shaped incisor the Mongoloid race is as old as *Sinanthropus*.

But the American Indian, the Amerind, must have "differentiated" long before the Sino-Japanese, Eskimo-Aleut Mongoloids. Even those who believe in no earlier American than the Clovisians could hardly find fault with that view. In the upper cave at Choukoutien, that same cave where *Sinanthropus* was found in the lowest level, were found the skulls of a man and two women assumed, not too seriously, to be his two mates. They are older than fifteen thousand years, but not indefinitely older; W. W. Howells calls them "unmigrated American

Indians," anthropologically of course. Here, therefore, in an undifferentiated, proto-Mongoloid population in which Howells and Birdsell see several strains from Caucasoid to Australoid, must lie the roots of the American Indians, and not genetically only. With the "Old Man" of Choukoutien and his womenfolk was an industry "of an evolved type derived from the old complex of earlier days of choppers and chopping-tools and flakes."

A great deal of energy and earnestness has been expended over the past few years in tracing the tools and flint-knapping technique of the Paleo-hunters from well-known European industries, such as the Mousterian and Aurignacian, by the spread of their influences across Central and Northern Asia. Whatever success these efforts have had in demonstrating such relationships, they overlook one set of facts. The Mousterians made hand axes and the Aurignacians did not; but both the Clovis and Folsom hunters, though distinctly advanced beyond the pebble-tool stage, and almost all American cultures for which there is a reasonably complete inventory, *except Eskimos and Aleuts*, made choppers. This trait is the shovel-shaped incisor of cultural genetics, and it must become the thread to be followed in American prehistory.

The next chapter will deal with the cultural evidences in North America of pebble tool-chopper complexes only, without stone projectile points, to convince the reader that the stone-projectile-point cultures are natural evolvements from the pebble tool-chopper stage by precisely the same process that developed hand axes out of choppers—i.e., by continuing the chipping process all over the basic chopper form until a bifacially worked blade took shape. There was this difference between the Amerinds and the Chelleans: it was a more efficient hand-held, generalized tool that the Chelleans were working toward, while the Amerinds knew about spears and wanted a more effective tip for them. Out of what was basically the same simple pattern, the two tools, which are quite similar in form though not dimensions, were manufactured for two quite similar ways of living; for the Chelleans were big-game hunters, who, according to Leakey, used the bolas to bring down game that was then slain with hand axes, while the Clovis hunters attached a smaller worked stone to a shaft, which then became a flying hand ax, and killed or mortally wounded at a distance.

Even as the American Indian has ample justification to consider himself to be of a clearly differentiated race, so does he have every patent right and title to the invention of his stone industry and other indigenous cultural developments, for he made them out of a pattern as old and as primitively hominid as aptly named Olduvai Gorge.

7

Fractured Evidence

In May, 1965, Sigfus Olafson (whose translation from the Icelandic opened this volume) and David L. DeJarnette of the University of Alabama, who began his professional career as coexcavator of the famous Tennessee-Alabama Pickwick Basin Amerind middens of freshwater shellfish in 1936–39, put in an appearance at the University of Illinois, Urbana, at the annual meeting of the Society for American Archaeology. This is the Cannes Festival of the American archaeological arts, where there appears annually and unfailingly, on crutches if necessary, every star and hopeful in the field of American archaeology, to evaluate the latest harvest of work, to see and be seen.

Olafson and DeJarnette bore with them in two wooden boxes 87 pounds (about 300 items) of pebble tools, representative of a collection of some 700 pounds of such tools gathered from eleven sites in Alabama. The collection was mainly the harvest of Matthew Lively of Birmingham, who had turned it over to Daniel Josselyn, spark plug of the Alabama Archaeology Society, who had in turn submitted it to Alex D. Kreiger of the University of Washington, a specialist on Early Man. It was Kreiger's suggestion that the lot be exposed to the scrutiny of the SAA assemblage. Olafson and DeJarnette had no illusions about the reception they could expect; in American archaeology pebble-tool industries not related to established stone-projectile-point industries are on the official index of forbidden subjects. Merely to possess such objects, let alone dignify them with a name (the Lively complex, after their discoverer), signifying acceptance as archaeological materials, is as reckless as was embracing Christianity in the reign of Nero.

But the conference headliner that year was to be Leakey, then lecturing at the university, and since his reputation had been made at the birthplace of pebble tools Olafson and DeJarnette thought he would not avert his eyes from the Lively tools out of fear that to be caught looking at them would compromise his professional image.

The Olafson-DeJarnette strategy was to lay their Lively-industry specimens before Leakey, solicit an opinion audible to a group of bystanders, and, if that was favorable, make sure that it was amplified for the benefit of this gathering at the fountainhead. The amiable Leakey, on a tight schedule of lecturing and conferring, had to forego lunch to make his inspection. Tall, authoritative, hearty, he quickly became, it is related, a cynosure among the celebrities as he bent over the stones being disclosed for his inspection in the lobby of the conference building where the meeting with him had been arranged. But as the crowd, its attention attracted by his attention, began to drift into a circle about him, when the foremost came within six or eight feet they halted as though they had suddenly discovered that what absorbed him was the deactivation of a bomb. And thus Olafson and DeJarnette were able to arrive at a measurement (7 feet $\pm$ 1 foot) of the proximity of approach to pebble tools allowed by professional caution. Any closer than that, and how could a virtuous professional deny that he had ever seen pebble tools? The crowd, once the object of scrutiny had been apprehended, broke up. To have remained longer could have been construed as voyeurism.

Leakey was apparently not even aware of the impropriety he was committing and went on with his study. Then he, who had seen more pebble tools than any ten American archaeologists, pronounced judgment. "Of course they're pebble tools. And why not? Why shouldn't there be pebble tools in America?"

Three years later he was to announce, with Ruth DeEtte Simpson of the San Bernardino County Museum, Bloomington, California, and Thomas Clements of the University of Southern California, that he had found American pebble tools, and where else but in California, where they have everything. But that is to anticipate the development of this chapter. Neither the Lively complex nor the pebble-derived flake industry found by Leakey and his colleagues in the Calico Mountains of California make up by any means the whole case for a pebble-tool period in American prehistory. Nor is the professional mind as closed to the probability that such a period did exist and did precede the established stone-projectile-point industries as the quarantine of the Lively industry at Urbana suggests. Too many excavators of unimpeachable reputation have seen pebble tools in the field and have reported them. But, it seems, they have not reported them with the missionary zeal that would make converts of those who have not encountered them *in situ* in the course of excavation, and there are, of course, a great many of these deprived unfortunates.

One of them must be he, who will be nameless here since it is his opinion, not his name, that interests us, whom the book editor of *Science* appointed to review *The Bering Land Bridge*, already much discussed herein. An archaeologist himself, the reviewer took issue with archaeologist Muller-Beck and with Hopkins for their informed judgment that man had pushed into America prior to twenty-two thousand years ago, thus:

Indisputable evidence for man in the New World of this vintage or older has long been recognized as one of the greatest discoveries an American archaeologist might hope to make. As a result there is a considerable search underway, and from time to time we hear enthusiastic claims of success. Granting the possibility that some of these may yet prove valid, it nevertheless seems to me that the discovery of early-early Paleo-Indians in the Americas is taking too long. By now their presence should have been firmly established

and repeatedly verified. . . . Without far more than the tantalizing
bits of evidence claimed to date, one may regard the matter of
20,000 year old man in America with considerable skepticism.

On display here, of course, is not the art of the reviewer,
which is to deliver an objective assessment of a book, but the
advantage taken of the assignment of a certain amount of space
to register a complaint that the book does not take the point of
view the reviewer would have taken had he written it. What
interests us about it is the reviewer's perfectly unselfconscious
statement of his attitude, without fear that he will be called to
account for it, in all its arrant casuistry. What he says, in effect,
is that if evidence is not "indisputable," that is, decisive, then
it cannot be considered evidence of any weight at all. There are
no gradations between negative evidence and invincible evidence
—no circumstantial evidence, no cumulative evidence, no inexplicable evidence. Beyond this, he sets a time limit on when
evidence that meets his specifications as "indisputable" may be
received; it is already too late. And finally he passes not a particular judgment on the archaeological sections of *The Bering
Land Bridge* but a general one on the whole of American prehistory. We can be in no doubt that he and the prevailing school
whose view he summarizes so boldly doubt not only Muller-
Beck's pre-20,000 B.P. migration of hunters but a Pacific-lit-
toral migration of the pebble tool-chopper folk as well.

What are pebble tools, that they are so publicly shunned and
rejected? Strictly speaking, any stone industry the material of
which is water-shaped pebbles and cobbles found along the
shores of streams and other bodies of water, or even dug out of
glacial till, can be said to be a pebble industry; but this is by
way of distinguishing it from those industries the raw material
of which is obtained by quarrying natural exposures. There is
not a major outcrop in America, and few minor ones, of the
chalcedony-flint-jasper-chert series, of obsidian, quartzite, and
even vein quartz, that does not show signs of long Amerind
exploitation. Prudently selected fresh material from an outcrop
is much easier to work than pebbles, the "rind" or cortex of
which is tougher than the interior stuff. But pebbles had the
advantage of occurring in the very stream bed along which the

Amerind lived, and every gravel bar was a supply depot of material in various sizes. It is not too much to say that well over half of Amerind stone tools were made out of pebble material.

The term *pebble tool* is much more restricted in meaning than this. It is a tool which is still, in the main, a pebble. A cutting edge or point or usable face or angle of work has been produced by the necessary chipping on the pebble block or core, and there is no further alteration of the shape except, occasionally, to provide a better finger- or handhold. All pebble-tool industries include a flake-tool element, the flake, struck off by a single blow, becoming a tool immediately by reason of the keenness of its edge. Sharper than steel, this edge is brittle and wears jagged very quickly in use on resistant material; hence the incidence of struck spalls in a pebble-tool industry is high. Obviously they do not look pebbloid unless they are rind flakes, but, as in the whole-pebble tools, there is little or no further alteration. It follows, from this cessation of work as soon as the essential edge or working angle is effected, that in pebble-tool industries, though there are repetitive tool forms, there are no finely developed or specialized ones. As soon as anything as elaborate as a hand ax or a projectile point begins to be made, the industry can no longer be called a pebble-tool industry.

That tool making must have begun with a pebble-tool phase, and continued for hundreds of thousands, even millions, of years in that phase, is as indisputable as it *is* disputable whether particular pebble tools under observation were made by man or nature. The environment or geological context should provide the answer, but, unfortunately, both nature and men have a habit of working at the same sites. Heat and cold, glacial drag, soil creep, waterfalls, and certain other violent behavior of water such as whirlpools can grind and batter pebbles into surprisingly plausible tool forms. Often enough these are found in gravel deposits in just those places to which man would have been attracted because of the abundance of pebble material and favorable camping circumstances, and it takes more than a scorecard to tell the artifacts from the naturifacts. The earliest or Eolithic ("Dawn Stone") phase of the African pebble-tool sequence, called the Kafuan, remains ambiguous in many sober minds because Kafuan "tools" are found in such profusion and in such places that it seems to them as if only nature could have had enough hands and time to make them.

To identify pebble tools for certain is not, however, hopeless. When flake-scarred pebbles are found scattered through stable soil, where no natural attritional forces have been in agitation, and struck flakes, showing bulbs of percussion, are in association, even the devil's advocates will change the subject. The bulb of percussion is a very localized swelling, a sort of pimple, on the flake at the point where the blow fell that detached it from the parent material. Its presence can be accounted for only by man's industrial effort. In instances where the signs are this good, they will probably improve immediately, for some of the pebble tools and chips will certainly show signs of use, even through a patina of age.

But if pebble tools may be confused at one end of the line with the random pseudomorphs of nature, at the other end they run the danger, in America especially, of being attached by standard opinion to standard industries. There are relatively very few "closed" sites in America, that is, sites used by one people and only one people over a period of their existence during which there was no cultural change. Most sites have been visited or occupied again and again by a succession of peoples over thousands of years, for the very good reason that they afforded habitational advantages and conveniences—air conditioning, running water, nearby meat and vegetable counters, fuel piles. These advantages might disappear for a time because of some mishap, such as a burn-over by a forest fire or damage by a tornado; but by and large, as at our Twombly Landing site, the resort of Amerinds before, during, and after the period of oyster abundance, the sites retain their assets of situation. Wherefore, on sites frequented by pebble-tool users will almost always be found the diagnostics of later, classified cultures; but the archaeologist who is agnostic about pebble tools grandly lumps everything together, which reduces the question of whether the pebble tools on the site are man-made to the simpler question, What difference does it make, since they're nothing startling anyway? This is how it is in Alabama, where the Lively-complex sites are as full as a fig tree of cultural discards from the last ten thousand years; and this is how it was, with a most unkind ironic difference, at Prickly Pear Hill, where I had my one experience with a pebble-tool industry.

Prickly Pear Hill is a broad, not too steep slope in the northern section of the village of Croton-on-Hudson, New York. From this hill Washington is said to have reviewed his Continentals after the Revolutionary War, and at the top is located the Institute for Motivational Research, whose director, Dr. Ernest Dichter, is credited with having discovered the sex symbolism of the hardtop convertible. These facts are of no consequence to archaeology, but they do give the area an ambience. What took us there was the report that it had been the farm from which a rich and varied collection of artifacts, now in the custody of the Ossining Historical Society, had been gathered some three-quarters of a century ago. Most of the farm had been bought in the late 1920's for development as a golf course, which was under construction when the depression of the 1930's stymied it; and it had lain expensively idle, taxes in Westchester County being what they are, and mostly bare, fuzzed over with patchy bush, ever since.

"The survey of the archaeological potential of what is purported to be the former Haines Farm" was undertaken by three female members of our Briarcliff College Center Group under the best possible conditions—a sunny March day after the ground surface had been scoured by the sluicing of melting snows and hard early spring rains. And, of course, there wasn't a sign anywhere of an artifact-yielding locus. There never is, we have learned, after years of tracking down confident assertions that at such-and-such a place all you have to do to fill your pockets with arrowheads is to know what one looks like. All the three searchers had to show for some fifteen hours of combined grass-roots scrutinizing was three flakes of quartzite; they almost didn't show me the flakes, in their mood of frustration.

There are millions of quartzite pebbles in the Croton River, a mile away, and a few in the Hudson, half a mile away, and tools of quartzite are found in shell-midden and inland sites all through the valley; and most of these are of the same shiny, grainy, gray-blue composition, with occasional flushes of red in it, that the surveyors had brought in. But what were flakes of quartzite doing halfway up a hillside on denuded ground, where the only agent other than man that could have struck them off was unlikely lightning? Was the agent man, golf-course maker, with a bulldozer? Prickly Pear Hill was just barely worth a second look.

We found the chip locus and went at it with skeptical trowels. The stuff was there; in a three-hour session of testing, we uncovered, in the cover of recent soil, about fifty pounds of it, in every size from a thumbnail chip to a ten-pound cobble. It had been worked, by man, with his hands, for, while most of the debris consisted of single-blow flakes or the blocks which yielded them, there were a couple of bifaces, spalls worked on both sides. These could have been incipient tool blanks, and they could have been choppers. There was certainly a workshop somewhere in the immediate vicinity. Whose, by the evidence? As we have said, everybody made choppers.

We laid out a pattern of five-foot squares. The evidence continued uniformly, and bulkily, the same: flakes, larger spall-offs, blocks broken and unbroken, and a biface now and then. The whole began to look more and more pebble-tool-industry-ish. We had dug up perhaps two hundred pounds of the stuff, over several squares, when the monotony of what we were finding suddenly excited me to implore, "Now don't anybody find a Levanna point."

Levanna projectile points are triangular in shape, and their appearance seems to mark the first use in this area of the bow and arrow, after the countless millennia of the javelin- or atlatl (throwing stick)-launched dart. It shows up well within pottery times, in what is called Late Middle Woodland, and represents immediately prerecent lateness. I would have been only too happy to encounter elsewhere a Levanna camp site, but here the aspect of things seemed to be very much at the opposite end of the time scale.

And, of course, this being the Brennan luck as contrasted

with the Leakey type, within ten minutes somebody did come up with a Levanna point—not any one of the fifty other varieties of point that might have been there, but a Levanna of depressing conformity to type. But I took a sanguine view. The point was of black flint, and, while a few pebbles of black flint were turning up in the soil, not one of them was worked, and there was not a single flint chip in the industrial scrap. I put the Levanna point down as the tip of that arrow that Longfellow had shot so carelessly into the air and that, since it fell to earth he knew not where, had not been found.

Directly under the Levanna the dig began to be a dig and not just a scrape. Up to that point we had been finding the quartzite in the topsoil, varying from two to eight inches thick, and in what we thought of as the plow zone because the slope was gentle enough to have been cultivated. Suddenly it began to come from lower and lower down, in concentrated quantities. We had come upon a pit, at its deepest about forty inches deep. It proved to be boat-shaped, about ten feet long and about four feet wide at the midpoint. There were no signs that it was a dug pit, and we concluded, after some guessing, that it had been the hole left by an uprooted tree. In this cavity some careful and forehanded Amerind or band of Amerinds had cached away all the quartzite he or they could gather together, so that there would be a supply of material to work on while they were sojourning here, some distance away from any other source of workable stone. The matrix of clay in which the hoard was now enclosed was the dirt washed off the tree roots together with that carried into the hollow by rainwater. So we concluded that here was somebody's buried hoard, somebody's accumulated wealth, somebody's savings against a tough tomorrow.

But there was not one piece in the final tally of about half a ton of quartzite that related it to any known industry, no broken or half-done rejects, no misplaced finished pieces, no cache of blades or blanks of the kind Amerinds roughed out at the mine to be transported back to camp. The bifacially worked pieces— not many, but enough to prove that this was a stone industry and not an odd but explicable white man's doing—were heavy and strange, unless you construed them as pebble tools, as

we did. In the center of the pit was a large cobble, shaped like
a loaf of bread, flat on top, about a foot long and six inches
thick, with knicks in it—telltale knicks, for this was an anvil
stone and it showed us as plainly as a numbered diagram how
all this chippage had accumulated, like hair around a barber's
chair. The chipping or breaking method was that called block-
on-block. The stone to be chipped is swung down against a
larger one, the anvil stone, firmly based on the ground—the
oldest and simplest method in the book. Actually it should not
be called chipping at all, but shearing, for the spalls are almost
sliced off the down-driven stone. Had the contents of the pit on
Prickly Pear Hill been found in Choukoutien Cave, where much
of the industry was quartzite, the only cause for remark would
have been the provenience of the material itself.

As soon as we had found a half-dozen cobbles and pebbles
of this material, we knew they were not river stones. They were
coated with the patina of weather exposure, like water-worn
rock, but they did not have the roly-poly shape of river pebbles.
Instead they were faceted, the faces meeting in sharp angles as
though they had been planed at random. We concluded that
they had been planed by glacial grinding. They must have been
ripped out of a seam of quartzite, been transported by ice drag
across the earth's bare-rock surface, and deposited somewhere
on dry land without ever having been near a stream. So they
were not pebbles from the Croton or Hudson bars. But where
were they from? Beyond a radius of about twenty feet from the
pit, there was not a chip or pebble of any variety of quartzite
that we could find in the whole expanse of the hill. The contents
of the pit had not been gathered from the neighborhood like
walnuts being picked up; on the other hand, some of the blocks
were too heavy to have been carried very far. We still don't
know where they came from. But they certainly qualify the
Prickly Pear Hill workings to be counted, on the score of
material source, as a pebble industry, albeit not the usual kind.

As it happens, the pit is only thirty or forty feet from a small
stream which courses down the hill into the Hudson beside a
high knoll or bluff where we had once dug a productive site in
our shell-midden series. Many of the tools—projectile points,

choppers, knives, scrapers—appeared, at first glance, to be made of the same rather lustrous gray variety of quartzite as the cache material, and we had to face the likelihood that the cache was the locally stored supply of raw material for the band that camped seasonally on the ridge. A thirty-minute walk up the hillside, a half-hour's banging away, and a twenty-minute walk down hill would provide enough tool stock for a week, or perhaps a month. And if this were so, then the cache was not a pebble-tool-industry site but the material backlog of rather late people, on the order of four thousand years old.

But this, it soon appeared, was not likely. One of the odder shapes of quartzite found in the pit was a series of rusty, pocked-looking rods. They seemed to have been the cores cut out by a core drill, except that they were of differing diameters. We thought, fleetingly, that they were perhaps the products of quite modern activity, until we found some of the rods still in the quartzite, where they looked as though a thin pipe had been driven into the stone, like Excalibur, and had then oxidized away—which was manifest nonsense. These rods had to have been foetal in the quartzite when it was in formation. And that was the answer. The rods were, we discovered, a fossil of probably Devonian age called *Scolithus erectus*, which sounds without translation like what the rods look like, a stick of stone. Their presence identified the cache quartzite as not of the same deposit, certainly not from the same locality, as the riverbank quartzite, and it relieved us of the obligation to relate the former to the latter, that is, the speculated ten-thousand-year-old material to a known four-thousand-year-old industry.

Of such simple but potent ingredients of fact are compounded the cocktails that exhilarate the imagination of the diggers. In answer to our pleas, Dr. Don Dragoo of the Carnegie Museum, Section of Man, dropped in on the Prickly Pear Hill diggings one November day. He had recently examined the Lively-complex materials and had become one of the growing number of Eastern archaeologists persuaded to believe in them after approaching them closer than 7 feet ± 1 foot. (He is editor of a monograph about them to be published by a society devoted to the dissemination of discoveries in science in the broadest sense.) What we did not know until then was that he had been excavating his own pebble-tool problem, at Wells Creek, Tennessee. Our cache industry, he told us, was much like the Wells Creek industry, except that it was cruder, undoubtedly because the quartzite itself is a rougher material than his flint, as tweed is rougher than linen. He showed us a simple test for the riddlesome forms that we were not quite sure were tools or cores: you turn the form in your hand until you find the grip on it that feels comfortable; opposite that, where the working edge should be, there will be a working edge, almost always with some sign of cutting, scraping, or battering. We had such tools. What we needed, Dragoo said, was what he needed at Wells Creek: "indisputable evidence," that is, something datable.

It seemed possible that we had that, too. There had been crumbs and smears of charcoal all through the clay fill of the cache, but it had so obviously been washed into the hole that we were not inclined to spend any money, or waste a laboratory's time, on having it dated. We had hoped, though it did not seem likely if the cache was simply a store of materials, to find a hearth in the bottom of the pit. There was none there, but on the lip of the pit, where we excavated last, we came upon a handful of charcoal that was clearly the remains of a small, controlled fire. The long-dead flame instantly inspired us to see an ancient quartzite worker sitting on the edge of the pit between the fire and the matting of tree roots upturned as a shield against the wind off the Hudson, hammering away at his Paleolithic chores. True, the charcoal was not in the pit; it was only eight inches under the present soil line, in the glacial-till subsoil, but there were chips of quartzite all around and half a ton of the stuff almost within arm's length. Of course we sent the charcoal off to Yale.

It came back beautifully dated, which is to say that what we had dug was dated by it, with an age nobody could quibble with. But what it dated, in such a way that we never had any doubt about it, or the precision of the Yale Laboratory, was the Levanna point; the age was 1,140 years, the date A.D. 910—

which, since Levannas have been soundly dated and placed, fixes the Levanna with the exactitude of a family Bible.

Such is life, one thing on top of another and post hoc begetting fallacies of propter hoc. Not in a hundred years of patient pleading the evidence would we be able to convince anybody that what had been C14-dated was not the workshop at all, but only the campfire of a solitary hunter who had stopped there to roast a collop of venison after a long day's hunt.

Still, this is only a minor instance of a pebble-industry horizon undone by a projectile point. There is a much more famous one. At Prickly Pear Hill our sorrow was the lack of indisputable evidence. At Lewisville, Texas, there was indisputable evidence, almost literally by the bushel, in some twenty-one hearths, from basins two feet in diameter to circular surface spreads of five feet in diameter, with plenty of charcoal for C14 tests. These have been run again and again, every time there is an improvement in the method, and they have consistently given ages of about forty thousand years. But Lewisville also was illegitimatized by a projectile point, and the learned and judicious Gordon R. Willey, who is receptive to a forty-thousand-year-old New World population in his *An Introduction to American Archaeology* (1966), can do no more for it than, "The Lewisville finds are a possible but not a proven datum in the case for man in the Americas in early Wisconsin times."

The Early Man horizon on the Trinity River near Lewisville, Denton County, occurred twenty feet down in a gravel terrace the top of which was seventy feet above the river at normal stage, and it was exposed by earth-moving machinery when fill was needed for an earthen dam. According to Wilson W. Crook, Jr., and R. K. Harris, who led the excavation party and reported on the site in the *Bulletin of the Texas Archaeological Society* (1957), the terrace "has been geologically correlated with an interstadial or interglacial period of the Late Pleistocene, possibly within, or just preceding, the Wisconsin stage, depending upon the eventual definition and evaluation of this stage." In short, the geology supports the C14 date series obtained by the Humble Oil Company's Houston Research Center.

And so does the fauna. It included such extinct mammals as the mammoth, the horse, the camel, the Taylor's bison, the glyptodon, a large turtle and terrapin, and the dire wolf, as well as the full range of animals now found in the area. Much of the bone was almost certainly associated with the hearths, particularly the large hearths. The smaller hearths seem to have been used for food of lesser bulk: birds' eggs, snakes, mussels, rabbits, and hackberries.

The pebble-tool character of the site of the hearths is established by a gray quartzite pebble chopper apparently of the slasher type, in which the length of cutting blade is on the longitudinal side of the tool, which is pointed. Two flakes of this quartzite were found, and a flake and a retouched-flake scraper of white flint and a Clovis fluted point of the same material.

When first found, the Clovis point was the occasion of the kind of rejoicing that the discovery of a Paleo-hunter site usually brings to the heart of the archaeologist. It was only when two dates of "more than 37,000 years" were reported by the Humble Laboratory (37,000 years was then the practical limit of testing; the age has since been determined by Humble as about 40,000 years) that amazement began to grow. No Clovis site, of the several that have been C14-dated, has yielded an age of as much as 13,000 years; an age of 15,000 years is the maximum that even the most generous estimator is prepared to accept for the Clovis spearmen.

One immediately suspects that the point was planted. For some five years before the discovery of the hearths, bones of an obviously Pleistocene fauna had been eroding out of the terrace without accompanying evidence of human presence. The hearths changed all that; but the meager recovery of artifacts was not doing much to give them a cultural identity or archaeological importance. It seems possible, therefore, that somebody with a benevolent nature decided to sacrifice a Clovis point he had been hoarding to salt the site and enhance its importance. There is no incongruity in an association of a chopper with a Clovis point, since pebble choppers have been found before at Clovis sites, notably at the Lehner Ranch site, where mammoths and extinct bison were slain and butchered. As a matter of fact, the

Lewisville assemblage, excluding the Clovis point, is exactly that of the Levi Rock Shelter site near Austin, Texas, where a chopper, a scraper, and two utilized flakes were found in a zone under one dated at 10,000 ± 175 years B.P.; there was a Clovis-point fragment in the dated level.

Crook and Harris vigorously deny the possibility of implantation, as well as that of a displacement of the Clovis point from a higher level, since it was found *in situ* in a hearth, they insist, with a caliche incrustation on it and traces of the surrounding burned red earth in its flake scars. Only they knew enough about the site in time, they say, to have perpetrated the hoax. By thus denying the likelihood of a hoax, however, they have presented archaeology with an anachronism, an impossible forty-thousand-year-old Clovis point. The official verdict is that the hearths, despite the evidence of meals cooked at them, and the small ember logs occurring in them, are preserved hot spots from a Middle Pleistocene prairie fire. It is a facile but more than a little hackneyed explanation, and one still looks in the background for that benign third party who had dreamed up a surprise for his friends only to discover, when the C14 results came in, that he had hopelessly compromised the only site in America with the "indisputable evidence" of a laboratory-confirmed age of forty thousand years.

The validity of a site even older, geologically pre-Wisconsin, has been nullified by the same natural burn-over argument. At the Texas Street site, San Diego, in 1956, Dr. George F. Carter, at the time head of the geography department of Johns Hopkins University, discovered "fire areas" under forty feet of alluvial overburden in a bank exposure. The fire areas were about two feet in diameter, that is, hearth-sized, and contained animal bone, marine shells and percussion-broken rock—quartzite cores that might be choppers and flakes in the form of blades—all to be expected about a hearth. Of the hearths Carter, who draws professional animus like a lightning rod, wrote in 1965:

This fire area situation has been grossly misrepresented. I said [in 1957] that hearths cropped up laterally for more than 100 yds. This has been interpreted as meaning a continuous fire area, hence the remains of a forest fire. The hearths are normal in size and scattered through the deposit, vertically and horizontally, just as in other comparable sites. The only thing missing is a piece of human bone. What I would give for just one human tooth!

The site remaining toothless, so does its impression on American prehistory. The chipped stones are denounced as nonartifactual, and the hearths have been attributed to that elusive arsonist, Mother Nature. What else is there to explain? The burned animal bones? Fire burns animals, too, doesn't it? And the shells? Gulls drop mollusks from on high to break them. But if the rest of Texas Street has been explained away, what are a few old shells?

It took a thirty-two-ton Allis-Chalmers earthmover, two International Harvester bulldozers, and an outlay of some $42,000 to efface the claims of the first-discovered and most famous site, Tule Springs, Nevada, to the status of a camping ground of pebble tool-chopper man. It had acquired that reputation in 1933 when a party of paleontologists collecting fossils in the vicinity known as Vegas Wash, eleven miles northwest of Las Vegas, came upon a bed of charcoal and ash, broken bone, and a struck obsidian flake five to eight feet down in the valley fill. The material was not disturbed; instead, Finlay Hunter, financier and leader of the expedition, cased up the association intact and sent it to the American Museum, where it remained in storage until the advent of $C14$ dating. The intact block was then "excavated" in the museum and the charcoal extracted.

The site, for purposes of further archaeology, had been turned over to the Southwest Museum, Los Angeles, whose director, Mark R. Harrington, immediately organized a survey. He found the Hunter site and two other sites, labeled Ash Beds 1 and 2. Bones, including some cut and polished fragments, were found in the beds. The charcoal from this dig was combined with that from the museum block for an adequate sample, and the University of Chicago result—this was in the early, solid-carbon days—was "more than 23,800 years," with the probability of an age of 33,000 years.

This dating stimulated a second exploration, in 1955. It confirmed that the ash beds, now numbering three, were localized hearth areas, within which were abundant inclusions of bones, as would be expected at camp sites. The bones proved to be of camel, mammoth, ground sloth, and extinct horse. The areas of exploration were extended; and eventually seven areas, each with one or more ash beds, all containing bones, were mapped and tested or thoroughly dug. This region, now desert, had once been well watered; there had been a lake in the valley, along which the sites had been strung for at least a mile.

During this second expedition, and a third, only one artifact was discovered in a hearth, a handsome (to the archaeologist) scraper of orthoquartzite two inches in diameter. But within the bounds of the site as a whole were recovered three side-blade choppers or slashers, other scrapers, flakes, and bone implements. A new C_{14} date brought the age up to about thirty thousand years; and this time no anomalous Clovis point, or any other kind, intruded in the pebble tool-chopper inventory.

Tule Springs now loomed like a fog, or a cloud, on the Early Man horizon. Was it a cloud that would pass, or a fog obfuscating large structures of evidence? In 1962 Dr. Richard Shutler, Jr., curator of anthropology at the Nevada State Museum, applied for and received a grant of $42,200 from the National Science Foundation, supplemented by support from Allis-Chalmers, to resolve the question. With the earthmover picking up twenty-five to thirty tons of fill at a bite, the critical areas were trenched, in some places to fifty feet below the surface. Flakes and bone tools were found, but nothing that could be added to the character already given the site by the pick and shovel (helped by small charges of dynamite) of the Harrington expeditions. Out of a study of the geology came apparently (no definitive report has been published on the site at this writing) a conclusion that the bearing deposits could be either thirteen thousand or thirty thousand years old.

The C_{14} test said thirty thousand years, but that was not the end of the matter. Was what was being tested, despite its look and feel, really charcoal? It was analyzed chemically, and the analyst, Dr. S. F. Cook of the University of California at Berkeley, wrote in *American Antiquity* in 1964 as follows:

The conclusion is warranted that not only in Sample No. 1, but in Samples No. 2 and 3 [from Tule Springs] we are dealing primarily with vegetation residues which are in a relatively active stage of alteration and which include considerable amounts of organic matter produced by micro-organisms through past centuries and still being reworked at the present time. There is little evidence of advanced carbon or of much true charcoal of any kind.

Bugs in the brush, creating fake thirty-thousand-year-old carbon—this is a new one. There are many exceptions that could be taken to the decision imposed by this analysis on Tule Springs, but they all sound defensive, and none of them has been taken. The verdict on Tule Springs is that its human occupation, which is unquestioned, was between 11,000 and 13,000 B.P.

But does this not leave us something—a non-projectile-point, pebble chopper-flake industry during a period when Clovis points were being made in that region? It does; the fauna is that which was regularly preyed on by Clovis spearmen, and the absence of Clovis or any Paleo-hunter-style point in the three hundred thousand tons of earth moved under the eyes of a twenty-five-man crew is more than merely negative evidence. It defines and describes the culture of the Tule Spring campers: it was a bone and probably wood industry, with stone only a subordinate element; but the stone used was pebble, a telltale trait surviving from a pebble-tool-industry past.

Of the accumulation of evidence for what he calls the American Paleolithic, Willey in his *An Introduction to American Archaeology* (the best illustrated and mapped book in the field, and fine reading) says:

As things stand now the "pre-projectile point horizon" will not be demonstrated beyond reasonable doubt until a complex or assemblage of materials attributable to it are found stratigraphically beneath artifacts of the well-known, 10,000 to 12,000 year old, bifacially flaked lanceolate or leaf-shaped point class, or failing this, until the crude, non-projectile point complexes are found in indisputable association with middle or early Pleistocene deposits and convincing radio carbon datings. No amount of forceful argument, on the basis of present data, will change this situation.

Since this is the clearly stated obvious, it is acceptable to archaeologists and in resolution form would be passed by acclamation at a convention of the professionals, without further thought. Its very obviousness renders it innocuous until the last sentence, where we suddenly become aware that what has seemed to be only a statement of a desideratum is actually an ultimatum. Until the conditions are met, it is proclaimed, ears will be closed to argument, no matter how forceful. This would have to mean dialectic argument; surely it cannot mean the weight of evidence, which now runs to the ton. There is an age group of which this simple "I want, and nothing else is acceptable" is expected; archaeologists are supposed to have passed that age. What it has not provided cannot be demanded of investigation, and equally the data it has provided cannot be ignored. To impose such a standard on the investigation of American prehistory is not to investigate that prehistory, but to legislate it; prehistory is what is found and what can be made of that. Closing the eyes for a moment and picturing thousands of pre-stone-projectile-point-industry tools being swept under the rug will place the matter in perspective.

This is not a Ph.D. thesis, and the writer has no intention of reviewing exhaustively the American manifestations of the pebble-tool industry; the reader would certainly not put up with that. But I do have an obligation to document my thesis that the first Americans were the Chopper people. So let us begin at the beginning, which is Alaska. If at all possible the sampling of sites should begin in Alaska, through which pebble-industry people had to pass if there is to be an authentic pebble-industry horizon in more southerly regions. And it is possible.

The late J. Louis Giddings, probably the most perceptive of the workers in Alaska—which has attracted many of his quality —dug up the evidence in 1960–61 on the Palisades of Cape Krusenstern overlooking Kotzebue Sound on the northern shores of Seward Peninsula. He was digging there to continue a project that had begun with one of the most remarkable natural chronological records on the face of the earth. At sea level on Kotzebue Sound is a series of parallel ridges, 114 of them, each of which was once a beach at the edge of the sea. These are not raised beaches, out of water now because the sea has receded or the land been upthrust. They are all basically at the same level, ridge after ridge paralleling the present shore, like waves turned to sand, for about two miles inland.

Nobody told Giddings the secret of these ridges because they had never even been noted before, much less speculated upon as to how they were formed. But after excavation of a couple of sites, he thought he detected the simple and, when he thought about it, obvious pattern: each successive ridge inland was older. Testing quickly proved this to be true; for on most of the ridges there were occupation sites identifiable by their material culture, and they were in as good chronological order as an archaeologist could wish. For some five thousand years the shallow sea, driven by the prevailing winds and with the help of tide and currents, had been busily throwing sand from its bottom up on the beach until a ridge had been formed. When this ridge became so high that waves and tide could no longer reach it, it became a permanent topographical feature and the sea began its next sandpile. Usually the sea chews away at a beach and swallows it; at Kotzebue Sound it regurgitates it.

As a ridge became high and dry, it was occupied by people of the Eskimo tradition who made their seasonal living out of the sea. Starting at the seashore you could walk through Alaskan prehistory. But at the 114th beach inland, Beach 1 in the order of formation in time, the record came to a stop with a known culture, the Denbigh, of about six thousand years ago, which Giddings had himself discovered on Norton Sound about 1950. This beach survey proved many things of archaeological significance, including the continuity and probably American origin of American Eskimo culture, but it added nothing to the time depth of Alaskan prehistory.

But now Giddings knew where to look for sites older than the Denbigh: they would be upland and farther inland. He found his next site on a high terrace, called the Palisades, on Ingitkalik Mountain, facing out across the beach ridges, Kotzebue Sound, and the Chukotka Sea. There were two occupations here, both older than Denbigh. The lower, older one Giddings called Palisades I. It consisted of "five whole and one axe-like or 'chopper' tools made of beach pebbles, the fragment of a single-shouldered blade and 38 substantial chips, some of which have been used as cutting tools. The larger pieces are flaked on both faces to achieve an end-sharpened implement resembling Asian chopping tools."

No hearths or datable bone were recovered with this industry, but the tools show their age on their faces. The chert or chalcedony of which they were made is so weathered as to have been chemically altered. Giddings says, "The dating of this older assemblage, called Palisades I, is purely conjectural beyond the fact that no other artifacts in the region appear to be chemically altered in this manner."

Palisades I meets one of Willey's standards, that a pebble-tool assemblage be found under a projectile-point horizon, for above it was Giddings's Palisades II cultural layer, ninety artifacts and fragments and several hundred flakes, mainly of internally unaltered chert and chalcedony—this qualification being offered by way of contrast with the Palisades I material, which was *chemically altered throughout.* The Palisades II lithics are, "however, somewhat encrusted with lime and nearly all show a degree of patination." But the Willey standard was more restrictive than that; he specified that the projectile-point horizon over the pebble tools must contain "bifacially flaked lanceolates or leaf-shaped" points. The Palisades II points are bifacially flaked, and would be lanceolate or leaf-shaped in outline except that the outline has been interrupted by notching. They are, therefore, side-notched points and belong typologically to the Archaic of North America, the period *subsequent* to that of the lanceolate and leaf-shaped styles.

Whatever Willey thinks of these, Giddings, after a review of Alaskan materials in a landmark study, *The Cultural Continuities of Eskimos* (1961), made no bones about what he thought:

In summary of these selected horizons (there were 9 of them covering the whole prehistory of Alaska) it appears that the earliest human leavings yet recognized in the American Arctic are cobble chopper-tools and percussion bi-facing, followed *much later* [italics mine] by notched points, then by the micro blade-and-burin combination [the Denbigh pattern of so-called Arctic small-tool in-

dustry], then regionally by whaling and deep-house [semisubter-
ranean] building, then by pottery and first midden mounds, then
by elaboration of engraving art and ceremony and, finally, by a
specialized but utilitarian "Eskimo" form of culture.

Nobody had a better right than Giddings to project such a
succession, and he had confirmed much of it and was adding to
it and filling it in when he died as the result of injuries received
in an automobile accident in December, 1964. He had already
discovered and had spent a season at the twenty-foot-deep Onion
Portage site, about 125 miles upstream on the Kobuk River,
which empties into Kotzebue Sound. It is the best stratified
site in the Arctic, made up of more than seventy occupation
levels which have been related to eight horizons or "bands"
with from three to fourteen occupation periods per band. In his
only season at Onion Portage, Giddings had just reached Band
8 and had had a tantalizing glimpse of its industry; and the
anticipation of things to come was written large in the last
chapter of his posthumously published *Ancient Men of the
Arctic* (1967).

One of Giddings's students at Brown University, Donald D.
Anderson, took over the site and published his first summary
report of work in progress in *Scientific American*, June, 1968.
Tools that were the counterpart of Palisades II were found in
the top of Band 7, counting from the top, and in Band 6. They
dated, by interpolation from C_{14} dates, from about 6000 B.P. to
about 4500 B.P. Band 8 was divided into two time levels, the
upper with C_{14} dates placing it slightly earlier than 8000 B.P.
The industry of the lower level, named Akmak by Anderson
from an Eskimo word for chert, is earlier than 8500 B.P. Because
it closely resembles Siberian industries of about 15,000 B.P.
and, by Anderson's correlation, Beringia was closed between
14,000 and 10,000 B.P., he calculates that Akmak first entered Alaska around 15,000 B.P.

But this is exactly the time that the fluted-point makers
should have been in Alaska, according to the prophets of their
Asiatic nativity. And they were not in Alaska. Anderson says,
"Nothing from any occupation level at Onion Portage shows any
hint of Paleo-Indian influence." But in that sequence no pebble

tools turned up, either. We would not have expected them to; when Giddings said that Palisade II was "much later" than Palisades I, the "much" converts into at least ten thousand years. By 15,000 B.P. the pebble-tool makers had long since cleared out of Alaska and had scattered over other regions, among them Venezuela.

José M. Cruxent of the Instituto Venezolano de Investegaciones Científicas had first reported a Venezuelan Paleo-hunter assemblage, which he called El Jobo (after a village with a population of sixty), in 1956. It consisted of lanceolate, leaf-shaped and double-pointed projectile points with, among other tools, choppers. The points seemed to fit congruously into an "horizon style," that is, a motif prevalent over wide regions contemporaneously, of such points in the Western plains about eight thousand years ago; though later, when some three thousand El Jobo artifacts had been collected, stemmed and demi-stemmed points were found among them. Cruxent noted that the material was mainly quartzite, a stone not used for points in the later Venezuelan industries.

For the next several years he pursued every clue to the makers and age of the El Jobo collection, sending out several interim bulletins on it to *American Antiquity* and in 1963 in that same journal, with his collaborator, Dr. Irving Rouse of Yale University, summing up the fruit of their labors thus:

Cruxent discovered the first Paleo-Indian sites in 1956 at El Jobo, some 5 miles inland from Muaco [near the Caribbean coast of northern Venezuela]. He located over 45 sites in this vicinity and collected some 20,000 artifacts from them. Subsequent geological studies have made it possible to classify the sites into four successive complexes, Camare, Las Lagunas, El Jobo and Las Casitas, which are correlated respectively with the uppermost, upper middle, lower middle and lower terraces of the Rio Pedregal. The sites of the Camare complex yielded no projectile points, only crude chopping tools, scrapers and other flakes of quartzite. The Las Lagunas artifacts are smaller; the diagnostic form is a bifacially worked blade which could have been used as a hand ax or knife, or else have been hafted in a thrusting spear. The El Jobo complex has lanceolate projectile points, to which a few stemmed points are added in the Las Casitas complex.

In 1961 Cruxent discovered another Paleo-Indian site at Manzanillo, a suburb of Maracaibo. Its artifacts are smaller than those of
the Camare complex but, like the latter, it lacks blades and projectile points. It has yielded only crude choppers, scrapers and
flakes, made mainly out of fossil wood.

(It is worth mentioning here that one of the Southeast Asian
chopper industries, the Anyathian, used fossil wood. It was perhaps two hundred thousand years earlier than the Manzanillo
materials, but clearly this material, which does not flake well
enough to make good tools, satisfied the stone-tool requirements
of these early Venezuelans.)

From choppers and flakes to smaller, better-worked hand
axes that might have been hafted (note that the material of
this developing sequence is workable quartzite), thence to lanceolate projectile points which are in workmanship only lighter,
slimmer hand axes, then to stemmed points which are a further
reduction of the hafted end and are a form of notching, with
the chopper as such threading through the whole sequence like
a brand mark—this is a diagram, and a lesson that may never be
repeated, in the lithic industrial revolution that took place in
America, rather rapidly it would seem, between 20,000 B.P.
and 12,000 B.P. What stone working had become by El Jobo
times was what stone working continued to be, south of the
Arctic and Arctic-influenced areas along the northwest coast,
until the Stone Age came to an end. American stone workers
did learn how to strike bladelike flakes (strip blades, to use a
highly descriptive term applied by Kenneth Oakley, since the
core is "stripped" and the flakes look like strips of stone) from
cores especially prepared for that purpose, either by invention
or emulation or both. But the sophistication of techniques and
the highly specialized industries that proliferated in hand-ax
territory in the Old World are not found in sub-Arctic America
—which is far from saying that it could not produce handsome
results.

The choice of the span 20,000 B.P.–12,000 B.P. for the lithic
revolution is deduced from C_{14} dating. In 1959 Cruxent had
excavated near Muaco a site at a spring that had been the
watering place of extinct animals and, by the signs, of men.

Among the animal bones found there were those of the mastodon, American horse, and *Megatherium*, and some of these bones had been cut, split for marrow, and burned. Human association was proved by the recovery of several hammerstones, a possible knife, a fragment of a scraper, and a fragment of an El Jobo lanceolate point and a complete point, the latter found eroding out of the deposit. The only datable material at the site was burned bone, which has been found to give reliable ages where unburned bone does not.

Samples were sent to two laboratories, the Humble Oil Company and the University of Michigan. The age determined by Humble was 16,375 ± 400 years, and by Michigan 14,300 ± 500 years. Taking the most cautious view, Cruxent and Rouse would say only that these ages might apply either to the El Jobo points or to the other tools which typologically would fit into one of the earlier, pre-stone-projectile-point industries of the Rio Pedregal terraces. A second possibility is that both dates are accurate and are for separate events 2,000 years apart; neither the bones nor the artifacts are out of synchronization for what seems to the historically minded a very long period.

Regardless, the dates are of one stage or another of the Camare-to-El Jobo developmental sequence, and even if they apply to the pre-projectile-point stage and El Jobo points are as late as about 12,000 B.P., as Rouse has stated to me he thinks they might be, we must allow enough time for the development of at least three stages, with a possible date of 16,775 B.P. (16,375 + 400 years) fixing one of them. To say, then, that the development must have taken place between 20,000 B.P. and 12,000 B.P. is to allow no more plus-or-minus error than is statistically permitted to a laboratory.

Warned against argument, we can pursue the implications of the Muaco-El Jobo sites Socratically. Our points may be out of order, but shouldn't our questions be answered?

How is a crude chopper industry like the Camare at 16,375 B.P. compatible with the first settlement of America after 13,000 B.P. by expert flintsmiths working with selected flints and turning out fluted points?

How could any people living in America in 16,375 B.P.

have got to Venezuela if they had not come by 25,000 B.P.
at the latest, before the last major advance of the Wisconsin?
Is it proposed that the Camare-Las Lagunas-El Jobo sequence is only an aspect of the North America fluted-point
hunters? And if not, who were the people of that sequence?
Willey does not have to answer these questions. His *Introduction* is only the first volume of a two-part work, with the second
volume to be devoted to South America. But he must already
have answered the question, Can you scissor the subject of
American prehistory into two parts for no better reason than
convenience in managing the material, when nature did not
sunder the two continents and they are, in consequence, one
land mass, the Western Hemisphere? Evidently he has, despite
Camare-El Jobo, answered affirmatively, thus putting Camare-
El Jobo in its place. But what about the Cerro Chivateros site
and the "Andean Biface Horizon"?

In November, 1967, Edward P. Lanning and Thomas C.
Patterson reported in *Scientific American* on the Cerro Chivateros site, about a mile inland from the coast in southern Peru
in a range of hills affording abundant sandstone and quartzite.
There were revealed at the site "five major strata, each representing a different period of time, and somewhat different climatic conditions." In the lowest stratum, called the Red Zone,
is a flake industry, but a specialized one of scrapers, perforators,
and a few burins, small chisel-point tools for working bone and
wood. The Red Zone is topped off by a hard crust, called the
Lower Salitre, containing a few Red Zone pieces, followed by
a wind-deposited silt. Here occurs the assemblage called Chivateros I, consisting of "many thick, pointed bifacial tools, large
tools with serrated edges and heavy unretouched flakes that
were simply struck from a bigger piece. There are also a few
large scrapers, notched stones and bifacially flaked spearpoints
and knife blades."

This assemblage is assigned to Lanning and Patterson's
"Andean Biface Horizon" (ABH), which is "a single widespread cultural stage" in South America that includes Cruxent's
Las Lagunas phase and similar assemblages discovered by the
authors on the Central Peruvian coast, by Father Gustavo Le

Paige in the Atacoma desert of Chile, and by Eduardo Cigliano in the Argentine Andes. The diagnostics of the ABH are "elongated chopping tools and spear points coarsely flaked on both sides by percussion." The choppers are of the slasher or side-edged type.

Andean Biface.

Above the Chivateros I horizon is another crust, the Upper Salitre, into which the Chivateros I industry continues; it produced enough wood for C_{14} tests the average result of which was 11,4000 years. Chivateros II, equated with El Jobo, follows and ends the Cerro Chivateros sequence. By geologic extrapolation from the Upper Zone Chivateros I age of 11,4000 years, Lanning and Patterson give Lower Zone Chivateros I an age of about 12,000 years and the Red Zone assemblage below it an age of 14,000 years.

Here, it would seem, Willey's prescription has at last been satisfied, a pre-stone-projectile-point industry "stratigraphically beneath artifacts of the well-known, 10,000 to 12,000 year old, bifacially flaked lanceolate or leaf-shaped point class." The Chivateros I assemblage includes leaf-shaped "bifacially flaked" spearpoints, and the Red Zone assemblage is safely beneath it by two climatic periods. But it would be rash to assume that the case is proved; we have overlooked something, the qualifier "well-known," by which is meant Sandia or Clovis or, at the very least, Folsom. It can't be anything novel—the novel being a form of fiction.

So far the sites described have been of only modest antiquity, except Carter's Texas Street hearths. For these he suggests a Middle Pleistocene date (by the new order, at least 500,000 B.P.) which gives everybody, even me, the shudders. This limited antiquity requires only that the people who occupied these sites, or their cultural ancestors, made the trip from Asia while the land bridge was still passable before the onset of Wisconsin III, that is, before about twenty-five thousand years ago. If the Lewisville hearths are man-made, as we believe, then the Lewisvillians may have arrived here in the late stage of Wisconsin II, just before the land bridge went under during the following interstadial. But we have not advanced any evidence for an earlier influx. We are about to. Leakey had not been in the United States a year before he, being disposed by experience to look for the earliest men, found them.

Leakey himself selected a likely site in 1964 in the Calico Mountains of California, and excavations were financed over the next three years by the National Geographic Society, which had munificently funded his Olduvai Gorge work. The first report, signed by Leakey, Ruth De Ette Simpson, who was one of Harrington's party at Tule Springs, and Dr. Thomas Clements of the University of Southern California, discoverer of an enigmatic flake industry on the terrace of an extinct lake in Death Valley, appeared in *Science*, May 31, 1968.

Since 1955 Simpson has been collecting from the edge of the Mohave Desert near Barstow, along the shores of the dead Manix Lake, "an assemblage of large, crude, generalized artifacts, including coup de poing-like [hand-ax- or chopper-like] implements." Under further study some of the coups de poing seem to be large, leaf-shaped points, and the collection further includes large end choppers and side choppers with edge retouch, bifacial discs, flakes, and retouched flakes. The choppers and coups de poing and/or leaf-shaped points lay at or above the strand line of the highest level of the lake during the dampest phase of the Wisconsin, both singly and in workshop loci. The choppers were usually found away from the workshops, suggesting diverse centers of activity.

Tufa from just below the high-strand beach has yielded two C_{14} results averaging 19,500 years. Such an age accords well with the estimated climax of Wisconsin III, during which it would be expected that, after 4,000 or 5,000 years of high precipitation, inland lakes would be full to the rim of their basins. There were hundreds of these, because the region is relatively flat and lends itself to collecting runoff water in lakes rather than draining it off in river systems. Great Salt Lake is the residue of the largest of these, the enormous Lake Bonneville. It was only to be expected that this well-watered region would have supported a population, despite the probably uncomfortable climate. The question is, how long had the population been there? Since the pre-Wisconsin III interstadial? or before that?

The beach-line discoveries indicated that there should be other outcrops of this primitive industry in the vicinity; and Simpson set out to explore the nearby Calico Mountains, as Giddings had gone to higher ground for older occupations. In a fifteen-foot-deep prospector's open excavation in water-laid gravels in a dry wash, she found flake implements from top to bottom. Since this region is now all desert, the dominant geomorphic force is erosion—downcutting, not aggradation. The gravel deposits had to date from the period, probably before ten thousand years ago, before the setting in of the current aridity. About the time Leakey came on the scene, another exposure, in an alluvial fan near Yermo, began to exude pieces of the Manix industry, as Simpson had previously named it, and on Leakey's recommendation a dig was begun.

Over the next few years a pit twenty-five feet by twenty-five feet was dug thirteen feet into this fan, which had not been previously disturbed, and 170 specimens positively identified as artifacts, as well as several hundred others less positively identifiable, were dug up. The artifacts include large "Clactonian" flakes with bold bulbs of percussion and "simple bifacially worked tools" of the chopper type. In some cases the flakes had faceted butts; this means that a preparatory flake had been detached from a pebble to prepare a ledge or surface called the striking platform, in order to strike off a flake controlled in size and shape. Generally speaking, the flakes displayed all the characteristics of having been industrially produced.

Aware that the attribution of these finds to human workmanship would be challenged, though the Clactonian flake industry of Clacton-on-Sea in England, which is similar, is unquestioned, Simpson, as director of the dig, tested other areas in the fan. One large pit, at some distance from the main one, yielded nothing artifactual-looking. In smaller pits near the main pit there was recovery of a few recognizable specimens. All materials recognized as of human manufacture by Leakey, Simpson, and Clements show selectivity of material, being made of the better grades of the abundant chalcedonic pebble stuff. The evidence described an area of limited activity, a camp site or workshop.

Nothing datable came out of any of the pits, and the dating problem was then turned over to the geologists. In their estimation the fan had been deposited at least 40,000 years ago, during a period of stream activity in the gully, but the gravels could not, using conventional chronology for the Wisconsin, be older than 120,000 years. The most probable age, they thought, was between 50,000 and 80,000 years. Since it was not stated that the flakes and tools occurred at a consistent depth or level, they must have occurred throughout the thirteen-foot dig, and occupation must have therefore been constant or intermittent during the buildup of the fan.

To nobody's surprise, this geologic dating has been challenged, as has the human production of the pebble industry, despite its endorsement by Leakey, who not only has seen more pebble tools than all Americanists put together but has manufactured them and used them in the tasks of cutting, chopping, and scraping for which they were intended by those who made them culturally. One would think that at this stage of the game there would be norms for judging what is and what is not fracture by human agency. In theory there are such norms, among them the presence of bulbs of percussion on flakes and the occurrence of bifaces or "cores" with several flakes removed from more or less opposite planes. But acknowledgment that these norms are present is still an act of the will, and dogmatic skeptics have an easy out at the Yermo site: it meets none of Willey's specifications, none at all; it does not even show a stratigraphy. What is there is there, take it or leave it.

The more intellectually flexible view of Manix Lake-Calico Mountain archaeology is that the evidence outlines a long occupation of this once well-favored habitat by a pebble-tool people, beginning at least in Middle Wisconsin times with a chopper-flake phase and developing into an incipient stone-projectile-point phase at the height of Wisconsin III. The synchronization is not exact, but this is what we have already seen on the terraces of the Rio Pedregal. More, much more, than providing a mere compilation of a bank account of instances of pebble-tool industry in America, it has been the endeavor of this chapter to make it plain that not only was the chopper-flake tradition the industry of America's first immigrant groups but it was the legitimate parent of what American stone work subsequently became. Willey's specifications are adventitious; they are the conditions under which archaeologists feel they must find a basic stone-work phase in order to believe in it. But the central specification has been omitted. Must not the chopper-flake phase have existed because there was no other source from which the American stone projectile point and the stone industry associated with it could have evolved? Or, conversely, do not the pebble-tool evolutionary sequences we know of, regardless of whether their provenience is of itself sufficiently clear, provide exactly the industrial line of descent we need for both the Paleo-hunter fluted points *and* the more widespread and typical Archaic pattern?

The pebble-tool stage with which we are already acquainted is surprisingly varied in its development. The Camare of the highest terrace on the Rio Pedregal was a basic chopper-flake phase; it began to develop along the line of refinement of the chopper core into a true bifacial blade, and once that theme had been hit on, projectile points of lanceolate or leaf shape were inevitable. But the industry of the Red Zone at Cerro

Chivateros, for which Lanning and Patterson plead contemporaneity with Camare and of which there are other manifestations in Peru, has gone in the direction of flake tools, although it must have included choppers—a heavy, edged tool is certainly indispensable for hacking branches (the Red Zone people lived in wooded valleys) and disjointing bone. The flake scrapers and perforators and the spall burins are the implements of a finer, more controlled incision.

In far-off Alabama, tool development took a third line. There are no clues as yet, though there has been some deep excavation, as to where the Lively industry, the similar Wells Creek industry investigated by Dragoo, another like it discovered in Tennessee by Dr. T. M. N. Lewis (long head of the Department of Anthropology of the University of Tennessee), and, perhaps, our own Prickly Pear Hill, belong in the Early Lithic horizon. These are almost Kafuan pebble industries, with thousands of tools consisting of the bulk-pebble chunk from which were removed only the chips required to change it into a tool. The tools were practically a form of sculpture, with the workman "bringing out" of the pebble the tool latent in its natural form. Thus there is very little standardization of final form. The identification feature in most Lively-complex tools is a "nose" or blunt spur at the junction of two or more flake scars. Noses—the term comes from Old World Paleolithic studies and was not coined for the Lively industry—occur on choppers and scrapers and "end tools" of indecipherable usage and the most unusual and distinctive tool of the industry, a narrow, thick biface with an elongate nose at the end, apparently a drill or reamer or punch. But according to Josselyn, the only flakes used were those from the pebble rind, which, as we already know, is harder than the interior. As a whole the industry shows no tendency to evolve lanceolate bifaces or incipient projectile points, but one of its most curious features is that the striking off of long, narrow flute flakes—strip blades or flake blades—like the fluting in Clovis and Folsom points, is common.

Altogether the Lively industry is an original and independent variation on the chopper-flake theme, and it points out clearly that there is a Western—Rio Pedregal and Manix Lake—and an Eastern—Alabama and Tennessee—aspect to this ancient tradition. It is the most exciting turn that American prehistory has taken since the find of a Folsom fluted point in the rib cage of an extinct form of bison back in the late 1920's proved the coexistence of man and now-extinct Pleistocene animals in the New World, freeing it from the Hrdlickan view that there was no American population before 2000 B.C. It is not Leakey alone who sees the Alabama pebble tools as Paleolithic; it is also such authorities on the Paleolithic as Professor François Bordes of the University of Bordeaux, Dr. Laszlo Vertes of the Hungarian National Museum, and the expert on the Mousterian culture of Neanderthal, Professor J. Desmond Clark, now of the University of California but formerly director of the Rhodes-Livingstone Museum of Northern Rhodesia and author of *The Prehistory of Southern Africa*—prophets heeded in their own country if not in this.

The pebble-tool horizon in America was discovered in the 1960's; it will be up to the next decade to explore it.

8

Meridional America

ONE LEARNS not so much from one's mistakes as from the chagrin that follows, like a box on the ear, their discovery. Rather more than a few years ago I wrote, for delivery at a multi-state archaeological conference, a paper on choppers, the ubiquity of which in American archaeology had begun to seem to me highly significant. It was my notion, though I never expressed it directly, that the chopper was the distinguishing tool of the Archaic people and bound them together in an ancient and Pan-American tradition initiated by the Chopper-people firstcomers. I had persuaded myself, or been persuaded by the confident insistence of my betters, that the fine, bifacially worked, lanceolate or leaf-shaped blades, fluted and unfluted, of the Paleo-hunters were of another tradition and another ancestry altogether and had come out of Asia at a later time and under different conditions from those the Chopper people.

It required no wading through recondite references to draw up an impressive list of pebble-tool and Archaic sites with chopper-flake components. Choppers were everywhere in the artifact lists, but went unremarked in the analyses and discussions. The time spread was from Lewisville and Tule Springs to the Rupununi phase in British Guiana, which remained free of the influence of white civilization until 1925. The geographic spread was from the Firth River, shortly before its entry into the Arctic Ocean, to the Atacama Desert of Chile-Bolivia. The field was covered only as well as could be done in a twenty-minute paper, but delivered in the tedious manner and droning voice customary in such presentations, which make the papers seem twice as long as they are, that coverage must have sounded impressive if not definitive. Joffre L. Coe, an archaeologist whom I respect highly, who is the editor of the well-regarded journal *Southern Indian Studies*, immediately asked for the paper for a forthcoming issue. Flattered, I took it home with me to convert it from a reading script into something fit to print. The conversion required a bibliography of detailed references. Somehow I got a little off the routine track, and before I could defend myself I was bushwhacked; there on a page, as plain as a cigarette ad, was the fact that choppers had been found at the Lindenmeier site in Colorado, with fluted Folsom Paleo-big-game-hunter points.

Accidental? Atypical? No. The then recently published report on the Mammoth Kill Creek Site on the Lehner Ranch in Arizona listed a chopper among the eight tools, other than the thirteen Clovis points, recovered. And choppers were common on the Ecuadorian site of El Inga, where fluted (but not Clovis or Folsom) points occurred in a mixed bag of early point types assigned to big-game hunters contemporary with at least Folsom. And—but the best summary I can give of what I found when I began looking things up unselectively and with both eyes open is to say that in the fourth edition of Wormington's *Ancient Man in North America*, a catalogue of early sites of all kinds and aspects, there are twenty-four page references to choppers, from at least thirty sites. Everybody made choppers. And my thesis that the chopper-flake Archaic was a tradition separable from the Paleo-hunter lanceolate-blade makers fell apart like an unshelled egg.

I had not done my homework, and I had been guilty of the common error of imposing on material what I thought, instead of extracting from it what was there. The paper was never submitted to Coe, nor has he ever been told why I never submitted it—that I prefer silent repentance to auricular confession. But then was born the idea that infuses this book, which is—just as a reminder—that *all* the Amerind industries south of glaciated regions for which we have found evidence at 12,000–10,000 B.P. (that is, at the end of Wisconsin III) must have been developments, stimulated by exposure to this rich and diverse land during the fifteen thousand years that Wisconsin III occupied the Canadian landscape, out of what had been here *before* the onset of Wisconsin III. The chopper is the shared trait that signifies the family relationship of all immediately postglacial Amerinds. This time, however, I did not try to force the thesis to maturity. The data of the 1960's, from Venezuela and Peru in the south to Cape Krusenstern and Onion Portage in the north, has provided the nourishment it needed for growth, and it can now stand on its own, not a thesis any longer, but a synthesis.

That there is a difference between the school of stone craftsmanship in which the Paleo-hunters were trained for the production of their neat and symmetrical tools and that represented by the distinctly more rough-and-ready tools of the Archaic people is basically an artistic and subjective impression. Pains seem to have been taken in Paleo-hunter points to get the symmetry right and to execute details in a draftsmanlike manner. The blades are carefully retouched to effect a smooth outline as well as a sharp edge; and the few other tools in the scant stone inventory, the snub-nosed end scrapers with their regular pattern of parallel flutelike flakes at the end of long blade flakes, the tiny, needlelike graver spurs, the trimmed-down thinness of bifacial knives—and all these tools in fine flint—spell out high standards and patient execution. These lapidaries, it would seem, would rather have broken a piece in work by a strike to remove an excrescence than leave the excrescence, whether it detracted from the functioning of the tool or not.

In Archaic-tradition stone work, the projectile points and other bisymmetric tools are very often off the perpendicular and vast quantities of all kinds of tools are worked only to a degree sufficient for the day. Not that Archaic lithic technicians could not do trim and handsome lapidary work, but there was simply no quality control, outer or inner. Whoever decides, for other reasons, that the Paleo-hunters and the Archaic people are foals out of the same dam has certain problems in technological heredity to explain.

Alan L. Bryan's *Paleo-American Pre-history* was mentioned some few chapters back as taking a broad view of the subject not at essential variance with the one being explained here. Summarizing his view, Bryan says:

> To re-capitulate, the basic hypothesis of this study is that the large leaf-shaped [the generalized form] Point Tradition entered the western hemisphere sometime during the Wisconsin Age [note that this is not limited to Late or even Middle Wisconsin] after developing from the Hand-axe Tradition in Eurasia. At various times and places, after this technological tradition had diffused throughout the New World and formed a basic stage of organization, several secondary traditions evolved locally from the basic platform of organization. After developing from a single-shouldered leaf-shaped point [Sandia] the Fluted Point Tradition diffused throughout North America and on into northern South America. The Parallel-flaked Point Tradition expanded throughout western North America and *on into Northeast Asia* [italics mine]. The Willow Leaf Bipoint [both ends pointed] Tradition spread widely into South America and *Northeast Asia* [italics mine] from a Pacific Cordilleran center in southwestern North America. The Notched Point [the basic pattern of almost all early Archaic points] spread throughout North America and ultimately as far as South America *and Japan* [italics mine]. A tapering Stemmed Point Tradition probably developed indigenously in South America from a variant of the Fluted Point Tradition and eventually appears to have evolved into a Tanged Point Tradition on that continent.

This is not the language of comedy, but it cannot help but raise a brief little smile at the reverse twist Bryan has given to an old story. Certain prototype projectile points which the schoolmen have been bringing into America from Asia, Bryan is saying, actually traveled in the opposite direction, from America to Asia. It is not necessary to our thesis to believe this, but if there was any trans-Bering crossing by these points, it was very probably in the latter direction.

Bryan's thesis of American origin should be as demonstrable

by statistics as it is instantly appealing to common sense. Biologists assume that the region where a species occurs in the greatest numbers and the greatest diversity of subspecies is the region of its origin. In America the ratio of stone projectile points to all other formal stone tools found in excavation of preceramic and early ceramic sites will habitually run 5, sometimes as much as 10, to 1; and typologists have named and catalogued, like butterflies or sea shells, perhaps three hundred varieties, which include every conceivable variation on the five or six possible plane-form patterns. Whether America did export certain of its projectile-point types back to Asia we may leave to the next decade of research to verify. Our concern is what took place within the hemispheric ocean-limited borders of the hemisphere, and in pursuance of this concern we find a disputable premise in the Bryan thesis.

There is no necessity at all to postulate the development of the basic lanceolate or leaf-shaped biface, which is the first or nascent projectile-point type, from an Asiatic hand-ax tradition. Bryan believes that America's first settlers brought with them a chopper-flake industry, but, he says, "at present there is no evidence anywhere that large leaf-shaped points developed from pebble or cobble choppers." But what about the Camare-Las Lagunas-Las Casitas-El Jobo sequence in Venezuela? And what about Lanning's and Patterson's Andean Biface tradition? The phylogeny of chopper into biface into point is as clear as the ontogeny of larva into tadpole into frog.

The analogy is not from some rediscovered lecture notes in Biology I. I saw it happen, in stone work—an illustration of that axiom, or is it a scientific aphorism, that ontogeny recapitulates phylogeny—on the back porch of a farm home on the Ohio River. It took no more than ten minutes, because that is how long it takes to make a projectile point, from embryo to imago.

My second focus of archaeological attention is the broad bottomlands on the west bank of the Ohio River just below Portsmouth (where I was born), where, just at its big bend to the southwest the Ohio receives the important tributary the Scioto. Though these bottomlands are regularly, usually annually, flooded by the Ohio, they form a plateau sloping back toward the hills at from thirty to sixty-five feet above the bed of the river. Running parallel with the river through these bottoms (rich corn and tobacco land) is a series of ridges usually thought of as terraces formed as the river sideslipped its trench from the west or Ohio side of the valley to the east or Kentucky side. These ridges are natural levees, separated from each other by shallow swales, and sites of Amerind occupation lie so closely together on them that you can't always be sure where one ends and the next begins. Under the best collecting conditions, after the fields have been disced and rain washed, a circle with a fifty-foot radius will produce more worked stone than most of us care to lug the mile to the barn, though the temptation to pick it up makes one almost lustful. The sebaceous glistening of damp flints, startlingly tinted, some almost psychedelically variegated, does something seductive to the eye and will. You always pick up more than there is any rational purpose in owning.

Surface hunting is a recreation in these bottomlands, but it is also a necessity for anybody who cares about prehistory. Pot hunting—collecting prize specimens for display, sale, or trade—is open and notorious in Ohio, where all attempts to bring "amateurs" under control and discipline have failed, and sessions of the so-called State Archaeological Society are little more than commercial fairs. Ohio is the heartland of the spectacular Hopewell culture and the only slightly less spectacular Adena culture—both of these names are those of farms near Chillicothe, where rich mounds of these cultures have been excavated—and the entire southern half of the state crawls with surface hunters who are little better than poachers searching for Hopewell and Adena "goodies." Their sin is not that they take but that they have no idea of the archaeological value of what they take and keep none of the records that convert surface finds into genuine data. And even when they do keep records for their own convenience, they do not scruple to barter or sell from their stocks, destroying the integrity of the site inventory. It is little wonder that beyond the collector's-item cultures—Adena, Hopewell, Paleo-hunter, and Fort Ancient—the

prehistory of southern Ohio, still one of the richest archaeological areas in the country despite the assiduous vacuum
gleaning of its eye-level sites, is a series of blank pages in the
literature.

My short visits during the summer restrict me to surface
collecting, though we have located an horizon yielding Palmer
points (of which more later) on the order of ten thousand years
old, about which something serious is going to have to be done
very soon. But this vacation archaeology has not been without
its discoveries. I began to note in collections from sites some
thirty miles apart, east as well as west of the Scioto, the recurrence of stemmed points of an obviously homologous industry.
They were thick, heavy, made by broad percussion flaking so
that they looked crude, experimental, almost as if made by
children. The source of their material was the gravels of the
Ohio River; for many of them still bore patches of the chocolate
brown rind that is the coating of most Ohio River pebbles no
matter what the color of the flint inside. But there were far
too many of them, on far too many and too widespread sites,
for this not to have been the long-prevalent industry of a
thriving people very much at home in these bottoms and back-
country hills.

Besides, they had one "advanced" feature: they seemed to
have been given a sharp and even edge by pressure retouch. This
is a technique of removing pinhead-sized flakes from relatively
thin material by pressing down on it with the point of a rod of
hard material—a nail or a screwdriver or a steel punch is perfect for the job, but, being several millennia away from the
nearest hardware store, Amerinds had to use antler, bone, or
wood—giving it a twisting jab. This removes a flake not from
the contact face but from the reverse or underneath face, a
peculiarity of flint which will be explained later. The technique
is called pressure flaking, as opposed to percussion flaking, or
removal of chips by striking. Once you have learned it (I never
have), you can turn out forms in flint ad lib, as long as the
blank you are working on is thin enough. These forms do not
have to be projectile points; they can be beetles or buttercups, if
you like. Pressure flaking is rather like the artistic method

known as pointillism, except that you shape by subtracting dots instead of adding them. Just how early Amerinds knew about pressure flaking and how much use they made of it even after it was known is now questionable. It is seemingly the only possible technique for certain kinds of tight-corner jobs like narrow notching-in of blades and, perhaps, serration of blade edges, but the Friendship-tradition stemmed points presented none of these problems.

I had named this industry the Friendship tradition for a small community in the midst of the bottomlands where it was common, and my curiosity about it took me finally to the six-hundred-acre farm (four hundred of these in site-strewn bottoms) of the Cunninghams, Roger and his father, Roy, in the Friendship vicinity. Raised in the midst of fields where Indian relics turned up in every plowed furrow, Roger had had youthful dreams of being an archaeologist; but the land had to be cultivated, so he took his degree in agronomy. It had the same effect, however, of inculcating the scientific method. With a dairy herd of thirty cows and with four hundred acres of corn, tobacco, grain, and hay to cultivate, he had never done any digging. But he had given the ten sites on his farm designations and had catalogued by number and site provenience every artifact picked up, running into the thousands.

He, too, had noted the Friendship-tradition points, and, when I inquired about them, took me to the four-acre field from which most of his had come. The field was then in a thick stand of corn (it produced about 145 bushels to the acre that year), which did not favor surface hunting. A project was then agreed on. When the field was opened up the following spring by plowing and discing, Roger was to make an intensive harvest of everything that would provide us with an understanding of the Friendship tradition. The results were astounding. Within the six weeks during which the field was open, Roger brought in daily material by the two-gallon-bucket load, which sorted out into about two thousand recordable pieces and bushels of stuff of some interest for which there was simply no room in the house. There were over five hundred whole projectile points in the collection and another five hundred identifiable parts, with the rest points in work, fragments, knives, choppers (made out of tabular sandstone), "intermediate" bifaces, flake tools, and grooved axes. Since nearly every waste flake showed signs of having been used at least once, the material showing only this casual use wasn't even picked up. There are few Archaic stone industries in America that can be described from so much of the products and debris.

That it was a pebble industry—direct, simplified, and pragmatic—for the production of stemmed projectile points (and if some or many of these were knives, they were plunging knives, or daggers) is as clear from an inspection of the unfinished or broken pieces as from the statistics on points. The choice of material was a pebble with one flat face, which became the ventral, or underneath, face when held in the hand. The object was then to reduce the dorsal hump to a plane parallel with the natural ventral face. The chipping went on until that was accomplished—or it wasn't, because the material broke or it couldn't be worked any more and had to be given up as a failure. From the material Roger had collected we could lay out, in blow-by-blow order, specimens in progress by this method, from pebbles with one chip gone, through failures where the pebble had been worked all over into a lanceolate or leaf-shaped intermediate stage in which there were no more edges to strike against but the form was still too thick for use, through intermediate forms in which the stem had been partly worked in when, damn it all (or whatever Amerinds ejaculated at such times, since they never invented cursing), the stem broke, and up to the final finished point, with a streak of brown patina on the dorsal face and another on the base of the stem. It was from the common occurrence of pebble rind on the base of the stem that we deduced that the core was probably held in the hand during work.

There was nothing to it—no tricks of the trade, no gimmicks. You picked up two pebbles (in the Ohio Valley the hammerstone was usually flint, the same material as the hammered stone) and began cracking away at the one held in the left hand with the one held in the right—Indians and Amerinds seem to have been about 90 percent right-handed. That one end of the tool you are going to make is to have a point gives you the start of work on the design: the sides must diverge from this apex. To a degree, how the cookie crumbles, that is, how the stone breaks for you, will determine what kind of taper the sides take, arcuate as in lanceolate or leaf-shaped outlines, or rectilinear, as in triangular or cuneiform outlines; other factors are the shape of the pebble and how you "go with" that shape. Since you do not want the tool to be indefinitely wide, and the pebble block is not indefinitely wide to begin with, the divergence will soon have to be curbed and the sides then brought into near parallel. With most pebbles being rounded, following the natural outline is most likely to get you a lanceolate or leaf-shaped, or at least trianguloid, plane form when the thickness has been finally reduced satisfactorily. On this neutral or intermediate form you can elaborate in any way you like, by further reduction and detail. You can produce any projectile-point plane form found in America: lanceolates of the Clovis, Folsom, and related forms; bipointed points; stemmed points; and side- and corner-notched points. Only the notched points (in side-notched points the notches come in from the side with their axis at a right angle to the altitude or axis of length; in corner-notched points the notches begin at the basal corners and run into the blade at a forty-five-degree angle) require resort to another tool. Some side notches and corner notches, the wide and/or shallow ones, can be made with a small hammerstone; but the narrow, deep ones can be made only with a punch, either by the pressure method already mentioned or by indirect percussion—that is, by striking the punch with a hammerstone, as in driving a nail.

From selection of pebble block to completed product—finished is not quite the word—the Friendship industry is a continuity of simple, direct activity, which turns out the most wanted tools in about ten minutes at most, barring breakage. Nothing could be more basic, and hence more primitive. But it is in fact a synoptic tradition, condensing the whole evolutionary progression of the Camare-El Jobo sequence into a direct, brief process. The El Jobo people were the first to make narrow, lanceolate bifacial points, and the first not to stop there:

in the El Jobo collection are not only bipoints—points sharpened to tips on both ends, the first experiment in narrowing the base to fit a shaft—but recognizable deliberate, highly revelatory points with stems.

It was clear to us, after our study of the Friendship material, that it was "old-fashioned." Our estimate of its temporal placement (we have no C_{14} date as yet), from where and how it appears in the Ohio Valley, is from 5000 to 4000 B.P. Serrated and notched points which had to have been produced by punch methods, such as the serrated-blade Palmer type previously mentioned, are presumed to be much earlier on the Ohio banks, because their like has been dated elsewhere as older than nine thousand years, and they are types with clearly distinguishing attributes. Thrust into Ohio Valley prehistory at such a late date, the Friendship tradition can be explained in one of two ways: either it was developed by a people whose industrial roots were in the El Jobo tradition and had not deviated from it, who had filtered into the Ohio Valley from the south—as is very plausible, because the Ohio at that time joined the Mississippi in Louisiana—and settled down and flourished there; or it had evolved out of a more or less local pebble-tool industry related to the Lively complex. Both alternatives fit easily into what is beginning to be clear as the real real scheme of American prehistory, the gradual infiltration of northern regions from the south—a scheme that will rewrite the American prehistories of the near future.

What the Friendship tradition taught us, then, was that it was a truly seminal discovery or invention, this biarcuate biface that had been first made in South America, perhaps in Venezuela, where it first appears at the Las Lagunas stage, or perhaps elsewhere within the widespread territory of the Andean Biface tradition. Once this primary form of projectile point, with its protean potential, had been hit upon, the variations which could be made on it followed rapidly. In one direct line of descent were the lanceolates: Clovis and Folsom, with the probably borrowed (from Sandia) superficial detail of fluting, and the plain lanceolates, Plainview, Milnesand, Long (which the reader does not have to remember); in another, the bipoints;

and in a third, the demi-stemmed Sandias, followed quickly by full stems, out of which developed the notched blades. And all of these can be produced in detail by direct percussion with a hammerstone, except the deep, narrow-notched variety of blades as already noted. And this is true of the edge retouch in Friendship points that had seemed to me so technologically discrepant.

The discussion of the Friendship tradition in the Cunningham household—Roger's wife, Barbara, is as inquiring of mind as he is—did not include their teen-aged son, Rick.* He remained aloof from the whole subject, as a concern of the old folks and because he had other voices to listen to. He knew, and wanted to hear, no more about El Jobo than El Caudillo. But there was this constant preoccupation in the air, and he responded to it by deciding to become a self-taught flintsmith.

He asked no questions and consulted no references; the theory of stone fracturing as explained by a Leakey or explicated by a John Witthoft did not interest him. He knew from the prevalence of hammerstones and flint flakes in the fields that artifacts were made by pounding stones together, and that was enough to begin with. It interested me keenly that the first forms he achieved, without direction of any kind, simply by experimentation in controlled chipping, were palmate—that is, wide-at-the-base, leaf-shaped blanks—or trianguloid. He had set out to make projectile points, and it was highly significant to me that he had immediately discovered the inevitability of making the blank first. The stemless triangles are, of course, points in their own right, but they are the last form of point made east of the Mississippi, where they were the exclusive type at European-contact times; and why they were not made early in the game puzzles me to this day, though I believe it was because early points were big, and a triangle with a two-inch altitude is an impractical weapon head. Rick was satisfied that he had made points when he made triangles, but I was not, since they had no bearing on either the shape or chronological occurrence of the stemmed Friendships, and I had heard that

* He was killed in February, 1969, in a car accident after having taken his physical examination for entrance to the United States Military Academy at West Point, to which he had Congressional appointment.

stemmed points are difficult to make. So I asked him to make a stemmed point.

He hardly hesitated. Choosing a small hammerstone, oval, about two inches long, he began pecking away at the big end of a teardrop-shaped blank—perhaps *nibbling* is a better word. In three or four minutes he had not only bitten out a stem, but had touched up the blade edges with quick, pattering dabs of blows. It was a small point, not typical of Friendship points as to size, but exactly like the few small ones that do occur, and exactly like, except for material, the stemmed points we find in Hudson Valley middens of 4,750 years ago. The retouch would have fooled me if I hadn't seen it done. It was as delicate as pressure flaking, and I am now willing to bet that a great deal of flaking now called pressure flaking is done with a little old hammerstone and the fine touch of somebody who has the feel of stone work in both hands. There would probably be few takers—now. Bordes, the aforementioned French expert, has already shown that the "pressure" flaking of Clovis and Solu-trean (the Upper Paleolithic culture of France and Spain that produced paragons of flint work) can be duplicated by expertise with the right hammerstone.

This is not to say that Rick was an expert craftsman, but he had empirically proved the Friendship-industry technology. Its method is what Witthoft, probably the profoundest American student of lithology, calls "free flaking," which is, he says, "one of the most ordinary chipping patterns and is the only method which most modern experimenters ever learn to control." Rick had been "programmed" by my asking for a stemmed point, and he had, with a computerlike efficiency, proceeded to show that it was practicable, by the method at his command, to extract that shape from the raw material. That method led, naturally and unavoidably, through the leaf-shaped-biface inter-mediate form; there is no other way to do it *if*, like Rick, you already know what a stemmed point looks like. In the beginning nobody did; it is a form, therefore, that could have come about only after the leaf-shaped biface had been invented. But the leaf-shaped biface is not necessarily an intentional form; it is what happens to a lumpy pebble, as we have seen, when the process of reducing it to flatness is carried far enough. Its invention, or discovery, was therefore inevitable in a pebble-tool tradition—as it was not in non-pebble traditions, where it is a deliberate choice of form.

From the vantage point of the present it seems that the process took so incredibly long to be discovered that the question is raised, What effected that discovery when it was finally made? I have always been suspicious of dramatic inspiration, of the Eureka-I've-found-it striking upon the novel. Things evolve out of the drift of experience, it seems to me, in the direction of the inevitable. If, as we have been insisting, the subsistence pattern of the first human beings to enter America was basically foraging and scavenging of the easily obtainable, like shellfish, turtles, snakes, toads, rabbits, small burrowing animals, birds, vegetal roots, bark, nuts, fruits, and seeds, no very specialized stone tools were needed. But America was overrun by big-game animals, and even to butcher a carcass already downed by entrapment or by a predator that had been driven off from his kill by fire required implements of some weight and durability. The chopper served well for hacking, and flake edges for severing, but the more carcasses had to be cut up, the more experience must have shown that narrower choppers—those made on narrower pebbles—could be plunged more deeply into the flesh and, once there, could be made to rip the flesh if they had an edge on the side (which would be the slashers already mentioned). We must assume that the usefulness of one side edge inspired the idea that two side edges would be better, and this is the only inspiration that needs to be admitted in the development of the pebble-tool tradition. A narrow, slimmed-down pebble chopper with a chipped point for plunging and two chipped side edges for ripping is a leaf-shaped biface.

The patient reader must by this time be wondering whether all this was necessary. Isn't this obvious, simple, and direct method of working stone the only way? It is not. The Afro-European tradition follows a different pattern altogether: the preparation of the block, or parent material (it might be a pebble but usually was not), for the striking off of spalls of controlled shape and size, which were then further refined into the wanted implement. There was no continuous reduction of the parent block through the leaf-shaped-biface phase. The core was trimmed to a polyhedral shape, with a flattened end, called a striking platform. The spalls, rather confusingly called "blades" (the English vocabulary of archaeology is an argot, without the trade argot's vividness of terminology, but with the same effect of concealing meaning from the outsider), are detached by accurate blows on the striking platform, which is not precisely flat but is, rather, planed to take advantage of the fracturing characteristics of the stone.

These characteristics are surprising. Cryptocrystalline materials like flint, chert, chalcedony, and metamorphic cements like quartzite, are commonly said to break conchoidally, or like a shell (clam or scallop). From the bulb of percussion, where the blow falls on the block, a series of ripples can be seen to radiate, denoting how the force of the blow traveled through the block. The spall itself will be squamate or conchoidal, that is, nearly round, if the blow is simply one of uncontrolled impact.

But conchoidal fracture is only a partial, one-dimensional description of what takes place. If you were to strike a flat, slablike block of flint, not at the edge, but in the center, with enough force to drive out the spall, that spall would be a perfect cone, with the apex at the point of impact. There would be left in the flint a hole, not a break, that would look drilled as by a countersink or eaten out by a cuboid-headed termite— not too wild an analogy, since there are termites that devour concrete. This has probably never happened, in practice or experiment; but the pattern of shock waves from impact has been measured and charted, and it is like the wave pattern caused by dropping a stone into water, except that the waves not only travel out but down at the same time, three-dimensionally.

You cannot, therefore, strike a stone on the edge of its striking platform with a straight-line downstroke and effect a flat slice of a spall, like cutting bread. Such a stroke would send the waves of force into the stone, concaving it. Since the object in working a core is to strip off from it controlled flakes with a flat underside, the blow must come from an angle, or the core tilted, or a bit of both. And the striking platform itself is usually faceted. This is a very much subtler technology than that of the pebble-tool tradition, though method must not be equated with skill. Workers in the pebble-tool tradition could and did strike blades from at least Clovis times on, and they had a method of creating a striking platform by knocking off at one blow the rounded end of a pebble—which, detached, looks like a human kneecap—like everything else they did, simple, immediate, and direct. The difference is, not that the pebble-tool workers were thicker of wrist, but that they did not habitually make prepared cores for the production of shaped intermediate forms.

The prepared-core technology is as old as Acheulean times, 250,000 years ago in the short-term calculation of Pleistocene chronology, perhaps 750,000 years ago by later standards, and had, in Africa, an interesting origin. A group of already-advanced stone workers were isolated in an area where there were no gravels from which core material of suitable size could be selected and where the only available stone was large field boulders. This dilemma begot the so-called Victoria West technique, whereby a hand ax was pecked and trimmed in cameo on the face of a boulder, a striking platform was notched at the top of the cameo, and then a single accurate stroke on the striking platform delivered a whole and finished tool into the hands of the maker.

On a reduced scale this is the so called Levallois Flake technique of Europe; the "blade" or controlled spall, smaller than the usual hand ax, is dressed out on the prepared portable core and then sheared off as an almost finished tool, requiring only retouch, at one smiting. The Levallois Flake technology may very well have had its origin in the Clactonian Flake industry, independent of the African Victoria West method of "mining" boulders. Since the Clactonian began as a tradition for the random production of simple flakes, which are conchoidal in shape, and then advanced to a phase where these were retouched, it seems inevitable that experience with spalling flakes off a core would have taken the worker in the direction of shaping the core so as to produce the exact flake he wanted.

Such "discoveries" grow from the constant observation of repetitive results from action with controlled force against surfaces at certain angles. They are evolutionary stages in skill, such skill and dexterity, as Witthoft has pointed out, as a golfer acquires, and in familiarity with material and its "laws." If man at this time had codified in his mind the mensal habits of the moon and the annual habits of the sun, he was capable of observing and predicting the behavior of stone. Witthoft says it this way:

Flint tools were the manifestation of certain motor habits, traditional procedures and stereotypes, and unbelievably precise "muscular knowledge" of materials and forms; all of these were in no sense controlled by conscious planning or conception of processes and finished forms. Neither was innovation and invention the result of conscious designing for improvement, but were due to a factor of "drift" in the gradual modification of motor habit and stereotyped patterns, scarcely perceptible in the work of one generation.

It seems probable that, during the Acheulean, the path of Afro-European stone technology in the direction of prepared cores and unifacial blades was set for good. The Acheuleans made, by free flaking, large leaf-shaped bifaces which may or may not have been hand axes, the intermediate form which the pebble-tool people made so much of once they had it. But at that level of culture, man was not ready for the hafted spear or knife, and though he had the skill to make a lanceolate or stemmed or notched point, he had never seen any of these and was not, as Rick Cunningham had been, "programmed" for their production.

From the Acheulean onward, Old World lithic technology follows a line of development of prepared-core and controlled struck-flake methods until, in the waning days of the Mesolithic, it is producing very small tools in precisely outlined geometric shapes, attained by snapping the thin "blades" or flakes across. Blades had by this time become replaceable parts in permanent handles, like the blades in a safety razor, the principle of which is thus eight thousand years old and so not strictly patentable. Sickles for cutting grain were made this way, and it seems highly probable that man tried the edges on his own facial vegetation.

The tradition of the prepared core not only reached America, but, if Anderson is nearly right in estimating the date of Band 8 at Onion Portage, where it occurs, it reached here at the quite early date for America of fifteen thousand years ago. But it never got south of the ice, at least while the Wisconsin was still massing up the landscape. It remained in Alaska and either became in time what is called the Arctic Small Tool complex—a mini-sized version of the core-and-blade tradition, the blades being parallel-sided flakes like tiny table-knife blades —or died out and was supplanted by the Small Tool complex of later migration. Giddings, who discovered the first of these small-tool industries at Cape Denbigh, thought it probable that the Small Tool tradition originated in the American Arctic and spread circumpolarly from there back to Asia, in which case the industry in Band 8 may well have been the parent tradition. When the core-and-blade tradition is found outside the Arctic, it is found in peripheral regions and dates well after the Wisconsin had retired to the wings of prehistory. When cores and blades do appear again as an industry, the whole industry of a people, it is in the Poverty Point culture of Louisiana at about four thousand years ago, and nobody has been able to show that it was anything but an original invention there.

For all that has been written here about stone work, any impression that the subject has been exhausted must be erased. Stone work is a handicraft as intricate and various as weaving or ceramics. It can be dichotomized into what I have been calling the pebble-tool tradition of direct, out-of-the-block production of tools and the prepared-core, controlled-flake tradition. Thereafter, nearly any statement made about stone knapping is subject to qualification or quibble. Stone is not the only kind of hammer used, for instance. There is the "soft hammer," a baton of wood, bone, or antler which detaches a characteristic flat, thin, spherical flake. There is what may be called the fixed hammer: the stone to be chipped is the one held in the hand, and it is whacked against an anvil stone. Sometimes when the stone to be chipped is held in the hand, the give of the hand as the stone is hammered is necessary to the interplay of forces; sometimes it is held against a force-absorbent anvil, a piece of wood or firm ground; and in the bipolar technique it is held against or just above a hard stone anvil, with the flake produced between the upper and nether stones receiving two bulbs of percussion.

Indirect percussion by the use of a punch has already been defined, as has pressure flaking, except that Australian aborigines are said to be able to do it with their teeth. There is another technique which may be classified as either pressure or indirect percussion or a bit of both. It is accomplished by what looks like a crutch, a pointed shaft with a saddle-shaped crossbar at the proximal end. With a prepared core on the ground between his feet, the worker leans his weight on the crossbar, pressing the shaft down on the edge of the core, and—*voilà*, a blade strips off. It is a man-powered punch press, and can be assembly-line fast in blade production; but it needs a fine, nearly flawless material. Stone Age man knew every trick there is to skin the flint: he knew enough to store stone raw material in damp ground—to keep it fresh, that is, from turning brittle through loss of its water of hydration; and he knew how and when to heat-treat it; and—but I would not presume to take the subject any further than is necessary to the purpose of this chapter, not after rereading Witthoft, to this effect:

> I must remind the reader that flint-knapping is a long extinct art, and that we are quite unaware of all its subtleties; men who made flint tools throughout at least half a million years of human history had a great many techniques, procedures and designs which are completely strange to us, and we know almost as little of these matters as stone-age man knew of the technology of non-alloy metallurgy. What little knowledge we have of the lithic industries comes from the study of large, controlled series of artifacts (finished, unfinished and broken), attempts to reproduce the same types experimentally and comparison of our pictures of many such analyses. Flint typology is something to be approached with the attitude "I don't know"; not with the assurance of ignorance.

The purpose of this chapter must by now be strongly suspected by the reader. The premise has been established to his satisfaction, I hope, that the viable tradition in American stone work, as exemplified by its most numerous and diagnostically variable tool, the projectile point, developed out of a simple pebble tool-chopper-flake basic industry here, in this hemisphere and, more specifically, in South America. Ever since archaeologists began the study of American prehistory, they have been looking toward Asia for the roots of Amerind culture. It is true that the human population must have come thence. But when we examine the technology this population brought with it, we must say that it was hardly the roots; it was, rather, merely the seed. When technology begins to advance and culture to elaborate in the slightest, the advance and elaboration is on clearly American beginnings.

We can forget Asia, I think, as the cultural main office from which salesmen periodically took the road west with sample cases full of new products. Asia explains Alaska, because Alaska was a part of Asia aboriginally and up to the time of Seward's purchase. But America south of the Wisconsin—and it is now time to give it a fit name, which will be Meridional America—was another continent altogether, separated from Alaska-Asia by a barrier as wide as and much less traversable than that which separates England and New England, the ocean of the glacier frozen into mountainous, insurmountable waves. And Amerind culture had to have developed in Meridional America, or the land would have been as backward and as empty when Europeans discovered it as the hinterlands of Australia.

It is easy, when the Wisconsin is only an outline on a flat map on a black and white page, to open corridors through it and suppose that people poured through them like the sooners into Oklahoma Territory. But the Wisconsin was not only a vast and absolutely forbidding feature fluctuating across half a continent; it was an interdicting climate, too. Not only were it and its environs to be shunned, but those regions farthest from it provided fuller and easier living. Those few optimistic souls who were enticed into Alaska during a milding period were afterward forced south when the treacherous climate turned bitter again. They kept going and never looked back. Why should they have? They had attained the Garden of Eden, and what lay ahead of them was its peopling and exploration.

One may sincerely doubt that any of the inhabitants of Meridional America ever saw the ice mountains of the Wisconsin, or ever ventured into the boreal landscape fronting them, any more than we go looking for the glaciers of Greenland and Antarctica in the ordinary course of our lives. They were content to live where the food that they knew how to harvest was plentiful, in climes more summer than winter, more green than gelid white. When the Wisconsin began its withdrawal into permanent retirement, no Amerind could possibly have known what was happening—that the ecological zones in which they had been living were shifting northward, and that the nut trees and berries and the animals they hunted were extending their range by a mile or two northward in a decade or a generation. The Amerind had no sense of metes and bounds; his locality was the habitat of what he customarily ate, and where it was in relation to the poles and equator was meaningless.

What is being said here is that there was a time when Pennsylvania was in Alabama and Alabama in the Gulf of Mexico, and then the Wisconsin began to retreat, and the temperate zone dogged it, pace for pace, until Canada had left Pennsylvania and was back where it belonged. It is the job of the palynologist, the counter of pollen in soil profiles, to detect these changes in paleo-vegetation, but the faunal evidence is rather more dramatic. John Guilday of the Carnegie Museum, the man to whom archaeologists send the bones from their digs for identification, has analyzed the bone from deposits in a cave in Centre County, Pennsylvania, called Hosterman's Pit, and those in a sinkhole called New Paris No. 4—in neither case with evidences of man, since both places were natural traps. In Hosterman's Pit, $C14$-dated 9,240 ± 1,000 years (7290 B.C.), he found the southern flying squirrel, the southern bog lemming, the pine mouse, the rabbit, the Virginia deer, and the elk. At New Paris No. 4, only sixty-five miles away, the faunal assemblage, $C14$-dated at 11,250 ± 1,000 years (9300 B.C.), included the northern flying squirrel, the northern bog lemming, the collared lemming, the yellow checked vole, and the caribou. Guilday says:

Thus, within a probable time span of 2000 yrs. [9300—7290 B.C.] or within a maximum span of 4000 yrs. [10,300—6290 B.C.] the mammalian fauna changed from an assemblage of cold-weather species characteristic of central Canada today to the temperate fauna that still lives in the area. This, of course, implies a rapid climatic change. There is abundant palynological evidence for such a change within that period.

This evidence is to the effect that forests of deciduous trees, to which order the nut bearers belong, supplanted the predominant spruce-northern pine evergreens.

"Rapid" hardly seems the word for a change that covered three hundred to four hundred miles of latitude in at least two thousand and at most four thousand years. But it was inexorable; and in time it accomplished the closing of the circle: as the spruce forests invaded the taiga-tundra left behind by the diminishing ice, the Amerinds, who had been accustomed to hunt the caribou and its faunal accompaniment, ended up in Alaska, from which their ancestors had departed at least ten thousand years before and perhaps thirty to forty thousand. Thus Meridional America gave population to Alaska, not Alaska to Meridional America, because the sweep of nature was to the north, as life reclaimed for itself the territory that had been entombed so long beneath the whited sepulcher of ice.

Hypothesis and argument? Not at all. It is all there, in the bands at Onion Portage. Anderson writes of that sequence:

> Some time before 4000 B.C. we see the arrival at Onion Portage [just north of the Arctic Circle], of a forest adapted tradition that had its origins in the eastern woodlands of the U.S. The advance of the Archaic Tradition into Arctic terrain coincided with the postglacial shift in climate that allowed the forests to invade the northern tundra. With the re-expansion of the tundra at the end of the warm period [this warmer-than-present period within the postglacial period is generally called the Altithermal, that is, period of high heat] Arctic cultures again dominated.

And, furthermore:

> During the millenniums between 7000 and 3000 B.C. nearly the entire interval of the postulated contact between (or identity with) the Arctic and the Paleo-Indian cultures—nothing from any occupational level at Onion Portage shows any hint of Paleo-Indian influ-

ence. On the contrary, the influence in the earlier part of the interval is Siberian and in the later part Archaic.

There is more here than testimony to the effect of heat on the Amerinds of the Eastern Woodlands. Where were the Arctic-adapted dwellers of the Kobuk River while southerners were living at Onion Portage? Obviously they, too, had gone north where the cold was; once an Arctican always an Arctican. They were never coming south, no matter how many corridors were open.

The difficulty under which American archaeologists have been laboring since the first one picked up a projectile point and called it an artifact is that they have not been working with maps of the Meridional America that the Amerinds lived in. They are aware how much the Wisconsin canceled out of the present map of North America. They are not aware of what it added. It is only now beginning to be recognized how habitable was a dry Atlantic coastal shelf during the proved Early Archaic period. As large, or larger, is the coastal shelf in the Gulf of Mexico.

For seventy-five cents (it used to be seventy-five cents) you can buy H. O. 1290, the navigational chart of the Gulf and the Caribbean, and it might make an amusing evening to sit down and draw the outline of the land that was there about fifteen thousand years ago. It will be at about the 50-fathom (300-foot) depth of water isocline. (You will find that it makes little difference if you draw a 65-fathom isocline, which is where the shoreline was when the Wisconsin was at its most extensive; the Gulf drops off sharply after about 350 feet into a pelagic deep.) From about central Mexico across the Gulf states to Florida you will find a very sizable addition of land. I have guessed it to be somewhat larger than two Floridas, or about 115,000 square miles, and given it the name, for my own use, of Mextexida—Mexico-Texas-Florida.

Mextexida is, of course, another Beringia, a great deal more stable and much more livable. Add to it the fact that Florida would then have been high and dry, not the half-drowned land of the Everglades, and you have a vast region of temperate climate and inexhaustible resources. And practically in the heart of it is Alabama, with all those pebble tools and all that Archaic material dating to ten thousand years ago.

If I were forced to guess, under threat of torture, where the Archaic originated, it would be in Mextexida, just as I would guess that the big-game-hunting tradition originated in Venezuela. But I would not guess Asia for either of them.

9

The Users of the Fruits

THE TIME and effort expended in establishing that Meridional
America during Late Wisconsin and early post-Wisconsin times
was not the happy hunting grounds of the big-game Paleo-
hunters exclusively but also of more numerous contemporaries
living by a much different set of rules, may seem excessive
when the result is summarized in so simple a statement. Yet
this is the first law of gravity of American prehistory, and from
it follow all other laws. What archaeologists are digging up is
either the record of a succession of migrations from Asia, or a
composite histograph of regional developments of a fundamen-
tally primitive and generalized culture that could be stimulated to "invention" by the special environment in which it found
itself.

Most, and by now that is perhaps 99 percent of, American
archaeologists, have abandoned the succession-of-migrations
view. But they have not espoused the only logical alternative.
By clinging to the last forlorn hope that the Paleo-hunters will
prove to be the first migrants and that they went busily to work
dropping woods colts all over the continent, from which sprang
the regional facies, they reveal their emotional bias. They want
this to be the way it was. This is nostalgia, not science, a kind

of White Russian longing for the old days, accompanied by a certain counterrevolutionary plotting to restore the monarchy by such ploys and devices as showing that struck blades found with Paleo-Indian industries are the same as blades struck by somebody on the shores of Lake Baikal in Siberia at or somewhat before the same time—as is true. The blades look alike, but nobody has as yet been so bold as to propose that the Paleo-hunter industry was in the prepared-core-and-struck-blade tradition. Because it wasn't.

This is already a sufficiently kicked dead mule. Yet it is not enough to trace the phylogeny of lithic technology. What concept of cultural formation could possibly apply to both the overland-nomadic big-game hunters and the essentially sedentary peoples of the pattern of living that is called, with the usual academic talent for the misnomer, the Archaic?

It is really not a very difficult observation to derive from an acquaintance with the data the perception that the content of a culture is directly and immediately adjusted to the physical environment (desert, Arctic, jungle, woodland) and shaped to procure the food, animal and vegetable, afforded by that environment. At its broadest and most obvious, it is the almost fatuous statement that we live in the world we live in. It becomes rather more meaningful when stated as, We live in the world we live in, according to its rules and our necessities. It becomes truly educative when you first have to describe the world lived in, like the oyster-zone locale of the lower Hudson, and then deduce the felt necessities that this locale satisfied by the means employed.

But in the hands of the environmental determinists, this very useful principle or divining rod becomes an instrument of ontological distortion. Reducing culture to its materials, its shape responding as inevitably to the forces of wind and weather as a rock or tree—a proposition few would disagree with—the environmental determinists feel themselves justified in suppressing all other factors: physical and cultural heredity and human temperament, the great X factor. This has all been argued before, in the great Jukes-Kallikak debates of two generations ago, pitting the environmental determinists against the hereditary determinists—which nobody won, because environment can have a determining effect only on what heredity places within its influence; heredity determines whether there will be a succumbing or an adjustment to or a rebellion against the circumstances in which it finds itself. Soft and soluble rock is more quickly sculptured than the adamantine by attritional forces.

There is no heredity in culture, that is, tradition, which did not come from some other environment than the one in which it exists at any given time. If we have learned nothing else so far in this study, we have learned that the environment, the climate and all that is meant by that, is in a constant process of change, toward intensification or reversal. If people move as they did when they came to America and then spread over the hemisphere in order to remain in touch with certain aspects of environment, they have to lose touch with other aspects. Probably the most rigidly environmentally determined culture ever was that of the Arctic hunters, because the penalty for the slightest maladjustment was death. We have seen how they had to leave Onion Portage when that Arctic Circle habitat became a little too warm for them, because warmth, a boon to us, was bad for their business. They had to stay with the temperature environment because the animals they knew how to hunt and to utilize belonged to that environment. But by staying with that environment they had to change their geographic environment, resituating themselves on a flat coastal plain as compared with their former inland, mountainous habitat. What they took with them, however, was their artistic tradition of ornamentation and decoration of tools and utensils, a tradition that is almost nonexistent in the peoples of Meridional America. It is very difficult to see how that tradition in the north and its absence in the south were in any way environmentally determined.

Environmental determinism is like gas; it needs to be constrained in order to exert its influence. The terms of restraint are that the immediate or microenvironment be described and the group behavior within it ascertained; only then can you detect the pressures of economic determinism. There are thousands of microenvironments in America; and group behavior, industrially, socially, and psychospiritually, differs in detail with each. The more primitive the level of culture, the more likely to be similar are the cultures within differing environments. But as soon as sophistication sets in, and by sophistication is meant control, then coercive environmental tyranny is relaxed, and the X factor of human temperament introduces variations. It is not easy to define temperament; man is, individually, a complex operating mechanism of emotional motivation, innate mental capabilities, and an endowed fund of psychic and physical energy. Societies may assume their character from the average of the temperaments of their members—restless to stolid, sanguine to resigned, artistic-spiritual to experimental-practical—or from the example and direction of one or two superior members. As more and more individuals became more and more individual, the temperament of a society made itself manifest in the way it dealt with its environment, which is culture; and the rigidity of environmental determinism is seen to be not rigid at all but permissive of almost infinite alternatives. What is seen as environmental determinism is actually man's temperamental limitation and frustration. But the tensions within man's consciousness and self-consciousness, his dissatisfactions (so let us call man the dissatisfied animal), have continually developed his temperament—never to be thought of strictly as intellect—to where he has defeated environment on some occasions and allied himself with it on others. For environment is both his enemy, in that it will dispassionately kill him, and his friend, in that it has taught him all he knows and nurtured him while he learned. (It may even have taught him too much, because man is now engaged in utterly selfishly and suicidally destroying it as a sphere for human continuation.) Had it not been for this process of man versus environment, man cum environment, we would still be uncultured apes.

The chopper-flake culture that entered Meridional America was very nearly opportunistic only, that of a hand-to-mouth, beggarly existence. The tools made by its people were mainly, as far as we can deduce from the material remains, only those needed to hack up the food that came their way for immediate transfer to the mouth. These human animals were foragers for live food, vegetal and animal, and scavengers for what nature or predators had killed. They were food pickers in the sense that we use the pejorative "garbage pickers." The invention of the stone projectile point changed all that, and was the first important cultural leap forward in the Western Hemisphere.

It is extremely probable that the first American projectile weapon was a simple wooden shaft with fire-hardened point; it is certain that spear shafts were then fitted with bone or horn points. Such points, probably suggested by the sharp-ended splinters of bone split for marrow and then formalized by industrial methods, have been found in pre-Clovis strata and continued to be made in small numbers for thousands of years. With the innovation of the stone projectile point, one new way of life, one departure from the old pattern, became possible. So confident were the Paleo-hunters of the efficacy of their stone-tipped weapons that they did a daring thing: they left the fixed locale they had been scrounging over, where they knew every turtle pond and rabbit hole, and committed themselves to the shifting environment of the big-game herds. This environment was, of course, always the same ecologically, the grasslands or the lands of low shrubs and bushes where the big herbivores pastured; but that kind of environment spread from the Rocky Mountains to the Atlantic coast during Late Wisconsin and early post–Wisconsin eras—not totally but much more extensively than now, with Ohio in the north and Alabama in the south then being eastern extensions of the prairies, and the coastal plains of the Great Lakes and the Gulf of Mexico filling out the distance to the oceanic shore.

It was an environment two thousand miles long east-west and one thousand miles wide north-south, and there is no record, even in the vast Asiatic-Russian steppes, of a single identifiable people as mobile as the fluted-point hunters of the Clovis tradition over so vast a territory. In South America, big-game-hunter points, lanceolate of blade, with a flaring "fishtail" stem and an occasional flute, are strung from El Inga, Ecuador, to Fell's Cave overlooking the Straits of Magellan—as long a run but not as wide. It is not stretching meaning and intent in the least to say that the environment the big-game hunters chose for themselves, when they decided to go on the road with their spear-throwing act, was from Fell's Cave to the Debert site in Nova Scotia. Yes, they were stringently regulated by this environment after they adopted it, but they did adopt it, and it was not the only choice opened up by the invention of the stone projectile point.

Stone projectile points came into the hands of other groups, too, but they chose not to leave the boundaries of the district they knew so well and most likely loved. What the stone projectile point meant to them was that they could live a little better and more securely where they knew the locale intimately. They could more certainly and more often kill bigger animals— deer, elk, bear—and they had a weapon against enemies, animal and, if there were such, human. Their culture still continued to be environmentally determined in every way known to us— even their mythology and cosmology were structured about the little universe they knew—but they had determined the environment a little, too. It was not the same environment; it was more productive, more controlled, safer. When these same stay-at-homes later developed the mano, or hand grinding stone, out of the pebble hammerstone, inventing the use rather than the tool, probably while cracking nuts, the environment enlarged by another slight degree. Man cannot escape the prison of his environment, but his culture is what he has invented to make him freer and more powerful within it, a determinant as well as the determined.

It is the stay-at-homes, small bands dwelling within a district of a few square miles, which we may think of as a kind of ecological and social parish or clan-stead, with whom we will now be concerned. Theirs was the pattern of living that made America totally inhabited by ten thousand years ago, if not earlier, with every square foot of it, from marginal-subsistence desert lands to the coastal verges, claimed by one band or another as its patrimony—not densely populated, since the yield from hunting and foraging is not many meals per acre, but thoroughly explored and thoroughly, although not exhaustively, exploited. These are the people whose continuous occupancy of the land for upwards of ten thousand years has been proved in the sequences at cave home sites and riverbank camp sites in every section of the present United States except the Northeast. The Paleo-hunters were gone by about 8500 B.P., with the extinction of the gregarious grazers and browsers, the mammoth, horse, and bison (even though modern buffalo, *Bison bison*, seems to have been taking over the savannas and prairies at the time), and the less habitually hunted big-game animals such as the sloth; as a matter of fact, that is a definition of the Paleo-hunter, that he was a hunter of beasts now extinct. It is possible, even probable, that some of them were converted to the semisedentary district life of the Archaic, but the conclusion that must be archaeologically drawn from the disappearance of their way of life is that they, too, became extinct. Nowhere are Paleo-hunter points found under circumstances indicating that they converted from chasing big game to Archaic districtism, and it is a little hard to believe that they would change their point styles, like growing a beard as a disguise, just because they had stopped running around. We do not find Paleo-hunter-tradition points in shell heaps or in caves with Archaic sequences. By the time the Paleo-hunters disappeared, the Archaic people were well established everywhere.

The term *Archaic* is one of those terminological mistakes American archaeology made unwittingly in its youth that, like cigarettes, it now refuses to give up. It was first applied by Dr. William A. Ritchie, now New York State Archaeologist, to a preceramic-pottery culture he found at Lamoka Lake, New York (the site already mentioned as having been misdated by the solid-carbon method), and its discovery was one of the turning points in American prehistoric studies. Ritchie first used the term *Archaic* in a 1932 report, only five years after the discovery of a fluted point in the rib cage of an extinct bison found at the Folsom site had demonstrated, the tetrarchs of American archaeology (Ales Hrdlicka, Daniel G. Brinton, W. H. Holmes, and Herbert J. Spinden) to the contrary, that America had been humanly occupied in preceramic times. Archaeology was therefore in a receptive mood for an Eastern type of preceramic culture.

The Lamokans were plainly not fluted-pointed hunters of extinct big game; they used a small stemmed point, and they killed deer and small game, fished, collected river mussels and ate acorns (after leaching out the tannic acid) and a variety of other vegetal foods. And, though they were older than the trait of ceramic pottery (making only fiber baskets, which they used as cooking vessels by hot-stone boiling), they were plainly younger than the Folsom people, judging by the associated fauna. This was recent, of the kind that Guilday found had entered the region *after* 9000 B.P. When Ritchie came up with the term *Archaic* for the Lamokans, he meant it to apply both to this pattern of culture and to the time period, i.e., between the Paleo-hunters and the subsequent ceramic period. It was thirty years before it became evident that these dual usages of the term were incompatible.

In 1964 the Society for American Antiquity (SAA) held its annual meeting at the University of North Carolina, in Chapel Hill, where three men pointed out the contradiction that research had disclosed in this double entendre. Joffre L. Coe, who had just completed the excavation of a sequence of cultures in the Carolina Piedmont extending through ten thousand years (as head of the Department of Anthropology at the University of North Carolina, he was on his own grounds), wrote, in the abstract of his delivered paper on the Archaic of the Southeast:

Today it appears that there were some "archaic" cultures that were co-existent with some Paleo-Indian culture in the southeast. There is no longer reasonable doubt that the concept "archaic" covers a long period of time and that it must be defined in terms of content as well as time.

Melvin Fowler of the University of Southern Illinois Museum, who had just completed his work on the Modoc Rock Shelter in Illinois, where there had also been a ten-thousand-year habitational sequence, was even more specific in his paper on the Archaic of the Midwest. His abstract, which is a good, memo-style description of the Archaic pattern and so is quoted in full, reads:

The area discussed centers around the Middle Mississippi River Valley and the various tributaries. The cultural materials which underlay Archaic in the Midwest are Clovis. There are no data to present, with the possible exception of Graham Cave (in Montgomery County, Missouri), that shows Archaic developing out of Clovis. Archaic cultures are clearly established by 7000 B.C. and, therefore, are contemporary with Folsom in the southern Plains, Plainview in the northern Plains and Plano in the Prairie. Archaic materials are associated with Plano-like points in the Midwest, namely Dalton in southern Illinois and Plano- or Plainview-like in central Illinois. These are part of the Archaic assemblage but may represent technological carry-overs of the Clovis Tradition. The development of the Archaic in the Midwest is one of gradual ecological adaptations to specific environmental zones. The seasonal cycle of food getting was developed and well established by the Archaic peoples. Late in Archaic sequences there is evidence that the cultivation of local plants, such as the sunflower, augmented the subsistence base. Several regional traditions or cultures are recognizable in the Archaic of the Midwest. This is probably a direct reflection of the localized food getting techniques and the *seasonal cycle which localized the territoriality of the Archaic peoples and limited the contacts they had with other groups* [italics mine]. The Archaic of the Midwest is the basic cultural expression upon which the elaborate ceremonial complex of the tomb builder cult was added.

Quite fortuitously, that 1964 conference reached consensus on the Archaic. It was not, as the Neo-Hrdlickans had been crying up as the number 2 plank in their platform, a mulligan stew of hobo cultures from that part of Asia from which the fluted-point spearman had come—which was plank number 1. It was as homegrown as the paw-paw. Conference reports on local populations beginning at ten thousand years ago and leaving their marks through subsequent generations up to the gunpowder crack of history were given by:

Richard D. Daugherty, Washington State University, on the lower Snake River, Washington, where "research in this region has led to the development of a cultural sequence extending from early post-glacial times to the present. . . ."

Wakefield Dort, Jr., University of Kansas, on Indian Head Cave, Idaho, where there was a C14 date on charcoal of 10,000 B.P., which may have been two thousand years too late.

Jeremiah F. Epstein, University of Texas, on "A Long Stratified Sequence from Nuevo León, Mexico, from Terminal Pleistocene times to the 16th century."

John W. Griffin, National Park Service, on "The Archaic Sequence in the Ocmulgee Bottoms" in Georgia, where the occupation, "as now known, stretches virtually uninterrupted from Paleo-Indian through Historic Creek times."

Wesley R. Hurt, Indiana University, on the continuity of the population at 10,000 B.P. at Lagoa Santo, Brazil, and the depositors of seashore shell mounds of 7000–3000 B.P.

Carl F. Miller, Bureau of American Ethnology, on Russell Cave, Alabama, where the sequence is from 10,500 B.P. to white-contact times.

William J. Wallace, Long Beach State College, on a survey of Death Valley National Monument that disclosed "evidence of a lengthy aboriginal occupation, beginning about 9000 years ago and continuing into the time of White contact."

David L. DeJarnette, University of Alabama (who took the Lively-industry tools to a later SAA conference), on the Stanfield-Worley Rock Shelter and the Asbury Rock House, Alabama, with ten-thousand-year sequences.

When Ritchie introduced the concept of the Archaic, it was regarded as native only to the Eastern Woodlands; and it was in this sense that Anderson used it, properly qualified, for the influences from the South that arrived at Onion Portage. The term is no longer that exclusive: at the 1964 SAA conference, in addition to the foregoing citations, it was conferred by E. Mott Davis on a culture period in the Great Plains; by Roger I. Grange on a site at Spring Creek, Nebraska, dated 5860 B.P.; and by Claude N. Warren on the hunting and food-gathering stage in California. In short, the term *Archaic* may now be used for everything everywhere that is preceramic and not Paleo-hunter—which permissiveness drew from Earl H. Swanson, Jr., of the Idaho State University Museum, as near an epigram as is likely to come from the pen of an archaeologist. His contribution to the 1964 conference was, "It seems clear that an American Archaic cannot be both age and stage."

In logic it cannot: as an Archaic "stage" or pattern of living, it begins at least coevally with the Paleo period; and so you find yourself trapped in the necessity of using the two-headed or Siamese-twin chronological term Paleo-Archaic, with Archaic referring to a group living the district pattern and Paleo referring to the time level at which it existed. Ridiculous, but one has to adjust to it, as one adjusts to (1) *pop* as he who supplies the pocket coin for the fizzy treacle (2) *pop*, which goes (3) *pop* when the bottle is opened, which bottle, empty, may thereupon become an element in a certain art caprice that was, when this was written, passing (4) *pop*ular.

This all could have been avoided if someone not verbally tone deaf had, in the beginning, paused to think out what was the Pan-American pattern of living during the time period that seems to me to be quite properly called Archaic, since it is a term of temporality. The best that archaeology has been able to do in descriptive nomenclature for the pattern is *foraging*, defined in the *American College Dictionary* as "the art of searching for provisions of any kind"; but foraging is far from accurate, in that the Archaic people were not searching for food— they knew, and had known for generations, where each food-producing "patch" in their district was—and they were not, as is the connotation, raiders and invaders from elsewhere. The flat and more limited but more accurate terminology is the *hunting and gathering stage*. What it lacks is perspective and contrast.

Ten years ago I found a term which seemed to me much more evocative of the relationship of the pre-Archaic, Archaic, and post-Archaic (when most aborigines were still only semi-agricultural) to the food-getting "philosophy" of the Amerind and to the source from which he got his living. There has been no rush to adopt it, though there is nothing in the poverty-stricken archaeological vocabulary that has its coverage; the principal objection is to its polysyllabic "strangeness" and its derivation from legal language. The former is unavoidable, and the latter, it seems to me, adds a dimension to its meaning.

The word is *usufructian;* it breaks down the way it looks into *usu,* "use," *fructus,* "fruit," and the suffix *-ian,* for "he who uses the fruit," in the general sense. The dictionary-approved noun for such a person is *usufructuary*, only one syllable longer than my construction, but that one syllable seems to me to mark the difference between the barely possible and the clearly unspeakable. The *American College Dictionary* gives this definition of *usufruct*: "From Roman and civil law; The right of enjoying all the advantages derivable from the use of something which belongs to another, so far as is compatible with the substance of the thing not being destroyed or injured."

The Amerind did not, as is widely known, regard himself as the owner of the "something," that is, the land, all the advantages of which he enjoyed; he regarded himself only as having rights to hunt and gather food and other necessities there, which rights were shared by all the animals and plants, streams and hills, that were also present. The land belonged to Manitou, the Manitou of human beings. But each order of beings—animal, plant, and inanimate—had its Manitou, who would sternly punish those abusing the members of his order. The Amerind, therefore, restricted himself to using what he needed, his need being the "legal" principle on which he based his right of use. For anthropological purposes a qualification must be made that is not expressed but is certainly implicit in the definition. The usufructian Amerind harvested and gleaned the fruits of the earth within his district, without attempting to manage, cultivate, or produce them. He exploited the plants, animals, and supplies of raw materials without seeking to increase their amounts, except by magic and prayer. The use of the fruits of his district of earth was all he wanted, and he shaped his culture to an efficiency in taking them. It was so with the chopper makers, and it was still necessary in the vegetal-food-producing days of horticulture and agriculture, in order to acquire adequate protein; for no aborigines, at any level, were ever animal husbandmen. The only animal they ever raised for food was the dog—also a beast of burden, a pet, and a hunting companion—and, in some rare instances, fowl such as the turkey.

Though it was barbarous and sometimes, when nature was having a bad spell, precarious, in the right climatic zones usufructianism was a far from impoverished life, and was often superior to the settled village life of the food growers, whose diet was usually short of protein. Joseph Caldwell has suggested that the reason the cultivation of corn-beans-squash came so late to the Eastern Woodlands—about 900 A.D. in New York, for instance—was that it afforded few if any advantages appealing to the eyes, the appetites, or the dispositions of people who had within plucking or hunting range all the nutrition and variety in their diet they needed for sustenance and relish. In the Pacific Northwest, where the abundance of natural food was virtually inexhaustible, the only crop ever grown was a little tobacco for ceremonial use, because it was not native to the region.

Harold E. Driver of Indiana University and William C. Massey of the University of Washington, in their compendious *Comparative Studies of North American Indians*, comment, "Subsistence areas show a definite, although not perfect correspondence to natural vegetation areas." (So much for environmental determinism as an absolute.) They mean, of course, animal and vegetation areas, as they proceed to show. In the Arctic the principal "fruit" of the region is sea mammals—seals, whales, polar bears—and the culture is materially designed for and by their hunting. In the sub-Arctic forests, moose and caribou provide the bulk of the diet and the rhythm and implementation of the culture. On the Plains the buffalo, supplemented by elk or wapiti and deer, was the staple, but this kind of culture had been in the spectacular equestrian phase best known to us for scarcely two hundred years before it ended with the wiping out of the last herd by a Sioux October hunt under Sitting Bull in 1883. Along the Pacific Northwest coast, the Pacific Slope region bordering the bounteous sea in the best-watered region in the American temperate zone, where a precipitation of 175–200 inches a year supports a veritable rain forest, fish, fresh and smoked or dried, was the basic meal all year round. In central California the acorn, its harmful tannic acid removed, ground into a flour that served all the uses of wheat or the cereal grains, from boiled mush to baked pancakes or "bread," was the staff of life.

These are the patent examples of usufructianism in regions

where there is one dominant fruit of the earth. Generally speaking, in the rest of America what went into the pot varied seasonally, with a fluctuating ratio of the vegetal and the animal, and amounted to what nutritionists would have to admit was a balanced diet, over the year if not day by day, and a far more healthful diet than the Indians of our day, ghetto dwellers, and the poor anywhere ever sit down to.

Animal flesh was eaten as a matter of course in every form in which it was available, since man, despite his supposed ancestry as a fruit- and nut-eating ape, has a highly efficient animal-protein digestive system; about 90 percent of animal protein can be broken down into usable amino acids, and flesh affords all the essential vitamins when the whole animal, including entrails, is eaten and the blood used. The protein content of meat assays at half or more of its weight, more than twice the protein content of any vegetal food. An analysis of the food refuse in certain shell middens in Florida has revealed the popularity of snails and rattlesnakes—not surprising, since both are considered delicacies to this day, the rattlesnake being one of the meatier species of snakes and, by report, toothsome. Our lower-Hudson middens were, of course, monuments to the human animal-protein consumption, not only aquatic but from birds, terrapins, muskrats, woodchucks, bears, deer, and elks. But all this is obvious. Probably nothing animal which the Amerind ate would turn the stomachs of modern man, except certain grubs, slugs, and insects. Speaking for myself, I think I would probably eat them if I had to, and might even learn to relish them; when all is said and done, the consistency of the slug is not too different from that of the oyster, and all tastes are acquired.

Vegetal foods are less nutritious, and none of them provides a sufficient diet; but they are often tastier, more easily preserved, more portable, and, above all, quantitatively and geographically more available. Without them man would not have survived, in all probability, to enjoy his present menus of breakfast cereal, spaghetti, potatoes, and cake-pie-Danish pastry. Man's vegetarianism opened the way to civilization, as is by now widely known. But the vegetals we eat in such bulk are a paltry

few by contrast with the hundreds that we could be eating and
that the Amerinds did eat.

From Driver and Massey's survey of wild plant foods in
known use at the time of white contact and from other sources
we get the following assessment of the larder of the usufructians.

Amerinds north of Mexico made use of 31 genera and 90
species of the Liliaceae, or lily family, including the lily, onion,
smilax, mariposa, yucca, camas, and Joshua tree. Parts eaten
were shoots, stalks, berries, fruits, seeds, pods, flowers and
leaves, heads, buds, and hearts. (Of animals you can't eat the
hide, hooves, horns, or hair; of plants there is nothing you can't
eat.) Liliaceae species were eaten in every culture area where
they occur.

Of the Asteraceae, the aster family, 45 genera and 92 species
were eaten, including the aster, sunflower, dandelion, goldenrod,
and sagebrush. In addition to food, they provided leaves for
brewed tea and chewing gum.

Of the Gramineae, grasses, the most important species are
Zea mays, or corn, which was eaten wild before it was domesticated, and wild rice, a staple in the Minnesota-Manitoba area
and an important food wherever it grew, from Louisiana to
Ontario. The grasses supplied 27 genera and 27 species. The
grasses we know best, wheat, oats, barley, and true rice, did
not grow in America, but some of the grain amaranths produced nearly as much edible seed per acre as cultivated oats or
barley.

The rose family, Rosaceae, to which belong blackberries,
service berries, raspberries, strawberries, rose hips, and many
of the cherries and plums, supplied 18 genera and 102 species.
But there were other berries, the huckleberries, blueberries,
salal berries, and cranberries of the Ericaceae family, and
gooseberries and currants of the Grossulariaceae, which were
not only eaten out of hand but, as often as not, used as an
ingredient in combinations for sweetness and tang.

The curious family Solanaceae includes the Jimson weed
(named for Jamestown, Virginia), a narcotic rival of peyote but
probably used before white-contact times only as a pharmaceu-

tical; the deadly nightshade, from which belladonna is derived; tobacco, which must have been smoked first as a wild weed, probably in the late Archaic, along with a dozen other combustible weeds and fibers, such as the inner bark of the red willow, called kinnikinnick; the potato, a complex hybrid which must have shown some promise in the wild state before being improved by cultivation; and the tomato, which we know only in the form improved by cultivation.

Gourds, pumpkins, cushaws, squashes, watermelons, and cucumbers belong to the family Cucurbitaceae. Pumpkins and cushaws joined beans and corn eventually, to become the great trinity of aboriginal agriculture. Gourds, of course, provide nothing to chew on but do make good utensils.

The Leguminosae are the pea-bean-peanut-mesquite family; they furnished 22 edible genera and 69 species, with roots, tubers, seeds, pods, stalks, shoots, leaves, and flowers all likely to appear on the bill of fare in season.

The trees were tonnage producers. The oak, 27 species of which yielded palatable nuts after being de-tannined, grew in vast groves all over North America in the area of deciduous trees, and everywhere they grew, the nuts were eaten as a main, or a regular though minor, foodstuff. In lean years they were a hedge against starvation, since, even if the crop was poor, the prevalence of *Quercus*, the oak genus, insured quantity. The buckeye, or horse chestnut, not so inclined to grow in great groves, is found from Massachusetts to California; it drops a luscious-looking, plump, velvety-brown nut marred by its content of poisonous hydrocyanic acid. But the buckeye has a high protein content for a wild plant, about 23 percent of dry weight, and when the cyanide (used as a fish poison) is leached out, with its starches and fats it can do the job of preventing not only starvation but malnutrition.

The benign nuts, the chestnut (of fond memory), the hickory, the walnut, the butternut, and the pecan of the South, were regularly gathered but apparently were never as important as the soft-shelled, solid-meat acorns. All through usufructian cultures in the area where these trees grew are found the nutting stone, an anvil stone with a "cup" in it, into which nuts were placed and then cracked open; when so cracked, the meats came out in intact sections. In my boyhood one of my annual autumn chores was to gather, hull, dry, and crack the black-walnut crop from our summer place for the culinary use of my mother, an indefatigable cookie baker. This usually amounted to two or three buckets of hulled nuts. I think I know why Amerinds did not bother with walnuts: the nutmeats hardly pay for themselves in the energy expended to get them on the table. Hickory nuts, of ineffable flavor, to be sure, for the same labor give only half the reward of walnuts.

The pawpaw may be counted a tree or a bush, depending on whether you are a child or a man. Rarely mentioned in the literature on Amerind delicacies, its seeds, which in my youth we used in a game much like the Indian game of hand, have been found in late Archaic-Adena sites; and it is inconceivable that the pawpaw, shaped like a blunt banana or a very large bratwurst, with its almost cloyingly sweet taste and juicy pulp, would not have made a festival of eating during the two weeks in August of its ripe season. I was never allowed to eat more than one a day when I was young, because there was supposed to run in my family a tendency to "pawpaw face," a swelling and slight inflammation which would now be recognized for what it is, an allergy. Whether the pawpaw fruit or foliage produces an allergen I don't suppose we shall ever know, because I can't imagine anybody's being concerned about something so clearly doomed to dietary extinction. It is a peculiarly evanescent fruit, not susceptible to any kind of preservation; you have to eat it almost as soon as it is plucked, and probably not one person in fifty thousand ever gets that close to one.

The cacti or Cactaceae are, according to Driver and Massey, "indispensable in the greater Southwest," where 12 genera and 40 species produced fruit, pulp, leaves, buds, and blossoms for desert and semidesert dwellers. The 170 species of the agave, mescal, or maguay produced fiber and food in the same general area.

There is a long list of miscellaneous items to be added to the foregoing: the sweet potato of the morning-glory family, manioc (which, like the buckeye, is high in hydrocyanic acid and has to be de-venomed), the papaya, the guava, the pepper, the vanilla bean, chocolate, and the Jerusalem artichoke. No list can hope to be definitive, and the developing branch of fecesology, the examination of ancient feces, is always turning up something new that passed through Amerind digestive tracts, such as the greens of the Chenopodiaceae or goosefoot family and the seeds and stalks of the giant ragweed. The thousand or more fossil quids from Danger Cave, Nevada, were, before being spat out as exhausted, the rhyzomes and leaves of the desert bulrush, chewed not only for nourishment but, in that hot and dusty area, oral hygiene and, possibly, separation of the fibers to make cordage. There are, in the American botany north of Mexico alone, at least 120 families, 444 genera, and 1,120 species of plants; it is hardly an exaggeration to say that what the Amerind could not eat of these (700 plants are poisonous in some degree, up to fatal, but this did not prevent the use of some of them, like acorns and buckeyes) or somehow use (15 species have been found to have been used for fish poisons), he turned to medicinal purposes, remedial or magic. This is usufructianism. He, that is, she, never developed out of all this a great cuisine—she was a boiler and stewer and everything-goes-in-the-pot cook, and the only Indian dish I can think of with any relish is succotash—but nowhere in the world was there such an a la carte choice.

The concept of usufructianism has by now been so stuffed with data that, like environmental determinism, it looks to be coming apart at the seams of meaningfulness. So Amerinds ate what nature set on the table for them to eat; that calls for sesquipedalianism? As long as nature's was the hand that supplied the table, it does. Usufructianism ends, according to our definition, when cultivation begins. But this was not a stopwatch distinction. What happened was that one plant would be first domesticated, that is, encouraged to grow in certain patches by intentional dropping of seeds at harvest, and later cultivated by preparing the ground, intentional planting of seeds, and, at a minimum, keeping the weeds at bay. Sunflowers, probably because they quickly outgrew surrounding vegetation, and some grasses like the grain amaranths, because they crowded out other growth, were certainly among the domesticated plants. And so were corn, beans, and pumpkins before they were cultivated, as we shall see. Except for the one cultivated crop, the food store was obtained from wild plants; the living pattern changed very little.

What we need as the terminal date for usufructianism is a material clue that will tell us when plant cultivation did permanently alter the living pattern; and this would be, not a single artifact of tillage purpose, but structures that require community effort and community social organization to erect. Villages do not quite meet this specification, though fortified villages might; but the best such structure is the mound, burial and ceremonial, because it is not, strictly speaking, utilitarian. When large grave mounds began to be built, where principal persons were buried with grave furnishings as in the Adena culture, or when extensive embankments like those at Poverty Point were thrown up for a purpose not yet fully understood, then usufructianism came to an end by, as it were, its own commission—and not before.

With its old-fogy habit of making mistakes and then insisting that they have been sanctified by usage and are therefore untouchable, American archaeologists have gone on teaching that the Archaic ends with the appearance of ceramic pottery, after a transitional period of stone bowls and pots. This is a hangover from the days when it was thought that plant cultivation and pottery were partner traits. But it has been known for quite some time now that ceramic pottery was being made in the Southeast before four thousand years ago, probably two millennia before plant cultivation there, and that the people of Poverty Point, in Louisiana, who were potless, must have been practicing plant cultivation very successfully in order to have the free time to build their monumental mounds and extensive earthworks. So we are right back in the age-stage dilemma. Pottery is as good a trait as any to use for marking the end of the Archaic as an age or period, but when you use it for that purpose, you've struck your match; it is no candle to be burned at both ends. If you want further illumination, it will have to be by finding a substitute for usufructianism.

Archaeologists dote on pottery because it is a complex aggregation of stylistic variables—manufacturing technique, decoration, and vessel form—the modifications of which have chronological significance. In short, when an archaeologist comes on a pottery site, he can begin to tell time, in units of centuries or less, and he feels himself in touch with diurnal concerns; a touch of broken crockery makes the whole world kin. There can hardly be any doubt that to the Indian woman pottery was of the order of the invention of the vacuum cleaner; she no longer had to cook by the laborious boiling-stone method of heating stones and plopping them in the stew held in a watertight basket. On the other hand, she had to carry the pots when the household moved. I have dug up sherds in shell middens on the Hudson from a vessel about twelve inches across at the mouth—and not bone china, either, but thicker than a flowerpot; and the complete vessel must have weighed as much as a dinner service for eight.

Pottery added something to the amenities of living, no doubt; it gave people something to sit around during meals, and it undoubtedly drew the family together. And it had another curious effect: on the camp dogs. During the excavation of Sheep Rock Shelter, in Pennsylvania, it was observed from analysis of the feces of dogs that an abrupt change had occurred in their diet. Whereas during the Archaic, dogs had dined, as is the custom of proper dogs, on the bones of deer and other such land mammals, all of a sudden, at a given archaeological level, they had rejected such fare and taken to a catlike diet of fish heads and bones. The level was observed to be at the advent of pottery. Analysis of the spurned deer shins was indicated, and it very quickly cleared up the mystery of the haughty hounds. The introduction of ceramics had made it possible to boil bones so thoroughly that when they were ready for the garbage heap they had been distilled to a residue of chemical calcium, no more nutritious than a clinker of limestone. I still wonder how the dogs knew they were being so insidiously starved before they all perished from pellagra. Starvation, it seems, will take doggedness even out of dogs.

Any further divagation on the endlessly fascinating subject

of pottery will, however, take us too far from our preoccupation
with the Archaic as a useful tactic in American archaeological
strategy. It is that, but only when redefined to bring it into
some kind of congruence with the pattern of subsistence that
must be called, for want of a saltier term, usufructianism. We
know when this pattern ended, when bands stopped making the
seasonal rounds of their districts, having found a relatively
stable food source that enabled them to settle down more or
less permanently at one site, coagulated into multiband villages
capable of executing community works. In Mexico usufructianism, and hence the Archaic, terminated about thirty-five
hundred years ago; in other places it never terminated.

But when did the Archaic begin? Usufructianism was the
way of life of America's first settlers. It would be unrealistic,
however, not to recognize that it can and should be divided up
into periods by reason of the immediately recognizable difference in artifacts. The break comes, as has already been shown,
with the invention or innovation of stone projectile points, for
they introduce a significant stage in lithic technology as well as
provide a new tool for environmental exploitation. To begin
the Archaic here would not meet with the approval of the
men of the archaeological cloth, because it would include
the Paleo-hunters in the Archaic—a shocking solecism to them.
So be it. As professional vagabonds and hunters of extinct big
game with their own stone-working traditions, they deserve a
classification apart, but not one which exempts them from being
designated what they were: specialists only.

But they have already been accorded meet treatment, while
the typical dwellers of the Archaic still have that coming.
Archaic studies got off on the wrong foot from the beginning,
with the failure of students to recognize that the projectile point
was to the prepottery Archaic what pottery is to the following
ceramic period—or the length of skirts to the twentieth century:
the most stylistically variable artifact in the culture, and the telltale clue to temporal placement. This failure can be specifically
as well as generally documented, and it is, unfortunately, on
public display in nearly every museum in the country, especially
the most marmoreal, where the projectile-point displays are still

in 1930-style arrangements, and are unforgivably misinforma-
tive.

An early draft of this book was read by an eminent American
archaeologist whose renown extends beyond hemispheric borders
because he has spent most of the past decade digging up a
Neanderthal sequence in a cave in the Near East, where he
has made some highly important finds. In a marginal note,
meant kindly (I have known him for many years), he said something to the effect that I was being far too obsessive about
projectile points, and was overstressing their importance. I was
not repressed—not merely out of native irrepressibility, but
because I knew that preoccupied as he was with Neanderthals,
where there are no variant forms of projectile points to speculate about, he was telling me only what he had been taught in
his university days: that during the Archaic, projectile-point
styles had about as much diagnostic value as has a headache as
a specific diagnostic for illness. My friend, like many American
archaeologists, apparently, had not heard of, or at least taken to
heart, the story of the excavations of Joffre Lanning Coe, published in August, 1964, by the American Philosophical Society
as *The Formative Cultures of the Carolina Piedmont*.

The first phase of Coe's work was begun in 1939, when, with
the aid of the WPA and the NYA (National Youth Administration), "an intensive program of site surveys and excavations was
carried out in the Piedmont region of North Carolina," and was
ended in June, 1942, by World War II. This work resulted in
the successful definition of the regional historic and proto- or
late-prehistoric cultures; and when the second phase was begun
in 1948, the emphasis shifted to a study of the cultures preceding these, with the question still open of whether or not they
were directly ancestral.

Coe's procedure was what he, like my Neanderthal-oriented
friend, had learned in the classroom. He describes it thus:

During the following year [1949] a thorough study was made
of collections from over a hundred sites in the Uwharrie area in an
attempt to see whether the presence, absence or repeated association
of specific traits on those sites could identify a recurring cultural
complex. It was assumed that if a significant number of traits were

found to occur together on a series of sites, then they were probably the physical remains of the activities of a particular group at a particular period of time. The first results of this effort appeared to be rewarding, and the Guilford and Badin foci were first defined on the basis of this assumed association of traits.

The Guilford and Badin foci soon became an archaeological canon when they were described by Coe, as the leading scholar for his region, in the tomic survey *Archaeology of Eastern United States* (1952), edited by Griffin. They did not long remain such—nor did much else in that handsome and ambitious volume, full of the passé and the fascinating, like an Egyptian tomb—and Coe was one of the chief profaners. Even as *Archaeology of Eastern United States* was in press, he was digging the Doerschuk site at the fall line (where the mountains begin to break down to the coastal plain) of the Yadkin River, and had begun to suspect that the Guilford and Badin foci were more the products of academics than of Amerinds.

Over the next several years he dug a series of riverbank sites near the fall line in the Yadkin, Pee Dee, and Roanoke rivers, all of them stratified by flooding and as interrelatable as cousins, by means of projectile points. The stratification had been created by the deposit during high water of a sterile layer of silt over an occupation layer, thus separating it from the subsequent occupation after the water had receded. Coe says that "when an occupation zone can be found that represents a relatively short period of time the usual hodgepodge of projectile point types are not found—only variations of one specific theme."

Coe is not an emphatic stylist; his choice of *hodgepodge* over *mixture* or *miscellany* or *diversity* carries a deliberate charge of feeling, since too many of the "complexes" so confidently established in the literature on the Archaic inventory are just such hodgepodges—among these, his own Guilford and Badin foci. After he had correlated his Yadkin-Pee Dee-Roanoke columns and obtained some key C_{14} dates, Coe found that his Guilford focus, which he had originally assigned as the earliest in the Piedmont because of the occurrence of lanceolate blades, was actually near the middle of the sequence, with a date of about

6000 to 5000 B.P., and he had erroneously included in it points of the earlier Morrow Mountain type. But the Badin focus was the most flagrant gaffe; he had assigned it to a pottery horizon about fifteen hundred years old and listed in its trait list points from the Hardaway period of about 10,000 B.P., from the Kirk period of 8000 B.P., and the Stanly period of 7000 B.P.

What had misled him, and many another archaeologist who has not as yet seen the error of his ways, he points out succinctly: the materials that had, on excavation, appeared to be in association were of the manufacture, not of one people, but of the succession of peoples who had set themselves down at the same location for thousands of years because, as usufructians, they lived the same kind of life and found the same locations useful and convenient. But the soil of these locations, on knolls, was thin because of erosion, and a soil twelve to fifteen inches deep had to contain all the droppings of ten thousand years.

Academic archaeology had been mildly aware of the possibility of mixing of materials and had devised the technique of seriation to unmix them. The theory behind seriation is that the level at which most points—or other diagnostic artifacts—of a style or type are found is probably the level at which that type was most popular, and that when items of that type are found above or below the level of greatest popularity, they are assumed to have been displaced, or to have been present as minority types. In actual practice the latter explanation was the one preferred, for the very good reason that no excavator wanted to lay himself open to the criticism that he had no proof that projectile point styles were not eclectic and a matter of personal choice; why couldn't the same hunter have made several styles of points with a different purpose for each style? Of these seriation studies, after his riverbank stratified-site digs, Coe said that they "are primarily clerical exercises and contribute mainly to compounding confusion."

Those readers who may feel tempted someday to dig a site may be interested in the treacherousness of topsoil as a context for interpreting what they find. The principle on which archaeologists work is "Last in, first out," or, that what is on top was the last to be deposited and is therefore the most recent. This is a

very unsafe rule to follow in many instances, especially in sites
on slopes, where downslope materials are often stratigraphically
reversed. What happens is that the materials first deposited at
the top of the slope are the last to be carried down by surface
erosion. They are, it is true, the most recent deposit where they
are found, but that is not where they were deposited by the
human depositors with whom we are concerned. On the other
hand, you can't be sure when the displacement happened and so
allow for it, because it is random and adventitious. I once found,
on a quite gentle slope, in a yellow seeming subsoil with a well-
established forest topsoil over it, sherds of the same pot scattered through a vertical depth of ten inches. The sherds and
crumbs had plainly been conveyed downhill from where the pot
had been smashed, sherd by sherd, by erosion and other dis-
lodging forces, over a matter of decades, perhaps hundreds of
years. This phenomenon rendered that whole yellow soil deposit,
which I had naively assumed to be a stable soil horizon, totally
unreliable for placing anything. Yet I know an archaeologist
who tried to make something of the comparatively rich materials
in it as though it were the soil of primary deposit and not the
offscouring of erosion and soil creep from above.

But our subject was the topsoil, that part of the ground on
which we walk that is still "alive." It receives annual increment
from dropped leaves, vegetation, dust, and other chance materials. These elements, just under the whole leaves of the most
recent fall, become a duff of two inches, more or less, of soft,
partially decayed materials. (I am obviously speaking of
wooded, or partially wooded, uncultivated areas, or areas lapsed
into the wild state.) The soil under the duff, in what is called
a "forest brown" profile, ranges from dark to light brown,
shading into a yellow or a reddish yellow if there is iron in
the bedrock outcrops or boulders extruding from the underlying glacial till. The depth of this soil may be a few inches,
over bedrock upthrusts, or several feet, in cuplike enclosed
locales at the foot of slopes from which there is no outlet. But
in most places in the rocky, hilly Northeast that are not the
bed of dried-up bog, pond, or stream and not in a primeval
forest, this soil is rarely more than eight inches deep over the

basement of bedrock or till. This eight-inch layer is the net or residue of soil-aggrading and soil-degrading forces since the withdrawal of the Wisconsin glacier. In nonglaciated regions there is a similar net or residue, usually deeper, but I have seen reports from Alabama which stated that eight inches is the average depth in many formerly forested sections of the state.

This residue, which I prefer to think of as metabolic, a product of catabolism and anabolism, is as constantly being subtracted from as added to, and at about the same rate, except in specific locales where either the erosional or the incremental forces have a temporary advantage. The least understood forces, which are the forces that most effect the placement of artifacts, are those of diminution. Surface erosion is easy enough to observe; but where the ground is well covered with leaf fall and leaf mold, the rain penetrates into a porous or spongy layer before contact stops it and changes its direction. If it falls on anything but dead-level ground, when the duff and subsoil are saturated some rainwater is going to gravitate downslope. Some particles of loose earth will be moved mechanically, others in solution.

Artifacts of any size or weight are not likely to be budged by this subsurface erosion of gravitating water, but they will shift downhill with the creep of the whole layer, also subject to gravitational pull. But, more to our point, artifacts in eroding subsurface soil will sink down through it as it is removed or dissolved under them, or is depleted, since the most active factor in diminishing soil is the vegetation that feeds on it, the roots of which keep it in a broken-up, loose tilth or condition. What with drawing their nutriments from it and probing through it, roots keep soil in a slow but constant stir, strongly assisted by the activity of earthworms, which move astounding amounts of earth from lower to higher levels; it is said they can move a ton of earth per acre per year. Nor does this include the burrowing of larger animals, from moles to woodchucks.

In this inconstant element, artifacts sink more or less as they would in water, until they meet something resistant, a hard lens, a rock, or a root. I remember well the most convincing evidence I ever saw of artifact descent through a topsoil. We were excavating a tiny, flat knoll-top site, the knoll having been caused by an upthrust of the gneissic country rock. The soil on top of this rock was only five to eight inches deep, and under it was a kind of granular sand, which was the detritus of the gneiss as it decayed. In a five-inch-deep spot we found a fine, undamaged spearpoint about four inches long, standing straight up, its base resting on the detritus, its tip pointed at the sky. A very simple experiment showed that this is how it would sink in water, the heavy basal end first. By type the point was four thousand years old, and it had probably spent thirty-five hundred of its years in that position, poised to sink an adderlike fang in the foot of the transgressor.

The profile of a forest brown soil does present a specious-looking stratigraphy, but this layering of black-brown-yellow is nothing more than a spectrum of weather chemistry. I have gone back to sites dug five years before and seen this spectrum reestablishing itself. To confuse diggers further are the sediment lenses or layers that accumulate for some reason or other throughout a soil profile; sometimes they are clay placques, sometimes areas where sand grains and small pebbles have settled together to give a look of stratification. And I suspect that from time to time these have fooled diggers into false assumptions. The fact is that the topsoil root zone is a single system in continuous ferment, to which gravity on slopes is a powerful auxiliary force for movement, and what this ferment does to the placement of artifacts is as unpredictable as Puck. And it will remain "alive" for thousands of years, until some natural or human agency actually kills it.

Coe's archaeology was not dependent on this kind of reasoning, however. He found his sequences in fixed zones of relatively short-term occupation, the artifacts culturally pure beyond quibble. Many Archaic sequences have been dug in America, some beginning deeper in time, but none has so clearly demonstrated the axiom of "one specific theme" per one limited culture-time unit. Most Archaic sequences come from caves where the stratigraphy is seldom sharp, mixing is to be expected, and the yield of artifacts at any one level usually too sparse for comparative studies. The strata at the Piedmont river sites furnished all the points the student needed to demonstrate the validity of the one-specific-theme principle.

It is a principle that holds up cross-country. In 1963 Bettye Broyles, who had dug under Coe and who is now West Virginia State Archaeologist (and almost certainly the only living archaeologist who ever led an all-girl dance combo), began digging a site on the bank of the Kanawha River near St. Albans, West Virginia, that corroborates not only Coe's axiom but the regional distribution of his early point types. Discovered after a washout of the riverbank—my ubiquitous friend Olafson was present when the site was disclosed by the discoverer—it has been shown by drilling to have charcoal present to a depth of 36.5 feet, making St. Albans the deepest stratified site in America at present. It has been dug only to the 18-foot level so far. At the 20-foot level it is below the river, the height of which has been raised by a dam; and the problem of seepage into the excavation will have to be coped with, inasmuch as current excavation has plumbed 9,850 ± 500 years into the mine of past time. With more than 18 feet to go, St. Albans is the site in Meridional America most likely to match, and perhaps overmatch, the Arctic Onion Portage site and to take us back through the stone-projectile-point boundary into the era of pebble tools.

One horizon at the St. Albans site can be traced by the line of charcoal and occupation discoloration like a black stripe made with a paint brush, for a mile along the face of the riverbank. This is the horizon that dates from about 10,000 B.P., and both Coe and Broyles refer to it as the Kirk horizon, that zone from which came points of variant outlines with serrated blade edges in the Piedmont excavations. This saw-toothed blade edge is as distinctive a feature and as telling in tracing technological "heredity" as blade fluting or Paleo-hunter points. Points of the Kirk family of serrated blades have been identified, since Coe's recognition of them, from Alabama to Michigan. Their distribution is through the whole Woodland region east of the Mississippi (one showed up at our Twombly Landing site), and, since they fall into the 10,000–8,000 B.P. interval, their makers must have been the people who spread northward with the improving climate and the change in flora and fauna that Guilday found

at Hosterman's Pit. We are safe, I think, in considering these
Kirk people denizens of the deciduous forests, adjusted to a
habitat different not only from the still-practicing big-game
hunters', but from our shell-midden coastal people's. (The serrated point of Twombly certainly preceded the deposit of any
oyster shell there.) In the Kirk family of serrated blades we
have the bright thread that traces the motif of the Archaic, the
shifting of environments across the map of Meridional America
with the exit of the Wisconsin, and the shift of population with
them. There can be no doubt, from the evidence of the mile-long
Kirk zone at St. Albans, that at least the Eastern Woodlands
were well enough stocked with human beings that they could
use the lebensraum.

Kirk Serrated.

The Kirk family of points is not the earliest of Coe's discoveries in the Piedmont. Lowest in the sequence were the
Hardaway family of three varieties: the Hardaway blade, which
is a not very prepossessing lanceolate form; the Hardaway-
Dalton, a stubby point with a deeply yoked base thinned by a
kind of fluting flake; and the Hardaway side-notched, in which
the yoking and the side-notching effect basal corners that
look like turned-up toes. There are those who profess to see in
the Hardaways a degenerative transition from the Paleo-hunter
fluted points, by reason of the occasional occurrence of short
fluting. I will take it on myself, in order to protect the innocent,
to doubt this, because it is based on the gratuitous assumption

that any point style of more or less lanceolate outline is related
to the fluted lanceolates. Too much labor has already been
spent on the proposition that the lanceolate outline is a form
that inevitably grows out of the bifacial shaping of a core, and
is a preform for any more elaborated styles, for us to accept that
assumption just because it is rife.

But more archaeologically persuasive is the probable age of
the Hardaway. By retro-polation from a C14 date in a higher
zone, Coe has estimated the Hardaway family at about 9000
B.P. This is overly cautious. Broyles now has a C14 date on
an early Kirk variety, possibly the Palmer, of 9,850 ± 500
years; the points were actually in and around the dated hearth,
in the zone seventeen feet below the surface. The one point she
found in the eighteen-foot zone is broken beyond identification,
and this zone is, at the moment, the basement of the St. Albans
excavation. But there has been recovered from the riverbank
about twenty-five feet downriver from the dig at twenty-three
to twenty-five feet below the surface during low water, a fluted
side-notched (not lanceolate) point that Coe regards as transitional from the Hardaway to the Palmer. Since Coe has laid
out a series of points, on display at the Research Laboratories
of Anthropology at the University of North Carolina, showing
a nice and convincing gradation backward (or forward, if you

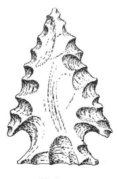

Palmer.

like) from Palmer through the three Hardaway variations to
the lanceolate Hardaway blade, we can project the early Harda-

way horizon, without fear of sharp contradiction, to a time
level of near 11,000 B.P. But that dating makes the Hardaway
horizon the full contemporary in the East of the Folsom fluted
in the West, and, to repeat an earlier quotation from Coe,
"Today it appears that there were some 'archaic' cultures that
were co-existent with some Paleo-Indian culture in the Southeast."

Hardaway–Dalton.

This is the interpretation placed by Bryan, in *Paleo-Indian
Prehistory*, on the lowest level at Graham Cave, Missouri, excavated by Wilfrid Logan, where the C_{14} date on a hearth per-
tains to a mixed bag of points that includes some fluted lanceolates *and* some fluted side-notched and stemmed points. This is
the only possible interpretation, of course, and it is fatal to any
assumption that the fluted lanceolate points are the Adam and
Eve of the family tree of American projectile points. Fluting
may have been a copied trait, or it may have been simply one
of the technological practices of basal thinning known to flint
workers generally during its period of popularity, which ended
at about 9500 B.P. It is, therefore, a horizon trait most commonly found in lanceolate points older than 9500 B.P., but not
exclusively in them. Across the South—from Missouri, through
Alabama, where variations of the Hardaway-Dalton occurred in
the Stanfield-Worley Rock Shelter (C_{14}-dated at 9,640 ± 450
years) excavated by DeJarnette, to the Carolina Piedmont—
fluting is a trait diffused in both the usufructian and the Paleo-

hunter traditions, by reason, probably, of their coexistence but not their acculturation by miscegenation.

We shall close our discussion of the relations between the usufructian and Paleo-hunter traditions with a statement from *The Archaic of the Middle South* (1959), by T. M. N. Lewis and Madeline Kneberg Lewis, who worked out of the University of Tennessee for over a generation on the archaeology of the Tennessee-Alabama region. They write:

> To date it has not been possible to demonstrate any continuity between Early Lithic [their designation of the Paleo-hunter tradition] and Archaic; however, the two groups may have been coeval to some extent.
>
> The two groups reveal different patterns of ecological adjustment; the Early Lithic peoples probably hunted prairie fauna [the prairie extended across Tennessee into Alabama in those days] while the Archaic people hunted forest fauna. The difference in their economy is not likely to have led to conflict (or contact) between them, since they were not competing for either space or type of subsistence. If there was any interaction between them, it is not reflected in the cultural remains. Such similarities as exist in tool technology, for example, unifacial scrapers, merely indicate some remote, common, Old World tradition which is an antecedent of both cultures.

The Lewises had in mind, I think, an Old World antecedent tradition in the form and fashion of pre-Clovisians, but the statement stands just as well for that chopper-flake industry we have long since nominated and seconded for New World primacy and which was present here regionally, in Alabama, as the Lively complex.

There was nothing functional that the Paleo-hunters and their cousin usufructians could borrow from or teach one other. Functionally their tools were the same or equivalent. From the Hardaway and Kirk zones Coe lists only projectile points, quarry blades (or preforms), drills, scrapers (eight types, of which one, I feel sure, is a chopper), and seven types of hammerstones (some of which I would guess are grinding stones). You can distinguish the points, scrapers, and drills from their Paleo-hunter equivalents by their styles and not by any designed

difference of purpose, with the trivial exception of certain
Paleo-hunter scrapers with delicately worked "graver spurs."
One suggested use of these is as tattooing needles. It is certainly
a possibility, but the usufructians could have scarified themselves with what Coe calls pointed scrapers or, for that matter,
with any waste flake that turned up with a snag end. The tools
which were not represented in the Hardaway and Kirk zones
are also alike. The most significant of these is the misnamed
bannerstone, a weight for the atlatl or throwing stick to give
that spear-casting device balance and thrust. Evidence for the
atlatl does not appear until about 7000 B.P. Tools of bone and
antler are assumed to have been used by both Paleo-hunters
and usufructians, but only by the greatest good luck could
complete inventories of these have survived the thieving acids
of the soil. Bone awls appear in the lowest level at Graham
Cave, where they may be associations with the fluted points
or the side-notched types, or both—probably both; for Graham
Cave is the only site so-far excavated where fluted-point Paleo-
hunters and contemporary usufructians, who by nature, as the
Lewises have explained, lived in segregated and noncompetitive
environments, mutually resorted. We are not at all surprised to
find them contemporaries and, being contemporary, such cultural compeers that if you could live the life of one, you could
undoubtedly adjust immediately to that of the other.

What kind of life was this? Probably no citizen of any current civilized society could have lasted a year in any of these
environments despite their richness of food resources. Many
an archaeologist might know in theory exactly how to go about
it, but he would be fatally lacking in practice. He could probably manufacture in a day all the tools needed and in a week
have surveyed as much of the locale as would provide him with
a living. Perhaps it would take him a day to get a fire going
and several days to find or provide himself with a shelter. But
sooner or later he would neglect something, fail to make an
observation, not foresee a contingency, or fall victim to mis-
chance, and the human species would disappear from the fauna
of that place.

We know of nothing to refute the probability that the

Paleo-hunters disappeared from the Eastern Woodlands and the prairies alike with the extinction of the big game they hunted and that they were always so few that there came a time when they simply failed to reproduce themselves and dwindled out of existence, perhaps not entirely as a people but as a culture. The last remnants of them may have joined usufructian bands; it would be hard to believe that they founded usufructian communities. For the usufructians were a flourishing people of many strains, who knew the Woodlands environment and its dangers and resources as a stockbroker knows Wall Street. We have already mentioned the mile-long Kirk site at St. Albans. The peripatetic Olafson has reported to me a series of "ridge top" sites at what are called "bear wallows," tiny ponds or natural catch basins, on the mountain range trending from West Virginia to North Carolina and, if you follow certain slopes, into Tennessee, where there are Archaic projectile points, including numerous Kirks, in such abundance (about two thousand have been found to date) that the population density and distribution patterns of the Archaic will have to be reassessed. In this mountainous country there were two locations of the forest en-

Big Sandy.

vironment that could supply a living, the river valleys and the ridgetops, and the population during the Archaic of ten thousand years ago was sufficient to have explored and exploited both of them. The usufructians were in no danger of extinction as long as there was a forest to live in.

But the Kirk people may not have been the main Archaic tradition at all. In the lowest level at the Stanfield-Worley Rock Shelter, cheek by jowl with Dalton points, were broad notched blades, with the notches ground, regionally called the Big Sandy I type. The reason for grinding the notches is self-evident enough: to dull them so as not to cut the lashings of the point to the shaft. This practice has already been met with in the fluted and other early big-game-hunter points, where the lower edges of the blade were blunted. It has been suggested that the basal grinding of fluted points was to provide a striking platform from which to drive the flute flake, but no such reason can be advanced for smoothing down the bases of other types, and I have not seen a satisfactory explanation of it. Like buttons on men's coat sleeves or bands on hats, it may be only the persistence of a feature the utility of which is obsolete; but for the archaeologist it serves the very useful purpose of differentiating the early side-notched points from the later ones, since this pattern has a long history and a wide dissemination. As a matter of fact, it is so widespread that one gets the fleeting impression the points may have been ordered from all over the Eastern Woodlands out of an Archaic Sears Roebuck catalogue, with the usual choices in style, color, and quality.

The Palmer points which initiate the Kirk family certainly owe their shape to the same designer who started the Big Sandy side-notched tradition, and they are the outlier of the tradition to the southeast. Across Georgia and Alabama and northward into Tennessee and Kentucky, the type name Big Sandy is retained, and the points themselves, as distinguished from other types to which they obviously gave rise, are found through perhaps three thousand years of the Archaic. They are the side-notched points that are associated with fluted lanceolates at Graham Cave; and two of them are the lowest points found at the Modoc Rock Shelter in southwestern Illinois (reported in 1959 by Fowler), where they came from the twenty-six-foot level, about four feet below the lowest Dalton. There is some question about their age at Modoc, because of an apparent reversal of stratigraphy in the lower levels, on the evidence of C_{14} dates, but the oldest date of 11,062 ± 602 years does not seem out of line for the Modoc side-notched points that came from well below it. (The lowest artifact, from the twenty-seven-foot level, was a chopper.)

The tradition's earliest northernmost outlier in Meridional America is at the Raddatz Rock Shelter, Sauk County, Wisconsin, reported in 1959 by Warren L. Wittry. A C_{14} date of 11,602 ± 600 years from charcoal in the lowest level does not apply to any discovered cultural material, but extrapolation from the column of dates would give the Raddatz side-notched points an age of at least 8,000 years, with their use extending through the following 4,000 years at least.

Raddatz.

But when we relax the strict Big Sandy form and consider all early side-notched points as a pattern, we can take the tradition all the way to Alaska. Giddings found side-notched points in his Palisades II level, and they show up at Onion Portage "before 4000 B.C." Giddings's guess is that "this side-notching appears to be as old in the Arctic as 6000 or 8000 years and to mark a simultaneous spread across various parts of America." "Simultaneous" is to be interpreted as within two thousand years.

The K I site in Rutland County, Vermont, produces Big Sandy-like side-notched, ground-base points that Ritchie calls

Otter Creek and relates to the Wisconsin type. From the resemblance and from geologic evidence, he estimates a date of 7000 B.P., certainly no overestimate, for the Otter Creeks, and, except for the quartzite of which they are made, they could have come from Wisconsin. Indeed, this was probably the line of march, through the birch-spruce forest zone that still must have been lingering at this latitude at this time.

Otter Creek.

It is almost certain that they did not arrive in New England by direct route from the south, as the Raddatz-point makers very probably arrived in Sauk County by trending up the Mississippi Valley. It has been one of the unexpected discoveries of our digging in the lower Hudson that the broad notched-blade tradition stopped its spread southward out of northern New York at the upriver limit of the oyster-producing zone. We have no site in our area of quite the age of Raddatz or Modoc or Graham Cave, but no matter. We have no broad notched-blade points to reckon with, except at the Haverstraw Bay end of the lower Hudson. There was a four- to five-mile penetration here by notched-blade makers, for all the world as though they had slipped into oyster-eater territory just for a look around while the oyster eaters, makers of stemmed points, were away from the river; but the penetration was not so deep that the invaders could not make a run for it if discovered and set upon.

Once it was thought that population during the Archaic was

so thinly distributed that there was not much chance of groups'
jostling each other, but now I am of the opinion that the whole
Eastern Woodlands had been staked out in district claims by
8000 B.P. and that spears and knives were as much side arms
as hunting tools. The oyster eaters may not have held the lower
Hudson that early, but it is beginning to seem that the Kirk
people might have; unlike the Paleo-hunters, they were very
decidedly competitors of the notched-blade makers for favorable
territories.

The side-notched tradition even entered big-game country,
while the big game and their hunters were still there. A cremation burial with grave goods consisting of projectile points of
the Eden-Scottsbluff late Paleo-hunter type was excavated by
Ronald J. Mason and Carol Irwin in 1960 at the Renier site in
Brown County, northeastern Wisconsin. Only one other type of
point was found in the burial; it was in fragments, but one
fragment was the basal end, with side notches and the telltale
grinding. It is similar to the side-notched points at the Modoc
Rock Shelter and to those reported in 1960 by Dr. George A.
Agogino and Dr. W. P. Frankforter from their dig at the

Modoc Rock Shelter.

bison bed called the Simonsen site near Quimby on the Little
Sioux River in Nebraska. The bones in the bed were those of
Bison occidentalis, now extinct, and the C_{14} age was 8,421

± 520 years. This discovery made it possible to place two sites in Iowa, the Turin and Hill sites, both of which produced similar side-notched points, and the Logan Creek site in Nebraska, in an early horizon of side-notched-point excursion across the Mississippi into the Plains. That these Simonsen

Simonsen.

people really were Eastern usufructians and not Paleo-hunters who, as some would have it, had had a change of viewpoint about projectiles every time there was a slight change in the species of the animals they hunted, rests on the evidence at the site of concentrations of hackberry seeds, wild-plum pits, bird bones, turtle bones, and snail shells. Wherever you find this appetite for two- or three-course meals, you have the usufructian cuisine.

Agogino and Frankforter conclude their Simonsen-site report thus: "Certainly the discovery of such seemingly ancient cultural horizons as have been mentioned here indicates a far heavier preceramic occupation in this region than had been suspected in the past."

This is what Dr. Jesse D. Jennings was saying eight years later, in *The New York Times* of July 9, 1968, about a region farther west, at the edge of the Great Salt Lake Desert in Utah, a territory which, according to long-held doctrine, had been abandoned by man because of its aridity and unproductiveness during the hot, dry post-Wisconsin phase. Jennings was the excavator of Danger, Juke Box, and Raven Caves (reported in 1957), also on the edge of the Great Salt Lake Desert, which did for the desert West what Coe did for the Eastern seaboard: proved that there the usufructian pattern of culture, with its own tradition of projectile points, was fully contemporary with the fluted-point horizon.

In Level I, the lowest at Danger Cave, was found in association with one of six hearths in that level a narrow lanceolate point not only unfluted but narrowing at the base to an incipient stem. (A couple of chips out of each side at the shoulder would have turned it into a Friendship type.) The hearth was C14-

Danger Cave.

dated at 10,270 ± 650 years. But from the same level there also came dates on mountain-sheep dung of 11,453 ± 600 years, 11,150 ± 570 years, and 11,000 ± 700 years. It is decidedly not to be passed over that in Level II, with a hearth C14-dated at 9,789 ± 630 years there were nine side-notched points that might have been shot there all the way from the Big Sandy area in Alabama or Tennessee. These points increase to twenty-one in Level III and continue through Levels IV and V. Jennings thinks they may be knives, but the form, not the use, is the thread of the evidence.

Nowhere among the nearly forty varieties of projectile points at Danger Cave is there one, or the suggestion of one, of the Paleo-hunter types. The itch to compare leads us, rather, to the Eastern Woodlands, where the same forms of notched, stemmed, and shankless points are scattered across the breadth of the landscape and through the depths of Archaic time. Conventionally it would be assumed that projectile-point-shape influences reached the Utah area of the Great Basin from Oregon, where there is also a long, deep sequence of occupation. But actually the sequestration of the Danger Cave area, and the parochial habits of its usufructians, gives us to think something else: would not any people working from the lanceolate-ovoid blank in isolation but in a millennia-long continuous tradition of technology have been likely to hit upon all the general forms extractable from that highly workable preform? It is not probable that we shall ever know the answer.

Danger Cave produced other surprises: basketry from Level II, almost ten thousand years old, other evidence of fiber textiles, and the harvesting and milling of grain (in this case, pickleweed). The eighth millennium B.C. is as far back as there is archaeological evidence for basketry and twining anywhere in the world; and confirmation of the age comes from Fort Rock Cave, Oregon, also in the Great Basin, where a cache of woven vegetable-fiber sandals was discovered under a volcanic pumice dated at 9000 B.P. (With the sandals were side-notched and corner-notched points.) But for all its evidence of a strongly entrenched band of usufructians with a viable culture that lasted down to the twentieth century, Danger Cave might have been no more than a stronghold in a singular and somewhat weather-beaten oasis, if Hogup Cave had not been discovered.

It was the results of the excavation of Hogup under Jennings's direction that the *Times* story treated, and it is a repeat of the Danger Cave situation about seventy-five airline miles southwest. The latest occupation evidence is from A.D. 1600; and a C14 date from the fourteen-foot level, the lowest dug so far, is 6400 B.C., or about 8300 B.P. Jennings finds that desiccation was not as severe as had been postulated for the so-called Altithermal (high-heat) phase, from about 7000 B.P. to 4500 B.P. (our Hudson River period of high oyster production), and that these people of what has been called the Desert culture were in no continuing peril of extinction. Yet the life was so hard, Jennings says, that he expects never to find the skeleton of a woman older than forty years. Childbirth was the least of a woman's labors.

Hogup Cave adds nothing to the cultural picture already detailed at Danger Cave; what it does is to help fill in the archaeological map in a region where human occupation had been thought to be a near impossibility. What we are now faced with is the probability that this marginal country was fully occupied, to the limit of its resources, to support cultures adjusted with maximum ingenuity to use them all to the utmost. We, at our present stage of technology, do not inhabit these regions; but when we do move into them, it will be done as it is now being done in Arizona, whose cities are swelling farther and farther into the desert: not by living in the prevailing environment, but by constructing a new one. If Amerinds lived the harsh life of the Great Basin, it must have been because they had to. They had been born there, but that need not have coerced them to stay; there was, for them, simply no place else to go. True, there was a certain environmental entrapment: the Desert-culture people knew how to live in the desert, its sky was home, and they were sure of themselves under it. But their tools and ways were not efficient in the desert alone; in better country they would have produced a better living. The Desert-culture people would have been fools not to know this, and they were not fools.

The Great Basin is by no means the totality of the desert West, we are reminded. The heat- and drought-blasted region of southern California and Arizona, extending across parched New Mexico and scorched Texas, can lay claim to as many habitationally repellent square miles as any place in the hemisphere. It was not always so, as we have seen from the sites of big-game-hunter kills already alluded to; and when it was slightly less so, the usufructians were there, along with the big-game hunters, even as in the Eastern Woodlands.

The best- and oldest-known of these usufructian Southwesterners are the Cochise (named for the Arizona county, not the famous Apache chief, for whom the county itself was named) of southwestern Arizona and southwestern New Mexico. The Cochise cultural sequence begins in a phase known as the Sulphur Spring, with a $C14$ date of $9,706 \pm 370$ years but believed to date from appreciably earlier, because of the geologic context and the occurrence in the earliest deposits of the bones of the long-extinct dire wolf. It did not lose its hereditary identifying features until three thousand years ago, when it dissolved into other phases. For several years the Sulphur Spring-phase inventory was believed to include only milling stones (which were present by the hundreds), choppers, and scrapers; later a few points, some leaf-shaped, some stemmed or notched, indicated a probable transition from self-tipped wooden spears. It can hardly be argued that the Cochise were in any way related to the Clovisian mammoth killers of Naco, in the same territory, whose $C14$-dated campfire (scattered in fragments about the kill site) was $9,243 \pm 300$ years old. Two more dissimilar cultures at such a time level could hardly have been imagined. The Cochise were hand millers of seed, who hunted a little for diet supplement, much like the Danger Cave people. But when they did begin to make stone projectile points, they did not make them in imitation of their neighbors and contemporaries, the Clovisians; they borrowed—if indeed they did borrow, and did not work out as best they could their own designs in stone points, once they had grasped the idea of a stone point—from some usufructian culture with which they had come in contact.

Much closer in aspect to the Cochise were the people whose tools Frank Hibben found eroding out of the banks of rivers and arroyos in the middle Rio Grande Valley, near Albuquerque, New Mexico. Apparently these sites, at Albuquerque, Rio Puerco, and Comanche Springs, collected at, rather than dug, in the late 1940's, have been forgotten; and, though hearths were observed, the charcoal seems not to have been preserved for $C14$ dating. The stone industry ran to a heavy chopper-flake tradition, so that these sites could easily be assigned to a pre-stone-projectile-point era, were it not for the slab metates and the manos. These utensils relate them to the mush- and hoe-cake-eating Cochise, while the absence of stone projectile points argues that they were not hunters of the animals whose bones were found in the same horizon: mammoth, horse, camel, and a large unspecified cat. The snatching of scraps from the table of killer carnivores like the large cat, probably of the jaguar family, is the most plausible explanation of the associated bones. Jennings has advanced the probability that the domestication of small grain was a practice of his Desert-culture people as early as anywhere in the world and was not discontinued until replaced by corn cultivation. The Cochise and Albuquerque-area finds serve to make the insight convincing; the only difference appears to be that the Arizona-New Mexico usufructians depended on the grain amaranths, which might have become as civilized a preference as wheat or oats, if they had only stuck with them. One wonders when some of these grains will be rediscovered and put into cultivation.

The Archaic of Texas is so typically Archaic in pattern that it has been forthrightly labeled Archaic and requires no further description, though what can be said is that it partakes about equally, depending on the local environment, of Eastern Woodland projectile-point patterns and Arizona seed-milling habits. At the McCarter site near Muskogee, Oklahoma, James B. Shaeffer found a complex of grinding stones and scraper planes in the pebble-tool tradition that tied the area in with the Cochise and the widespread Balcones phase of the Archaic in Texas; it included side-notched points. The Hardaway-Dalton style, called the Meserve west of Oklahoma, is found all across Texas and Oklahoma. But the style that seems to give a certain unity to the South, from Nevada to the Carolinas, is the Gypsum Cave point, a triangular-bladed point with a short, dwindling, usually pointed stem. These points were first found in Gypsum Cave, near Las Vegas (where some still make their points, the hard way) with hearths, of which one was dated at 10,455 ± 340 years. The cave seems to have been occupied alternately by men and now-extinct ground sloths, whose dung had a preservative effect on some unique artifacts, including painted foreshafts of the compound dart. (This kind of shaft was probably, though not necessarily, used with an atlatl; the shaft consists of two parts: an arrow-length foreshaft and a heavier, spearlike backshaft, into which the foreshaft fits. The two parts separate when a hit is made, the backshaft falling away and being recoverable.) This Gypsum Cave design becomes the Gary stemmed point in the Middle South, and is the Morrow Mountain style in Coe's sequence of about six thousand years ago.

There is another instance of this kind, where it is a little harder to tell which way the wind was blowing when the style was disseminated across the country. Discovered in 1933 near Twenty-nine Palms, in the Pinto Basin of southeastern California, was a striking-looking style with a deeply notched base; some specimens are so deeply bifurcated that they look like effigies of short-legged pygmies. Somebody missed a great chance to distinguish himself as a phrasemaker when he unimaginatively named these Pinto points bifurcate-base points instead of two-toed tips or, better still, tipped toes. Their California age is figured at between 9,000 and 7,000 years. They are found throughout the Southeast, where they are called Le Croys, but the best series of them comes from Broyles's St. Albans site, where the earliest variety, called St. Albans, has been C14-dated at 8,830 ± 160 years; and the archetypal Le Croy, which is all tip and toes, is dated at 8,250 ± 100 years. No student has so far addressed himself to the problem of how these bifurcates were spread across Meridional America without

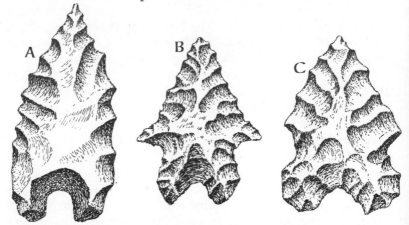

(*a*) Pinto. (*b*) Le Croy. (*c*) St. Albans.

the aid of mass-media advertising or a network of Avon representatives.

With Pinto points at the Stahl site, only a hundred miles from Los Angeles and just beyond Death Valley, are milling stones, and house patterns indicated by post molds, the oldest-known fixed dwellings in America. No nomadic hunters, these Pintoans: they had home addresses, if only for the winter season. This Archaic usufructian pattern of stone points and milling stones occupies all the territory between Arizona and the coastal ranges, including the now insufferable Death Valley and the brick-kiln-like environment of the Mohave Desert, which is in part the bed of an extinct glacial-period lake now called Mohave. Found with the assemblage of choppers and manos (but no metates) were two kinds of points (which had also occurred at the Pinto sites) called the Silver Lake, from the name of another extinct lake, and the Mohave. These are crude and of almost featureless design, hardly more than crude preforms—as though the idea of stone points had just been grasped, but not the exact technology for making them. There has been a great deal of controversy about the dating of Silver Lake and Lake Mohave types, since no hearths have been discovered at the many sites of their provenience. But "environmental dating"—that is, geologic study of the period of shallow lakes and grasslands when the region would have supported a usufructian culture, as well as C_{14} dating of materials (peat, snail shells) from the period—gives phase dates of 10,000 to 8000 B.P.

This is a region that certainly could have been influenced by both the Desert culture and the Cochise milling-stone tradition. But Emma Lou Davis of the San Diego Museum of Man has worked out a series of sites, at which are found ovate and "long-stemmed, weak-shouldered [actually single-shouldered and Sandia-like in outline] points," choppers, knives, and "scraper planes," that extends as far north as Lind Coulee, Wyoming. This assemblage appears at Lake Mohave, Death Valley, Panamint Valley, and Borax Lake, all California localities. The San Dieguito "complex" extends this tradition to the Pacific coast. If I understand current opinions on the San Dieguito culture (which seems to be the overall name for the tradition and its associations), although it existed in the Great Basin it kept rather farther to the west of that geologic province and was a predominately hunting culture; and it is distinct from the Desert culture, significantly lacking milling stones. The distinction is probably valid and archaeologically important, but the location of the camps so far excavated, always at what was the water's edge of the ponds or lakes of the time, is that of a people interested in getting something out of the water besides a drink. Few Paleo-hunter sites are found in such circumstances: near springs or small streams, of course, but hardly ever near fish-bearing bodies of water. The San Dieguito sites probably were seasonal and may well have been like the spring sites of our Hudson River oyster eaters and the Sanpoil.

In this point-by-point survey of the usufructian Archaic, we have finally closed in on the Pacific coast. Let the reader pause here to make a quick sketch, on the page margin, of his guess as to the outline of the pattern characteristic of the early phases of point making in the region, the only hint being that it has not appeared so far in this compendium of styles.

The pullulating center of the Archaic along the Pacific coast seems to have been in Washington and Oregon, and the traditional form of this stage, while it was general and before its specialization toward fishing in the salmon streams, is called the Old Cordilleran. The delineation of the Old Cordilleran was first advanced by B. R. Butler of the University of Idaho in 1959. The Northwest has not only yielded more and more corroborative evidence that the concept is realistic, but evidence of an increasing time depth. In the April, 1968, issue of *American Antiquity*, there appeared a brief note to the effect that the Old Cordilleran had popped up at a site near Waterton, Alberta, at a level that has to be on the order of thirteen thousand years old.

Because it seems to have been a hunting culture at the time, a full contemporary of Clovis, it makes a very plausible parent for the San Dieguito hunters of the coastal-range foothills of the Great Basin; at one of its later stages it does produce the "weak-stemmed" or half-stemmed points by which Davis traces the range of San Dieguito. We are very interested, therefore, in what style of point the Old Cordilleran produced. Called the Cascade, the style is a bipoint, that is, pointed at both ends, sharp-tipped not only at the blood-letting or distal end, but more or less so at the proximal or fastening end. It is clearly both contemporary with and earlier than the fluted-point lanceolates, but any theory that the Cascade "willow-leaf" lanceolate is the technological forefather of the fluted lanceolate or any of the other Paleo-hunter lanceolates comes up hard against the fact that the Paleo-hunter lanceolates are manufactured from straight-based preforms even when these are somewhat contracting toward the base. The flute flake could not have driven off the base of a Cascade, as it was off the Clovis-point blank.

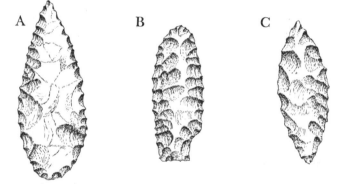

(*a*) Lerma. (*b*) Sandia I. (*c*) Cascade Bipoint.

To understand how the fluted lanceolates could have evolved from the double-pointed Cascades, we have to imagine some sort of intermediate form, and one that would serve is the Sandia I, or earlier Sandia type. It will be remembered that the Sandia I is a single-shouldered style in which the "stem" below the shoulder contracts to a pointed base. It is, therefore, in outline only a step away from the double recurvate symmetry of the bipoint; and that step, we can imagine, came about because of a mistake, that is, a simple mis-hit in chipping. A slightly too energetic blow on the edge of a bipoint, or a slight weakness in the material, will cause a jag or indentation, which, if it occurs about a third of the length of the point from the base, gives it in effect a shoulder. To the maker's eye such an indentation would be a slip and a flaw; but sooner or later somebody must have noted that the flaw, in use, gave an advantage in hafting, and thus would be born the tanged point. If we read it: Bipoint into Sandia I, Sandia I into Sandia II (with straight base and fluting), and Sandia II into Clovis fluted, we have an alternative line of evolution of the Clovis— the other being out of the Andean Biface-El Jobo line, which I still prefer, simply because it is less devious.

The Old Cordilleran lacks grinding stones, or at least the unmistakable milling implements of the Cochise tradition, but its second most characteristic tool is the pebble chopper. If the estimated 13,000 B.P. date for the Waterton site is authenticated, we would seem to have come upon here a second instance of the invention of stone projectile points by a pebble-tool-stage people, rivaling the Andean Biface tradition in age. The invention must have happened about 13,000 B.P. In the bottom stratum of Wilson Butte Cave, in regionally adjacent Idaho, Dr. Ruth Gruhn of the University of Idaho has found bones of extinct horse, camel, and sloth showing knife cuts, C14-dated at 15,000 ± 800 years ago. Idaho, the nearly forgotten state, has also yielded a widespread industry of "hand ax-like bifaces based on large flakes," not yet time-tagged. This, together with the Clactonian-flake "hand-ax" (chopper-tool) industry first discovered in the middle 1930's by E. B. Renaud in Black's Fork Basin, southwestern Wyoming, now provides in this region a pre-stone-projectile-point background for the Old Cordilleran.

The Black's Fork material had its initial exposure during American archaeology's Prohibition era, that generation of scholarship between 1920 and 1950 when the mere mention by a professional of an American "Paleolithic" of hand axes or pebble tools was regarded as a symptom of public intoxication. So thoroughly was its reputation blackened that there is probably not an academically trained archaeologist today who would even dare review it, or who has not been so preconditioned against it that he cannot review it objectively. While Renaud seems to have cast too wide a net in finding traces of a Clactonian industry in individual pieces all over Wyoming, Colorado, New Mexico, and Oklahoma, the American experts who said that his "hand axes" are mere workshop cores are squarely at odds with European Paleolithic specialists, who found them authentically Paleolithic in form and execution. Here we have an earlier instance of Leakey and the Lively complex.

Since a great deal of work is being done in Washington, Oregon, Idaho, and the contiguous Canadian provinces of British Columbia and Alberta, and with the 1968 discovery of Marmes man, we may anticipate with a certain complacency the positive demonstration by data of a pre-stone-projectile-point horizon in the region. Marmes man is a handful of skeletal fragments, including bits of skull, found under a rockfall in a canyon of the Palouse River, a tributary of the Snake River, in the state of Washington. The finder was Roald Fryxell of the University of Washington; the director of excavation was Dr. Richard D. Daugherty, also of the University of Washington and an Early Man specialist; and the announcement was made under the auspices of the U.S. Corps of Engineers, the Smithsonian Institution, and the National Science Foundation, in the office of Senator Warren G. Magnuson of Washington. The poor lad whose defiled bones (defiled not by the excavators but by his neighbors, who had cannibalized him) could hardly have dreamed that he would be resurrected in such exalted company.

The Marmes-man site has been geologically estimated at between 11,500 and 13,000 B.P., but this would appear to be too conservative, in view of the fact that the artifacts discovered were a bone projectile point and a section of bone shaft. There seems little doubt that the Old Cordillerans were using stone points as early as twelve thousand years ago, perhaps thirteen thousand; and Earl Swanson of the Idaho State University Museum has found near Shoup, Idaho, an industry of fully stemmed points made on blade flakes that he estimates at 11,500 B.P. Marmes man would hence appear to have been somewhat backward if he were using only bone points later than that. But, of course, that may be why he was the dinner and not the diner. The Marmes site (named for the owner of the ranch where the find was made) is believed to be a camp site because of the occurrence of charred deer and elk bones in association. Charred bone is C14-datable, if nothing else datable turns up in the continuing excavation, and it now seems that Marmes man is just the man we've been looking for all these years. It may take a while, though, to find all of him. Excavation of the Marmes site began in 1965, and at the moment he consists of some pieces of skull, a leg bone, a vertebra, and some wrist and finger bones, enough to prove that he was here, not enough to say how Mongoloid he was.

(This is, by the way, not the only Marmes man. In 1963 the partial skeletons of two adults and an infant were taken from the Marmes Rock Shelter. But they are only half the age of the bone-point spearman, about 6,200 years old.)

The demonstration that there was a culturally progressive group in the Pacific Northwest which independently invented stone projectile points will not surprise, and can only make happy, those of us who believe that the main migration route of the earliest Americans was along the Pacific coastal shelf. It will be noted by those who are map readers by inclination that the Fraser River of British Columbia and the Columbia River between Washington and Oregon are the first two great river systems to be encountered by south-trending peoples along the littoral that would have given them entrance to the interior of the continent. The Columbia's tributary, the Snake, which rises in Wyoming and travels south, and its northern tributary, the Clearwater, are pathways into a node of valleys and waterways that can be followed into the Great Basin and through the Rockies to the High Plains. When the Great Basin was a relatively well watered region and its now extinct lakes were standing fresh and fecund, its penetration by hunter-gatherers was inevitable.

The Fraser River, which enters the Pacific (the Strait of Georgia) at Vancouver, is somewhat far north for inland travel during advanced ice periods and would not have been ice free until about 11,000 B.P. Nevertheless, at the East Yale site on the Fraser there is an assemblage of cobble tools and scrapers based on flakes that has every appearance of being a pre-stone-projectile-point industry; it is at a consistent level through several thousand yards along the riverbank. In the Fraser Canyon, not far from East Yale, Charles E. Borden of the University of British Columbia has been working on a deep (about twenty-five-foot) stratified site since 1960. Its earliest level has been dated at 9000 ± 150 B.P.; and a lanceolate point and one of Davis's "weak-shouldered" points have been found, with wild-cherry pits (and choppers, of course). The wild-cherry-picking season coincides with the salmon run, and a "fossil" midden has produced salmon bones. The site stacks up from 9000 B.P. to about 3000 B.P.; but, though the levels grow steadily richer in both quantity and variety of artifacts, the choppers and the cherry pits are recurrent from beginning to end. It is a perfect Archaic usufructian sequence, from a flake and chopper plus stone projectile points to pipes and carved figurines, a regional duplicate of Coe's columns in the Piedmont.

The Columbia River provides evidence of the same sequence, with its most important site at Five Mile Rapids in The Dalles Reservoir on the Oregon side. Excavated by L. S. Cressman, the Five Mile Rapids occupation had its beginnning about eleven thousand years ago, and the midden yielded additional evidence of usufructian habits and bird and small-mammal bones. Bipoints were in use from the first phase until about seventy-five hundred years ago. A corresponding sequence was found by Butler on the Washington side of the Columbia at Indian Well. The bipoint is found down the California coast through a succession of locally adaptative cultures and, it is believed, was carried inland at about San Diego, across Death Valley (then no worse than a short-grass prairie) and into Mexico. There it is known as the Lerma, the signature style of the earliest Mexican hunters; but whether the Lerma is the Cascade bipoint or a cousin to the El Jobo points, which are the scions of the Andean Biface tradition, the reader is in as good a position as I am to guess.

With this commingling our cross-country tour must end, there being no place to go but down, that is, southward, where there is a different story to tell. But the reader must not be left with the impression that the Archaic was nothing more than a phantasmagoria of projectile points. The stylistic mutations within patterns and the peregrinations of traditions do not yet make a decipherable scroll; points are the alphabet, but we do not yet know the language. They tell us what, in general, was happening: there was movement and multiplication of population, directed pretty much by the way the wind blew and the sun shone. What we do not know is whether there were migrations of whole groups over long distances with the intent of seizing and occupying new lands. Was something taking place like the succession of tribal movements out of eastern Asia into Europe that began with the Battle Ax people, who probably brought the Indo-European languages to the shores of the Atlantic, and that was followed by a long list of peoples with more familiar names, the Huns and the Goths and Visigoths, the Celts and the Teutons? Probably there was no such general upwelling and outpouring of any people; the structure of usufructianism, an association with a given microenvironment almost like that of an oyster clinging to a rock, was against it. Yet there was a remarkable spread of new ideas throughout Meridional America during the Archaic, and, it seems to me, remarkable progress.

If the premise is accepted that America was settled by a people with a primordial pebble-flake stone industry, who were disseminated through it generally but spottily, and who then achieved stone projectile points around 14,000–13,000 B.P. by invention, then they telescoped some 1.75 million years' progress into the next 7,000 and almost caught up with the rest of the world during what we have been calling the Archaic. At the time of the invention of projectile points Amerinds are industrially not much beyond *Zinjanthropus* or *Sinanthropus*. But by 9000 B.P. the Danger Cave people were milling "domesticated" small grain. Robert J. Braidwood of the University of Chicago, who has been digging for the roots of agriculture in the Near East, where it began, estimates that village life based on raising small grain began about 10,000 B.P. Had the Great Basin improved instead of deteriorated as an environment, small-grain field agriculture might have begun right there. The first genuine cultigens, cultivated plants, occur archaeologically at about 7000 B.P., perhaps a little earlier, in Mexico. There were farming villages in Mexico at about 4000 B.P. and an enigmatic mound complex in Louisiana at the same time. The Olmec center of San Lorenzo Tenochtitlán, Vera Cruz, dates from about 3100 B.P., and shortly afterwards the Adenans of Ohio were beginning to erect the first of the burial mounds that mark, by our definition, the beginning of the end of the Archaic. These matters will be the concerns of the next two chapters. The concern of this one has been to show the state of things as they were during the Archaic that worked up to these achievements. The homogeneity of usufructianism and the uniformity of tool inventories, milling stones, projectile points, knives, scrapers, choppers, drills, and in the later phases bannerstones, axes, adzes, gorgets, and some specialized tools like the so-called plummets, make it seem that during the Archaic little or nothing was happening. But it was. During the Archaic the Amerinds acquired numbers, identity, traditions, and a profound and intense knowledge of the world they lived in. That knowledge does not show too concretely on the archaeological record, but it brought to fruition in America, both South and North, cultural efflorescence both high and unique. The Archaic of the Americas was one of the most extraordinary cultural epochs in the history of the world.

10

The Conservifructians
and the Cultifructians

Until North America had a prehistory of irrefutable antiquity, obviously Mesoamerica and South America could not be permitted by the archaeological cardinalate to have one either. The trackways to these deeply interior regions of the hemisphere were through the future Alaska, Canada, and United States, and the end could not be as old as the beginning. That the Incan of Peru and the Aztecan of Mexico were vanished civilizations at all, and not polities to be dealt with by the European powers of the sixteenth century through embassy and treaty and such guile, like the principalities of India, was owing to the accident (plainly the will of Christendom's God) that the first Europeans to confront them, Pizarro and Cortes, had destroyed them utterly, not merely as states but as societies, in a brigand's adventure after gold. (De Soto's vicious filibuster through the southern United States was dissimilar only in that it found no treasure to loot; the health of the high, though non-literate, culture of the region was stricken as though by a plague—and the plague was literal.) This was instant prehistory. Incan and Aztecan records were destroyed on the pretext that they were works of the Devil, and those who might have testified to the contents of those records were slain as the Devil's disciples by those whose sacramentals of piety were gunpowder and disease. It is easy to see how these destroyers and their masters, whose own sense of history went no farther back into time than the birth of Christ, slightly preceded by the Greeks, and for whom the biblical Jews were the peoples of prehistory, with their origin in the Garden of Eden, would conclude that the Incas and Aztecs, and the somewhat less recently passed Mayan apogee, had roots in time no deeper than their own— which was true, but not as they understood themselves. In those days, of course, the human race and the firmament could be shown by sacred document to have existed for less than six thousand years.

We shall skip over the doctrines of the mid-nineteenth century that broke open this time capsule like a peanut shell: Charles Darwin's demonstration that life itself was eons old; Louis Agassiz's demonstration that the present face of the world had been scarred, not by Noah's pluvial flood, but by another kind of deluge, ice; and finally Boucher de Perthe's demonstration of a Stone Age in man's history unaccounted for in the Bible. These had only a brief effect on America before the Hrdlickan-Smithsonian ax fell and claims, both wild and reasonable, for Amerinds as old as Genesis in South as well as North America, got it in the neck. Nobody went to Mexico or Guatemala or Peru to dig anything but Aztec, Maya, or Inca ruins. And nobody went for knowledge's sweet sake, as archaeologists; they went as collectors for museums or as explorers for the National Geographic Society. What philanthropist would have put up the money for an expedition to look into the caves where pre-Archaic and Archaic usufructians might have lived and left behind the evidence—as in Danger Cave—of their first domestication of the wild plants that were to become the cultivars of American civilizations: pumpkins, beans, and corn?

For twenty years or so after the Folsom apocalypse, during which the Ritchie concept of the Archaic was taking shape, south-of-the-border archaeology was restricted to the classic monumental sites, and to the annual meetings of archaeologists and anthropologists, where the digging done was by the diffu-

sionists and the autochthonists—into each other. The former ar-
rayed the evidence extracted from Tikal, Bonampak, Monte
Alban, La Venta, Cuzco, Machu Picchu, and other sites so as
to prove that there had been decisive foreign intervention in
the Maya-Inca-Aztec territories, with the interventionists streaming in from you know where like an Asiatic Peace Corps.
The latter are ourselves, the readers of this book, the convinced
ones, who see Amerind culture as an Amerind product, from
projectile points to corn.

Strangely, as it seems now, the American origin of corn—
botanically *Zea mays* Linnaeus—was in dispute, because nowhere in the New World could there be found for it a satisfactory ancestor. Neither could one be found in the Old World;
but it was cultivated in India before A.D. 1435, and there are
Chinese records of it in A.D. 1414—both dates being well before
the Columbian voyages, and both records presupposing earlier
cultivation. It was not beyond reason that ancestral maize was
a bashful and retiring grass growing even now in an obscure
valley in Southeast Asia, since in a fairly primitive popcorn
form—in at least one case, in the Naga Hills of Burma, exactly
like that grown early in corn history in Peru—it is grown even
today in Burma, Sumatra, Java, Borneo, and as far north as
Formosa.

The late J. Alden Mason, one of the most cultivated and
equable minds in American archaeology, wrote in 1957, in his
classic *The Ancient Civilizations of Peru*, as follows:

> Maize or corn, which became the great staple food of much of
> aboriginal America and a great world crop, is generally admitted to
> be the most domesticated of all plants, without known wild relatives,
> and incapable of self propagation. The origin of corn has been hotly
> disputed for years, and the best agronomists hold conflicting opin-
> ions. Only five years ago one of them could write that the original
> home of maize was a greater puzzle than ever before.

Obviously only the discovery of wild corn could settle the
origin question, and—since the cultivated corn we know would
be completely helpless if left untended because its husks prevent
its seed from scattering for the following year's growth—the
botanists did not even know what it looked like. The task of

discovery was clearly archaeological; but archaeologists showed very little enthusiasm for it, preferring to dig temples and pyramids—and who can blame them? As between trying to resurrect and preserve the magnificence of once-great cities and trying to find the pollen grains of a plant that might not even have existed (since one theory was that maize was a hybrid involving the related grasses of teosinte and *Tripsacum* and, possibly, a third grass), it was not hard to decide how to expend scarce excavation funds.

Yet one cannot help but see a certain failure of will in the neglect or shirking of a program of search for wild corn; it would not have been a "safe" kind of program, insuring reputation for whoever claimed to have found it; the finder would, on the contrary, be more likely to find himself hailed before a court of critical inquiry, so churlish was the mood of the establishment in those days. The wording would be not "lucky" but "unlikely finder." Let us recall what happened to Helmut de Terra as late as 1947.

It was de Terra's misfortune to find in the Valley of Mexico a fossil human skull and most of a skeleton of a geologic age of about ten thousand years with the aid of an interferometer, an electric dowsing apparatus, the first time such an instrument had been used in archaeology. He had been looking for exactly what he found, but still he came on it unexpectedly, since the underground "anomalies" that the dowser had been registering, as he scanned the surface with it, had proved on two previous tests to be of merely geologic origin. The digging of the test pit where the skeleton was found had been interrupted by a storm. Work was resumed by the hired local laborers against de Terra's orders before he had returned to the scene, and it was they who first saw the bones of Tepexpán man—"the first man from the late glacial strata of Central America," as de Terra called him, for the skeleton lay beneath a crust of calcite that was the dividing line between the older and younger clay strata at the edge of an extinct glacial-pluvial lake.

Prating priggishly about the "sloppiness" of the excavation, a judgment based on photographs, American archaeologists, in the kind of unison they achieve only when on the attack, tried

234 AMERICAN DAWN

to rebury Tepexpán man. He was not of a glacial age; he was not a contemporary of the mammoths found in the same geologic position about a thousand feet away; he was an intrusive burial; the bones had dropped down an animal burrow—anything but the obvious. Finders weepers, not keepers—get this dead body out of sight!

Then, in 1952, at Santa Isabel Iztapán, about a mile and a half away from Tepexpán, a mammoth skeleton with artifacts, including two projectile points (one of which was a bipoint), was excavated, not "sloppily," from the same formation and C14-dated at about 9000 B.P., a minimum date. It is not on record that anybody apologized to de Terra, as Sir Arthur Keith made amends to Dart for his mistakes about the australopithecines.

There had been one earlier excavation of Early Man material in South America that might have drawn the same kind of scorn. It was the work by Junius Bird in 1934–36 in Fell's and Palli Aike caves near the Straits of Magellan, where he found stratification of cultural deposits, with projectile points and bones of extinct horse and sloth in the lower levels. But Bird was prudent; despite the presence of extinct species, which might be accounted for by late survival in that nethermost region, he gave the sites a maximum age of 5,400 years. This modest guess stepped on no official toes, at a time when only fluted points were permitted to be 10,000 years old. But the C14 age of Palli Aike turned out to be 8,639 ± 450 years, and of Fell's Cave 10,720 ± 300 years.

The Tepexpán-man explosion was, however, the end of an era that was surrendering not with a whimper but a bang. The Age of Enlightenment had already begun, quietly, almost stealthily, with a survey by Richard S. MacNeish, then of the National Museum of Canada, of Tamaulipas, a Mexican province on the Gulf coast directly south of the horn of Texas. In the preface to the report of the survey, *Preliminary Archaeological Investigations in the Sierra de Tamaulipas, Mexico*, not published until 1958 though covering work done in 1945–46, 1948–49, and 1952–54, MacNeish writes:

One of the most important problems tackled was that of the non-ceramic [prepottery] cultures in Meso-America. When the survey was first planned in 1944 and begun in 1945, no single expedition in Meso-America had concentrated its efforts on finding sites of Early Man or pre-pottery occupations, though much verbal interest had been expressed concerning these problems.

What he forgot to add was that there had also been no concentrated effort—or any effort at all--to investigate the incipience of agriculture or the domestication of the plants that became America's cultigens. But the Tamaulipas digs themselves missed nothing, from a pre-stone-projectile-point horizon to the Las Pasitas Indians, who occupied Canyon Diablo of the Sierra at the time of the Spanish conquest.

Most of the materials came from dry caves (330 caves were investigated) in that now very dry land, and so were in relative stratigraphic positions. In Level 6 in Diablo Cave (Tm c 81), beneath an horizon of Lerma bipoints regarded as Paleo-hunter because one of them had recently been found with the Iztapán mammoth and because they are in pattern with El Jobo points, MacNeish found an industry he named the Diablo complex. It includes "crude ovoid knives, large pebble scraper, large crude flake scrapers and choppers made from flint cores," on which he comments, "I have considered it a separate entity." Such an inventory requires no further comment in a book in which at least two chapters have been devoted to a pebble-tool chopper-flake Amerind technological past. It was certainly not a big-game-hunter complex; but, MacNeish points out, "all the tools but the pebble scrapers are known in later horizons," including the choppers.

The Lerma points were found in Level 5, and the C14 date on Floor X, the upper of two "floors" in Level 5, was 9,270 ± 500 years. Again we are confronted with that strange, and too frequent to be coincidental, veil that seems to fall on the C14-dated beginnings of stone-projectile-point usage. The reader will not have failed to notice that for the initial stages of projectile-point usage in long sequences in every part of the land covered so far, when there is a C14 date, it falls roughly between 9,500 and 11,500 years ago. No matter how evident it is that the initial dated manifestation cannot have been the initial technological phase, the C14 apparatus clicks out an answer that

gives one the eerie feeling it has come up against a barrier. In
the August 16, 1968, issue of *Science*, C. Vance Haynes of the
University of Arizona submitted the results of several C14 tests
of bone and teeth from the Lehner Ranch mammoths; these
were not routine time tests but were chemically predesigned to
ascertain the reliability of bone for dating by quantitative analysis of its carboniferous components. The double-checked result, after the components had been satisfactorily isolated, was
11,260 ± 300 years. This is probably the most nearly accurate
age we will ever have for the Lehner Ranch site and its Clovis
hunters, corroborating the University of Michigan date of
11,290 ± 500 years and the University of Copenhagen date of
11,180 ± 140 years, both on charcoal, and casting in somewhat
dubious light the University of Arizona date of 12,000 ± 450
years. The most recent of the Arizona mammoth-kill sites, at
Murray Springs, reported by Haynes, has a precisely contemporary C14 age of 11,200 years. Wilson Butte Cave, already
mentioned, with its age of 15,100 ± 800 years, breaks the barrier, but with bone tools and not stone projectile points. The El
Jobo date of 16,375 years seems to break the barrier, but it
may apply to the pre-projectile-point sequence, while another
date (favored by Rouse and Cruxent) of about 11,000 years
applies to the stone points. The one date that breaks the barrier
is that of 12,530 ± 370 years, announced during the summer of
1969, on a cave in Orange County, New York, where a fluted
point had been found.

A collusion of several factors may be the cause of this mysterious stymie. One is the disappointing absence of datable material from key strata, as in the carbon-sterile Sandia-point level
at Sandia Cave and Level 6 at Diablo Cave, where the geology
is clear-cut, and the unfortunate ambiguity of association, as at
Lewisville, where the material is in good supply. A second factor, not yet testable, is one with which we have already met in
the 10,000–2200 B.P. interval, the disparity between C14 and
solar time. Though we have been assured that C14 years and
solar years are approximately equivalent at 10,000 years ago,
such assurance cannot be given for the interval preceding. Now
that it is known that disparity can occur, the whole range of

time for which C14 is useful beyond 10,000 years falls under suspicion. Ernest Antevs, the geologist whom most American-ists consult on glacial and postglacial geology in the West, has consistently overestimated the age of Early Man sites by about 2,000 years. While geologic estimation is nothing to time an egg by, it does have its chronological structure; Antevs could easily prove to be correct, when all the counting is done.

But regardless of the date in years at which the barrier oc-curs, there does seem to be a hemisphere-wide simultaneity—within 2,000 years—about the appearance of stone projectile points, as patent in South America as in the ground we have covered in North America, even though we have argued for the "invention" of stone points from the Andean Biface tradition. What we must have here, in this two-millennium phenomenon, is the period of adoption of stone projectile points by people to whom they came as a new idea; but, as before suggested, the idea was executed only as well as could be within the existing technology, rather than copied from a model. The farther from the center of origin the diffusion of the trait of making stone points, the more aberrant the form. Though the fluted-lanceo-late-point makers did found a tradition, it is unthinkable that all styles everywhere are branches off that family tree. Thus we find that in Mexico and Central and South America the earliest point-producing horizons are within the 11,500–9500 B.P. bracket and that, though the modes are necessarily similar, the stylistic attributes and the sequences are of a system of their own. This did not become evident, however, until 1961, when the first synthesis of South American Early Lithic industries appeared, the work of Edward Lanning, whose 1968 concept of the Andean Biface tradition has been so often referred to, and Eugene A. Hammel.

They say (in *American Antiquity*, October, 1961), "The only early lithic forms which seem specifically similar to North American types are the Clovis-like points from Ecuador and the lanceolate points from El Jobo in Venezuela"—some of the El Jobo points being bipoints like the Lerma and the Cascade. There are, of course, no real Clovis points in the Ecuadorian El Inga collection: only two fluted bases, which may be of lanceolates, or only slightly off-form basal fragments of the "fishtail" stemmed lanceolates that also occur at El Inga, a few specimens having flutes, and in Bird's Straits of Magellan caves as well, in the latter site without flutes. The El Jobo-Lerma bipoints, as has already been suggested, would seem to have been derived from the Andean Biface tradition, while the Cascade bipoints are of independent origin, despite the similarity in outline. It would be much easier to trace the Lerma-like points found in the Stanfield-Worley Rock Shelter, and elsewhere in Alabama, to Mexico than to the Old Cordilleran region.

At the time of writing, Lanning and Hammel considered the El Inga-Magellan fishtail lanceolate the oldest of the typed projectile points in South America, probably as old, about 11,000 years, in Ecuador as the Clovis in North America. But probably of equal age, and at least 10,000 years old, the Lauricocha I industry, from twelve thousand feet high in central Peru, features long, slender lanceolate points made on flake blades, which remind us of the Shoup, Idaho, stemmed points made on flake blades, estimated by their discoverer Swanson to be 11,500 years old. It will take a great deal of dirt moving to relate these two, however, though the technology of making uniface points is an uncommon one.

The Lauricocha Caves, as in the case of the Carolina Piedmont sites, provides a long sequence, up to the time of Christ, but their projectile-point tradition, unlike the Piedmont sites, keeps to one pattern, the leaf-shaped. At that altitude the Lauricochans must not have had many visitors, or any neighbors dropping in with new ideas. Though a stemmed point with a rounded base, approaching the Gypsum Cave-Morrow Mountain style, evolved from this, it did not replace the leaf-shaped style and is only a concomitant. The one new style, a triangular point from Lauricocha II, estimated at 8000–6000 B.P., is easily seen as a variation of the leaf-shaped pattern; but at about this time level, triangular-bladed points begin to appear in several places in South America. It is possibly of significance that a few long, narrow triangular points named the Stanfield triangular type were found in the 9,600-year-old Dalton-Big Sandy level at the Stanfield-Worley Rock Shelter; at least, it is significant to us who have been maintaining that as a temperate climate moved north in late glacial times, the general movement of peoples was with the climate. The Stanfield triangulars are so out of key with the rest of the Stanfield-Worley point styles that only an actual visitation by a band of campers with near relatives south of the border can account for them.

There was not, it seems, a great deal of movement or cultural diffusion in the other direction, from north to south, across the present United States-Mexican border, and the reason would be that desiccation had begun to set in seriously in northern Mexico. Lanning and Hammel assign seed-grinding manos and metates to their Period III, from 6000 to 3000 B.P., several millennia later than at Danger Cave and in the early Arizona-New Mexico cultures. It is not until the latter part of Period III that the typological unity of South American points begins to break down. This unity is seen as the clustering of all stylistic variations, including the long-stemmed forms of El Inga and others of pentagonal outline, about the basic leaf design, which runs concurrently with a simple hunting way of life. This life was transhumant in rhythm, summering in the mountains and wintering in the valleys. In the light of the Sierra Tamaulipas caves and those of southwestern Tamaulipas, of which Mac-Neish investigated sixty-eight, the subsistence of these hunters, to whom the Lermans are related by the design of their points, must have been definitely usufructian.

Despite the find of a Lerma bipoint with the Iztapán mammoth, the Lermans were not big-game hunters of Clovis habit. The food-animal remains found in the Sierra Tamaulipas caves were those of red deer, white-tailed or Virginia deer, and beaver, the climate then being in a distinctly watery phase. But MacNeish finds that meat was never the whole of their diet, sometimes falling as low as 40 percent and constituting at most about 70 percent. It would be safe, I think, to apply these same ratios to the early Archaic of the Eastern Woodlands and all the surrounding big-game territory.

The Lermans remained in their Sierra Tamaulipas caves unchanged for a thousand years, then disappeared without a trace, leaving a hiatus in the record. It is an interval of climatic change, with one aspect of which we are already familiar in Guilday's study of faunal change in the Pennsylvania bone deposits. It is the period during which Jim J. Hester, then of the Museum of New Mexico, in his 1960 study *Late Pleistocene Extinction and Radiocarbon Dating*, found the termination of what we now regard as the typical Pleistocene bestiary: the mammoths, Columbian, imperial, dwarf, and woolly; the American horse; the camel; the bisons, *antiquus* and *occidentalis;* the dire wolf; two species of ground sloth; and, perhaps, the musk ox, the cave bear, and the four-pronged antelope.

There has been as much written about this abrupt termination, called the "great extinction," of Pleistocene big-game animals, such as mammoth, horse, etc., as about the disappearance of Judge Crater and, it seems to me, with as little subsequent penetration of the mystery. The efficiency of hunters using stone-armed spears and darts has been blamed for the decimation of game species, but during the populous Archaic, hunters with the same weapons did not wipe out the deer or *Bison bison*, the modern Plains buffalo; it took firearms and commercial hunting to do that. By the same token, it could not have been destruction of pasturage by climatic change, since *Bison bison* appears on the record as early as ten thousand years ago and prospered in the millions, despite fire drives and other mass-slaughter practices by the Indians and despite the Altithermal, that millennium at 6500 B.P. hotter and drier than today. There was even an Eastern Woodlands form, the last specimen of which east of the Mississippi was recorded as having been killed in 1790 in Tennessee. It is not clear how the change of climate of 10,000–9,000 B.P. could have brought about the extinction of megafauna, since it had survived such climatic reversals before, but the fact that it did disappear during this time of climatic reversal cannot be ignored. Such few spearmen as there were could not have wiped out species that were not already on their way to oblivion.

The Lerman diet ratio—that being what it amounts to—continued unchanged, as MacNeish sees it, from 10,000 to 8100 B.P.; but this may be something of an illusion, because there is no evidence in eastern Tamaulipas of an occupation immediately succeeding it, to show what the Altithermal, the higher-heat, less-rain climatic shift, was doing to the Lermans. The next period, in time though not in direct cultural line of descent, is found in caves in Infiernillo Canyon in southwestern Tamaulipas. Called the Infiernillo phase, it has been C14-dated at 8,540 ± 450 and 8,200 ± 450 years ago, and apparently occupies the two millennia between 9000 and 7000 B.P. MacNeish says that the choppers, scrapers, and points (one form, called Abasolo, is leaf-shaped with a rounded base, while another is a bipointed diamond) bear a resemblance to Lerma. But the rest of the Infiernillo remains are something else altogether. The people of the Infiernillo have passed rapidly through usufructianism and are now conservifructians.

MacNeish writes, "The food remains of the earliest phase, Infiernillo, show that these people were basically food gatherers who did considerable hunting. *However, even at this stage small amounts of their food, such as gourds* (Lagenaria) *domesticated squash* (Cucurbita pepo), *peppers and small runner beans* (*perhaps wild*) *were domesticated* [italics mine]." This was not agriculture nor horticulture, any more than the small-grain domestication at Danger Cave was farming, but it is beyond the Danger Cave plant domestication in that the foods domesticated did become the cultigens of horticulture and agriculture. Just as at Danger Cave, however, there was no breaking of the usufructian pattern of existence. It was usufructian with a little extra care taken to insure that there would be fruits of the earth to use. Since this extra effort was more conservationist than cultivational, it seems fair, if not very imaginative or glib, to call the Infiernillo stage conservifructian.

The Infiernillo, preserved in dry caves in a mummifying atmosphere, is a revelation of the nature of the early Archaic, possibly even in the Eastern Woodlands, where no perishable materials were preserved on open sites and few enough in rock shelters. There were the standard lithics—hammerstones, points, choppers, scrapers, scraper-knives, scraper-planes, gouges, abraders or rubbing stones, and a great deal more: snail beads, bird-bone and other basally drilled bone awls, atlatl foreshafts, pointed sticks of unknown usage, one-over-one woven mats, overhand knots of yucca fiber, two-ply Z-twisted maguey cord, S-twisted cord, wooden wedges, wooden fire tongs, "Fuegian" net bags with rod foundations, interlocking-half-stitch woven baskets with rod foundations, wound-loop baskets on rod foundations, and twilled mats with square corners. Cave dwellers these Tamaulipans were, but not cavemen. We can stop talking about stone industries and begin talking about crafts; we can stop worrying about survival and start counting the centuries until the people who have this firm a grasp on their own destiny will begin to congregate in societies that will become villages and, inevitably, cities. The discoveries in Tamaulipas would have stunned Ales Hrdlicka and his Smithsonian colleagues. We can only be thankful that they were made when his day had passed and that of Libby had come, for Hrdlicka was never at a loss for a slash at what he did not like that left it permanently disfigured. One can imagine what vituperation he would have summoned up against the idea of incipient agriculturists in America at 8500 B.P.; in our present state of knowledge this is only about two thousand years later than the same stage of culture in the Near East.

Small-grain domestication at Danger Cave is, of course, of the same order of age as small-grain domestication in the Near East, but it is not, at Danger Cave, incipient agriculture. Nothing ever came of this conservifructian inspiration in the Great Basin, and of the crafts that, as we now see it, were invented by the Desert culturists. Nothing, that is, but their probable diffusion to places like Tamaulipas, where there were the plants and the conditions for the initiation of horticulture, garden-plot rather than tilled-field. Small grain—wheat, barley, oats, millet —does not yield to the kind of cultivation Amerinds could provide, planting by dibble and digging stick and tillage by hoe. It requires true agriculture, that is, field cultivation, and the Amerinds never had the draft animals to drag the plows that break the fields for sowing. What they did have, in the semitropical zones, were the wild plants—beans, pumpkins, corn— that yielded well to planting in hills, each hill being a tiny garden of its own.

Since the textiles at Danger Cave are the earliest American

textiles we know of, it is only reasonable to suppose that the
know-how spread from its Desert-culture center in all directions,
including southward to Tamaulipas. Accompanying it may have
been the idea of domestication of whatever plants the usufructians of any given environment had been accustomed to gather.
The Infiernillo phase is a transplanted Desert culture, lacking
only grinding stones, which are not necessary implements in the
food preparation of the kind of plants domesticated in Tamaulipas. Gourds were used for utensils, squash and pumpkin seeds
are soft enough to grind dentally, and beans have no husks to
grind.

In the Sierra Tamaulipas, after the hiatus that is filled in
southwest Tamaulipas by the Infiernillo, appears a phase called
Nogales, twenty-five of whose twenty-nine traits, including some
Lerma points, are holdovers from Lerma. One new trait of the
Nogales is grinding stones, but it has a general appearance,
compared with Infiernillo, of being behind the times. It is usufructian and usufructian only, its economy being about 25 percent hunting and 75 percent wild-plant gathering. It is a widespread phase, extending to northern Tamaulipas and the Texas
border, and it is notable mainly because it is so typically usufructian yet individual, in that it had trade relations of some
kind with the Gulf coast, where shell for beads was obtained,
with a suggestion of contacts with Texas in the find of a Plainview lanceolate point (a point type named for the type site in
northwest Texas, where it was found in a bone bed, probably
resulting from a stampede or drive, of extinct bison).

The Nogales lasted unchanged for two thousand years, from
7000 B.P. to 5000 B.P., though in part contemporary with and
in part later than Infiernillo, with which it shared the Abasolo
round-based point and little else. Yet it was in the succeeding
phase in the Sierra Tamaulipas, called La Perra, into which
there was a carry-over of Abasolo round-based point type and
the quite similar Tortugas triangular, that MacNeish found the
first and earliest Tamaulipas corn. Rather surprisingly, it was
not wild corn or even novel corn, but of the variety called Na-
tel, one of the four so-called Ancient Indigenous strains still
cultivated in Mexico today. Even more surprisingly, although

La Perra's contemporary phase in southwestern Tamaulipas, called Ocampo, which followed Infiernillo there, had "domesticated" squash, peppers, small runner beans, and a newcomer, common beans, to the point of horticulture, it was entirely innocent of corn. Corn did not appear in southwestern Tamaulipas for another five hundred years, about 4150 B.P. in the Flacco phase; and then it was not Na-tel, but Chapalote, another of the Ancient Indigenous strains, at a rather late stage in its development. The first Chapalote had just been found (1949) by Herbert Dick of the Peabody Museum, Harvard University, in Bat Cave, New Mexico. The then-new technique of dating by carbon 14 gave the earliest Bat Cave corn an age of about 5,600 years, one of the few solid-carbon dates that have not been revised. It was primitive enough: the ears were nubbins about one inch long, and it was a pod popcorn; that is, the kernels exploded when exposed to heat and were enclosed in glumes rather than the full husk as we know it. Upward through the seven feet of deposits in Bat Cave and onward through time, the Chapalote strain improved in size of ears and rows of kernels and progressed in its botany toward its present state of absolute dependence on man for survival.

Corn, of course, is no more able to fend for itself in the wild than an egg, to the shell of which the husk may fairly be compared. The husk packages the kernels so tightly that they cannot fall to the ground as seed for the new crop. Wild corn could not possibly have been like its coddled descendants. Paul C. Mangelsdorf of Harvard University, whose feats with corn entitle him to be called the amaizing, outlines the problem thus:

The absence of a wild form has been conducive to speculation— sometimes reaching the point of acrimonious debate—about its probable nature. There has, however, been general agreement that modern corn is unique among the major cereals in its grain-bearing inflorescence (the ear) which is completely enclosed in modified leaf sheaths (the husks), the plant being thus rendered incapable of dispersing its seeds. How, then, did wild corn, which to survive in nature must have had a means of dispersal, differ from modern cultivated corn? Where did it grow? How did it evolve under domestication? These are some of the questions that comprise the corn problem.

Because corn as we know it cannot propagate itself on its own, and because no amount of searching had produced a wild ancestor, the suspicion was abroad that it had no wild ancestor, but was some sort of doubled and redoubled cross between its two nearest relatives, the grasses teosinte and *Tripsacum*. When experiments to demonstrate this did not work out, a third grass was hypothesized, but it proved as elusive as corn itself—until its pollen was discovered by Paul Sears in drill cores two hundred feet down in the sediments of the ancient dried-up lake on which Mexico City now stands. The pollen was finally and positively identified by Elso Barghoorn, also of Harvard—corn being thus pretty much a Harvard thing. It was wild corn: the mysterious X factor in the ancestry of corn was corn. There was no question about its having dropped down an animal burrow. Modern corn pollen was in only the top six feet of the core. The two-hundred-foot level was estimated by Sears at eighty thousand years.

The facts did not admit of alternative explanations. Wild corn had been marked for extinction almost the moment that man had taken it in hand and begun to domesticate it, and it was gone now forever, like the mammoth and the mastodon and the saber-toothed cat. But knowing that it had existed was a beginning, and the clues as to what it must have looked like were in Mangelsdorf's hands. He had the Bat Cave pod popcorn and MacNeish's Tamaulipas material, and he, in his own words,

undertook to produce a genetic reconstruction of the ancestral form of corn by crossing pod corn and popcorn and backcrossing the hybrid repeatedly to popcorn. The final product of this breeding was a pod-popcorn bearing small kernels enclosed in glumes on ears arising from the upper joints of the stalks. This reconstructed ancestral form had two means of dispersal: seeds borne on the fragile branches of the tassel and seeds at high positions on the stalk, which at maturity were not completely enclosed by husks. The reconstructed ancestral form served another useful purpose in showing the archaeologist approximately what to look for in seeking prehistoric wild corn.

The archaeologist who undertook the search was MacNeish. He had by this time exhausted the information afforded by

Tamaulipas, from the Lerma hunter-usufructians through the
conservifructians to the cultifructians. In the Sierra Tamaulipas
the La Perra phase was followed by the Almagre, from about
4000 B.P. to 2500 B.P., during which 70 percent of the bill of
fare came from wild-plant gathering, 20 percent from cultivated
plants, and 10 percent from hunting, and during which wattle-
and-daub houses were built in villages that were probably
occupied most but not all of the year. Next came the Laguna
phase, from about 2500 B.P. to the time of Christ, which
brings us to the end of the scope of this book: precivilization
in the limited social-organization sense of the word. During the
Laguna phase, community structure is that of permanent villages up to two hundred houses in size, centered on a temple
mound, the whole pattern based on an agricultural economy,
with minor dependence on wild-plant gathering and hunting.
The Amerinds have left the wilderness and have created their
own physical environment. The social environment has passed
the dividing line between band mores and the necessity of imposing the kind of discipline that amounts to law on large
groups where the members live in fixed abodes all year within
the sound of one another's voices; under such conditions behavior has to be much more strictly governed than in free-
roaming bands, in order not to disturb the functioning of the
whole community. Individual conduct and family interests are
now subordinate to what has become, no matter what its size,
the state; and state interests are now supervening.

In southwestern Tamaulipas the Flacco phase, in which corn
is found, developed into the short-lived Guerra, which evolved
into the Mesa de Guaje, where pottery appears earlier than in
Laguna but which is otherwise very similar. The agricultural
produce now included cotton and several strains of corn and
lima beans. The boundary between Guerra and Mesa de Guaje
is at the appearance of pottery, but it was not an "invention"
there, merely an innovation. And, indeed, nothing in the Tamaulipas sequences was an invention.

It was because the Tamaulipas sequences were average,
typical exemplars of what was going on in dozens of localities in
Mexico, Mesoamerica, and, to an extent, in South America, that

they are so highly illuminating. This territory is subdivided into literally hundreds of confined locales by its rugged mountain systems, as the United States and Canada are not. In each locale there was an independent sequence of development, as in the case of the Sierra Tamaulipas and southwestern Tamaulipas; yet, stage for stage, the trend is average. What happened in one locale sooner or later happened in another—obviously by contact of some kind, but intermittent contact. The Sierra Tamaulipas cultures and the southwestern Tamaulipas cultures resemble each other, yet there is no correspondence. For a long time the projectile points are, like those of South America, variations on a leaf-shaped theme; but when this theme is forgotten, and new ideas about hafting and weapon types are adopted, the points begin to diverge into shapes that seem to be northern imports, from Texas and New Mexico. The Sierra Tamaulipas corn, Na-tel, was grown there twenty generations before corn, of another strain entirely, appeared in the archaeological column in southwestern Tamaulipas. This delay was very probably due to the fact that the southwestern Tamaulipans had something going for them in their squash and beans, and that corn, at that stage of development, was nothing much, while to the Sierra Tamaulipans it was an asset to a usufructian economic base.

It is clear enough that ideas did get around through the Mexican-Mesoamerican valleys, but by a tortuous circulation system, not by simple contiguity contact. The Sierra Tamaulipas was laggard in picking up the squash-beans cocultivars, while southwestern Tamaulipas, when it did take to corn, adopted a strain that had been doing well at Bat Cave, several hundred miles to the north, for at least 120 years before and was not primogenial even there. It is not to be wondered at that several cultural climaxes were achieved in Mexico and Central America: the Olmec, the Zapotec, the Oaxaca, the Toltec, the Highland and the Lowland Maya, and as many others; and each climax in turn had its expansion effect on all others. Here were the centers, the key areas, the regional nuclei, according to A. Palerm and E. R. Wolf, "of massed power in both economic and demographic terms." Tamaulipas had never achieved a cultural climax; what MacNeish was looking at there was an extremity of the circulatory system.

Not that he was researching the sequences leading up to a cultural climax—that takes teams of experts, large sums of money, and years of work, as we shall see shortly. MacNeish, with Mangelsdorf's encouragement, was looking for the last wild corn and the first domesticated corn. What he had already learned was that practically the only place it was likely to be found was in dry caves, and the guess was that wild corn had been a highland grass. With these specifications in mind, he undertook a Tamaulipas-like survey in the mile-high Tehuacán Valley in the state of Puebla on the outskirts of the Valley of Mexico, whence had come that eighty-thousand-year-old corn pollen.

For thirty-eight caves nothing happened. At the bottom of the heap were the Lerma bipoint hunters of what he called the Ajuereado phase, at about 10,500 B.P., or a little earlier than in Tamaulipas. By 9000 B.P. these hunter-gatherers had become gatherer-hunters, with seed-grinding mortars and pestles as well as manos and metates among their equipment, a very early appearance for these implements. Animal bones were few, and the food remains were mainly vegetal. They consisted of maguey, agave, opuntia-cactus fruit, and, significantly, wild grasses; before the end of the phase, called El Riego, about 7000 B.P., squash was probably being domesticated. The Tehuacans were a millennium in advance of the Tamaulipans, despite the fact that, as the crow flies—if a crow could fly over mountains ten thousand feet high—the distance between them was roughly comparable to, say, the distance from the Carolina Piedmont sites to the St. Albans site (between which points there may easily have been annual visitation, to judge by the artifacts). The El Riegans were making string nets, coiled baskets, and what must have been the status equivalent of a mink coat, twined blankets of plant fibers—all of which were buried with the dead. This constituted more than a suggesion of burial of some ceremony, which is entirely absent from Archaic burials in the archaeology of the United States till about 4500 B.P. One child burial hinted at either cannibalism or ritual sacrifice, possibly the beginning of a practice that grew through the ages to become the horrid climax of the Aztecan liturgical year, when the heart of a young man especially chosen for his beauty, after a year of high honor and pampering, was cut out of him by a priest on the high altar before the assembled populace and, still streaming hot lifeblood, shown to the multitude.

New insights, new comprehension, new evidence: all this, but no corn. The 1959 work was done, and it was February, 1960, when the thirty-ninth cave was opened—and there it was, corn of Bat Cave age and evolutionary stage. At first glance Tehuacán Valley was not a climax or nuclear area, nor, through the first thirty-eight caves, had it seemed a likely place to find corn; as Mangelsdorf said, "In earlier speculation about where wild corn might have grown we did not associate it with such plants as cacti and thorny leguminous shrubs." But the rainfall of about twenty inches per year came in the Tehaucán Valley during the growing season, from April to October, which was ideal; the drought season was winter, when seeds should be dormant anyway, and the springs of the valley were perennial.

The survey was now over; corn had been in the Tehuacán Valley early enough to have been there before man had taken an interest in it, which was enough to attract the financing for an ambitious project of high resolve. The funds, spent on botanical, geological, ecological, and pollen specialists, were not wasted. Five caves dug during 1960–62 yielded 23,607 specimens of *Zea mays*, of which more than half were whole or nearly whole cobs. The richest cave, Coxcatlán, gave its name to the phase which follows El Riego without cultural break; its C14-dated span was from 7150 B.P. to 5350 B.P. In a Coxcatlán deposit of about 7000 B.P. there came to light some half-inch cobs so genetically infantile that it is still undetermined, and may be indeterminable, whether they are wild or domesticated. Mangelsdorf thinks they are wild, but the common ancestor of both Na-tel and Chapalote. They are the earliest corn now on record, but they may not always be.

The cobs from the five corniest caves, beginning with the Coxcatlán phase and ending with the Venta Salada phase of

A.D. 1536, have been sorted into six major and five minor strains. Mangelsdorf and his assistants have classified 252 cobs "as possible first generation hybrids of wild corn with various cultivated types" and 464 cobs as "backcrosses of first generation hybrids to the first corn." During the classification routine it was noted that at the end of the Purron phase, which began at about 4200 B.P., following Abejas which followed Coxcatlán, there was a significant increase in the size and botanical attributes of the corn remnants; a distinctly new strain, larger and more productive, and not in the orderly evolution of the original strain, had indubitably arrived in the valley. It had been hybridized with teosinte, which does not grow in that area; it had, therefore, to have been imported from somewhere else, where there could have been a natural cross-pollination of wild corn and teosinte or teosinte and early domesticated *Zea mays*. If the site where this marriage took place can be found, there may be recorded an even earlier date than 7150 B.P. for the earliest hand-sown maize. But it will not be really important. Wild corn and its first conservifructian form have been found, with all that these discoveries demonstrate: that there was in fact a wild-corn grass, that it was indigenously American, and that the usufructian habit of exploiting the total resources of the environment had turned it up as inevitably as gold dust was noticed in the gravels at Sutter's mill.

There could have been no inkling at the time of what a treasure corn was. Its produce could not have made it any more sought after than other vegetals, because it was an inconspicuous plant among others that yielded more showy fruit and greater bulk of edibles, like the squashes and beans. One would guess that a sweet and inimitable flavor—modern, chalky-tasting field corn, raised for every purpose except the human palate, is a post-Indian development—kept it on the Amerind grocery list. It was collected wherever it was found because people liked it, and because its explosion, when heated, into fat and toothsome snowdrops was unique, fun as well as filling. All plants pay good wages for the labor of cultivation; indeed, there would be no civilization anywhere if they did not—if, on the contrary, they turned sickly or sterile when kidnapped from their natural habitats by man. Corn is the most extravagant paymaster of them all: modern hybrid corn grown under conditions for which it was designed gives returns that Monte Carlo and the stock market never heard of—1200 to 1. From the beginning it has been, with any encouragement at all, building toward that prodigality; but in the beginning nobody knew it. Not until it began to peak ahead of its fellows in the production competition did man's attention focus on it; and when he did finally realize what he had, American civilization was conceived and born. Its spurting ahead was due to something no Indian could have known anything about: its extraordinarily protean gene pattern, which responds amazingly to hybridization. Today it comes in more shapes, sizes, and colors than any other grain raised by man; and if there were any call for further attributes, it could be bred to have them. Mangelsdorf is authority for the statement that there are now eight thousand varieties; in Columbus's time there were at least seven hundred, all developed from one strain of *Zea mays*.

But not from *Zea mays* alone; involved in its genetic structure, like a miscegenative father, are teosinte and probably *Tripsacum*—which, though it is a wild grass, is thought by Walton Galinat, Mangelsdorf's collaborator, to be a cross between teosinte and *Manisuris*, another wild grass. There is nothing in the plant kingdom to compare with the vigor of the reaction of *Zea mays* when it is crossed. Why, then, did wild corn become extinct?

Mangelsdorf suggests, briefly, that domesticated corn killed off the wild strain by the deadly mechanism of crossing with it, so that it acquired the helplessness of domesticated corn and could no longer reproduce itself. We have already mentioned what the practice of "domestication" of grain amounts to: the deliberate dropping or leaving behind of seeds while gathering from wild plants, to insure the next year's growth—in that same locale. Since the simple experience was that certain plants grew in certain places, it was most likely that when domestication intensified into cultivation by planting, weed killing, and watering, the locus of the garden would remain in the vicinity where the plant had grown wild. As soon as cultivated corn began to take on the new look, it transmitted to all the barbarian corn in the neighborhood that infectious refinement that improved it right out of existence. Since corn pollen is wind disseminated, over the centuries the pristinity of every stand of corn within an area circumscribed by mountain walls was violated constantly. Wild corn did fight back, as Mangelsdorf's 464 cobs "backcrosses of first generation hybrids" to the wild form give testimony. Even when the alien corn, carrying the hybridized tripsacoid (the term covers crosses with either teosinte or *Tripsacum*) genes, was introduced into the Tehuacán Valley, there were backcrosses to both wild and pretripsacoid parents. But it must have been a losing battle.

How, precisely, the wild corn became extinct is not known. Eventually that stage may have been reached where the bastardized wild corn could not reseed itself, or it may have been sexually disturbed. In the corn we know, the male stamens constitute the "tassel," at the top of the main stalk, and the female pistils are what we call the "silk" of the cob. In wild corn the cob was bisexual, the tassel of pollen-bearing stamens growing out of the top of the ear. One can easily imagine wild corn reaching a stage where the transfer of stamens away from the cob resulted in a maladjustment, by which reproduction was seriously disrupted. People are not the only life forms with sexual problems. Mangelsdorf's conclusion is that "repeated contamination of the wild corn by cultivated corn could eventually have genetically 'swamped' the former out of existence."

The archaeology in the Tehuacán Valley records the decline of wild corn. The remains of the maize of the Coxcatlán phase are probably all wild, with a few possible exceptions. In the following Abejas phase, beginning at 5350 B.P., only about 47 percent of the cobs are of wild plants, but cobs of apparently wild corn (probably backcrossed a hundred times) appear as late as the Palo Blanco phase of A.D. 250. Mangelsdorf surmises that the last uncultivated corn may have actually disappeared only when Mexico began to be overgrazed, after the white man brought horses, cattle, and sheep into the country. He doubts that any wild corn now exists or could exist.

Undoubtedly the Coxcatlán will always remain as the prime

reference in the literature on the earliest corn, and once corn fell into the hands of its usufructians, the pace at which civilization could be achieved was incalculably accelerated. Horticulture was bound to be achieved once beans, the cucurbits (squash, pumpkin, and so forth), and other indigenous plants began to be domesticated; but true agriculture, as an economic base for civilization, required a major grain. Corn was not that major grain in the beginning, but it became major as its vigor and variety were evoked by hybridization and cultivation. Yet, from the beginning, there seems to have been something stimulating about its very cultural presence.

An anthropologist with a panoptic view of all existent cultures at 7000 B.P. would not have hesitated about predicting that Coxcatlán man would reach the agricultural stage that would cease to be called cultural and begin to be recognized as civilized. The Coxcatlanites were well into conservifructianism; with the earliest corn, wild and/or domesticated, were avocados, gourds, and chili peppers, to which were added, as the phase progressed, tepary beans, grain amaranths, squash, and sapotes. The macrobands no longer dispersed seasonally into microbands, but each little community had its fixed living site. And Coxcatlán man was making hard vessels. These were of stone, not ceramic, but they marked the achievement of a model of a nonleaking, permanent, noncombustible container. They were first used probably for storage and as mortars for seed grinding, but some of their advantages as vessels over the lighter, more transportable baskets must have been realized. The manufacture of more and more craftsmanlike stone vessels continued through Tehuacán phases subsequent to Coxcatlán, and when the first ceramics appeared, the pots were copies of the shapes of the traditional stone ones. Ceramic pots were very late in the Tehuacán sequence, about 2300 B.P., and the reason must have been that the stone vessels had been serving well enough the purposes of ceramic pottery.

Corn, beans, and squash, hardware vessels, fixed abodes— the very holotype of American civilization—and all this at between 7000 and 6000 B.P.; yet the Tehuacán Valley was a fringe area that never became "nuclear," never reached the climax of a monument-constructing, politically complex system of civilization. But by now the attitudes toward archaeological strategy in investigating Mesoamerica had been permanently influenced by MacNeish. In 1966 the Oaxaca valley, with its fabulous prehistoric ceremonial city, Monte Alban, where the Zapotecan climax had burgeoned, was selected for a comprehensive study project headed by a team consisting of Kent V. Flannery of the Smithsonian, archaeologist (he had worked at Tehuacán); Aubrey W. Williams, Jr., of the University of Maryland, ethnologist (I once worked for his father in the National Youth Administration); and Dr. Michael Kirby, geomorphologist, and Mrs. Anne Kirby, geographer, both of Cambridge University. The Oaxaca Valley was one of the five physiographically definable provinces that had been from the beginning and continued to be "areas of massed power"—all of them, with the exception of the Maya area around Guatemala City, strung out in a north-south line, beginning with the Valley of Mexico and its eighty-thousand-year-old wild corn.

The sequence begins at the familiar ten-thousand-year horizon—the actual C_{14} date being 9790 B.P.—but with the most strongly entrenched usufructian economy we have met at this early date, with the exception of the Cochise. The period, known as Guila Naquite from the cave where it was found, covers the millennium between 10,000 and 9000 B.P. Within its refuse, still intact though desiccated, were acorns; piñon nuts; mesquite beans; fruits of prickly-pear and organ cactus, maguey, and several other species; along with squash and small black beans. There is little difference between the second phase at Oaxaca and the Coxcatlán at Tehuacán, wherefore it has been labeled Coxcatlán; but it, along with corn, appears to be later at Oaxaca, and this may be significant. The usufructian-conservifructian folk of Oaxaca kept to the higher-altitude zone of the valley, to the caves at the borderline between the piedmont (literally, "foothills") and the high mountains; they did not descend to the bottom of the valley until the full agricultural phase at about 3200 B.P. The reason, as divined by the Oaxaca team, was that on and just above the piedmont, where rainfall is up to forty inches per year, grew "the richest and most varied assemblage of edible wild plants of the entire region," but only the high and low alluvial plains of the Atoyac River, which drains the valley, and the lower piedmont were suitable for field cultivation of corn.

The Oaxaca Valley had been able to build steadily toward a cultural climax because it had the resources for the production of corn at all stages of corn-cultivation technology. The valley is arid, with from twenty to less than thirty inches of rainfall per year, and the technology was hydrological. The first step had apparently been what is called pot irrigation, which was possible because the water table in the high alluvium is only five to ten feet under the surface. Wells are dug into this water table, and the water is dipped out in large jars and poured by hand on the growing corn. The number of wells per acre may run as high as ten, and three crops per year are produced in the frost-free climate of the valley floor.

It is easy to see why this would have been the first methodological stage. One of the first practices of the conservifructians in the domestication of plants must have been watering, with water obtained from nearby springs or streams; the perennial springs of Tehuacán must have been highly influential in the early development of corn in that valley. But Amerinds were also experienced at digging for water in stream beds when the streams themselves had dried up. Wells or water holes, therefore, were no novelty, and when the conservifructians came down out of the hills to grow corn in fields, they brought with them the techniques they were already accustomed to use.

(*Riego a brazo*, or pot irrigation, is something I performed in my youth without the faintest suspicion that I should ever encounter it in anthropology, because I thought my mother had invented it to make my life miserable. In those days we had a summer place in the country, and large-scale—so it seemed to me—truck gardening was my mother's sole recreation and therapy. Theories about raising children being what they were then, her brood, principally myself as the strong-armed eldest, were pressed, not to say impressed, into service for her extensive projects. I hated to see that evening sun go down during the July and August dry spells. With the evaporating power of the direct solar rays off the ground, it was time to pick up a two-gallon pail and spend the next hour or so at the treadmill job of scooping water from the creek that separated the early garden from the late garden and sprinkling every plant that was still or about to be in bearing mood. Of course the waterholes were never close to where the plants were. So I grew up an odd child, with a precocious and inordinate fondness for cloudy gloom and the pitter-patter of the rain. But irrigation by arm does work. We had greenstuffs while the neighbors were still eating out of the root cellar.)

The early pot irrigation worked so well at Oaxaca that the increasing population began to look for more land. With all the pot-irrigable soil taken, the move was to the piedmont, where the streams leaving the mountains could be diverted into irrigation ditches; some of these ditches were in use so long that they became "fossilized," from the travertine precipitated out of the water as it was slowed and held to a stand. The cultivatable flatland plots were then enlarged by terracing with dry-stone walls. With population continuing to increase because of the effectiveness of these measures, dry farming with fallowing on the slopes was the next step; and it was successful, within its limits, because of the low erosion rate. Eventually every square foot of arable land came under cultivation by an appropriate method, from dry farming on the dry hillsides to flood farming in the bottom lands. And then? Then civilization became really civilized, and expansion took the form of imperialism, the accession or annexing of new territory by state power. The sculptured scenes of the Monte Alban I period at that state ceremonial-monumental capital show slain and mutilated captives being brought to the seats of the mighty, their conquerors and lords. Thus anthropological barbarism has become historic civilization, in the strictly denotative, not connotative, usage of that term.

The thoughtful reader may have spotted one slight flaw in the plausibility of the foregoing summary of how civilization came to the Oaxaca Valley: What caused the conservifructians to abandon life in the piedmont-mountain zone, where there was "the richest and most varied assemblage of edible wild plants in the region," and take the plunge down, so to speak, to the valley floor? The same kind of population pressure, one might guess, that caused the valley farmers to adapt to use every possible corn-bearing acre. Yet it would be a naïve answer. How were they to know how it was going to work out down there? Flannery, who worked not only the Tehuacán Valley project, but a later one on lowland sites along the seacoast, is of the opinion that the conservifructians had to learn from somebody else how to live the village-agricultural pattern. With Michael D. Coe as senior author, he wrote, in *Science*, February, 1968, "It probably was not until maize was taken to the alluvial, lowland littoral of Mesoamerica, perhaps around 1500 B.C., that permanently occupied villages became possible. . . ."

He and Coe had excavated at a site called Salinas La Blanca, near Ocos, on the Pacific coast of Guatemala only a few miles from the Mexican border. The corn found, of an unhybridized Na-tel strain, was, nevertheless, "considerably more advanced than the maize which was then being grown in Tehuacán." The time was 2500 B.P., and the degree of advancement can be accounted for only by a long history of intensive cultivation. The excavation of the site, consisting of two mounds of refuse and debris "representing house foundations of a succession of hamlets or small villages," adumbrated this conclusion. Much plant material was found, with bones of small animals and the remains of shellfish and crabs. But not a single stone projectile point turned up. So we have come full circle, from pebble tool-chopper days, without stone points, through a long, long era during which the stone projectile point was, in varying degrees, the tool on which man relied to survive, to the day when it is no longer needed. It is the usufructian, not the hunter, who has been on the true road to civilization all the time.

But how long did it take to make the one simple change in the pattern of living that made all the difference? The usufructians had moved all over the landscape to the places where nature had seen fit to allow this or that food plant to grow. The cultifructians finally learned the trick of making their staple foodstuffs grow where they wanted them to—that is, where they lived. Man had not quite, it is true, imposed his will on nature, but he had learned to create significant exceptions to the environment that nature had imposed.

The artifactual yield at Salinas La Blanca was mainly ceramic pottery, a telltale indicator of the sedentary life. Here was a village, then, that had grown up in exactly the spot where the people of that area had been accustomed to exploit, like all usufructians, several habitats or microenvironments. The seashore, the estuary of the Naranjo and Suchitate rivers and their lagoons and swamps, a tropical savannah, and a tropical forest: each of these had its own produce of edibles. Then the regional inhabitants had begun to restrict their exploitation of these multiple environments with the flourishing of corn, first domesticated and then cultivated. The more successful the corn crops, the less occasion to go abroad in swamp and forest with spear in hand; the corn of the fields now could meet the demands of a growing population simply by the addition of new fields, since there was unlimited surrounding land in that moist, mild sea-level climate. At Salinas La Blanca we have our color-slide demonstration of usufructianism into cultifructianism into cultivation into civilization, albeit a humble one.

Coe and Flannery wrote, "There never was any such thing as an 'agricultural revolution' in Mesoamerica, suddenly and almost miraculously resulting in village life." The argument from the example of Salinas La Blanca is persuasive. The arterial circulation system of traits, of "inventions," had brought corn out of Tehuacán or an adjacent high valley, where it was a native grass, along with the practice of domesticating it, to the coastal plain. There were the optimum conditions, and there was the land where its full potential as a principal food crop would be realized. But this realization had consequences beyond the mere fattening of bellies (and the introduction of dental cavities); it evolved a whole new pattern of society.

To say that the Oaxacans observed these consequences and then hastened to imitate the nearest lowland-village agriculturists would be absurd. But what must have not gone unremarked is that corn could be grown with highly satisfactory results in places where it did not grow as an indigenous grass. Once the

Oaxacans had been encouraged to try the more open and spacious territory of the high alluvium, their future, given the domestication methods they were already using, was assured. In the Tehuacán Valley there was no area like the Oaxacan high alluvium with a water table near the surface; there were only the perennial springs, and the Tehuacans fell behind in their social development. But the Oaxacans had the land and the resources.

Flannery *et al.* open their 1968 report "Farming Systems and Political Growth in Ancient Oaxaca" as follows:

> During the last 15 years an increasing number of anthropologists and geographers have turned their attention to the pre-Hispanic civilizations of Mexico and Guatemela. The evolution of these ancient complex societies is of general theoretical interest because it seems to have taken place independently of the early Old World civilizations.

On this, the only comment called for is, Indeed, indeed! Agriculture is not only what is cultivated but the practices of cultivation. In neither what was grown nor the ways in which it was grown do American agriculture and horticulture resemble cultivation in the Old World. MacNeish's discoveries have demonstrated forever that there was no immigration from anywhere of green thumbs who brought with them the idea of agriculture and then chose by instinct from the American flora, as from a seed catalogue, the plants to be raised and the proper methods for their raising. Usufructianism, conservifructianism, cultifructianism: the terminology may be improved upon, but the organic unity of the American agricultural system, the logic of its maturation—by analogy that of infancy, adolescence, and adulthood—is beyond archaeological cavil.

As it was in Mexico and Mesoamerica, so it was in the seminal areas of Peru and Ecuador, where conservifructianism is as old as in Mexico, and in the Central American territory of Mayan efflorescence. It seems that conservifructianism was not an "invention" or an innovation that required to be diffused from a center and picked up by the alert or the hard-pressed. It was a kind of inevitability, given the premises of usufructianism and the cultural disposition of the Asiatic immigrants who arrived here with only a chopper-and-flake industry to make a living. It was, considering the circumstances, all they needed, and what it tells us is not that these migrants and their Amerind descendants were ungifted novice craftsmen in stone (they did in time invent the stone projectile point, and the big-game specialists became expert), but that the way they lived required no more in the way of lithic equipment than choppers and the edges of flakes. After all, did anybody need a monkey wrench before nuts and bolts were invented?

The very uniformity of the evolution of the usufructians, from pre-stone-projectile times to the Ocos villagers, has made it almost unnecessary to give an account of the preagricultural sequence in Peru, where conservifructianism seems to have begun early, with the domestication of beans, squash, gourds, chili peppers, sweet potatoes, peanuts, and the nondietary but highly useful cotton. Corn, the great food staple of agriculture there as elsewhere, as the cultigen *Zea mays* arrived in Peru, giving it the push toward civilization, about 4200 B.P., slightly ahead of pottery. Though there are some duplications of domesticated plants, corn alone seems to have been an import. Out of what kind of background did this conservifructian-cultifructian tradition emerge?

Again we have recourse to Lanning, to a 1963 report titled, aptly, *A Pre-Agricultural Occupation in the Central Coast of Peru*. The data for the report came from more than fifty camp sites and from two areas, one north and one south of Ancon. The environment of most of the sites is something we have not met before, the *lomas*. These were (and still are) small patches of vegetation in an otherwise arid region, the plants of which flourished in winter on the moisture that rolls in as fog from the Pacific. Thus the lomas were winter camp sites, while summer, the rainy season, was spent in the mountain valleys. Lanning thinks the first discernible followers of this up-and-down way of life date "back to the Pleistocene"; he does not specify Late Pleistocene, and we may take it that he means from ten thousand years ago to some indefinite boundary near his fourteen-thousand-year estimate for the already-mentioned Red Zone

people of the drainage area of the Chillon River, which passes
through this loma zone. The stone-tool inventory looks that old.
Lanning says, "The most outstanding feature of the sites in this
area is the great quantity of flakes of green stone on the surface
. . . evidently struck off for use as tools without further modification. Of the same material, of course, are the cores from which
they were struck, and also a series of round cores with wavy
bifacial cutting edges and flat butts." These "round cores" were
the choppers.

"Extensive research has turned up only two fragments of
crudely percussion-chipped projectile points," Lanning says,
without specifying the form, which is apparently unidentifiable;
and among the cobble hammerstones were "a few large, thick
milling stones, small mortars with unshaped exteriors and basin
shaped bowls and cobble pestles." In brief, this is another area
like that of the Desert culture, but so far from the Great Basin
that what happened here had to have happened independently
and spontaneously.

The Desert-culture sequence is duplicated in the phases following the founding one: that is, a sequence of changing
projectile-point forms marks the passage of time, as various
projectiles are adopted—javelins and darts—and chipping grows
progressively more competent. Lanning says, "The seriation
of these later industries is based on their projectile points,
pointed tools (considered to be awls and perforators) and mortars." It should not have to be emphasized that mortars are
seed-grinding equipment, and that while vegetal remains, so
abundant and informative in the Mexican caves, have long since
disappeared, the nature of the lomas is such that the only food
they could afford over a winter's camping season would be roots
and grain seeds. In the last preagricultural phase, the Encanto,
which correlates with a nearby village through identity of projectile points, there was an abundance of bone and plant refuse,
grasses, seeds, gourds, cordage of sedge—and cotton. It is not
surprising that the Encanto is characterized by "the large number of milling stones and manos—more than in all other sites
put together."

Several factors had combined to effect a change at this time,

about 5000 B.P.: the introduction of cultivated plants as food
and for textiles, the village pattern of settlement, and a change
in the circulation system of the Pacific Ocean. This change
caused the loma-watering fogs to come ashore at high altitudes,
and the low-level lomas disappeared. But the circulation shift
was benign; the Peru current now brought fish schools inshore,
where they could be taken; the fish attracted shore birds, which
became a calculable element of diet; and shellfish began to
thrive. Thereafter, with summer crops to tend and a productive
sea at their doorstep, the ancients of Ancon ceased their seasonal
migration and settled down in permanent communities.

This is a fascinating sequence, its mutations dependent on
factors we have not met before—fog-swigging verdure and a
vagabond ocean current—yet it is by now a familiar cultural
epic. Whatever the climatic vicissitudes of the region, they were
worked into the way of life that was itself an incessant drive,
pushed and powered by the exigencies of increasing population.

The food-producing efficiency of the stone projectile point
brought home more bacon than had ever been in the larder
before, and the additional nutrition kept more hunters alive
longer—so many, in fact, that the demand for food outran the
ecologically limited supply. It was probably a matter not only of
normal breeding arithmetic, and of more infants being kept alive
longer by more contented mothers, but of an extension of life-
span. It requires considerable food, even at this level of feast
and famine, to keep an adult alive one year longer than actuarial
tables for that time would have predicted. With the woods not
being that full of meat, the more mouths that had to be fed
longer sought appeasement by taste testing everything chew-
able; the tribe having increased on the profits of these experiments to the limits of vegetal capacity to feed it, the next step
was to trick plants into higher, more certain yield. What archaeology proves for the American hemisphere is what archaeology
everywhere proves, the most obvious of self-evident truisms:
that man owes his preeminence among animals to his willing-
ness to go to any lengths to satisfy his appetite. Actually archaeology is a branch of demography.

This lesson having been repeated the Aristotelian thrice,

this book might end here, except that nothing has been said about events leading up to the end of the Archaic in the Eastern Woodlands of the present United States, where the story was decidedly different.

The development of a village agricultural society in the Great Basin area, as we already know, was aborted by the absence of a major grain like corn and such staples as squash and beans, and by the climatic mischief-making which left only small patches for the growth of the grain amaranth pickleweed. The hunting peoples of the prairies went right on hunting, probably because they liked the life, and because their numbers never exceeded the amount of meat they required. The descendants of the Old Cordilleran in the Pacific Northwest would probably be usufructians yet if white civilization had not broken up their playhouse. So handsomely did the Lord, through the instrumentality of the Pacific Ocean, provide there that it would have been almost blasphemous to try to improve on his work by agriculture; it would have been the tyro impudently competing with the master.

The Eastern Woodlands were almost as well favored; probably the warm, dry Altithermal served to air out the dank climax forests and to dry off some of the swamps and bogs into verdant leas, like the rest of the present United States. Though the region lacked a major cultivatable plant—of all the plants that are today's cultivars, only the berries are native to the region—there could hardly be said to be a lack of food. It hung high and low, from acorns to crawdads; and the land was so traversable, far and wide, that a seasonal local dearth was not as likely to be fatal as in the tight valleys of the montane West, Mexico, and western South America. When the Eastern Woodlanders began to domesticate plants, no earlier than three thousand years ago at best, it was desultorily and probably more out of convenience than necessity; and it was more likely to have been the result of "volunteer" plants growing up in clusters around caves and other habitation sites from seeds accidentally dropped than from any preconceived intention.

The post-Archaic archaeology of the Eastern Woodlands adds nothing to our usu-conservi-cultifructian theme and continuum—no new cultivar, no new technology, no new form of society—yet it is the most engrossing of all chapters of American prehistory. For the Eastern Woodlands are the region of the Mound Builders whose earthen monuments have been the subject of a half-dozen bestsellers of the past century, both fictional and scholarly—or pseudoscholarly. And that literature has kept viable one classic reference, Plato's lost Atlantis; added the word *behemoth* to the language; and brought about the founding of a native American religion, Mormonism, and through that religion, the addition to the union of the prosperous state of Utah.

11

Rise and Fall of the Shamans

THE PATENTLY MAN-MADE EARTHWORKS and tumuli that white Americans encountered in Eastern America, from Ohio to Georgia, as soon as they began to move westward from the coastal plain (the great Thomas Jefferson excavated one, quite scientifically, in Virginia about 1780) were instantly recognized as the antiquities of America, its equivalent of the ruined and vanished glories of ancient Rome and Greece. They are the most impressive and enduring of the works of prehistoric Americans, outside of the cliff communities of the Southwest, north of the Valley of Mexico.

In his excellent and readable *Conquistadores Without Swords: Archaeologists in the Americas* (1968), Leo Deuel says:

From the days of the early Pilgrims onward, the "Mystery of the Mounds" was enshrined in the romance of prehistoric America. . . . usually the mounds were ascribed to one or another of the great civilizations of the Old World, while more imaginative antiquarians conjured up a primordial indigenous American man. At any rate, the view prevailed for a long time that northern America had been inhabited eons ago by a great vanished race, the so-called Mound Builders, who had unaccountably disappeared from the land even before the advent of the Indians.

This succinct précis has been expanded by Robert Silverberg, with equal excellence and readability, into the full-length book *Mound Builders of Ancient America: The Archaeology of a Myth* (1968). He examines the history of theory about the origin of Mound Builders, from the first white-supremacy-biased fancies that a group of the human race, dispersing after the Tower of Babel contretemps, had found its way to America, or vagrant Welsh or Romans or Scandinavians or Greeks or the last tribe of Dan had fled here (though some few also favored the less-than-lily-white Chinese or Polynesians or Egyptians), to the current knowledge about them: that there are four different kinds of mounds, barrows, tumuli, and earthworks, and four or five separate periods when they were built. Taken quite seriously in its day was the notion of Ignatius Donnelly, newspaperman and politician, that the survivors of the catastrophe that sank the lost continent of Atlantis under the sea had made it to America and become the Mound Builders. They even inspired some attempts at serious art.

"Behemoth" was the name given to a gigantic, rampaging mammoth which harried the Mound Builders in Cornelius Matthews's "Behemoth: A Legend of the Mound Builders" (1839), a valiant attempt to give America a native epic. It derives thematically from the myriad European folktales of lands being ravaged by dragons or other menacing monsters and being freed by St. George, or the Little Tailor; and had it been better written—much better written—we might be reading it today.

Of lasting impact was the Book of Mormon, which describes how, after the Confusion of Tongues, the Lord himself guided to America a colony of fleeing Israelites, called eponymously the Jaredites. These exiles built magnificent cities and filled the land with population, only to wipe themselves out in a great internecine battle said to have taken place in upstate New York. Came then another influx of Israelites, of the tribe of Joseph, in flight after the destruction of Jerusalem by Nebuchadnezzar; they also prospered and built mighty cities, to fill this depopulated country in which the Lord had taken such a personal interest. Factionalism soon developed, however, and the descendents of the prophet Lehi split into the Nephites, the good, God-fearing party, and the Lamanites, the recalcitrant idolators. For their impious ways the Lamanites were struck by the Lord with melanism, that is, their skins became darkened, though they could recover their former white hue by repentance. These, according to the Book of Mormon, which is held by Mormons to be of authority equal to that of the Bible, became what the pioneers were to know and fear as the murdering redskins, or Indians; the civilized, Caucasian-type Nephites were, of course, the Mound Builders. The inevitable war between the good Nephites and the bad Lamanites culminated in a battle on the same battleground as the first American Armageddon. But, because the Nephites had in the meantime fallen below the standards he expected of them, the Lord permitted them to be totally destroyed. The mounds are their tombs. But the Lord of Heaven was not to be put off by the two failures of his chosen ones. He had his angel, Mormon, reveal this history to Joseph Smith, a New York State farm boy, by way of appointing him to head a third effort at founding a godly society in the New World. Beautiful Salt Lake City testifies to the successful execution of Joseph Smith's mission; but the war between the light skins and the dark skins, if you want to carry the analogy that far, has begun to erupt again, in skirmishes throughout the nation.

It is most appropriate that the Mound Builders should have sowed the seeds of made-in-America religion, since, with the exception of some Ohio Hopewellian fortifications and the possible habitation embankments at Poverty Point, Louisiana, they were all erected out of a belief in the immortality of man's spirit and/or in the control by the Almighty or a pantheon of almighties over human destiny. The two great bird-effigy mounds at Poverty Point and the nearby conical funerary mound, with which are associated six concentric systems of embankments in an enormous arrangement of octagons (the outer octagon is three-quarters of a mile in diameter) suggest, in concept if not in exact plan, the great ceremonial centers of Mexico, like Monte Alban, heart of the Zapotecan church-state. The burial mounds erected by the Adena people bear witness to their belief in the transference of the spirit of the deceased to another world, and these burial mounds appear, rather more elaborately constructed, in the partly contemporary Hopewell culture. But the Hopewellians, who are the people with probably the best claim to the Mound Builder title, heaped up prodigious piles of earth, the only monumental building material they were equipped to work with, in intricate complexes of embankments, sometimes surrounding pyramids and other tumuli and sometimes not, to create what are generally regarded as "sacred precincts"—a way of saying they were temples without roofs.

Effigy mounds are those which have animal or bird shapes; the two bird effigies erected by the Poverty Point people, the earliest builders of mounds, have the distinction of being the first examples on record of three of the four principal types of earthen structures. They are religious in that, at the very least, they invoke the protection of the superspirit of the clan animal, or a zoomorphic supernatural power. The largest effigy mound is the Great Serpent Mound in Adams County, 1,254 feet long, 20 feet wide, and 5 feet high, considered to be of Adena construction; but smaller, less conspicuous effigies dot the Midwest by the thousands and were being built into historic times, possibly as property markers and certainly as talismanic guardians with inherent superhuman powers.

The religious motivation of the temple mounds of the Mississippi Valley and the Southeast, including Florida—the Adena and Hopewellian mounds are Ohio Valley phenomena—is implicit in their classification. They are pyramids on the order of ziggurats, rectangular though not usually square, with flat plaza tops whereon were erected wooden "temples" (by size they rate being called chapels only, but we incline, by education, to call any sacred place a temple if the worship there was "pagan") and other structures, probably the dwelling places of priests and headmen. Monks Mound in Madison County, Illinois, in the flood plain called the American Bottoms, where the Missouri and the Illinois rivers join the Mississippi at St. Louis, is not only the largest temple mound in North America but the largest earthen structure north of Mexico (the larger of the two Poverty Point bird-effigy mounds being the second largest). It is 790 feet east-west by 1,037 feet north-south, and 100 feet high, containing 21,976,000 cubic feet of earth, according to the latest calculations—there has been no significant erosion for at least a century—and it is so huge that the Illinois Park Department has built an automobile road to the top. But it is only one, though by far the largest, of some fifty-five mounds on the site, called Cahokia. One of the structures that was built on it was no chapel, however, covering a floor area of 11,347 square feet.

Even during the nineteenth-century era of wildcat speculation about aboriginal mounds, uninhibited by any excavated data, there were some who saw a relationship between the mounds of the United States and the great raised structures of Mexico, some of which are earthen, some stone, because of the ziggurat form. They were divided between those who saw the Mound Builders migrating to Mexico and carrying their building activities there to more splendid heights and those who saw the movement of population and earth heapers the other way. It is now incontestable that the ideas that produced the Mississippi period in the present United States arrived from Mexico by a route not visible to the archaeological eye, which means that they probably were transported across the Gulf of Mexico or along its shoreline in boats. But the Mississippian covers only the period of construction of temple mounds, the first one of which was built about A.D. 500. By this time the Hopewellian cultural climax had faded into oblivion, the Adenans were scattered, and the Poverty Point people of circa 1000 B.C. were long dead and forgotten. Where, then, originated the urge or sense of objective, uniting the Poverty Point, Adena, and Hopewell communities, to put forth the communal effort to build high on the earth?

The reader does not have to be told, not at this late date, that the first and for a long time the only idea that occurred to anyone was that mound building was a thought carried in somebody's head from somewhere in Asia. It had to have been a thought only, because there is no dotted line of mounds laying out a track across Canada, through Alaska, through the Chukotka, and into a cis-Asian home office. This idea produces exactly the same embarrassment suffered by the promoters of Asiatic originators for the big-game-hunting fad. Gathering together all the C14 dates relating to Poverty Point, Adena, and Hopewell, James Griffin, in his *Chronological Position of the Hopewellian Culture in the Eastern United States*" (1958), came to this conclusion: "The known time span of Hopewellian and the increasing evidence of a gradual cultural development, which differed in various geographic regions, have made all migration theories obsolete."

He meant not only migration from Asia but from Mexico and Central America. Poverty Point, Adena, and Hopewell have to be explained as having grown from seed to bud where they stand; only then may we look for evidences of cross-pollination.

How do we begin, as archaeologists, to find this seed? By defining the first evidence of the sentiments of religion that sought expression in mound building. We are not, in this chapter, merely tidying up the American prehistoric house by relating what followed the Archaic in the Eastern Woodlands. We are trying to understand prehistoric American society in its bone and spirit. It has been our objective from the beginning to discover what prehistoric Amerinds were like, and how they came to be; and we have discovered, in almost every instance, that they made themselves and their cultures out of the materials they found here—always assuming that they were fully human and, as such, innately disposed to act in certain ways when they came. That they eventually discovered in themselves and/or developed religious notions about the supernatural is not surprising in the least.

In the preceding chapter, the emphasis was on the evolution of food production to the agricultural stage, without which the complex social development we call civilization is not possible; civilization came into being in Mexico, Mesoamerica, and South America, as it did everywhere else in the world, as the expression of the idea that the production of food was as much a function of good relations with the supernatural, as maintained by a priesthood, as of planting and cultivating. There are no primitive atheistic societies; the supernatural, whatever the exact anthropomorphic or zoomorphic character this power is assumed to have, must always be propitiated and its benevolence sought. Only in our present state of knowledge about the mechanics and structure of the universe could the God-is-dead doctrine have arisen.

Man, in his weakness, first conceived of supernatural power, both benignant and maleficent, as emanating from beast gods, since the beasts of the earth were animate beings like himself, whose flesh fed him, on the one hand, and whose teeth and talons killed him, on the other, and whose attitudes toward him were enigmatic, to say the least. When, probably after the domestication of animals, the inferiority of beasts came to be understood, man came to think of the supreme power as being the fecundity of woman, to which he owed his individual being, and then as man, the inseminator of that fecundity. The first male gods were the Zeuses and Jupiters, gods of the thunderbolt and of divine caprice, followed by the Hebrew Jehovah, the stern deity of justice and of stone-engraved rules, and finally the grandfatherly figure of Christian iconography, with a long white beard, dressed in a Roman toga, who tempered justice with mercy. The explorations of the universe by cosmic physics can find neither a heavenly abiding place for this All Highest, whose name was once too dread and too sacred to be spoken, nor an active role for him to play in the operation of the system. He may have been the intelligence that conceived the universe according to the formula $E = MC^2$, with himself as the E of the equation, in which case we are back to that answer to the catechism question "Where is God?" which is "God is everywhere." But there is this difference: God is everywhere, not as the great overseer and recorder of personal conduct, but as the universal immanence and sustainer of the system, the substance of which it is created; he is the universe. A case could be made for this being nearer the feeling about divinity held by primitive societies than the Kingdom of God, with its divine Emperor surrounded by angelic servitors and saintly courtiers and populated by a citizenry whose loyalty to the sovereign has been tested and proved.

Until man attained self-consciousness—the realization that

he was an individual separate and apart from all other individuals, no matter how close the resemblance, that he was an agent responsible, physically if not morally, for actions he initiated, and that he had feelings, desires, and ideas that were entirely his own—there could be no religion. And if there are those who want to say, "*Vraiment*, this is what happened when Adam and Eve were cast out of Eden, and what you are talking about is really Original Sin," I will not deny that the punishment inflicted for the hubris of Original Sin is the awakening of the conscience. "The knowledge of good and evil" is the hair shirt of self-consciousness, by another, slightly different, name. The human race became psychically modern when it learned this about itself, and the secret seems to have been known for a very long time.

One might not think that this is a proper subject for archaeology, yet it is, and could not be otherwise. For, in what seems to have been an instantaneous reaction to the discovery of the personality within, the human mind conceived the notion that that personality would never die—was too precious, having once been summoned from the abysm of obliviousness, ever to be consigned to it again. To mark his belief in his immortality, according to whatever rite seemed most likely to insure for the deceased the honors and prestige earned in this life for the duration of its sequel, he began to bury his dead.

Interment is both a social act, recognizing the loss to the group of a contributing member, bound to every other member by ties of mutual obligation, and a reflex of self-consciousness: some day I, too, will lie there on the bier. Inhumation nowadays is as much a matter of health and sanitation as anything; in primitive society, when the corpse could easily have been disposed of by leaving it to vultures or other carrion eaters, to bury the dead was the ultimate tribute that could be paid to an individual—and to the concept of men as personalities, rather than man as a species. That it was a tribute of respect, not merely a do-unto-others routine, seems to be the meaning of the Neanderthal burial discovered by Solecki at Shanidar Cave; the skeletal remains of the deceased were discovered to be surrounded by the pollen of the flowers with which he had been either covered or surrounded. They were doing this about sixty thousand years ago, these first flower people, and were burying their dead perhaps as early as a hundred thousand years ago, with food and implements to see them through their first days in the next life. As the first certain believers in individual personality, they deserve to be classified *Homo sapiens*, no matter how their foreheads slanted.

These Neanderthal obsequies are found only in the Middle East and in Europe. The Far Eastern Neanderthals remained innocent of any such expression of feeling about death, as did their descendants, or whoever it was, who made it to America. As previously mentioned, it is at present impossible to know the physical anthropology of the earliest Amerinds, because of the paucity of osteological material. Since all of that material— Marmes man, Midland man, Tepexpán man, Minnesota man (a girl sometimes called Minnesota Minnie) the Vero Beach and Melbourne, Florida, fragments—has been the remains of victims of fatal accidents who died where their bones were found, it is a highly probable conclusion that interment was not a habit at that time level.

Intentional, ceremonial burial appears first among the early Archaic usufructians, and, as might have been expected, in caves. What may be the earliest is found in Graham Cave, where an adult of, as nearly as could be determined, the 9700 B.P. occupant group had been laid away with a slab of limestone under his shoulders and another over his face; with him was a perforated wolf canine, a possible antler flaking tool, a bone awl, a hammerstone, a projectile point, and a worked chunk of hematite, an iron ore used for tools and as a source for red paint. In the Stanfield-Worley Rock Shelter, two burials were found with Morrow Mountain projectile points which would date them at about 6000 B.P. These are examples of a rather more ritual kind of burial than the skull at Hogup Cave found wedged in a crevice in the rock and the bone pile found in Hawver Cave, California, at the bottom of a deep cleft, merely stowed, it seems, beyond the reach of immediate animal despolation. What was general, then, during the Archaic, is going to be forever impossible to say. Undoubtedly

thousands of interments will never be discovered, and other
thousands have moldered away without trace, leaving us to
wonder whether only some groups honored their dead by inhumation; whether some interred and others made other dispositions, such as elevated exposure; whether only the revered,
or favored, were given special funeral attention; and, finally,
what ritual disposal of the dead by any means conveys about a
sense of religion. But it can be said that intentional burial with
evidences of ritual does seem frequent enough during the Early
and Middle Archaic to give us to think that it originated among
the usufructians in Meridional America and that it was insti-
gated by the metaphysical motives arising from religious
concepts.

The thread of evidence of mortuary rite that we want to pick
up begins at the Renier, Wisconsin, site mentioned a few chapters ago. Here, in 1959, Ronald Mason and Carol Irwin found
a most interesting association of the base of a side-notched point
of the Big Sandy theme, which apparently originates among
the Eastern Woodland usufructians, and fragments of fine paral-
lel-ripple-flaked Eden and Scottsbluff points of late big-game
hunters with the cremation burial of a young man. The situation, with a concentration of fire-cracked rock, gives a picture
of the cremation of a skeleton, rather than a corpse, and the
intentional inclusion with the remains of "killed" artifacts, that
is, artifacts deliberately broken to release their spirits, or included because they were already broken and thus were "dead."

The practice of elevated exposure of corpses, usually on scaf-
folds, until the flesh has entirely disintegrated followed by cremation of the remains is of wide distribution and is documented
into historic times. The Iroquois periodically, about every five
years, collected the stripped skeletons of the deceased of the
community, threw them all together in a huge ossuary pit, lined
with fur robes or skins, and a miscellany of grave goods or
"furniture," ranging from medicine bags to kettles, and then
buried them. At Renier we probably have the earliest example
of cremation of a skeleton after exposure, and certainly this was
not the first, though Mason and Irwin date it at between 8000
and 6000 B.P. (with the older date the likeliest) by reason of

the presence of the Eden and Scottsbluff points, which are no-where else any younger than that.

But, always on the lookout for a clue to a thesis, we ought not to overlook the presence of the side-notched point. There is, of course, the explanation that will occur to a novelist: the young man was the offspring of an Eden-Scottsbluff big-game-hunting father and a mother coaxed or stolen away from a band of the resident population, who were makers of side-notched points. That they were contemporaries we know from several sites, including the Raddatz Rock Shelter of Wisconsin. The side-notched-point base, we will conceive, was thrown on the pyre as a memento of the young man's maternal heritage. Such things happen, and mothers do act this way.

We are also not precluded from suspecting that the big-game hunters who, in Wisconsin, are somewhat eastward of their wonted territory and within that frequented by the Raddatz side-notched-point people, may have been so impressed by ritual burial customs or attitudes of the established population that they emulated them; at the moment this is the only big-game-hunter ritual burial on record.

The Renier site demands our attention because it lies within the territory of the Old Copper culture, the first cultural focus in Meridional America to be distinguished for something other than stone work, whose people almost started a metal age and who were the first Amerinds to collect their dead in cemeteries. Two of these, at Oconto and Osceola, Wisconsin, have been excavated by Warren Wittry, who dug the Raddatz Rock Shelter, and Robert Ritzenthaler. Using first the native, almost 100-percent-pure copper occurring as glacially transported pebbles, and then copper quarried from the traprock outcrops on the Keweenaw Peninsula of Michigan and in Isle Royale in Lake Superior north of that peninsula, the Archaic stone-pro-jectile-point-making people of the region hammered out an inventory of tools and other items, beginning at about $7,510 \pm 340$ years ago, like nothing anywhere else in the world except in the Near East during what is called the Chalcolithic. Chalcolithic means, simply, the working of copper as though it were a special kind of stone and not as a metal which can be heated to the melting point and molded and alloyed. Whereas in the Near East the brief Chalcolithic phase was merely preliminary to the Bronze Age, the first of the metallurgical periods, when copper was alloyed with locally available tin and molded into tools and ornaments, the Old Copper American Chalcolithic, on approximately the same time level, went no further than hammering the soft copper nuggets into shape, either cold or after below-melting-point heating.

Old Copper-culture tools, and tools of native copper from the restricted Michigan area where they were to be had, like nuts, for the stooping down and picking up, had long been known to collectors, museums, and archaeologists. But the concept of an Old Copper culture, making, not copies in copper of tools and other items originally made of chipped stone, but new tool forms and even tools for new uses possible only in hammered copper, was an overlong time in taking shape. The reader will not gasp with amazement to learn that the first pronouncement about the Old Copper was that its routes of origin led back through Alaska and into the garden of Asia. The route was made plausible by sporadic finds of copper among late Canadian Indians and by the existence of an historic group called the Copper Eskimos who lived on the Coppermine River, where copper occurred as it did in Michigan and Isle Royale, and who as late as this century made tools of Old Copper type by traditional hammering methods. Taken with the occurrence of copper tools at post-Archaic Hopewell and Adena sites, this evidence pointed to a late arrival in America of an old-fashioned Chalcolithic practice, no later than, say, three thousand years ago.

No bells were rung, therefore, to announce the joyous arrival of truth and enlightenment when Wittry and Ritzenthaler announced that two C_{14} dates had been obtained on Oconto-cemetery charcoal, one of which was 7,510 ± 340 years and the other 5,600 ± 400 years. Instead of at least preferring the younger of the two, for which there was good reason, the academic establishment closed ears and doors to both and waited for the echoes to die down. At the time, 1956, it did seem that the 5,600-year age was the more reliable: it had been run on a single sample from a grave, whereas the 7,510-year result had come from a mixed- or composite-sample charcoal from two graves thought to be approximately contemporary. But the researches of the last ten years have been so kind to the older date that it is the younger which seems to have suffered from contamination toward recency.

In the first place, the Old Copper people made their stone projectile points in the side-notched Big Sandy pattern. Those found in graves are very handsome and may have been special mortuary pieces. The points in association with habitation debris are less well made, but the basic design idea of notching a preform blade in from the side is clearly executed. We know, from the survey of Archaic point patterns on which so much time has already been spent, that side notching of blades is at least eight thousand years old, from the Stanfield-Worley Rock Shelter in Alabama to the Modoc Rock Shelter in Illinois to the Simonsen site in Iowa to the Renier site. In addition, the side-notched points found by Wittry at Raddatz are so like the Old Copper points that he considered it necessary to write an apology for setting up a new Raddatz type; he considers the Raddatz Rock Shelter to be a probable occupation or hunting-camp site of the Old Copper people, with side-notched points showing up there at about 7500 B.P.

And, furthermore, George I. Quimby, in rummaging through some old reports from the 1930's, learned that in 1918 the geologic survey of Canada had reported the find of a copper spearpoint some forty feet below surface in Kaministikwa Valley, Ontario, in association with animal bones. The bones are apparently of extinct bison and the American horse. Thus the Old Copper culture must be an approximate contemporary of the Coxcatlán, or first corn phase, of the Tehuacán Valley.

What we found ourselves tracing in Mexico was a slow but steady growth in population, as nutrition improved with the domestication of squash, beans, and corn; a change in living pattern from seasonal shifting to fixed villages; and a complication of social structure resulting from both the more numerous population and the changed relations of the members of the population to each other and a developing new entity, a supersociety or "state." In the Old Copper area there was no change at all in food production from usufructianism—no domestication of any local plant, no mannalike new plant, nothing new at all save, possibly, a greater bounty of the native fruits of the earth by reason of a climatic optimum. Yet there was a cultural yeast at work on the population, for Wittry and Ritzenthaler estimate at least five hundred burials in the Osceola cemetery and probably a like number at Oconto, of "great diversity in burial types," but all in pits or graves.

Not too much should be made of the numbers; they almost certainly do not mean, not at this early date, that these were the cemeteries of populous villages such as only agriculture could support. They were the accumulation over centuries of the dead of mobile bands of the vicinity in traditional hallowed ground. But a great deal can be made of the continuity of the tradition so saliently different from everything else in the hemisphere and so technologically and societally on the move. It is a nice point whether coppersmithing was the natural result of a vigorous people very much at home in and adjusted to their copper-rich environment, or whether the spread of it over the area of occurrence of free copper drew scattered bands into a cultural and social harmony. If the Old Copper culture were only a bag of tools, however strikingly they contrast with the others of their time, it could be written off as an industrial sport stimulated by the peculiarly local occurrence of copper nuggets; but the accompanying cemeteries give us an entirely different view of its constitution. What we are bound to call religious impulses were released or awakened—without, it must be pointed out again, any change in food production—and it is reasonable to deduce that copper assumed some of the sacred character that corn had among its cultivators, or at least the properties of a powerful medicine. Man advanced toward civilization not only across fields of grain or between corn rows. It gives one to wonder what would have happened in the Old Copper homeland if there had been nearby deposits of tin. There might have been an American Bronze Age before there was a Neolithic, and metallurgy before farming.

It is just a little upsetting to a sense of congruity to come upon Old Copper-industry metal artifacts and realize that they were made by Stone Age people; there is a medieval look about them, and you can't help flights of fancy. Surely, you say to yourself, these are the tools of a haughty superior race who came marching into the forests inhabited by simple hunting and gathering folk who could not muster the force to resist and set up an arrogant and exploiting overlordship. A survey in 1929 listed some twenty thousand Old Copper artifacts of twenty-one general types as having been collected from Wisconsin alone. Since then, the area of provenience has been enlarged to include Minnesota, Iowa, Michigan, Manitoba, Illinois, and Ohio; the number of examples has more than doubled; and the number of types has been increased.

According to David L. Schroeder and Katherine C. Ruhl, who in 1967 made an analysis of the metallurgic characteristics of Old Copper tools, "The Indians appreciated some of the properties of copper and made use of these in shaping tools, weapons and ornaments of high quality workmanship," by the thousands, "beautifully shaped." They include awls, socketed and shanked projectile points, pike heads, gaff hooks, fishhooks, socketed spuds, celts, several kinds of knives, spatulas, ornamental crescents, clasps, rolled sheet-copper beads, a probable bracelet, and a finger ring. Rumors of this gleaming wealth and the people who possessed it must have spread throughout Aonao, The Land, as the later Iroquois called it, and not only of the wealth and the people, but of their practices and beliefs.

The Old Copper people were not the innovators of ritual burial, though there is an outside chance that the Renier cremation falls within the Old Copper era and is a component of at least its burial complex; but in the Osceola, Oconto, and Reigh (dug in 1953 by David Baerris and others) cemeteries was found nearly every kind of burial ever used by Amerinds: individual burial in the flesh, reburials of defleshed bones in bundles, single cremations, multiple cremations, burials with and without grave goods, and red-ocher burials, that is, burials of a corpse or skeleton sprinkled with red ocher or other red pigment. Here was the mortuary capital of Archaic America and, in consideration of what we have taken that to mean, a religious center—not in the sense of a Mecca visited by pilgrims,

though there were probably individual truth seekers who jour-
neyed there to observe and learn (the great Iroquoian religious
leader of much later times, the half-legendary Hiawatha, made
a trip west in search of enlightenment, it is told), but in the
sense of a lamp diffusing light.

It will be one of the major archaeological tasks of the next
decades to determine how influential the Old Copper culture was
in the prehistory of the Eastern Woodlands. If its span lies
within the C14 dates from Oconto of 7500 B.P. and 5600 B.P.,
then there is a long blank in the record between its termination
or decline and that of the next burial-cult phase at about 4500
B.P., the phase that gives us the ceremonial burial sites of the
Red Earth people of Illinois, the Glacial Kame people of Ohio,
the Laurentians of the Northeast, and the Red Paint people of
Maine.

The most vivid example of this blank lies in the Northeast, rather than in Wisconsin. Already mentioned has been the
morphological first-cousinship of the Raddatz-Osceola side-
notched points and the Otter Creek type found most abundantly
in the Lake Champlain, St. Lawrence, and Ottawa river valleys
(the St. Lawrence gives the whole Laurentian aspect its name).
Within the Vergennes focus of the Laurentian, to which the
Otter Creek has been assigned, is a broad range of copper
tools: toggled and socketed spearheads, spearheads with spurs
and shanks, awls, knives, spuds, gorges (a fisherman's item),
bracelets, and pendants. The richest sites of this Northeast Old
Copper are on Alumette and Morrison islands in the Ottawa
River, causing Ritchie, whose construct the Laurentian is, to
conclude, "It seems now fairly certain that the Ottawa Valley
was a very important, if not the major route of dissemination,
for the elements of the Old Copper industry of the Upper Great
Lakes area which have been found in Laurentian contexts in the
Northeast." The identity of these Northeasterners as advance
men of the Old Copper culture is not in doubt, therefore. Copper
tools they made, of Michigan or Wisconsin copper, but they did
not bury their dead; or if they did, it was not in cemeteries.

Wittry and Ritzenthaler remark, "Comparisons of the burial
complex of the Oconto site reveal close parallels in the burials of

the Brewerton foci [of the Laurentian aspect] of the New York Archaic." And again, "On the whole the Archaic burial complexes of the northern areas of Wisconsin and New York seem to be more closely related to each other than to those of the southeastern Archaic. There are, however, differences in physical type between these early populations."

It is the last sentence which puts the finger on the puzzle: the physical type buried at Oconto is longheaded, while the Laurentian physical type is roundheaded; the Oconto burials are dated 5600 B.P. at the latest, while the Laurentian burials with which they are compared are, at about 4500 B.P., almost a thousand years later.

Let us step outside the walls of hard archaeological evidence and take a speculative breath of fresh air. What were those Old Copper colonials doing in the Northeast? We can use a textbook response and say that population in the Wisconsin-Michigan region had grown to the limits of the environment's ability to support it in the manner to which it had become accustomed, and that some of the less-prospering groups departed for the great unspoiled East. Or we can note the failure of these expatriates to engage in sacred-ground interment and wonder if they were not truant groups of the disaffected. (It was under similar circumstances that the Pilgrims, and others, did an even longer walkout, across the Atlantic.) Perhaps they were outcasts, invited to move on, but this would need to have been by a more powerful central authority than could have existed at the time. Let us assume, therefore, that they went willingly, to remove themselves from the influence of a cult or leaders with which or whom they were in disagreement. Let us assume, further, that there were many others who found the cult onerous or its leaders unbearable who did not move and who simply turned their backs on the cultists and backslid into the contemporary equivalent of paganism.

The one reason that prehistorians would accept for the disintegration of the Old Copper culture, defined as a copper-working industry and related burial tradition, is, of course, a depression of climate. But a depression of climate need be no more than a couple of weeks long. To illustrate: *The New*

York Times of Sunday, September 22, 1968, carried a special
from Asheville, North Carolina, headed "Squirrels Starving in
Smokies Area." It related how squirrels were dying by the thousands either from starvation or from being run over by cars as
they left their woodlands in search of food; cornfields, orchards,
and even kitchen gardens were being invaded in the frantic
forage for day-to-day food and winter storage. T. N. Massie of
the North Carolina Wildlife Resources Commission called the
famine-emergency migration "the most extensive" he had ever
seen; on the threshold of winter, the squirrel population faced
disaster. The cause of it all was a late April freeze that had
killed off the year's crop of acorns, walnuts, and hickory nuts.

When people depended like squirrels on this kind of food to
tide them over the hard months, they would have been little
better off than the squirrels of the Great Smokies in 1968. Four
or five repetitions of this maladjustment of weather and growing season, of no lasting consequence to the forests themselves
and only a statistically expectable fluctuation in a normal
climate, could dissolve the loose tendrils by which usufructian
bands were beginning to entwine themselves into a society.
When the food environment failed, then the social environment
failed; but the latter is an entirely new kind of environment and
must now be accounted for in cultural equations.

The practice of burial in community holy ground must have
been supported, directed, and underlain by an ideology, both a
system of mythocosmology and a ritual sanctioned by it; but
such systems and rituals are always in the keeping of special
individuals—priests, shamans, medicine men, or however it is
the custom to designate them. The very real function of shamans is to make sure that the community is in such rapport
with the powers who are dominant in the mythocosmos that its
welfare, paramountly its food supply, is assured. It is possible,
therefore, to blame a series of calamities—killing frosts, plagues,
epidemics—on the failure of the shaman, or on the overthrow
of the community's gods by other gods, or on evil powers within
the same mythocosmos. The Iroquois, for instance, believed in a
Lucifer, called Tawiskaron, who was the bad twin of the Christ-
like son of the goddess Teharonhiawagon; and their demonology

zoomorphized or anthropomorphized harmful natural forces that would certainly have frightened Iroquois children into silence until the age of twelve: the Flying Heads (mysterious disappearance), the Great Mosquito (the mosquito plague), the Flint Coats (blizzards), and the Great Bear and the Serpent of the Lake (wasting disease).

The shaman always had the advantage of being able to protect himself, if he were at all canny, in ascribing calamity to failure of observance of taboos or prescribed rituals—as long as he was dealing with a guilt-susceptible people who believed in him personally. But even such people will turn away from the medicine men when nature, in an evil mood, exposes them for the false prophets, though not necessarily charlatans, they are. The evidence of shamanism in the Old Copper culture is not overwhelming: there are copper items of which the purpose is not known—the crescents, for example; but mainly there is a flute or whistle made of the leg bone of a trumpeter swan. It may be only a musical instrument, and then again it may be a shaman's pipe and/or sucking tube, the latter an instrument with the well-documented purpose of sucking the evil spirit out of the ill or afflicted. (The tobacco pipe—and as an inveterate pipe smoker, I am sometimes uncomfortably aware of this when a pipe stops up suddenly on an indraft—is believed to be a development of the sucking tube, the intermediate stage being the cigar-shaped blocked-end pipe, usually of Portsmouth fireclay or pipestone. Probably at this stage shamans were only learning their trade, which more nearly resembles that of the club magician-ventriloquist than the priest-celebrant of sacred mysteries.)

Along with the probably precarious position of shamans and the mythology they served, we must also consider that ideologies also have their cycles: early zealotry, followed by establishment as an orthodoxy, followed by sterility, resistance, and reform or rejection. If the span of the Old Copper culture is the nineteen hundred years from 7500 to 5600 B.P.—the beginning date is not as questionable as the final one—this is very nearly the span of Christianity. Its cosmology and theology—that is, the position of man in a geocentric universe, God's intentions

in creating it, man's delinquency and present trial existence—
became during those nineteen hundred years the established
dogma of the Western world, despite schisms over dogma. But
it will have to be admitted that over the past three or four
decades, Christian fundamentalist cosmology and theology have
been left little substance by science, and the last decade has seen
reforms and revisions that a fifty-year-old man would have
thought in his youth to be impossible. But it is no more possible
for religion to remain unchanged than for projectile points,
people, or society to go on forever the same; and once we see
Amerind bands drawing together into a tentative community,
the centripetal force of which is religion, we must assume that
there will take place the whole round of change to which this
aspect of environment is subject.

Nearly a millennium elapsed, then, between the end of the Old
Copper society, as archaeologically apparent, and the next positive evidence of communal burial practices, but it is clear that
the practice of ritual burial must have been kept alive somehow
in the North Central states and in the Northeast. Though the
Laurentian burials, to which the Oconto burials were compared,
are not the best examples of the new phase, they do provide
the link with the old. The new phase is probably best exemplified by a 1966–67 excavation by the Cohannet Chapter of the
Massachusetts Archaeological Society, with Maurice Robbins in
charge of the dig, of a charnel house at the Wapanucket site
on Assawampsett Pond, near the base of Cape Cod, Massachusetts.

During the early and middle 1950's, the Cohannet Chapter
had excavated a village site in the Wapanucket area C_{14}-dated
at about 4300 B.P., which was at that time the earliest true village on American prehistoric record and something of a refuta-
tion of the long-standing prejudice against permanent housing
for Middle Archaic Amerinds. There were seven lodges in the
settlement, approximately round, six of them from about thirty
to forty-five feet in diameter and the seventh, apparently a
council house, about sixty-six feet in diameter. Within the village boundaries were three cremation pits lined with sandstone,
from eight to twelve feet in diameter, in the charcoal and ash

of which occurred grave goods—only stone pieces, of course, surviving. Three cremation burials, apparently of the calcined remains from the crematories, also were within the community environs. Around 1962 another cremation pit was discovered, about a thousand feet from the village site, this one containing some handsome flint blades so large (about seven inches long) and so obviously unused that they had probably been made especially for the funeral occasion. (The manufacture of fine pieces to accompany burials is an outstanding Hopewell trait, which was carried to such extremes that apparently the whole Hopewell artistic genius went into preparation for death.) Red ocher had been sprinkled on the bone ash after the crematory fire had died down.

The charnel house was also about a thousand feet from the village, with the site designation of Wapanucket No. 6. It was a pit about three feet deep and twenty-five feet wide by thirty-five feet long in plot plan, with ramps leading into it from the north and south ends. Within the pit were stone slabs, eleven cremation burials, and grave goods of polished stone gouges, whetstones, a stone knife, projectile points, a polished stone "plummet," and lumps of red hematite, with "copious red paint" —probably ocher and hematite—spread over all. Some sort of structure—let us call it a temple, since it was roofed—in plan some sixty feet by sixty-five feet, judging by the post molds, had been erected about the pit; it had two doorways corresponding with the ramps. If one had to choose the ancestral prototype for the Hopewell burial rites of two thousand years later, with their cremation in large pits with puddled clay floors, red paint, and grave goods, including retainers or relatives of the deceased, this would be the perfect choice. The difference is that the Hopewellians erected log tombs about this charnel floor and buried it under an earthen mound.

The C14 age on the charnel house was 4,290 ± 140 years, almost the exact date of Wapanucket No. 6. One sees here, as a result of Robbins's excavations, a very rapidly elaborating ceremonial-burial tradition: from open-pit cremations no different from that at Renier, but with reburial of the remains, to a pyre in a special enclosed and roofed mortuary, which was the structural equivalent of the group's homes and principal building. Wapanucket No. 6 gives us to think that it must have been a stable and populous-enough community, in a reliable food-producing environment, to have gone in for such a social activity. Each of the six lodges probably housed a family that would have been, under more nomadic usufructian circumstances, a band of from 15 to 30 persons. The population at any one time might have numbered from 100 to 150, and the council-house village center gives the strong impression of a developing community government, in which the village fathers met and performed legislative, judicial, and administrative duties. The axiom that explains all this is: As economic autonomy increases, social autonomy increases.

The stone artifacts found as grave goods and in the village debris are very much in the Laurentian tradition, of which the Vergennes is the presently understood first phase. The chipped stone-projectile-point forms have evolved, to be sure, but the diagnostic polished stone tools, shaped by rubbing or abrading, are the same in form if not in full variety: gouges for woodworking, "plummets" of unknown purpose but thought to be fish gorges, bannerstones (atlatl weights), adzes, grooved axes, slate spearheads, and, above all, semilunar knives, so called because of their half-moon outline. What is to be read from the continuity of the polished-stone industry is that the new phase of ritual burial is an adapted or revived practice. There has been no disturbance of the long-resident local population, no invasion, no moving over to make room for immigrants, no hint of conquest. The burial cult and its embellishments were something itinerate, perhaps being "preached" through the region to communities now willing to listen and socially stable and vigorous enough not only to perform the rituals but to remember them as traditions. Diffusion by peaceable contact will suffice, perhaps, as an explanation for archaeological journalism. But one cannot help but wonder who made the contacts and how they were made.

Although our oyster eaters of the lower Hudson are of the same epoch as the Frontenac-Brewerton burials and the Wapanucket cult, we have not discovered, nor is there a report of anybody else's having discovered, intentional burial even, to say nothing of cult practices. This could not have been for lack of contact. I have found, for instance, from a site at the mouth of the Croton River (now the property of the Rockefeller-funded Van Cortlandt Manor Restoration) a deliberately halved ground-slate semilunar knife, and from other sites a smattering of Laurentian points and artifacts. The operative conclusion is that there was a boundary between the Laurentian and the distinctive culture of the oyster eaters that we call the Taconic at about the northern limit of oyster growth and that the burial ideology did not cross it. Perhaps the Taconic people were not in a state of social organization to adopt it; on the other hand, it is very likely that had they adopted it, the social organization to practice it would have followed on the adoption. What we see, therefore, is that the carriers, the missionaries of the burial cult, were not permitted to cross the boundary.

Those who are familiar with the literature on pioneer times west of the Appalachians—Conrad Richter's *The Trees* and Hervey Allen's trilogy *The Forest and the Fort, Bedford Village*, and *Toward the Morning* give their flavor—know what kind of community event was the arrival of the peripatetic preacher. Families were loaded into jolt wagons, or took to their horses and mules, or simply walked from miles and miles around, to come to the "preachin'," for what was a complex psychological experience that combined lecture, recreation and socializing, spiritual uplift, and the excitement of the emotions starved for drama. This kind of event, "the revival," was still seasonally recurrent in the Midwest of my youth, and I remember the storied Billy Sunday coming to our town, and the week—or fortnight, if the money was rolling in—of the fever of religiosity with which he inoculated the populace. One may look back on those days with amusement at the flamboyance of those spellbinders, and with anger at their shoddy and cynical bilking of simple people starved for spiritual exaltation; but they were, in anthropological parlance, agents of diffusion of cult—or, more properly, sect—ideologies and the masters of ceremony of affairs of high sociological potency.

I am not quite suggesting that burial-cult proselytizing was carried on by Billy Sunday-like shamans, but I am highly suspicious of cant abstractions like diffusion. Somebody who believed in these doctrines and who knew the formulas, the rubrics, had to explain them to those who did not. And those who sat through the explanation were under no constraint to believe, unless there was persuasion by demonstration and emotional appeal. The sectarian showman and the cult shaman are as alike in function as they are homonymously, and in their day served the purpose of what we now know as "media."

The second-phase burial cult, to repeat, extended from about the Iowa-Illinois border eastward across the Great Lakes corridor into Maine, along a trail of red "paint," ocher or hematite. The use of red paint in burials is as old as the Neanderthal, where it had, we deduce, the naïve poetic-literal symbolism we call magic: the same mysterious property that made blood red also made the pigment material red, and that property, which the pallid corpse had lost in death, could be restored by replacement from another source. (One would guess that the flowers placed around the Neanderthal corpse found by Solecki were red.) Still, that there is the slightest relation between Neanderthal red-ocher burials, or any such found in the Old World, and this apparently sudden popularity of red pigments is out of the question. We must keep the record straight.

Oswaldo Menghin of the Museo Etnográfico, Universidad de Buenos Aires, on a field trip through Patagonia in early 1951, found ten caves in the Rio Descado mountains, several of which had paintings of animals, symbols, and human hands on their walls. Two caves were excavated, and in the bottom of one was an artifactual association consisting of a paint-grinding mano, fragments of ocher, and fragments of a stone plaque with streaks of red paint on it; this combined evidence of paint gave Menghin to think that the pictographs had been done by the first cave occupants. Their spearpoints were diagnostic, the same expanded-stemmed or fishtail-form Bird had found at Fell's Cave at the southern tip of South America, which were dated circa 10,000 B.P. Since then (1957), further work had been done in Fell's Cave by the French archaeologist Joseph Emperaire and his wife (Emperaire died an archaeologist's death on this expedition, when a trench wall collapsed on him); and more fishtail points turned up, stained with red paint.

Of auxiliary interest to our general thesis was the isolation by Menghin of a "rudimentary stone industry from several sites [in the same area] typologically similar to that at Chou-kou-tien." This industry occurred among surface finds. Also to the point was the cave industry just above the fishtail points, of simple technology "comprised entirely of flakes with retouched edges." This Patagonian pattern of early settlement has been inexplicably ignored as a reference and premise. The failure to pursue it in the field is not so incomprehensible: not many archaeologists could promote the funds to explore Patagonia.

The use of red paint as a patent magic has been in America for a long time, but for hunting and living only, not for burials. There can be no suggestion of either a trade or trait relationship between these ultra–South American pigmentations and the cult of the Great Lakes. To call spontaneous the idea of applying the magic of redness to corpses and skeletons would be to guess, on the absence of evidence to the contrary; but it had been spontaneous once, among the Neanderthals. A second and independent "inspiration," granting the Amerind mind the same quality of imagination, is not too much to posit.

The particular archaeological manifestation of the widespread red-paint burial cult on which we will focus, because it occurs most spectacularly on the periphery of the Adena and Hopewell Mound Builder centers in Ohio, because it dates to the Adena era, and because it obviously contributed to both Adena and Hopewell, is the Glacial Kame culture. Known best from Ohio, it had, like the Old Copper culture, at least one outpost in the Northeast, in Vermont, where in the early 1960's Ritchie excavated the remnants of a Glacial Kame concentration, rather than cemetery, of burials.

Glacial Kame burials are always found thus, in remnants. The definition of *kame* is "a ridge or mound of detrital material, especially of stratified sand and gravel left by a retreating ice sheet." Such sorted sands and gravels are commercially valuable, and all Glacial Kame burials on record have been first uncovered by gravel-pit excavation, there being no above-the-

surface markers for these, the last of the non-mound burials.
Kames and eskers, deposits of outwash gravels from glacial-
melt streams, are not only easy to dig into but have excellent
subsurface drainage; but whether this latter advantage had anything to do with the choice of kames and eskers as burial
ground is not likely ever to be known.

In 1961 Raymond S. Baby, Ohio State Archaeologist, reported
on the salvage of a Glacial Kame burial locus discovered during
commercial sand and gravel operations in Logan County, Ohio.
By the time the official archaeological party arrived, only ten
burials, with twenty-three skeletons and some stray bones, remained of what had been extensive inhumations. The artifacts
with the burials included spoons of the shells of freshwater
mussels, shell beads and shell gorgets, copper beads, birdstones
(polished stone effigies of birds, usually stylized, of unknown
usage), bannerstones, and the inevitable bone awls. Later the
Ritchie excavation in Vermont turned up (in red-paint burials)
the same inventory, except that the shell was marine, plus copper adzes and cubes of galena, the shiny lead ore. All of these
items continue into Adena, which immediately follows the
Glacial Kame phase.

But the two most surprising Adena-like artifacts found at the
Logan County site were wolf skulls. They were artifacts by
reason of having been worked, the protuberances smoothed
down by cutting, breaking, and scraping, and by reason of their
having had a known purpose: they were mask-headdresses, with
the hide on, the wolf's-head regalia of shamans, as had already
been shown by excavation.

Now we have the explicit evidence of what everything else
about cult burial has alerted us to look for: the medicine men,
the priestcraft, the promoters and promulgators, the men at the
controls and their means of staying there. Almost as explicit is
caste burial, the elaborate ceremonial burial of chief men and
their lineage (assumed from the frequent occurrence of child
burials), with humbler interment for the rank and file. There
is no question about the Glacial Kame wolf heads: both wolf
and cougar skulls were used as mask-headdresses by shamans,

and Hopewell priests wore hoods of hide, trimmed with sewn-on pieces of human skull.

It is not too daring, I think, to surmise backward into Renier time, when the medicine man would be a working member of a hunting band, with the part-time function of incantation for good luck before the hunt and of prescribing the ritual at burial, after which he picked up his weapons and went out with his fellows to prey. Such bands could not afford a noncontributing member. But by Glacial Kame times, the medicine man had worked his way up to professional status, consulting on personal problems of love and fortune for a fee and being supported by the community for more general services in thaumaturgy, divination, and the supervision of the annual ritual round. Moreover, by this time, the sorcerer or shaman was probably becoming a political potentate, determining in some measure what the community should do with its labor and time.

The building of mounds over graves, which differentiates Glacial Kame from Adena in what is clearly a cultural continuum, did not require in its lowly beginnings, as Don Dragoo has pointed out in his *Mounds for the Dead: An Analysis of Adena Culture*, any great or sustained community effort. The first burial in the Cresap Mound, near Natrium, West Virginia, excavated by Dragoo, was nothing more than a shallow crematory basin, much like the charnel-house pit at Wapanucket, in which two adults had been placed, with enough earth over them for cover. This first "mound" could hardly have been more than a foot high, if that, and the Cresap Mound reached its final dimensions of seventy feet in diameter and seventeen feet in height only after repeated burials over several hundred years. Among the Adenans, mound building was a practice on the occasion of a funeral; but among the Hopewellians, with their engineered earthworks and barrows in grand designs, it was an industry, in which forced or tributary labor was organized and directed in the production of monuments that were not utilitarian, except as they were presumed to be pleasing to the supernatural powers of earth and air, because the ruling priestly caste of the church-state so decreed. The Hopewellian decline, after five hundred years of viability, was probably due to complex causes, among which the oppressiveness of a priestly tyranny may not have been the least.

Such undemonstrable conclusions aside, what we are witnessing in the slow efflorescence of burial practices, until they become the whole preoccupation not only of the community but of a coalescence of communities, is the development of the church-state just as it developed in the Near East. Apparently it is the natural and inevitable first form of polity, and we have it with us yet.

If we pay close attention to Dragoo's analysis of the Cresap Mound, we note that there is no sign that it was intentionally begun as a mound. It is an accretion of interments in the same spot, a kind of multistory cemetery, with annexes, a high-rise mortuary. What brought it into being as a mound was the preference of the Adenans of this vicinity for burials in what has to be interpreted not just as a sacred or hallowed locality— grove, field, soil deposit—but as a point at the crossing of lines of influence. In this sense the Adenans may not have been intentional mound builders at all, or at least not until the Hopewellians, who later became their contemporaries, or somebody else, introduced formalized earth heaping. The "somebody else" may have been the Poverty Point people.

Up to this moment we have not had to reach outside the North Central-Northeast region for an explanation of anything that occurred within the region, considered as a cultural province that defines itself by its burial traditions. There are positive reasons why we need not. The opinion has long been held that the Adenans, a roundheaded race, were of a strain originally established in Mexico and Central America and that they must have migrated as a people or infiltrated up the river valleys into Ohio, seating themselves in the ancestral territory of the longheaded pre-Hopewellians and Hopewellians. But how is the ancestry of the Hopewellians known?

Wittry and Ritzenthaler selected from their Old Copper-culture cemeteries one male skull from Osceola and one male and four female skulls from Oconto and submitted them for examination to George K. Neumann, one of the two or three foremost authorities on Amerind physical anthropology. Neumann's report states, according to Wittry and Ritzenthaler, that "in the light of the radiocarbon dates this is the most ancient cranial material that can be demonstrated to represent a variety of American Indian which can be linked to the Black Sand focus people of Illinois, the later Hopewellians of the Ohio and Illinois Valleys and the historic Delaware Indians." Craniometrically, they were longheaded, that is, the axis of their head width was less than 75 percent of the axis of their head length.

But the Adenans were broadheaded. Undoubtedly this was due in part to deliberate deformation by binding the head during infancy, and we may have an unbalanced view of Adenans because the skeletal remains recovered may be those of chief men whose bound heads were a caste attribute. Nevertheless, it seems certain that they were invaders into longhead territory. The question is, however, when? The Adenan sphere of influence is the Ohio Valley within 150 miles of the Adenan "capital" at Chillicothe, Ohio, on the Scioto River; and the most intensively occupied territory lies within an arc to the south, from West Virginia to western Kentucky. Portsmouth, Ohio, is about 50 miles south of Chillicothe, where the Scioto enters the Ohio; its environs, particularly on the Kentucky side of the Ohio, are thick with evidence of Adenan settlement. And this is exactly the area that is thickest with the stemmed points of the Friendship tradition described in an earlier chapter. No objective student would fail to see that the Adena "beaver-tail" points are the technically smoother descendants of the Friendships; and the patent development of the thick Friendships into the smooth, flat Adenas, without alteration of outline, can be easily laid out in a convincing series of specimens. And time favors this sequence: the Adena culture becomes explicit at about 2700 B.P., while the Friendship tradition is at least four thousand years old.

The Friendship-Adena tradition contrasts strongly, on inspection, with the notched blades of both "classic" and associated common Hopewellian types. It contrasts even more strongly not only with the Poverty Point dart heads but with the whole stone industry of that culture, which produced hundreds of thousands of microblades, small strip blades or lamellar flakes an inch or less long. And the contrast is enhanced by the approximate contemporaneity, as we see them now, of the Friendship tradition and the beginnings of Poverty Point.

Why, then, should we strain ourselves to try to find cultural ties between the Adenans of southern Ohio and the Poverty Point people of Louisiana? Quite simply because it must be there: centuries before Adena became what we recognize as Adena, and Hopewell what we recognize as Hopewell, the Poverty Point people had thrown up, by organized community effort (1) a conical burial mound, (2) two bird-effigy mounds, and (3) perhaps three miles of geometric embankments. They were a traveling or at least trading people, who used copper from Wisconsin, galena from Missouri, magnetite from Arkansas, and steatite from North Carolina; and the way into Adena country was open, wide open, to these traders, via the Ohio River.

The last, and the least publicized, major alteration in geomorphology that completed the map of what we now know as the United States of America was the breakthrough, at the Thebes Gap at Cairo, Illinois, of the Ohio River into the Mississippi about A.D. 1. Before that, the Ohio had joined the Mississippi at various places some 350 miles to the south, in the vicinity of Natchez, Mississippi, only 150 miles upriver from the Gulf of Mexico. From the first major thrust southward of the Wisconsin, the Ohio and Mississippi had been twin and more or less parallel streams coursing down a valley some 75, plus or minus a few, miles wide: the Ohio on the east, the Mississippi on the west. Considering that it carried the drainage it now carries plus all drainage from the western watershed of the Appalachians that now empties into the Mississippi, the Ohio must have been distinctly the more voluminous waterway, its entire length being through the moist Eastern Woodlands, while the Mississippi's principal tributary, the Missouri, wends almost entirely through more arid country.

The Poverty Point site, probably the ceremonial center of the culture of that name, is near the Mississippi, above the then juncture of the Ohio and Mississippi at Natchez; but the very

prolific Jaketown site is on the present Yazoo River, which
occupies the bed of what was, at the time of its settlement, the
Ohio, well upstream from the Natchez junction, on the way to
Adena-land. In his comprehensive survey of Poverty Point sites
appearing in the July, 1968, issue of *American Antiquity*,
Clarence H. Webb, the first descrier of the culture, lists fifteen
sites along the old Ohio Valley that certainly belong to it and
six sites possibly assignable to it, one of them as far upriver as
Indiana. In short, the Poverty Point people occupied the lower
Ohio Valley before and during the era. The Adenans occupied
the middle Ohio Valley and the valley of one of its larger tributaries, the Scioto, which heads up into Glacial Kame territory. It is not in the least plausible that they did not know and
relate to each other. But how?

If the colorful Poverty Point culture is the most inaptly
named in American prehistory, its most diagnostic artifact is
no more happily named "the Poverty Point object." In a report
on the Poverty Point and Jaketown sites in 1955, when they
were almost the only recognized examples of the culture, Ford
estimated that twenty million of these had been made. The
count is now thirty-four culturally positive Poverty Point sites,
thirty-two "possible" sites, and eighteen sites with some Poverty
Point traits. That's a lot of mud; because that is what the
Poverty Point object is: a chunk of baked clay about the size
of a snow ball, made in the cupped hands, yet far from hap-
hazard in design. This artifact has been classified into six major
and five minor types, some or all of which occur on all sites,
and seven unusual and infrequent types, most of which appear
to be decorated as if by some advanced kindergartener.

The myriads of Poverty Point balls suggest fierce battles with
brickbats between people who liked competition without fatal
bloodshed; but they are nothing so missile: they are, in fact,
substitute cooking stones. The alluvial plain of the two great
rivers is of bottomless clay, and there isn't a rock within miles
that could be used in the cooking methods of the day. One of
these methods, heating stones and dunking them in the soup in
the cooking basket, has already been described. By another
method the stones were placed on a bed of hot coals and the

food to be cooked laid on top of them. It may be surmised that
they imparted a special flavor to the menu, like broiling over
hickory charcoal, and that after so many heatings they lost that
flavor which would account for the millions; there are sites
where they occur though stones could be had in quantity.

From 1944, when Webb first noted the culture, until his
1968 summary and statement, nobody knew quite what to do
with the Poverty Point people. The C14 date from the Poverty
Point burial mound placed it at 2700 B.P. or synchronous with
nascent Adena, providing no clue as to which was the mother
and which the daughter culture and rather suggesting that they
were sisters. But C14 dates on Poverty Point sites in Lake
Pontchartrain, near New Orleans, now give the culture as early
a starting date as about 4000 B.P. Thus the Poverty Point
mound and earthworks appear as the climax of a development
long in the making. Suddenly we have on the cultural map
something that begins to look like a state, with a capital at
Poverty Point and the villages of its citizens spread over considerable territory. Yes, citizens: this is a complex society, the
members of which are no longer tribesmen or residents in
autonomous villages, but citizens—sociopolitical persons, with
duties and responsibilities to a commonwealth comprised of
many villages organized for its own continuance and protection
against not human so much as supernatural peril, the dis-
pleasure of the needed deities and the machinations of the evil
ones.

This is an extraordinary discovery, for the Poverty Point
culture is Archaic by the current taxonomic classification, pre-
crop-growing, preceramic. Despite the millions of solid baked-
clay objects made, apparently nobody thought of making a
hollow one of a larger size, which would be a pot; and pottery,
tempered with grass or vegetal fiber, appears only faintly at the
very end of the period. The Poverty Point society is usufructian
at the beginning and probably up to the last, climactic century
or so of its existence, when the appearance of pottery signals a
change in economy.

Webb says that agriculture or horticulture is not proved, yet
likely, from the observed occurrence of certain traits which

appear with agricultural traits from Mexico, specifically those from the Olmec center at La Venta on the Yucatán peninsula. But it is hard to believe that ceramic pottery would not have been imported at the same time as corn, beans, and squash, for they were a culinary complex at La Venta; the Poverty Pointers certainly knew enough about baked clay to grasp the principle quickly, and they certainly were in need of pots. No agricultural tools occur in the Poverty Point culture, though this is not decisive, since the silty bottomlands could be planted with the dibble, or digging stick. But in any event, La Venta could not have been exporting much before about 3000 B.P., when the Olmecs began to act civilized. The Poverty Pointers, then, had to have developed their complex society on the ancient hunting-gathering base.

Webb visualizes a flourishing usufructian population—and why would it not be flourishing, in the lush subtropical lower Mississippi Valley environment?—beginning to receive imports from the La Venta center, which, though it is located on the lowland plain of the Gulf of Mexico, is almost the full width of the gulf away. Why is this a possibility? With the sea level at 3000 B.P. very near the present level, a land route along the coast from La Venta to the Mississippi Delta would have been no more attractive than it is now, and it is hard to think of a reason why a party would set out from La Venta overland to what is now Louisiana. The great coastal plain of Mextexida mentioned earlier, along which it may even have once been customary to travel, would by now have been under fathoms of seawater. The only feasible route is by boat—feasible because the current and winds run clockwise and northward along the Mexican coast, and thence across the southern coast of Texas, Louisiana, Mississippi, and Alabama, and are then turned south again by the peninsula of Florida. It would have been a simple matter to take a boat at La Venta and ride this current to what is now New Orleans. The difficulty would have come in getting back. Without a knowledge of maritime voyaging, it probably couldn't have been done. Even a full clockwise circuit of the gulf encounters adverse winds and currents for the latter part. There is no archaeological suggestion of any kind of trade relations between La Venta and the Poverty Point people, and if there were, we would be hard put to explain them. The traffic was one-way only.

We are left with few alternatives. The Olmecs who departed La Venta departed for good, as exiles or fugitives, or as surplus-population colonists. No archaeology supports the last motive, but the pattern of Poverty Point acquisition of La Venta traits could be explained by either or both of the first two. Most striking, according to Webb, is the similarity between La Venta lapidary work and motifs and those of the Poverty Pointers in beads, pendants, and a great variety of objects of excellent workmanship and exotic materials—jasper, talc, banded slate, hematite, magnetite, galena, feldspar, fluorite, amethyst, crystal quartz, variegated quartzites, obsidian, and other colorful stones, from all over the central United States. These are highly crafted items of vanity and prestige, the kinds of things that always excite a people when they are introduced into a society that has been making do with humbler gewgaws, as white traders well knew when they went among the Indians with showy glass beads and other trinkets. But to transform a society of Archaic clansmen—even though, as at Wapanucket, they have reached the hamlet stage of the body politic—through adherence to a unifying burial cult, into the regimented society which produced the monuments to state and church at Poverty Point requires more potent artifacts, given meaning by an awesome ideology, and time, much time. Undoubtedly the powerful artifacts were corn, beans, and squash; and the ideology was sun worship, the placation of the climate- and weather-controlling astronomical divinities. But how long would this have taken, with the seeds of the basic cultivars reaching the lower Mississippi desultorily from La Venta and having to metamorphose an adequate usu-fructianism into cultifructianism before the Poverty Pointers could be converted to the tributary-labor society of the new worship?

The major innovations, Webb believes, were these: "strong religious and civil organization in ceremonial centers, with satel-lite villages; planned construction with solar orientation; mas-sive mounds with ramps and terraces; pottery making." These traits, in concentrated "pill" form suitable for transport, fed into the mouth of the Mississippi, being swallowed and traveling through that digestive tract, bifurcated as it was by separation of the lower Mississippi into its Ohio and upper Mississippi branches, into the continental belly, eventually and finally produced the truly amazing complex at Poverty Point. Only about half of the octagonal earthworks design remains today, missing sections having been cut away by meanders in the course of the Arkansas River and Bayou Macon at various times after the abandonment of the settlement. The octagons are interrupted at regular intervals by aisles leading into a central courtyard or large "square," where some of the convocation ceremonies took place that drew these throngs of Poverty Pointers. Though Webb and Ford interpret this amphitheater of dwelling ridges as a planned village, one tends to think of it rather as a place visited seasonally, like a county fairgrounds or the old chautauqua sites, except that the assemblages would probably have been at the winter and summer solstices, and perhaps at the spring and autumn equinoxes. These ridges, if they were all occupied at the same time, could have camped thousands, too many inhabitants for a permanently occupied village.

Besides the burial mound and the two bird-effigy mounds, the tail of the larger of which seems to have supported the temple, Ford considers it possible that there were two other mounds needed to complete the symmetry of the complex. The larger bird mound is directly west of the center of the amphitheater and the other directly north. A mound to the east and one to the south are certainly implied by symmetry, but the Arkansas River has been busy in those sectors. With the octagonal ridges occupied by hutments, thousands walking the swales between or the aisles, or gathered in the plaza, with the four great bird mounds placed at cardinal points of the compass about the massed center, there was not in all America north of the Valley of Mexico at the time a sight from the air or ground as arresting as this.

How does this accord with what we know of contemporary Adena society? Not at all well. There is nothing to dispose us to believe, not the settlement patterns nor preserved remains,

that Adenans were cultifructians until near the end of their era,
three or four centuries into the Christian calendar, and after
the Hopewellian certainly had corn, beans, and squash. A good
deal of Adena evidence actually comes from caves and rock
shelters, which is not where you would expect to find zealous
farmers. Robert M. Goslin of the Ohio Historical Society, in
his summary of Adenan food remains from both rock shelters
and mound sites, reports as the cultivars present only gourd,
pumpkin, squash, and sunflower—that is, the vining and the
top-everything sunflowers, neither of which requires much tillage. William S. Webb and Raymond Baby in their *The Adena
People: No. 2* describe Adena occupations thus: "Because of the
seemingly wide dispersion of the dwellings in any Adena community, there was rarely, if ever, a concentrated occupancy of
any small area. The result was that no deep village deposits,
with their intimate cultural remains, were left."

In short, no millions of baked clay lumps, no hundreds of
thousands of microblades, no great ceremonial center with satel-
lite villages, no heaps or pits of generations of trash disposal,
no mounds that took anything like the three million man-hours
of labor that went into the biggest mound at Poverty Point, and
no lapidary costume jewelry. On the contrary, the Adena stone
carvings are the famous and characteristic stone tablets or
plaques, with cabalistic designs or stylized abstractions carved
in bas-relief or incised on a flat stone face; these have, in some
instances been found with red paint in the grooves, from which
their use as stamps, probably for the body, has been inferred.

The Adenans and Poverty Pointers were alike, it seems, only
in that they were dirt heapers, but not for the same purposes.
The Poverty Pointers made lesser mounds, too—there are eight
small mounds at Jaketown, and several other sites have mounds
that seem to date to Poverty Point times—but they are not
Adena-type burial mounds, as far as has been ascertained. The
only resemblance with which we are left is the "sacred circles,"
simple circular embankments apparently intended to enclose or
mark off a sanctuary for ceremonial observances. The Adenans
made these, and so did the Poverty Pointers, if you call the
plaza within the octagonal earthworks at Poverty Point a sacred

circle; such sacred circles occur within the Poverty Point cultural span at several sites along the Gulf coast, particularly at Sapelo Island, where the embankment is of shell. Since the Sapelo Island circle is C_{14}-dated at 3798 ± 250 B.P., there was plenty of time for this trait to have reached Adena territory, but no particular reason to believe that it did.

There is one dubious bit of evidence linking Adena with Gulf-Mexican influences: the famous Adena human-effigy pipe found in a mound in the group on the Adena farm (the place name, not the name of its owner, who was Thomas Worthington, a governor of Ohio from 1814 to 1818), regarded by some as a portrait of the Adena physiognomy. The figure is that of a male either in a partial squat or dwarfed below the waist, well enough proportioned above, and with a strongly carved face of Mexican cast. This Mexican resemblance may be a subjective judgment, but the man does wear ear spools, which is a Mexican trait. It happens also to be a Hopewellian trait, and the carving of effigy pipes is a Hopewellian art, Adena pipes of pre-Hopewellian times being plain, cigarlike tubular pipes. I am far from alone in believing that the Adena pipe is not Adena, but Hopewell, but I may be almost alone in believing that the Adenans were not only non-Mexican but anti-Mexican.

We are now as ready as we are ever likely to be, in this book, to make guesses about the Adena reality. The stone projectile points of the stemmed Friendship tradition, which is so clearly proto-Adena, are very much in the style and of the same workmanship as the rather shambling category called Gary stemmed, which were made by the proto- and Early Poverty Pointers. By stone technology, then, and by physical type, as already mentioned, the Adenans were southern migrants into the middle Ohio and Scioto valleys, probably along the trackway of the ancient Ohio, of the same stock as the proto-Poverty Pointers but at least a millennium before La Venta expatriates reached the Mississippi Delta. (Just so did a short, dark Mediterranean people, ultimately related to the Egyptians, move north into the British Isles and seat themselves there among the thinly spread, lingering Mesolithic population.) They must have come without a religion, at least a satisfying one, for they quickly became converts to what we shall call the Old Copper cult, most vividly represented at the time by the Glacial Kame people.

Thereafter they remained staunch adherents to that cult, resisting alike any encroachment up the Ohio by the Poverty Pointers and, when the Hopewellians blazed up in the Illinois and Ohio forests, absorption by that powerful society. Their burial practices, the outward signs of their religion, were those of the region where they lived, not those of the region whence they had come; and, having once adopted these, the Adenans clung as faithfully to them as Ireland to the Catholic Church. One tends, however, to feel that these people, who maintained a cultural identity through about sixteen hundred years of prehistory (from about 1000 B.C. to A.D. 600, by extrapolations from $C14$ dates), resemble, rather, the Jews in their religious-ethnic integrity and in the fact that their Israel, too, ended in a Diaspora—for they actually did flee, as a people, eastward to the Delmarva peninsula of Delaware-Maryland-Virginia, and the evidence of shatter groups appears all along the Eastern coast and into New England. And this is the last we see of them.

Nobody knows what broke up the Adenans. They were an adaptable people who could live either in the hills or in the valleys. They occupied both banks of the Ohio, from the falls of the Ohio (at Louisville, Kentucky) to about Wheeling, West Virginia. If they did not control the use of the river, they certainly were in a position to. One might suspect piracy or preying on river traffic, the way the Shawnees preyed on the flatboats of westering pioneers on the Ohio in the last quarter of the eighteenth century, if there was any such traffic—and during the latter half of Adenan existence there was. The Hopewellians traded far and wide, west as far as the Rocky Mountains, south as far as the Gulf, southeast as far as Florida, and north into Michigan, for the exotic materials for their Egytian-like tomb cult; and the main trade route in and out of the Ohio Hopewell centers to most of the sources of materials was via the Ohio River.

Barring the discovery of a stronghold stocked with weapons and yielding caches of loot, from which the Adenans sallied forth to fall on treasure-laden homeward-bound trading parties of Hopewellians, we can never hope to prove that the Adenans were the kind of people of whom we have had other examples in history: pious brigands who find sanction in their religious beliefs and ethnic conservatism for robbing and raiding those not of their breed and kind. We think of desert Arabs as being thus, though they are hardly unique; the right to despoil and exploit by force and violence or by economic weapons those who differ from our ethnic or class selves is still assumed, unfortunately, to have been bestowed on us by whatever God or gods we trust. On the other hand, the Adenans certainly did not found their cult on such practices and may not have been aggressive at all. They may well have lived in interstices, as it were, in Hopewell territory, quietly pursuing their cult ways without challenge to Hopewell hegemony. Perhaps they were tolerated by the Hopewellians, perhaps ignored as heretics lost, perhaps despised. That they did not play a role vis-à-vis the Hopewellians was not possible, considering the centuries during which they were contemporaries.

The situation requires a brief recapitulation. As true inheritors of the Glacial Kame burial cult, the Adenans developed the only vivid and extensive cultural pattern we know of at about 3000 B.P.—that is, 100 B.C.—in the Scioto Valley and along the Ohio Valley both eastward and westward from where the Scioto joins the Ohio. For upwards of 750 years this pattern holds alone and without rival; at about 200 B.C., at the earliest, in exactly this same regional and geographical setting (the Illinois River Hopewell begins a little earlier and is different in significant ways), there appears a culture which, despite the similarity of its burial practices to the Adena, contrasts markedly in its community organization and level of achievement and is produced by a longheaded people, of that lineage which is traceable back to the Oconto burials of 7500 B.P. Ohio Hopewell performs brilliantly until about A.D. 450–500, and then suddenly collapses. But the Adenans live through the rise and fall of Hopewellianism, influenced by it, to be sure, but still "doing their own thing," until about A.D. 600 and flight to the east.

Some students approach archaeology as though it were a

branch of arithmetic, not anthropology, their curiosity going no
farther than counts and percentages of potsherds, and as
though culture is what the computer says it is. But I think we
must admit that we are here gazing in perplexity at cultures
determined by the unexcavatable facts of human character. It is
apparent that the Hopewellians expanded within Adenan territory, perhaps even dispossessing the inhabitants, and that Hopewellians and Adenans lived simultaneously within miles of each
other. More than mere disengagement and separatism is implied; there must have been barriers and resistance, and animosity, for barriers between people do not long stand up without animosity.

The possibility of active hostility exists on the evidence of a
clay figurine, realistic in execution, one of six recovered statuettes which have given us some idea of what Hopewellians looked
like. The figure is that of a warrior, and that warriors were a
special caste is inferred by reason of the dress (or lack of it),
accoutrements, and decoration. The probable castes would
have been the priest-shamans, the civil administrators, the artisans, the warriors, and the laboring peasant commonalty. The
warriors could hardly have been an honorary caste if they were
themselves merely conscripts from among the peons; they must
have had a professional function, for caste is hereditary profes-
sionalism. It would have been their duty to act as guards for
trading expeditions and as a standing army for home defense.
It is within the premises of Hopewell-Adena relations as we
now understand them that there were tensions between the two
groups that were never resolved.

But who were the Hopewellians? If there were a simple and
ready answer, the Adena-Hopewell enigma would long since
have been disposed of. As it is, we have to feel our way through
the shadowy forests of this era of prehistory. The people themselves were far from latecomers to what are now the North
Central states, and whatever novelty appeared among them had
either been in embryo there or was imported; it was not carried
into the region by a new people. Ceremonial burial, we know,
was thousands of years old among these denizens of the forests.
What was new about it was the accentuation, so that interment

became the supreme honor accorded to a personage who had held high office or exalted status in life. True, the Adenans had practiced this special mortuary veneration of chief men, but they did not have anything like the material and artistic wealth of the Hopewellians to expend.

James B. Griffin of the University of Michigan, one of the leading Hopewell authorities of the established generation, wrote in 1949 that Hopewell "is the cultural climax of the Middle Woodland Tradition and in many ways artistic levels were reached in this period which were not excelled even in the succeeding Mississippian stage."

Olaf H. Prufer of Case-Western Reserve University wrote in 1964 that "it is more appropriate to speak of a Hopewell cult than of a Hopewell culture. . . . The Hopewell complex cannot be classed as a *culture* in the anthropological sense of the word, that is, as a distinct society together with its attendant material and spiritual manifestations."

Hopewellianism, then, was the cultural insemination of certain of the Otamid groups (this is what Neumann calls this longheaded variety, the Adenans being Iswanids) of the North Central states at a time when they were not even conservifructians, at the right moment in their estrous cycle. Where this cult fertilization came from is no mystery: if it did not come from the Adenans, then it had to come from the Poverty Pointers.

There are two recognized Hopewellian centers: that in the Illinois Valley and that in the Scioto Valley, with its omphalos near Chillicothe. The Illinois center had an earlier beginning, was associated with a different pottery tradition, and never reached the creative vigor of Ohio Hopewell. Recollection of the bifurcation in the Ohio-Mississippi at this time supplies the reason: the trail that led out of Poverty Point up the Mississippi carried the gospel to the Illinois River; the trail that led up the Ohio carried it to Chillicothe, at a different time and under different circumstances.

Stuart Struever of the University of Chicago, one of the newer men in Hopewellian studies, describes the difference between the two Hopewells thus:

Hopewell mortuary sites in the Illinois and adjacent Mississippi valleys are numerous and more or less continuously distributed over long stretches of river valley, whereas the much larger and more internally complex Ohio centers are fewer and tend to be concentrated in localized portions of the Scioto, Miami and other valleys. The much smaller size and lesser complexity of the Illinois burial sites, together with their greater number and linear distribution, suggest a form of cultural system different from that which characterizes Ohio. In addition the clustering of Ohio centers strengthens the hypothesis that politics which integrate populations over a broad geographical area are represented. Localization of Illinois burial sites suggests politics of smaller scale, with mound groups serving communities within a more restricted area. . . . Most finely crafted Hopewellian items of stone and metal occur in Ohio in far greater densities than elsewhere and many occur there exclusively.

The differences stressed above are real and substantial; they are what happened to the gospel spread by different agents among different peoples. But in the beginning it had to have been approximately the same gospel that took these separate routes. One guess should be sufficient to tell us what that gospel, that semen, was: it was corn and its sisters, beans and squash.

When I wrote *No Stone Unturned* ten years ago, it was a matter of serious archaeological doubt that the Hopewellians had ever raised corn, but there was also a total absence of excavation evidence of village sites; the mounds had attracted all the attention, and habitation evidence is scarce in their vicinity, as would be expected. Having noted the distributional pattern and intensity of Hopewell occupation along river valleys, I was a firm believer in corn-beans-squash as the base of Hopewell prosperity; and as a native of that country, I knew where corn was raised. I said, therefore, that if it was habitation patterns archaeologists were looking for, they should search the bottomlands. That this would probably be a tedious and expensive search, because the Ohio and Scioto flood annually, sometimes twice annually, dropping inches of silt with each overflow, I was aware; but I was fully confident that this was the secret of the scarcity of Hopewell settlements.

I cannot claim that anybody paid any attention to this sug-

gestion, but when a Hopewell hamlet or compound was discovered, it was discovered in an annually flooded bottomland,
and Prufer, who did the excavation, was directed to it by the
farmer who owned the land. Searching for settlements, Prufer
had been about to close out his survey when the farmer, Alva
McGraw, persuaded him to test a bottomland cornfield about
two miles downriver from Chillicothe. In the foot-thick midden
were more than 10,000 Hopewell potsherds, corn grains, and
corncobs.

The reason for the "linear" distribution of both Ohio and
Illinois Hopewell is self-evident. Only in the bottomlands would
it have been possible to find the cleared land for extensive
cornfields. Not only do the annual floods renew the fertility of
the fields, but they keep them swept free of heavy growth. No
Amerinds ever had efficient tools for clearing away the magnificent stands of trees that comprised the Eastern Woodlands.
This was not Mexico, where land could be cleared by slash-and-
burn; it was the Big Woods, and the only place where agriculture was possible was on naturally deforested tracts.

Academic archaeologists draw many refined conclusions from
the fact that evidences of usufructianism are found in Hopewellian sites. An Ohio or Scioto valley farmer could enlighten
them about that, too. The floods in these valleys do not occur
on a chronometric schedule like those of the Nile. They can
happen any time during the spring, unfortunately, and if they
occur after May 10, there will be no corn that season. I had
occasion to be in Portsmouth during the middle of May, 1968,
when such a flood occurred; the Scioto-Ohio reached a height of
about sixty-two feet, with pool stage at twelve feet and flood
stage considered to be fifty feet. It was not only the loss of
labor, fertilizer, and corn seed that broke the hearts of farmers
(temporarily—they'll always be back at it next year); it was
that there would not be enough seed of short-season corn, even
in this day and age when the farmer buys all his seed (which
is hybrid) to replant. The only alternative was to plant the
fields in soy beans.

The Hopewellians had no short-season hybrid corn and no soy
beans, and the likelihood was that they committed all their

seed (including bean and squash) to the one planting. A late-May flood not only meant that it was "take to the hills" for squirrel meat and acorns for the flood year, but where was next year's seed to come from? One late flood meant at least two lean years.

But make no mistake about it: in the good years, which happen 10 to 1, corn grows as productively in the Scioto, Miami, Muskingum, and Ohio bottoms as anywhere in the world, and the luster of Ohio Hopewell has the verdant sheen of the corn from their fertile alluvium. So we must ask, How did corn find its way to these luxuriant valleys? We know that it must have been at Poverty Point during the great days of mound building there, about 800–600 B.C.; a thin trail of Poverty Point sites leads up the Mississippi to the Cairo-Cahokia area, where the Illinois enters it, and the extension of the corn-beans-squash complex into Illinois Hopewell country is almost on a straight line. But nothing identifiable as Poverty Point has been found along the Ohio beyond the Falls, the border of Adena territory. Did prophets of the corn gospel slip through the Adenan lines, or wander as footsore St. Pauls among the unheeding Adenans until they found willing ears among Otamids excluded from or disdainful of Adenan society?

The designation of missionary is not given lightly. Corn-beans-squash agriculture was not only seed; it was all the lore, practical and magic, religious and political, that was considered necessary to the successful raising and management of this sacred sustenance. If the lore did not reach the future Hopewellians by contact diffusion, then it had to reach them by the hands and through the preachments of the keepers of the mysteries, to whom the erection of mounds and earthwork sanctuaries was as important as the burial of the seed in little hills and the protection of the fields from birds and beasts. But it seems to me that recruiting zeal is less plausible an explanation of how corn priests spread the word in the Ohio country, since secrets and mysteries imply a certain desire to keep them out of the wrong heads, than that they were sought out and invited. The Scioto Valley Hopewell heartland was isolated from both the Illinois Valley Hopewellians and the lower Ohio Valley

Poverty Pointers, but we are forced to relate it directly to Poverty Point rather than to the Illinois branch, because it is truer to the parent. The Illinois branch erected few if any earthworks and no temple mounds; the Ohioans erected both, though earthworks seem to have been by far the most favored places of ceremony or worship.

There is a story here—not the kind we have up to now been endeavoring to tell, of cultures with denominations that are only our tags for filing, moving facelessly here and there with climate changes or fleeing hunger or pursuing game or content in a wonted environment. It is a story of persons with individual names who undertook missions and made contributions of moment and consequence to a large and complex society, which would have failed or never have been achieved without them. Among the usufructians and the cultifructians, what one knew everybody knew; but among the Ohio Hopewellians, there were experts and specialists, administrators, artists, engineers. It was somebody with a name and a face, a personal mien, and a public image who persuaded the non-Adenans of central Ohio to plant the first corn and build the first sacred circle. And he brought into being the straw bosses, the overseers of labor, the clerks who kept records on the days of labor done and still owing, the priest-engineers who staked out the mounds, the captains of the guard, the craftsmen, the traders, the keepers of the calendar, the celebrant priests, the medicine men, the traders, and the boatmen. They all had names and countenances and personalities, for when tasks are diversified and one man has this responsibility and another that, when decisions are made and projects undertaken for a populous society of interdependent groups of trades and interests, then men become individually different, in dress and address, habit and expression, ambitions and, most of all, self-consciousness. They become, in the novelist's or playwright's sense, characters, with names and roles in the plot, *dramatis personae*.

What the Ohio Hopewellians did to deserve this appreciation is today mostly a matter of a few artificial hillocks standing here and there (there are two in a public park in Portsmouth), some excavation records, and the survey of mounds, mostly

Hopewellian, by E. G. Squier, a newspaper editor, and Dr. E. H. Davis, both of Chillicothe. Private ignorance—destruction of mounds by plowing and bulldozing without realization of what they were; adult delinquency—looting for treasure or collection; and public folly—as when the army destroyed a mound group near Chillicothe to build Camp Sherman, a World War I receiving station—have left almost nothing for the modern archaeologist. But Squier and Davis were on the scene in 1845, with the backing of the American Ethnological Society, and they were uncommonly well fitted for the task. They opened over two hundred mounds, tested some hundred earthworks, and diagramed many others in whole or partial or evidential existence. This was only a fraction of the structures that existed even then, but Squier and Davis sought out the principal ones, and the "complexity" noted by Streuver for Ohio Hopewell building is deduced from their reports.

As far as I know, there has never been an attempt to evaluate the mound assemblages of the Hopewell by function, but it appears to me that none of the major concentrations duplicates the others—as though each river drainage, the Scioto, the Ohio, the Muskingum, and the Miami, had its own center or "metropolis," where similar activities, both religious and civil, were carried on by a locally self-sufficient community.

The mound and earthworks plan at Marietta, on the Muskingum near its entry to the Ohio, requires no fevered imagination to be pictured as the Rome, in the ecclesiastical sense, of the Hopewell faithful. A survey by one Charles Whittlesey, dated 1837, shows two rectangular earthworks-enclosed areas, one of fifty acres and one of twenty-seven acres. Within the embankments—25 to 35 feet at the base and 4 to 10 feet high, depending on the terrain—of the large precinct are four flat-topped pyramidal mounds, which probably had wooden temples on top. The largest of the four is 188 feet long, 132 feet wide, and 10 feet high; it is bordered by a graded pathway or, perhaps, no-trespass zone. From the river, about 680 feet away, there led into this enclosure a broad thoroughfare, 180 feet wide, within banks about 10 feet high, which has been dubbed the Via Sacra; and there can be little doubt that it was meant

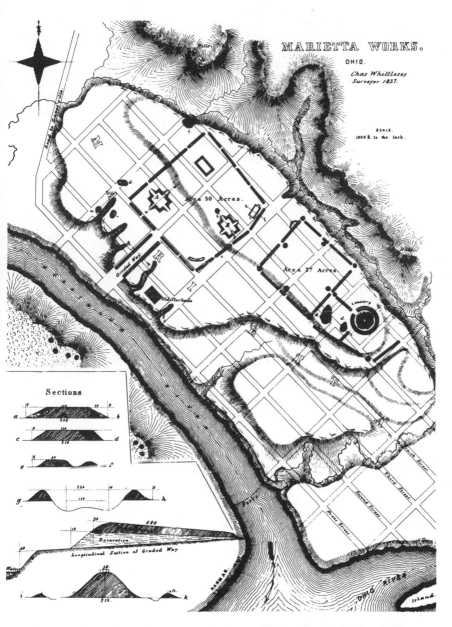

Mound and earthwork plan at Marietta, Ohio. (E. G. Squier & E. H. Davis: *Ancient Monuments of the Mississippi Valley*, 1848.)

to be a formal processional avenue for dignitaries and their retinues after disembarking from their barges at the shore. Giving main access from and to the river, the Via Sacra certainly suggests throngs of people traveling to this center of worship by water, which in turn suggests travel from considerable distances.

Just beyond the smaller enclosure, within which there were no signs of structures, was a handsome and symmetrical conical mound with the typical temple-mound flat top, surrounded by a ten-foot-high embankment, with other detached embankments in apparent if puzzling relation. One can only speculate about this clustering of "basilicas" at Marietta, whether each of them was used for a different kind of rite or, perhaps, for ceremonies at different seasons—the four mounds in the larger enclosure suggesting just that—or whether they were built one by one, used for a set period, and then abandoned. We are gazing at the monuments of a religion we do not understand, but we cannot mistake them for anything other than monuments of a religion.

Quite otherwise is the intricate layout of mounds and earthworks at Newark, about halfway between the Muskingum and the Scioto in central Ohio. There is nothing in either plan or mound form that suggests specific religious usage, no temple mounds, no rich burial mounds. One octagon-outline embankment, according to the Whittlesey, Squier, and Davis rendering done in 1837–47, encloses fifty acres and attached to it by a banked pathway, like an umbilical cord, is a circular enclosed area of twenty acres. This complex is related to another by a broad highway about 250 feet wide and about 4,000 feet long, protected or bordered by banks. The second complex is a near-rectangular embankment enclosing twenty acres, which is related by a bank-enclosed way to another circular enclosure in which there was a small effigy mound, the Eagle Mound. This is by no means the extent of the bank-enclosed figures and "highways." The entire enclosed area is about four square miles, despite which it is doubtful that the plan as known is the complete one.

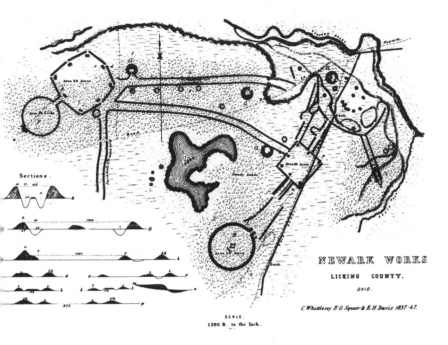

Mound and earthwork plan at Newark, Ohio. (E. G. Squier & E. H. Davis: *Ancient Monuments of the Mississippi Valley*, 1848.)

The earliest observers interpreted these structures as forts and ramparts, which fostered the fancies about a very numerous race of Mound Builders in a state of civilization far superior to the Indians of white-contact times, and about the embattled races of the Book of Mormon. But it can be doubted that the Hopewellians could ever have mustered the force to man these defenses; besides, there are indefensibly wide entrances to some of the enclosures, nor do they appear to be particularly insurmountable. Only the most thorough investigation of the Newark works in pristine condition would have revealed their use, and this was never possible. Almost surely they did not protect or define villages, there being no middens, that is, garbage re-

mains, within them. But if they are not religious, then they are
secular, and their very extent and their arbitrary pattern argue
for more varied purposes than the single one of religious com-
mitment. I would hazard a guess that here was the civil-admin-
istration center of the Hopewell hegemony.

The burial-mound concentrations are in the Scioto Valley,
particularly in the vicinity of Chillicothe, and most of the incredible treasure of Ohio Hopewell came from the elevated
sepulcher vaults of the Hopewell group, the central mound of
which is the largest Hopewell tumulus (250 feet long, 150 feet
wide, and 30 feet high) and the Seip group clustered about
the second largest. These were the cemeteries of the highest of
the hierachy and the repositories of the national wealth. Out
of them came hundreds of the sculptured platform pipes, usually
zoomorphic, probably the most positive of Hopewellian identifying traits; lapidary serpents; scroll designs in sheet mica;
hammered gold sheets; carved bone and antler; thousands upon
thousands of pearls, perforated and unperforated (the pearl of
the river mussel, not precious marine pearl); worked copper by
the hundreds of pounds, including breast plates, false noses,
and ceremonial axes; hammered silver; beautifully worked obsidian; jewelry and items of personal adornment of every obtainable material—from fossil shark's teeth and grizzly-bear canines
to terra cotta, cast into rings, and marine turtle shell; near-gem-
quality flints, not only from the famous Flint Ridge nearby at
Zanesville but from the Dakotas, Arkansas, and the Southeast;
pottery boldly decorated in a unique art style different from the
utilitarian pottery; and cloth dyed in many colors. The Hopewell
group is enclosed in almost three miles of embankments, some
three million cubic yards of earth dug with stone "spades" and
transported into place by basket or skin pouch, an enormous
amount of labor merely to erect the demarcation of what must
have been more than an Arlington—a veritable Westminster—
with burials at the place of the funeral exercises. Adenan
burials were potter's fields by comparison.

The reader may have missed one of the most significant items
in the foregoing list, the dyed cloth. It would astonish us, I
think, to return to Hopewell times for a convocation at Marietta.

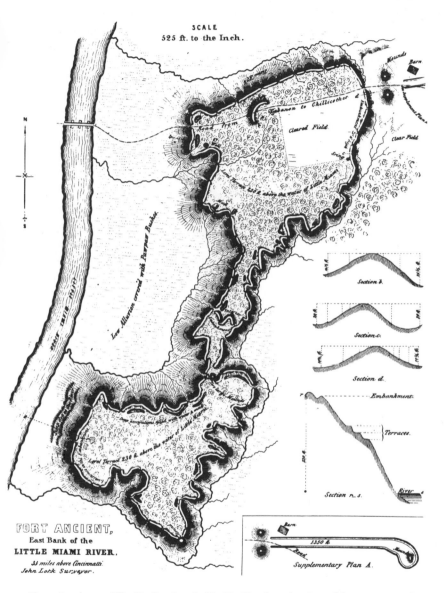

Fort Ancient. (E. G. Squier & E. H. Davis: *Ancient Monuments of the Mississippi Valley*, 1848.)

What would strike us first, while we were trying to make sense
of what was going on, would be the dress. We would hardly
be able to believe we were in mid-America in Amerind times.
The dress would not be the familiar leather uniforms that we
have been long accustomed to think of as Indian garb, but
brightly colored batiks, with South Sea-island sarongs for the
women and probably for the men as well, and togalike overall
garments. Designs in contrasting colors were done by resist
dyeing, treating the sections not to be colored so that they would
not take the dye. At least three colors could be attained in this
way; a burial shroud from the Seip-mound group is of a woven
fabric with a pattern of abstract forms in tan, maroon, and
black. One would guess that these were conventional funeral
shades, as melancholy black and angelic white are with us, and
that everyday and holiday outfits were gayer. Our stereotypes
being what they are, a glance would adjust our minds instantly
away from Hopewellians as being something out of a movie
Western.

If Marietta seems to be Rome, city of rite, and Newark
Rome, ruler of provinces, and Chillicothe Rome, site of the
catacombs, what are we to think of the citadel called Fort
Ancient thirty miles north of Cincinnati on the Little Miami
River? Within walled embankments up to 20 feet high in
places, faced with stone and built along the edge of an irregular
plateau 230 feet above the flood plain of the river, is an area of
about a hundred acres that, well provisioned, could have supported a beleaguered population of thousands. There appear to
be several entrances to this Quebec, which are believed to have
been closed by palisades with gates, and there was an em-
banked highway leading into it. The burial mounds within are
not the lavish mausoleums of Chillicothe and would not have
been the reason for this immense earthen stockade, a mile long
from north to south, with easily three times that length of wall.

There are some who see these defensive works and others like
them, such as that at Fort Hill in Highland County, between
the Scioto and Miami valleys, enclosing forty-eight acres, as
being from the declining phase of Hopewell, when it was beset
by enemies to whom it finally succumbed. It is an opinion held

on slight grounds. These bastions are not mere breastworks thrown up where battle was joined. They were erected at carefully chosen coigns of vantage, and the amount of toil that went into them, provided certainly by laborers who were also farmers and could work only periodically, argues for a long, deliberate term of construction. Nor is there any enemy known to archaeology who might have taken them by assault, certainly not the Adenans, who would have been at most guerrillas and bandits. What followed Hopewell, when it fell or was pushed, is a phase of low-density, small-band cultifructianism, during which pottery was made and corn, beans, and squash were grown by a people no more socially coalescent than those of Wapanucket No. 6. If Fort Ancient and Fort Hill were built as protection from enemies, they could only have been the enemies within, the Hopewell masses. Societies governed and exploited by an elite build such visible reminders to overawe the plebs; and when they fall, they fall just as Hopewell did, and as Rome did, leaving the land to the Dark Ages. Let us see Fort Ancient and Fort Hill as the Rome of the imperial legions.

By the standards just outlined, Ohio Hopewellianism was a nation, the first such within the present United States—indeed, the first United States. In its prime it was able to project its influences over a region with diameters from New York to Arkansas, from Wisconsin to Florida. It is not possible to be exact about what those influences were that turned up as Hopewell artifacts or Hopewell motifs. Perhaps they were nothing more than what gets Coca Cola known all over the world, some strenuous promotion and the palatability of the elixir; but one would think that it was something more. Armed might over these distances seems out of the question, though the Iroquois managed to exert their bellicosity as far south as the Carolinas and as far west as the Miamis; they exerted no cultural influences, however, merely leaving their enemies for dead. A show of arms and disciplined might, our assumed *raison d'être* of Fort Ancient, seems like a characteristic Hopewellian ploy. Still, there must have been something that lasted among the hosts after a visitation by Hopewell ambassadors: the Hopewell style, its stimulating creativeness, its glitter of affluence. In

short, wherever a Hopewell delegation went, the locals had
never seen anything like them and aspired to the secrets of their
success.

Prufer called Hopewellianism a cult, and we are not inclined
to disagree, but it was a cult with political power; it may be
likened to Spain sending out explorers to the New World to
claim its riches and win its inhabitants to Christianity. An offi-
cialdom of some kind sent, or equipped and assisted in going,
the traders, the Marco Polo-like travelers, the negotiating
agents, to far places—even to Mexico, whence the ear spools,
the weaving and dyeing of cloth, and some of the obsidian must
have come—with instructions about what to do and say, what
to look for, and what to bring back. Those officials were the
cult Junkers, whose sophistication would have been attained
from having made these same long expeditions in their youth.
Even so did the old-school-tie youths of England do their obligatory Continental tours before settling down at home to run
the British Empire from the Foreign Office. If it was the system
used to maintain the viability of Hopewellianism and the domi-
nance of its elite, it worked. The British Empire did not last
three hundred years; we have been a nation for less than two
hundred; but the span of Hopewellianism was that of the Roman
Republic and the Roman Empire combined. Perhaps they collapsed at about the same time; for the C14 date on the McGraw-
farm site is A.D. 450, and everybody remembers what happened
in A.D. 476. We would wish such longevity upon our own nation.
The Adenans outlasted their rivals, it is true, but as a culture,
not as a nation. And perhaps Hopewell collapse even gave
Adena a new lease on life; for there is some evidence, in the
Cresap Mound sequence, that Hopewellians, and we assume
they would have been the ousted elite, took refuge among the
Adenans.

There are the elements of a twilight of the gods in the Hopewellian collapse. Griffin thinks it coincides with a bad turn of
climate, and we have already seen that such a turn would not
have had to be prolonged to destroy corn culture. But there
must have been many bad turns of the local climatic cycle over

750 years which were somehow outlived. The hierarchy would not have given up easily. I have often wondered whether a pestilence did not decimate the population, or an uncontrollable pest attack the corn; in these days I hear of another corn malady or enemy every five years, it seems. Yet, ultimately, the collapse must have been political. We can picture the production of corn falling off to the point of starvation while the tributary exactions, the "taxes" imposed by the overlords, continued unabated, either starving an impotent peasantry to death or driving them to a bloody revolt, followed by reversion to the ancient usufructian pattern of living off the land even though there was some scattered cultivation. The fact is that almost literally nothing follows Hopewellianism, from Chillicothe along the Scioto to the Ohio and on both the Ohio and Kentucky shores of the Ohio from Wheeling to Cincinnati, from the Beaver to the Miami. When white men first came into the Ohio Valley, there was not a single permanent Indian settlement of record along this once-prosperous section of the Ohio. It belonged, on the Ohio side, to the Shawnees, whose principal village was at Chillicothe (a Shawnee word meaning "old town"), beyond the rugged, heavily wooded foothill country, while Kentucky was unoccupied, the Dark and Bloody Ground, hunted over and fought in by the northern tribes—the Shawnees, the Miamis, and the Delawares—and the southern tribes—the Cherokees and Creeks. The Mississippian temple mounds did not even reach there.

The temple-mound phase waxed from a budding at about A.D. 700 to full bloom about A.D. 1500 in the Mississippi Valley, during a known period of warmer climate with an increase in population estimated at ten to twenty times that of the post-Hopewell centuries—recollect the Cahokia mounds dating from this time—without a single tendril probing into the Ohio Valley. The contemporary occupants in the Ohio Hopewell country were the misnamed Fort Ancient people (they had nothing to do with the Hopewellian Fort Ancient), who lived in infrequent villages at the joining of the larger creeks with the Ohio, and who showed no interest at all in the priest-directed societies that were building raised temple complexes, from Aztalan in Wisconsin, through the rich but looted Spiro mounds of Oklahoma and the Etowah mounds of Georgia, even to the shell-mound temples in Florida.

Remembering that the Adena hegira from the Ohio Valley dates not too long after the Hopewell collapse, we can only wonder what really happened in the Scioto-Ohio region that laid it fallow for so long. The Fort Ancient people are the probable ancestors of the Shawnees, whose name is translated as "the Southerners," not because they came from the South but because they are the most southern of the Chipewyans, who include the Sauks and Foxes of Wisconsin and Michigan, of the Algonquian language group, and whose relatives can be found on the shores of Hudson Bay. It is tempting to play up the Fort Ancient people as fierce northern tribesmen who pushed south against the pacific Hopewell corn worshippers and eventually the Adenans, routing them from their homes, but it would accord better with the chronology to accept them merely as the people who, expanding southward, found an almost empty land. The bizarre civilization that the shamans had created from a mixture of ingredients out of a usufructian people had vanished as though by an evil magic that had extinguished it by a single malediction.

James Fitting, in a review of the symposium volume *Hopewellian Studies* (1964) by the younger group of Hopewellian scholars (in which, incidentally, nobody agrees with anybody), writes:

The word Hopewell is one of those terms which means all things to all people. Whether it evokes the image of a great religious movement or a finely made pot, there is scarcely a soul who does not rise to its utterance. In one sense or another, it applies to prehistoric materials found from the upper Great Lakes to the Gulf of Mexico, and from the Appalachians far out into the Plains. Today, the Hopewell phenomenon is probably of greater concern to more midwestern archaeologists than any other single prehistoric cultural manifestation.

So the feeling about Hopewell is not just personal with me —whose grandfather's father's house stood within the sacred precincts of a mound cluster in Portsmouth, where the leaf mold dated to the tread of shamans, then the kings of that hill before it was turned by the plow. It may have been that my mother was frightened by the ghost of a shaman in my prenatal months, but I doubt it. What I remember most vividly are her recollections of "arrowheads and axes" found in the neighborhood that were traded off at school or carelessly lost. They would have been heirlooms to cherish above all others. But Hopewellianism is not dead, not as long as corn grows in the Scioto-Ohio bottomlands and as long as two mounds, of the thirty or more that were once there, still stand on a hill in Portsmouth overlooking them.

Where the Ohio Hopewell once had been, a void was created when it collapsed as if it had been built over a chasm; but the sides of the chasm held. Hopewell styles and practices continued, through force of habit and tradition, among people who had not been disturbed as had the population of the Hopewell capital. These drifted into the Mississippian culture, not a revival of Hopewellianism—which had, nevertheless, prepared the ground for it. By this time the cultivation of corn-beans-squash had been long in the land, and much longer had been the ceremonial burial of chief men. All that was needed now was new stimulation, an updating of these ideas.

The stimulation came from Mexico, but there is no agreement on how. There was no movement of people; there is no trail of diffusion. And again we are forced back upon the explanation that groups of eloquent missionaries, perhaps no more than a small group headed by a strong personality—the St. Patrick of a bloody gospel—provided new leadership and rekindled the vision. (It may even have been the element of blood, of human sacrifice, like the Mayan and Aztecan rites of mollification of the gods by the offering of human victims, which gave the old religion its new vitality; we ourselves are presently in such a mood, when only violence relieves our tensions.) There are no trade routes between the Mississippi Valley and Mexico, and less reason to suspect trade than when Ohio usufructians began suddenly to wear ear spools and bury obsidian in quantity with their dead. But there can be no doubt about the derivation of the practices and their artistic expression. These are unmistakably Mexican, of that era when the intention of religion was to strike terror in the soul and fill it with incubi, not the *sursum corda* into spiritual serenity of (some) civilized creeds. The motifs are severed, amputated hands; staring eyes, disembodied or glaring out of heads, frequently tearful (the so-called Weeping Eye); the Feathered Serpent; skulls with brutally accentuated jaws; two-headed figures with one of the heads inhuman; heads with whiplike tongues; grotesque masks; rattlesnakes and horned toads—it all looks like something out of a preposterous horror movie. But there is nothing make-believe or synthetic about it; these symbols once had the power, it cannot be doubted, to freeze the blood and bend the will.

It cannot be said, however, that this bizarre and darkly imaginative symbolism of fear nerved the Mississippian peoples to a cultural level beyond Hopewellianism. Despite the Cahokia complex, with its eerie "Long-Nosed God" motif, and Aztalan, with its unmistakable evidence of cannibalism in this period, and despite Etowah (Georgia), Moundville (Alabama), and Spiro (Oklahoma), the richly productive centers of the art of the gruesome, no more earth was heaped, no more talent displayed, and no better organization attained.

Jesse D. Jennings wrote, in his contribution, "Prehistory of the Lower Mississippi Valley," to the 1959 publication *Archaeology of Eastern United States*, "Considering how generally widespread the evidences of the Mississippi culture are over the south there is surprisingly little systematic published work upon which to base a synthesis." Much work has been done since, particularly by A. R. Kelly, but a synthesis such as Hopewell lends itself to is still not possible. What the temple-mound idea seems to have done was to Balkanize mid-America. The temple mounds seem to have been not merely the centers where were conducted the necessary rites of the corn liturgy but the actual seats of government, and there were many of them. These political entities could hardly be called city-states, because the center was not a city, but it was like a city-state in that there was a social-political-cultural-religious, and even ethnic, core of gravity which held the surrounding territory together—a very localized, physiographically shaped territory. This is not Hopewellianism, with its *Lex Romana* and its segregation and dispersal of functions as we have seen them. This was a Disunited States.

Jennings writes of the Mississippian of the South, "Its abrupt disappearance has been credited to the simultaneous appearance of Europeans and smallpox, syphilis or the common cold. In any event it waned, to be finally observed in decadent form by the French among the Taensa and Natchez tribes."

This decline gives us to think that had the discovery of America been delayed for another century, the cultural level would have been no higher, the resistance to invasion no tougher, the respect exacted no more decent. Much could be written about the temple-mound period, about its artifacts and its ways of living as deduced from survivals among historic tribes, but it would all be lists and descriptions. The art—which is not the right word for the sacramental images produced to render corporeal the body and soul of some religious notion or another—and the state of mind and the grisly mythology that evoked it, are morbidly fascinating. But it falls short of the Hopewellian extrovertism and exuberant desire to see the world and absorb its multifariousness and perhaps overcome it with the cajolery of an idea. There is no vision in the Mississippian —only a grimly bizarre dogmatism, which was vindicated, not, as the faithful must have believed, by strict observance of precept, but because the Mississippi Valley and the alluvial plains of the Southeast were the finest of cornlands. Given time, the Hopewellians would have discovered Europe; they are the only people, it seems to me, despite the inferiority of their society to the Mayan, Aztecan, and Inca empires, who had that kind of curiosity and energy and that kind of basically scientific feeling about the earth, that it is here to be explored. The Hopewell shamans were men for all seasons; the temple-mound priests were content with their parishes.

Actually it is something of a violation of our intention that the Mississippians are in this book at all. Their *Zeitgeist* was Mexican, however it was transferred from Mexico, which was civilized, within our use of the term, at that time—civilization having been set as our finish line. But the Mississippian does bring to a conclusion our long narrative of what happened to

the chopper-flake people who ate their way to America, to establish the human species among its fauna. That part of Meridional
America which is now the United States is obviously the first
territory across which they could spread and which they could
populate and so be designated the First Americans. Where they
stood millennia later is at the "decadent form" of the Mississippian, among the Natchez and Taensa, without promise of anything great to come but another dark age like the one that separated them from the Hopewellians.

The capabilities of the chopper-flake strain of humanity
reached achievement, of course, in the great civilizations of
Mexico and Central and South America. They are outside the
scope of this book, simply because they are subjects for books
of their own and it is a distortion and demeaning of them to
treat them at lesser length. They belong properly to history,
like the Babylonians and Assyrians and Egyptians, though that
history cannot be known except through archaeology. But we
know they had a history, as long and internally eventful as that
of Greece or Rome, or ours.

The great states fell first, with appalling suddenness, to the
desperate sorties of Pizarro and Cortes, and within two decades
all their records had gone up in flames in a book burning that
accomplished what Hitler never did, the total erasure from history of a whole nation. The chopper-making big-game hunters
lasted almost four hundred years longer. To give a name to the
last one, it was the Sioux chief Sitting Bull, last Indian resistance leader, born in 1834, in the days when the buffalo were
hunted with stone projectile points and butchered with stone
choppers and stone flakes. The day he died, the day the sun
fell, was at the ebb of the year, December 15, 1890, almost
exactly four hundred years after Columbus had raised the first
land in the Western Hemisphere. He was shot to death by Indian
Agency police making an arrest. The police were themselves
Sioux Indians, but wearing the white man's uniform, taking his
wages, and carrying out his orders. They were of the progressive faction of the Sioux who had seen the uselessness of fighting the white man and had taken his road. But Sitting Bull was
a conservative, the last Old Stone Age man.

12

Sea Change

THE MODEL OF American prehistory that we have herein constructed is simple and straightforward: Asiatics of an archaic Mongoloid "race" crossed the then-imaginary borderline between Asia and America with a primitive chopper-flake industry before the third and last advance of the Wisconsin glacier, that is, before circa 25,000 B.P., as we now reckon Wisconsin time. The chances are at least 50-50 that America was entered before the previous Wisconsin advance, Wisconsin II, say before 40,000 B.P. There is a distinct possibility, on the Leakey-Simpson evidence from the Calico Mountains, that the entrance was before Wisconsin I, say 80,000 B.P., subject to future revaluation of Wisconsin time. Migrants so early would have been so few and their industry very likely so ambiguously Eolithic that it will be difficult to demonstrate, without skeletal material, their presence in that period. We neither accept nor reject, as yet, this aboriginal occupation, since it will not essentially amend our model.

However early the first coming proves to be, nothing more is required to explain the cultural development of Meridional America than an initial colonization of an immensely rich hemisphere by human beings able to make choppers and flake knives and scrapers. All else, the specialized hunting of the big-game spearman and the total exploitation of fixed environment by the usufructians, evolves, naturally and inevitably, into conservi-fructianism, into the preliterate "empire" of the Hopewellians and the literate states of South and Mesoamerica.

The only other population-culture influx of any significance was that of the Eskimos, whose advanced or classic Mongoloidism contrasts so sharply with the incipient Mongoloidism of the Amerind that the Amerinds may claim to be of their own race. They arrived here at about 10,000 B.P., remaining until this day in the circumpolar environment to which they were industrially and physically adapted, and contributed little or nothing to the usufructians of Meridional America, where the kinds of food produced by nature dictated a quite different adjustment.

There is a disposition among many prehistorians to believe that a group called the Athapascans or Athabascans breached Eskimo territory at a quite late date, say about A.D. 500, and drove southward as far as Mexico, the southernmost representatives being the Apaches. The presumptive evidence for this incursion is language and certain cultural traits such as the wearing of headbands and high, buskinlike moccasins, which are Mongol in pattern. Though Athapascans still live in Canada and reach into southern Alaska, they appear to be Indians, not far-scattered Mongols, and archaeology does not support a theory of migration. If they were latecomers, they brought no cultural innovations with them—significantly, they introduced no metal —and fell immediately into the usufructian ways of the natives. In any event, we need take no stand about the Athapascans; for their coming, if they prove to have been migrants, in no way modified what was Amerind.

So far, what we have considered has been pedestrian migration into America via the Bering-bridge overland route, though the Athapascans, arriving long after the submersion of the bridge, would have had to boat or be ferried across the Bering Strait. (This is one of the strongest arguments against them as Mongol transplants, since they were a strictly dry-land people as Americans.) What we now have to face up to is the question of the innoculation of Amerind cultures by transoceanic voyagers, such as the fleeing Jews of the Book of Mormon, or Donnelly's survivors of the catastrophe of Atlantis. Such events would not set askew our model before about five thousand years ago, when coastwise trade and short open-sea hops begin to appear on record in the Mediterranean and the Indian Ocean— unless it could be shown that the mariners came in some force and numbers and established here, as did the post-Columbus colonists, their own kind of culture, or that they were traders, in which case what they had to sell could only be the products of their own culture.

Had any such contact been made, we should expect to find artifacts of Western European or Eastern Asiatic origin, or at least simulations of these, as proof of the adoption of new traits. It will always militate against the likelihood of transoceanic contact that, except in a very limited area in Peru, America never had a metallurgy: cast copper, bronze, or iron. Had transoceanic colonists made landfalls in America after the time when crafts became capable of an ocean voyage, they certainly would have brought with them metallurgically made tools and weapons; and had traders offered their wares, metal tools and weapons would have been the first to catch the barbarian eye. While the originals may have long since corroded away, it would be unlikely that they would not have engendered a metal tradition of some kind. In tinless America a bronze age was not possible, but cast copper and iron were certainly within the means at hand.

This absence of metal rather vitiates the somewhat more plausible evidence that pottery may have been introduced from abroad into maritime areas in America. This evidence does not controvert the proposition that pottery is an independent American invention, however, and merely adds to the picture possible sources for some ceramic traditions. Amerind pottery will be discussed presently, especially that from Valdivia, Ecuador. Pottery making is, to be sure, a much older human accomplishment than metallurgy, and metal tools, weapons, and ornaments need not have been in the cargo of marine travelers. But by and large, the art of the shipwright, as contrasted with the handicraft of building dugouts, rafts, and other such water transport, does not seem to have long preceded metallurgy. As a matter of fact, metal tools were almost certainly needed to dress planks and timbers for real seagoing craft. The proper tools had to be in the hands of the artisans, who only then conceived the more ambitious projects that could be executed with them.

It is obvious that a distinction must be made between deliberate voyages, with a known destination in mind, and accidental ocean crossings (Valdivia is an example of this, if it is an instance of transoceanic contact) by boats blown out to sea. Of the latter there must have been many occurrences dating from the time that Mediterranean traders first ventured into the Atlantic as far west as Ireland. Though this kind of voyaging was mainly pilotage, seldom out of sight of landmarks, ill winds and sudden, blinding storms were always a threat to all navigational plan and control. Once it is driven beyond known waters and safe harbor, a craft is flotsam, to be carried wherever the currents and winds, not always in unison, happen to be going. We must suppose that most craft which were so unfortunate as to be blown into the open sea broke up before ever seeing land again, or that the crews, not provisioned for extended journeying, perished. But we must also suppose, since there are records of long survival at sea, like that of Captain Bligh of the mutinous ship *Bounty*, that some few did make it to America. But would the crews have gone ashore in any shape to defend themselves against attack by the aborigines or, if hospitably received, to contribute to the culture of those aborigines?

Deliberate voyages, it is clear on reflection, presuppose not one but three transoceanic crossings: the first accidental crossing and the happening on America; a return voyage to the port of embarkation; and then a retracing of the original route, with trade goods or colonists, to the newly discovered land. It is hard to believe that if such a trilogy of voyages ever took place, the information about the exotic New World, peopled by a race heretofore unknown, would not have been disseminated and retained in oral tradition somewhere, until picked up by a Plato or a Herodotus and set down in literature. This is what happened in the case of Eric the Red, which opens this book. Using the standard of lack of documentation, surviving tradition, or mythologic reference to anything that may be now identified as America, we may discount the likelihood of pre-Columbian trade routes to America—or even trade voyages, with a manifest of items to be bartered to American barbarians—or its discovery, in the sense that it was found, its existence made known, and its products returned to Old World markets.

One compilation of proposed and actual pre-Columbian contacts is that made by Charles M. Boland, who, in his *They All Discovered America* (1962) lists eighteen landfalls for which there is claimed to be some archaeological or documentary support. The chronology is modest enough. Only one of the eighteen contacts is assigned a pre-Christian date: it is said to be either Phoenician, at about 480 B.C., or Megalithic, contemporary with Stonehenge, England, at about 2000 B.C. Of the remaining sixteen, one is Roman, at A.D. 64, one is Chinese, at A.D. 499; one is our old friend, the Irish monk Brendan, at A.D. 551; and the rest are at A.D. 1000 or later. With the exception of the Phoenician or Megalithic visit (supposed to have terminated in a settlement called Pattee's Caves, or Mystery Hill, New Hampshire, which will be briefly treated in this chapter), none of these came in time to have had any impact on American prehistory. Had they done so, there would now be no dubiety about them: one of them, instead of the Columbian voyages, would have been credited with the addition of the New World to geography and history.

This is pallid stuff compared with Donnelly's romantic Atlanteans, the Book of Mormon Israelites, the supercivilized race that inhabited James Churchward's Lost Continent of Mu (the Pacific counterpart of the lost Atlantis) and is said to have jaunted about in airborne cars, and the whimsical notion of Harold S. Gladwin that part of the fleet of Alexander the Great got sidetracked on a voyage to India and ended up on the west coast of Mexico. Even so, archaeology has had little success when it rolls up its sleeves to investigate thoroughly such evidence as the Kensington Stone and Pattee's Caves, alleged to prove that America had been harboring pilgrims and refugees centuries before 1620. There is one notable exception to this experience, however: the discovery of Leif Ericson's Vinland the Good by Helge Ingstad and his archaeologist wife, Anne Stone Ingstad.

Discovery is not really the appropriate term, perhaps: the correct word is identification, the authenticity of the Norse sagas relating the founding of the Vinland colony having been accepted by most scholars. The search for trace of the settlement had been pursued for decades, before Ingstad found it at Lancey Meadows (L'Anse au Meadow at the northern tip of the island of Newfoundland), just where the sagas had said it was. It had been a rather substantial wilderness community, consisting of several houses—the exact number remains for complete excavation to determine, but there were at least ten, with two about thirty feet long—an iron smeltery and smithy for the working of bog-iron deposits from a nearby swamp, and a "great hall," seventy feet by fifty-five feet, which was very likely a combination church (Leif Ericson was a Christian), town-meeting hall, tavern, and market. There is abundant evidence of human activity at the site: stone-lined cooking pits, ember pits for holding fires overnight, hearths, a quantity of charcoal for the iron furnace, and one artifact—a soapstone spindle whorl from a loom. The charcoal was C14-dated and, allowing for the age of the wood in growth, corroborated the traditional date of the founding of Vinland: A.D. 1000.

In those days, during a climatic phase milder than at present, Vinland (the word *vin* is now agreed to mean "grassland" or "meadowland," rather than "vine") was fair and productive country. The Ericsons—first Leif, followed by his brother Thorvald, who was killed there by an Indian arrow, and finally half-sister Freydis, a female berserker who murdered all the women in her party with her own ax—sojourned in the prospering colony. But Thorvald stated the situation exactly as he lay dying with the Indian shaft in his vitals: "There is fat around my belly. We have a fine and fruitful country, but we will hardly be allowed to enjoy it."

During the first days of the colony, relations with the Indians, the Skraelings, had been amiable enough, even to the point of trade. But for some reason not known—could it have been Freydis and her ax?—the Skraelings suddenly attacked in great numbers. According to the account they catapulted into the Norse defenders missiles that we now conceive to have been hornets' or wasps' nests. Convinced by this display of hostility that the attack was no mere passing peeve of the Skraelings, the Norse evacuated Vinland forever, and gave up all claim to the vast territory that might have become their New World homeland.

Which brings us to the Kensington Stone, a tablet of calcite, on which are inscribed 222 runic characters reporting an Indian attack on an expedition of Norse explorers, presumably from the Vinland colony, in the vicinity where Kensington, Minnesota, now stands. It is a likely story from what we know of Vinland history, but the stone lacks something of the story's plausibility. Found in 1898, on the farm of Olaf Ohman, the stone immediately came under suspicion by runic experts, who found its language pretty much of a mishmash, a sort of runic dog Latin. Shrugged off as a probable fake, the stone was forgotten until 1907, when it was acquired by an energetic Norwegian-American, Hjalmar Rued Holand (who thus could have had nothing to do with any possible hoax involved at its inception). For the next fifty years, Holand (still alive at this writing) promoted the historicity of the Kensington Stone with an indefatigable zeal, until it was accepted by the Smithsonian Institution for public exhibit -a reward of a kind for Holand's labors.

It hardly merits such a place of honor, according to scholars, except as the triumph of a hoax. What it is worth was assessed by Eric Wahlgren in *The Kensington Stone, A Mystery Solved* (1958) a 228-page labor of loath. The runes, the experts found, vary from those in use in A.D. 800 (favorable) to those of A.D. 1800 (damning); the phraseology is modern and the grammar and numerals late nineteenth century. But Wahlgren went beyond the internal evidence; he discovered that the affidavits of witnesses to the finding of the stone were executed before a notary public in 1909, eleven years after it was discovered and two years after it came into Holand's possession.

Moreover, the commission of the notary public was not valid. The Kensington Stone is neither a genuine artifact nor was it recovered under irreproachable circumstances.

It was not Holand's only Viking preoccupation. Almost single-handed, he revived the legend of the Newport Tower. This structure still stands in Touro Park, Newport, Rhode Island, protected and respected as a monument—though to what, is far from certain. By colonial tradition a mill, it certainly does not suggest one; it is a round edifice of stone supported by colonnaded arches. It entered literature as the setting of Longfellow's poem "The Skeleton in Armor," in which the assumption is that it was a Viking fort or keep. Colonial records mention it as early as 1677, but with no hint that it was considered odd or out of place at the time; nor is there any mention of it as of other than unremarkable origin. The controversy over whether it was colonial or Norse sprang up 168 years after its first mention as real property, in 1835, in Longfellow's time, when it became an issue in, of all things, state politics. The then governor, Gibbs, was, like Longfellow, of the Norse faction. But the only dirt archaeology done during the furor was a certain amount of mudslinging, and while the Norse faction seems to have won at the polls, it was the usual victory of sentiment, not science. When Holand decided, almost a century later, to put his considerable fervor to work for the Norse cause, he used much of the material from the earlier controversy, and he soon had another one going. But this time an archaeologist was called in by the Preservation Society of Newport County. He was William S. Godfrey, then of the University of Chicago; and a committee of SAA was detailed to supervise the work. During the digging seasons of 1948 and 1949, with everybody looking down his collar, Godfrey ran his trenches through Touro Park and as close to the tower as he dared. He found nothing, incredible as it may seem: absolutely nothing, not a broken tool from the labor of construction, no artifact lost during what must have been the long period of use of so substantial a building. Nobody had misplaced anything there; nobody had discarded anything. There cannot be many sites of human activity in the entire world so devoid of refuse of that activity. O frugal New

England! Oh, yes, there was one discovery. It was colonial: a bootprint—not the heel or sole or even a nail, just the print.

Historically, then, the Newport Tower is a documented colonial-period structure; by the archaeology it is not precolonial. It was Godfrey's opinion that the explanation of the whole controversy is social. In his report for *American Antiquity*, the SAA journal, he wrote, "The roots of the controversy [of 1835] may lie in the growing class consciousness of the area, and in the rise in interest in early explorations of the continent. This period coincided in New England with a concern in genealogy and the invention of family trees." O proud, genteel New England!

Pattee's Caves, like the Kensington Stone and the Newport Tower, owe their celebrity to the industrious huckstering of one man, in this case the late William B. Godwin. This celebrity also evoked professional excavation, by Junius Bird (of Fell's Cave fame) and Gary Vescelius, both of the American Museum of Natural History; and, as in the instance of the tower, nothing was found to support Godwin's belief that the "caves" (really stone underground cells), had been constructed by Irish monks, or a second theory that they had been built by lost Phoenicians, or a third theory that they are of Megalithic-missionary origin. But here, it seems to me, we are confronted with a puzzle much less simple than the hoax of the stone or the exaggeration of age and significance of the tower.

Fourteen structures and features undoubtedly do exist on Mystery Hill, clustered within an area of about an acre. In keeping with the Megalithic-missionary hypothesis, these have now been given such appropriate names as the Mensal Shrine, the Lost Souls Dolmn, the Well of Crystals (because quartz crystals were actually found in it, and can only be explained by intentional deposit) and the Sacrificial Table. *Megalith* means "great stone," and the Megalithic missionaries were so called because they spread over Western Europe a religion of sun worship and belief in life after death that required the erection of monumental stones to define their sacred precincts, or open-air temples, and the burial of the dead in stone-lined vault graves, entered through a passage or by a shaft from above.

Stonehenge is probably the most famous of these Megalithic temples, and some of its sarsen stones, brought from twenty-four miles away, weigh forty tons. As it now stands, Stonehenge represents three periods of construction, all under Megalithic-missionary influence, with the last period definitely Bronze Age, at 1500 B.C. The earliest layout has been C14 dated at about 3800 B.P., a little later than the first appearance of Megalithic missionaries in Britain, estimated at about 2000 B.C. The always quotable Geoffrey Bibbey, in his *Four Thousand Years Ago, a Panorama of Life in the Second Millennium B.C.* (1961), writes thus about the spread of the Megalithic religion and its burial customs:

Along the whole course of the voyage here described, in Malta and in Sicily and in Sardinia, on the west coast of Italy and the south coast of France, along the south and west coasts of Spain and Portugal, in Brittany, Wales, Ireland and Denmark, a remarkable type of burial monument is found, beginning at all these points in the century or two or three prior to 2000 B.C. This burial monument consists of large tomb chambers for communal burial, sometimes built of dry stone walling with vaulted roofs, sometimes of upright slabs of stone roofed with similar stone slabs. . . . It appears clear that a burial practice native to Crete and the Aegean is introduced about 2200 B.C. into areas to which it was foreign, all the way around the coasts of Europe, but not inland, from Italy to Denmark. [The extension of the Megalithic religion inland came later: thus Stonehenge at 1800 B.C.]

We cannot help being reminded of the way the Hopewellian cult of burial spread throughout the heart of the present United States. Had the Hopewell culture been centered in New England instead of Ohio, Pattee's Caves would have received attention from more than one party of archaeologists after Godwin, who had owned the property since 1934, died in 1950.

The correspondence of structures in the Mystery Hill compound to Megalithic building has been explained in a paper in the *New York State Archaeological Association Bulletin* (March, 1963) by Andrew Rothovius of Milford, New Hampshire, who, with the late Frank Glynn, has tried to keep the site from dropping entirely into the class of tourist attraction.

At least one stone, the 4.5-ton Sacrificial Table stone, is mega-lithic, by Rothovius's account; and the double-entried shaft-bar-row (that is, mound) termed the Y Cavern is constructed very much in the style of the passage-shaft graves. Rothovius de-scribes it thus:

> The Y Cavern or great barrow mound is entered through a door-way at the left end of the crossbar. Along the inner edge of the crossbar is a "couch" carved out of the bedrock which Godwin in-sisted was the "Abbot's Bed." Its resemblance to the initiate's couches of the Mediterranean mystery religion of antiquity is ap-parent. Immediately to its right is the opening of a channel that cuts through the wall of the barrow and emerges 8 ft. away, above the "Sacrificial Table." Through this, one's voice is carried rather eerily to the outside.
>
> In the right end of the crossbar is a hearth, or what appears to be such, though no charcoal has been discovered in connection with it. Above it is an opening cut through the ceiling. In this a louvered stone was inserted that acted as a damper and draft controller. This, unfortunately, was vandalized several years ago, but its existence is a matter of attested record.

Of the utmost significance, if it could be verified somehow, is Rothovius's claim that "what appear to be chiselled outlines of the labrys or double-axe" have been noted in several places. Bibbey says, "The ship and the ax are the two most popular designs in the graves of the megalith-builders."

Certainly no Amerinds ever built like this; and if any Yankee ever did, it was only one, Jonathan Pattee, the original owner of the property. This was the conclusion that Bird and Vescelius (a valued acquaintance of mine) came to after disposing of Godwin's Irish-monks theory; but in order to reach it, they had to propose a gratuitous premise, that the Mystery Hill complex of structures, without peer or parallel, was eccentric because its builder, Jonathan Pattee, was an eccentric. How they knew this, they did not say. But the conclusion rather begs the question of the premise, archaeologically. It cannot be proved that Pattee was eccentric unless it can be proved that he built these structures, as an unusual or eccentric way of dealing with a problem of shelter or for an eccentric purpose; and it has not been shown, archaeologically, that Pattee built them. He used them, as any thrifty New England farmer would have if he had found them on his land, but would any New England farmer, however eccentric, have built a passage-shaft barrow for any New England farming purpose?

Grant the enigma of the site, however, and you still must ask yourself the question: And what did the Megalithic missionaries do then, after establishing a headquarters for their faith in New Hampshire? Known proselytizers, Bronze Age Jesuits, if you will, they had no effect at all on the Amerinds of their region; there was no sudden interest in building mortuary barrows, in erecting megaliths, or in masonry. Only in Ohio, a thousand miles to the southwest, does anything like this burial-mound complex occur, but not for at least five hundred years; the Adena mounds, earth heaped up over burials, and the Hopewell mounds, burials in log tombs which were then covered with earth, are not much like passage or shaft graves. The Adena timuli, which, at 750 B.C., are closest to contemporary with the Megalithic, are least like the barrow graves, while the Hopewell mounds and sacred precincts, which do resemble Megalithic practices in fundamental conception, are almost a millennium and a half younger.

If there is a thread of sun worshipping and open-sky cathedral building connecting Western Europe and America—and if this should be so, it would be a matter of enormous interest to archaeologists, historians, students of comparative religion and the history of ideas, and philosophers of the universal brotherhood of mankind—it will take more than Pattee's Caves to authenticate it, even if Pattee's Caves are themselves authentically Megalithic.

But we have not quite finished with New England as a port of entry for imports from Western Europe. Perhaps we never shall be, until that improbable yet not unthinkable time when every event of human movement that ever occurred is deposited in the data bank of an omniscient computer. For New England lies, to the map-reading eye, tantalizingly close to the Old World's western outposts, and one can devise several clever island-hopping stratagems by which man could have made his way between the two land masses. What has to be answered is not so much whether man could have made the journey as under what circumstances he would have set out on it.

The reader will undoubtedly remember the discussion about the effect of the massive withdrawal of water from the sea during glacial periods. With the last Wisconsin-Würm maximum lowering the sea by at least four hundred feet and exposing vast areas of the continental shelf of both hemispheres, Eastern America and Western Europe approached each other perhaps a thousand miles closer in places than the eighteen hundred miles or so of today. Nevertheless there still was a great deal of water between the two land masses; and undoubtedly it seemed then to present an impassable barrier, because, as far as we know, the very idea of seagoing craft had never entered the Paleolithic mind at 20,000 B.P. The cultural level was mostly the hunting of periglacial big game in those parts of Europe not covered by ice, as the present British Isles were.

But glacial melting began to refill the sea, causing a constantly retreating coastline. Some uplands were left as islands off the coast, and on some of these, we may assume, hunting bands must have been isolated before they knew it. With the sea persisting in its rise, these islands were reduced in area and food resources, until any population living on them had to change its subsistence plans. The inhabitants must have turned to the sea for their daily meat, and developed some sort of fisherman's knowledge of boats. Came then the very rapid rise at about 6000 B.P., about which most geologists are in agreement and in which Fairbridge finds the origin of universally recurrent myths about a deluge which we think of as Noah's Flood. The rise was so rapid that one man in his lifetime would notice the menacing encroachment of the sea and become alarmed about it—with good reason, since there must have been hundreds of postglacial low-lying islands, as safe-looking as Long Island is today, that were inundated from 20,000 B.P. to 2000 B.P.

We have only to suppose, then, that a group of islanders, apprehensive about a drowning future, took thought for escape, built a fleet of boats or a Noachian ark, and, when the invasion of the sea reached a critical marker or floated the ark, left their sinking homeland behind. Probably all knowledge of where lay the nearest safe land had disappeared, and westward was as good a direction as any; or wind and current determined the course: in any event, these seafarers lasted until they reached the American mainland.

Does any archaeology give us leave to engage in this speculation? Yes, the polished stone work that characterizes the Archaic of New England gives us encouragement to work on an hypothesis of a flight from some humble, ocean-swallowed Atlantis to an American haven. In the chapter on the Archaic, the side-notched projectile points of the Otter Creek style of the Vergennes focus of Vermont were related to the spread of the Big Sandy side-notched pattern out of the South. No other interpretation of the Otter Creek seems plausible than a derivation from the Raddatz points of Wisconsin, as a way station on the journey out of the South. But the polished stone tools, that is, tools shaped by abrading, of the Vergennes and succeeding phases are certainly not derived from the same sources. The polished-stone-tool element, which is highly distinctive, includes slate points, the plummet (possibly a fish gorge), the atlatl weight, the semilunar knife or ulu, and wood-working adzes, chopping axes, celts, and gouges. Whence came this trait of shaping most tools by grinding, and whence came some of the tools: the gouges, ulus, and plummets, for instance? That they came from the Eskimos, who use the ulu to this day, though in metal, or from any circumpolar culture, as had once been thought, has long since been disproved; the Eskimo and Northern-culture use of ulus and other polished stone tools is later than the New England industry. But there does not seem to be any other region from which the polished-stone inspiration could have reached New England; and either it is an *in situ* development, or we may be looking at the cultural pattern of Lost Atlantises that disappeared before history or tradition caught up with their existence.

Pursuing a theme similar to this, the Canadian archaeologist Frank Ridley took a long look at overseas bases from which the polished-tool complex could have come and published in the

Pennsylvania Archaeologist (August, 1960) his findings of parallels "between the Archaic implement complex of the St. Lawrence valley of northeastern North America and those of the Atlantic and Arctic cultures of northwestern Europe." The similarities included polished gouges, celts, slate knives, projectile points, and "the mortuary custom of covering the body with red paint." There are very strong manifestations of this red-paint burial complex throughout New England and extending down the coast to Long Island, though inland it did not penetrate our lower-Hudson oyster-eater country, only forty miles upriver from Long Island. The richest, most elaborate instance of this red-paint ritual burial is that of the Red Paint people of Maine at circa 4000 B.P.

Ridley finds his parallels as deep in time as about 7500 B.P. in the Gorbunov culture of the Ural Mountains of Russia and suggests that pressure from inland tribes forced the Gorbunov and later peoples to the Karelian Peninsula of Finland and to the coast of the White Sea, after which they could retreat farther only by boat. That they did this, some of them, and found themselves borne west across the North Atlantic, probably along the same route later used by the Norsemen, is implicit in Ridley's conclusion "that the northern European chronology of stone and pottery types extending upwards in time from the Gorbunov period to Karelian times [about 4000 B.P.] has, to a great extent, correspondence with the northeastern North American series of Archaic stone industries and its following Woodland pottery complexes." He has expanded this opinion to me personally.

Ridley's judgment was reached after he had visited the National Historical Museum in Moscow in 1959 and verified the correspondence in pottery treatment. But James B. Griffin, one of the leading authorities on Woodland pottery, who also inspected the Russian pottery, has told me that he saw no significant resemblances between the two ceramic traditions. Perhaps we have here an irresolvable difference in subjective interpretation between two men who both know the material; but I think there is a fatal flaw in Ridley's interpretation: there is no time correspondence. The first pottery in the American

Northeast, the Vinette I type, has nowhere been dated earlier by C14 than three thousand years ago, while the polished-stone industries of New England and Northern Europe do have a satisfactory contemporaneity. It is to be doubted that the Gorbunov or Karelian peoples would have brought their tools and not their pots. My sinking-island suggestion would solve this discrepancy. All we have to suppose is that the island people were participants in the polished-stone industrial tradition, but were cut off by the rising sea from the main body of the tradition before pottery reached it, and thus never had pottery to carry off when they evacuated their homes. But none of this fabric of supposition can be tested until we can investigate the bottom of the sea as easily as we can survey the land.

Ridley's search for an analogue to Woodland pottery is, however, the recognition of a problem in prehistory: where did Vinette I pottery come from? It is not at all like the pottery from the South: the Carolinas, Florida, Georgia, Poverty Point. Its paste is tempered with coarse grit aplastic, and it is made by the coil-winding method: that is, the vessel is built up by laying "ropes" of wet clay paste on top of each other like a coil of rope; these coils are then bonded together by malleating the outside of the vessel with a cord-wrapped stick or paddle, with a cord-wrapped block of wood or stone held on the inside as an anvil. Cord marking on the exterior and interior is the identifying feature of Vinette I, and the same cord marking, either on the inside or outside, in later styles smoothed over, characterizes the whole tradition.

The earliest pottery in the South, on the other hand, is tempered with vegetal fibers—grass, twigs, shredded stalks—and is hand modeled. The very earliest vessels were copied from soapstone vessels and bear simulated chisel marks, in imitation of the tooling by which soapstone vessels were shaped. This earliest pottery is dated at about 4000 B.P. from shell middens on the Gulf coast excavated by Ripley Bullen, and at 4564 B.P. from a shell midden on the Georgia-Carolina border. But its development did not take a direction that would allow us to think Vinette I derived from it at any stage: the earliest pottery, called Stallings Island, is plain, not cord marked; that of three thousand years ago, contemporary with Vinette I and called the Orange series, is decorated, not cord marked.

The reader is by now conditioned to guess on the first try where it was thought that Vinette I came from: Asia, of course. Unfortunately, no trail of sherds leads across Canada from the Bering Strait to the Northeast, or to the Midwest, where the Adenan's first pottery, called Fayette Thick, is the equivalent of Vinette I. MacNeish, the same who traced the ancestry of corn through Mexican caves, has taken up this matter in his *Introduction to the Archaeology of Southeastern Manitoba* (1958). Concerning the general agreement of students that the Woodland tradition must have entered the northern United States through southern Manitoba, he writes bluntly, "The present evidence is categorically opposed to such a hypothesis." The earliest dated Woodland pottery in the United States, he finds, is coeval with a cultural phase in Manitoba called Larter, which is preceramic. He says, further, "First of all, considerable archaeological surveying in the boreal forest of the Northwest territory, Yukon and Alaska has been done. All in all over 300 sites are known. Not one Woodland pot sherd has been found on or in any of them."

If Vinette I and Fayette Thick did not travel into the Northeast from Asia or from the Southeast or from the Southwest via Poverty Point, where the earliest pottery is fiber tempered, then Ridley's hypothesis of overseas origin must hold water. But there is one objection: no equivalent to Vinette I turned up in Moscow; Ridley's correspondences are between European and later Woodland types, including some Hopewellian styles. The objection is not fatal—European motifs could have been added into an already established Vinette I ceramics--but the Vinette I tradition, in which pots were being made in the Long Island-Connecticut area until historic times, remains unaccounted for, and with it, the whole Woodland pottery province: roughly, the northeast quadrant of the United States, from the St. Lawrence to Virginia and from Maine to Illinois, with later enlargement beyond the Mississippi and beyond the Canadian border. Vinette I pottery, a good many sherds of which I have found in the lower Hudson, does not look like an invented pottery, because of its advanced technique of manufacture; but, with its coarse paste and simple, baglike shape, it does look copied. But copied from what, which came from where?

Most experts, including MacNeish, still believe, despite the total lack of evidence across Canada, in an Asiatic incubator for Woodland pottery. Ridley believes it crossed the Atlantic from the east; and he has this advantage in the argument, that the lack of sites along the marine route can hardly be used as an argument against it. But nobody suggests that it was an offshoot of the indigenous American pottery that we find in the southern United States, which may have been invented there, or may have been a diffused idea from Mesoamerica, where pottery seems to appear at about the same time (if 4500 B.P. is a good date for the first Stallings Island ware). Yet who would find it plausible that pottery was the only trait to have been brought into the area by whoever brought it, Asiatics or Northern Europeans? But if we don't believe this, what other traits have we found among the Adenans and the Hopewellians and the Northeasterners that had not been there, *in esse* or *in utero*, for millennia?

Just how a pottery-seeding contact, and only a pottery-seeding contact, might have been made by boatmen, supporting Ridley's Europeans rather than Asiatics, is illustrated from Valdivia, a shell-midden site on the coast of Ecuador. The original excavator and the discoverer of the anomalous pottery within the shell deposits was the knowledgeable Ecuadorian amateur the late Emilio Estrada. The pottery, while *sui generis* and of a previously unknown ceramic tradition, would have been a relatively minor addition to archaeological knowledge had not the middens yielded the surprising C14 age of 4,450 $\pm$ 200 years. This was 500 years older than the oldest pottery then (1958) known in America, the Guanape; yet it was obviously no beginner's concept of ceramics, like Stallings Island; its decoration was that of quite advanced potters. To add to the puzzle was the fact that the cultural content of the Valdivia middens was not in advance of the seashore usufructianism of that coastal stretch, where contemporary dwellers were without pottery. Clifford Evans and Betty Meggers Evans of the Smithsonian were invited to look over the situation.

Their close examination of the 36,096 potsherds recovered revealed a patent mismatch: it was the decoration that was advanced, not the construction. They wrote:

For all its elaboration in shape and decoration, Valdivia pottery exhibits its primitive character by the thickness of the vessel walls and the imperfect symmetry of rim and body contours. The vessels were built up from coils of clay that sometimes were left visible on neck jars as an ornamental effect [not like the malleated coils of Vinette and the subsequent Point Peninsula ware]. The surface of most of the vessels was smoothed to a high gloss; about a fifth of them were given a red "slip."

This could not be a native ceramic tradition: there was nothing in America from which it could have developed, yet it had to be an imitation of a developed tradition. But whence had come the tradition that it imitated if it was the oldest pottery in the region? Could it have come by sea? and if by sea, then from overseas, across the Pacific? The possibility had to be considered, despite the fact that it seemed to be directly contradicted by the breadth of the Pacific, enormously greater at that cultural period than it is now (having skippered a small ship across it twice, I have personally experienced its present vastness). But the mind can leap these distances in an instant, and Meggers and Evans knew where there was an Asiatic ceramic tradition that produced pottery almost exactly like that of Valdivia. It was in Japan, some eight thousand sailing miles away, and it was called Jomon.

Jomon pottery, as the record now stands, is, at 9000 B.P., the earliest pottery in the world, the earliest Egyptian and other Middle Eastern traditions being about six thousand years old. Thus the Jomon culture, of seashore shell-midden depositors like the Valdivians, found on the islands of Honshu and Kyushu, had forty-five hundred years of pottery making behind it before something very like its ceramics appeared on the Ecuadorian coast. With the assistance of a National Science Foundation grant, Meggers and Evans went to Japan to discover just how like Valdivian pottery the Jomon pottery was.

As a long and evolving pottery tradition the Jomon had undergone a series of stylistic changes; the critical question, therefore, was: Did Jomon pottery of about 4500 B.P. look like what had appeared at Valdivia at that time? It did, in vessel shape and decorative techniques and in construction methods. With these facts before us, we can hardly help accepting a direct transfer of people with pots in their hands from Jomon to Valdivia, however unlikely the voyage.

It must, of course, have been an involuntary voyage, wholly accidental and, in the minds of the boat crew, a calamitous event. The Jomonians were shellfish gatherers, as were the littoral Valdivians and our lower-Hudson riparian campers of the same era, but the Evanses see them also as deep-sea fishermen. It is a sensible assumption: if they were fishermen at all, they had to be deep-sea fishermen, since the Japanese islands are mountains thrust up sheer from the depths of the ocean and deep water begins almost at the strand line. Once we begin to entertain the thought that the Valdivian pottery is Jomon inspired, we accept this premise as implied; only a craft designed and built from the beginning to withstand the heavy seas of open water could have made the long haul from Japan to Ecuador in one piece.

With the Evanses we now suppose that a Jomonian fishing boat is struck by a storm, probably one of the typhoons that sweep Japan—full or glancing, one or more annually—during the typhoon season from late July to late October. By the time the wind abates, the boat has been driven far from land and into the oceanic current that skirts the Japanese islands. As now charted, the main offshore current runs not southwest, transversely, between Japan and South America, but northward, toward the great eastward arch of Asia as it extends toward Alaska. The barrier of the two continents in near approach acts as a dam and turns the current east, toward the North American shore. That barrier then turns it southward, parallel to the continental shore but some three hundred miles away, to about the latitude of Ecuador; there it turns westward across the Pacific, joined by the southern Pacific countercurrent, and becomes the river-in-the-sea that Thor Heyerdahl's Kon-Tiki rode to Polynesia. How the Jomonian boat escaped the grasp of this current and was able to veer to port, toward the South American mainland, we shall never know. Like everything else about the voyage, this escape must have been adventitious, a timely wind or storm blowing onshore and pushing the boat to a landfall at last.

The current over this route averages about ten knots per day; with eight thousand miles to travel, we get a time-at-sea of eight hundred days: two years, two months, and ten days. Incredible, yes; impossible, no. As fishermen the crew could have fed themselves by using the skills that normally provided them a livelihood, and rain falls frequently enough all year round along the route as far south as San Francisco to have provided fresh water; below San Francisco the precipitation along the coast would be sufficient during the winter months. But rainfall could not have been so constant as to keep the crew in fresh water all the time, so we see aboard the boat as the indispensable gear, without which the voyage could never have been completed, a half-dozen jars or pots, leak-proof and sealable against evaporation, for water storage. When the Jomonians went ashore at Valdivia, they must have had an appreciation amounting to superstitious veneration of what their pots had done in getting them there.

What could the Jomonians have thought when they first sighted the shell heaps of Valdivia, so much like their own homeland? Possibly, despite the fact that the Valdivians spoke an alien tongue and had strange customs, that they had merely been going round and round in watery circles. That they had crossed the world's largest ocean the long way, they could not possibly have suspected. The Evanses point out that the cultural level, excluding ceramics, and the pattern of living of the Valdivians and Jomonians were similar, and the Valdivian cast of countenance and coloration might have made them look like kin to the Jomonians. (The Jomonians are not the ancestors of the Japanese, who are latecomers to the islands—at about the time of Christ—from continental Asia, but belong to a much older, less "Mongoloid" strain.)

It must have seemed to the Jomonian Argonauts that a "divine" demon wind had seized upon them for the violation of a tabu, had damned them to a watery hell until they had served

a term of punishment, and then, appeased, had returned them
to the land of the living but not to their own backyards, as a
final measure of retribution.

We see the Jomonians slipping in on the tide at Valdivia,
apprehensive as to whether the demon has been appeased and
deliverance is imminent or whether there are other persecutions
ahead in a land of monsters. To the Valdivians they must seem
superior beings, with their sturdy boat emerging from the mists
of the high seas, their weathered look, and their pottery. The
meeting is immediately reassuring on both sides. The Jomonians see that they have not been carried to the shore of Hell
across an oceanic Styx, but to a place of human abode, pleas-
antly recognizable. Relieved, they advance with diffident eager-
ness. The Valdivians, innately hospitable, fears allayed by the
scant numbers and gaunt condition of these newcomers, yet
respectful of their possession and handling of the boat, meet
friendly overture with welcoming response.

How long it would have been before there was language
enough between them for the Jomonians to relate their Sin-
badian adventures to the Valdivians we cannot even guess, since
it is doubtful that the Jomonians could ever have made com-
prehensible to the Valdivians what had happened, even so far
as they understood it themselves. But explanations must have
been asked for and given immediately, explanations that the
Valdivians wanted to hear expanded with greater detail. The
Jomonians had come, we may suppose, during a time when
food was plentiful enough for sharing with uninvited guests.
Probably the Jomonians very shortly began to justify their
existence by adding to the food supply with their boat and
fishing know-how. They became, at any rate, valued and established members of the community, and were permitted to take
wives and set up households. (The Valdivians apparently lived
in wattle-and-daub huts.) Into each new Jomonian-Valdivian
menage goes one of the precious voyage pots.

Since it does not seem likely that there were women in the
crew of the Jomonian boat if it were on a routine fishing run,
and if women were the Jomonian potters, when the Jomonian
husbands came to the point of instructing their Valdivian wives

in ceramics, they could impart manufacturing method only, not the tricks of the trade. Those had to come of practice, and, while the earliest pottery is inexpert, they did come: it did not take long for Valdivian pottery to become as accomplished as the Jomonian, and when they had got the hang of it, the Valdivian women began to make figurines in ceramics that had formerly been made, not too realistically, in stone. The figurines, comparatively well done, are rather like the Hopewell statuettes in that they tell us something about the look of Valdivian women. The faces have slits and holes for eyes and mouth, but chins and cheeks are modeled and the bare bosoms are in full relief. Where the talent is most lovingly laid on is in the hairdos: these are so elaborate and so varied that the twentieth-century mind suspects a beauty parlor in the community, with regular weekly appointments (and wave-setting sessions under a solar hair drier). Perhaps these coiffures came with the Jomonians, too. On the other hand, one woman among the Jomonian Argonauts could have done it all: set the hair styles, started the first pottery kiln, and cooked the first mollusk stew ever tasted by palates accustomed to eating shellfish raw. We can finish it all off by assuming that she married the chief's son and became a legend, the model for the figurines.

Had Ulysses been aboard the Jomonian boat and had the Valdivians carried the tradition into literacy, this transpacific crossing would now be one of the world's great epics. It was probably the longest voyage, in elapsed time, ever made by man: even with winds acting in concert with a ten-knot-per-day current and no navigation errors, it must have lasted at least a year, much more likely two; adversities could have prolonged it to three. The protraction is probably not important; once the regimen of survival had been learned, living off the sea was probably not much more uncertain than living off the land. But it was every bit as much so, and the fauna of the deep was a zoology beyond man's experience. How hideous the giant squid must have looked, how titanic the whale—for the whale-path had to be crossed. Yet, when we have done with yarning, and take to evaluating the hard archaeological facts, what did this Japanese invasion signify in American prehistory?

Even those Americanists who see it as the Evanses see it will hardly claim that the Valdivian is the ceramic tradition which spawned all other American ceramic traditions. Pottery came to the Valdivians at a time when they were ready to make it and use it (fragile, onerous pots are only encumbrances to hunting bands), and it bettered their lives, as it bettered the lives of any Archaic people to whose simple equipment it was added—but no more than that. That it was pottery in an advanced decorative stage was of no consequence; its usefulness gained nothing from its polish or its form. And this one new trait was the only discernible consequence of the Jomonian miracle. The Valdivian culture continues as the Valdivian culture; it does not become an Ecuadorian Jomon. There is not another single item of Jomonian form or flavor in the Valdivian middens: they yielded only the crudest stone industry of flakes and choppers, manos, metates, and net sinkers. Where were the polished stone axes of Jomon, the fine leaf-shaped blades, the antler harpoons, the rich bone industry? Did the Jomonian seamen remember only how to make pottery and forget how to do anything else?

The archaeology of Valdivia has given us a fine sea story, or excited us to imagine one, and for that reason alone it deserves a place in American prehistory. It is, moreover, a warning not to harden our hearts adamantly against transoceanic contacts. Nobody has proposed a better explanation of how the Valdivian pottery got to that isolated coast and was found in middens which yielded no signs of a rudimentary ceramics, such as mud balls or carved stone vessels, deposited by a people who gave no other sign of technological ingenuity. And if one trait was once washed up on the beach, others probably were—but like driftwood, not like seed, to take root and produce colonial fruit. That happened only after Columbus.

Jomonian Sinbads, Megalithic monks, an island folk in flight from their drowning homes under an unsung Noah—romantic as all these possibilities are, they are simple contacts of barbarian and barbarian, a meeting and mingling, even integration, of people who were really more alike in their standards of living than they were different, or, at least than they were irreconcilable in their differences. But let us assume a case where there was a contact from a mature and peaceful civilization in Asia with an entrenched and flourishing civilization on the west coast of Mesoamerica. What would be the effect if the contacting Asiatics came bearing the essence of their civilization as ideas in their heads rather than, like the members of the Cortes expedition, as guns in their hands.

The effect as perceived by a Mesoamerican specialist, Gordon Ekholm of the American Museum of Natural History, was described in a series of papers in the early 1950's, of which the summary paper appeared, under the title "A Possible Focus of Asiatic Influence in the Late Classical Cultures of Meso America," in Memoir no. 9 of the Society for American Archaeology (1953): *Asia and North America: Transpacific Contacts.* I have been at some pains above to state the hypothetical case of transpacific contact between civilizations obliquely, since this is what Ekholm has done: pictured and described the effects without speculation about how or why the contacts took place. In the Memoir 9 piece he wrote, "I do not hold strongly to a 'belief' that transpacific contacts occurred, only that the problem is an exciting and important one and should be thoroughly examined from all points of view." Thus Ekholm takes himself out of the heat of the argument about pre-Columbian contacts and leaves the beholder to conclude for himself why the statue of a seated lion from Java very much resembles a seated jaguar at Tula, Mexico, and why there are lotus motifs at Palenque that strongly suggest the sacred-lotus motif from India, when the sacred Indian lotus is not native to America.

Ekholm posed the problem thus: "When considering in a general way the possibility of some external non-American influence affecting the known sequence of cultures in Meso America one thinks first of those periods within that sequence where pronounced changes in the cultural picture occurred." He finds three such: (1) the Formative period, "where we have the invention or the introduction of agricultural and pottery making techniques and the accompanying change from a primitive hunting gathering existence to one of an early proto-civilizational life"; (2) the beginning of the Classic period, about the time of Christ, which "saw the rise of a new pattern of life with such features as a complex ceremonialism involving the erection of great ceremonial centers with corbelled vault arches and specific types of tombs and stepped pyramids . . . a well developed tradition of stone sculpture and a system of hieroglyphic writing combined with a mature calendrical and astronomical science"; and (3) the Late Classic period, about A.D. 700, when certain art motifs not related to any cultural change or advance became pronounced.

The last decade of research has not been kind to Ekholm's Formative period. We have seen how MacNeish's indefatigable canvassing of caves proved the careers of the most important agricultural plants, from the wild through the domesticated to the cultivated varieties, with domestication beginning as early as seven thousand years ago, well before anybody would believe that an Asiatic Peace Corps could possibly have reached America by any means of transport known for that time level. And as pottery begins to verge on five thousand years ago, Asiatic stimulus for its inception ceases to apply, despite Valdivia, which is not the main tradition of American pottery. The earliest C_{14} date for pottery is 2914 ± 170 B.C. (4864 B.P.) at a shell-midden site at Puerto Hominga, near Cartagena, Colombia. The pottery is vegetal-fiber tempered, like the Stallings Island ware, but considerably more advanced, being decorated with incising and stamping and having lug grips or handles of biomorphic design; this Puerto Hominga ware is obviously in a second or third stage of development, the primary stage of which must have occurred before 5000 B.P.

The parallelisms between India-Southeast Asia and Mesoamerica, executed mostly in stone, to which Ekholm directs attention for his Classic and Late Classic periods are certainly visible enough, being incorporated in large buildings as well as detailed statuary and carved design, and are most impressive when seen in side-by-side illustrations from Asia and America. It is beyond our scope to lay them pictorially before the reader, but we can list the principal categories. They are: the facades of buildings carved as the faces of monsters, with the doorway as the mouth; statues of divinities or semidivinities in semire-

cumbent position; stunted or dwarf atlantean figures as the
capitals of columns, their arms upraised in a U to support
massive lintels; long, vaulted exterior galleries running along
temple walls, with the walls bearing sculptured reliefs and the
galleries set off from a courtyard by column arches; low reliefs
of court assemblages of a dozen or more figures, with the
arrangement of figures generally alike; similar treatment of
phalluses, the phallus being a rare motif in America except in
Ekholm's Classic period; "tiger" thrones; lotus thrones, staves,
and panels; trefoil arches; the sacred tree or cross; serpent
deities and serpent columns; and the "diving God," a fierce-
faced, fanged personage or anthropomorphic spirit who seems
to be swooping down at the onlooker like a leopard attacking
from an overhanging bough.

To Americanists generally, Ekholm's analogies are art appreciation, not archaeology, apparent only to the eye of the
beholder. Willey gives them no weight in the succinct but
comprehensive survey of Mesoamerica in his *Introduction to
American Archaeology: North and Middle America.* Robert
Wauchope, director of the Middle American Research Institute
of Tulane University, in his *Lost Tribes and Sunken Continents*
(1962) lumps Ekholm's resemblances (as well as the Evanses'
Valdivians) with such old-fashioned science fictions as the Lost
Atlantis and the Continent of Mu, and such stunts as Thor
Heyerdahl's fine Viking derring-do in proving that the Pacific
could be crossed by doing it backwards, archaeologically speaking, in the company of the scientifically outcast. Ekholm has
invited such treatment by not lifting a finger to hypothesize
how Asiatic religious-art concepts could have been induced into
Mayan and Mexican thinking and public works.

To be sure, no simple Valdivian boatload of castaways would
suffice, but a band of seafaring Megalithic-like Asiatic missionaries might. They would have been swallowed up in the populace, and their influence would show only as they motivated the
populace to build and sculpt and draw as they directed. But
against this may be set the fact that Ekholm's resemblances are
really those of attitude, posture, choice of subject: the style
and, above all, the substance is Mayan or Toltecan or Aztecan.

The mythology and religion within which the American member of the paired resemblances is depicted are not Hinduism nor any of its offshoots, nor is there any immanent Asiatic feature. It would be difficult, one would think, for missionary directors of the work not to include in it something of the substance of the original of what they were teaching as they had learned it. The problem yields better to another explanation: American artists and artisans went to Asia to learn techniques and pick up ideas and returned to work them out within the canons of native theology. But, so far as I know, this has never been suggested.

Though the Ekholm resemblances hang suspended in the air, rather like a rainbow, they hardly deserve the dismissal given them by Wauchope. We should not delude ourselves that we know that much about Pacific archaeology. Something that asks for an explanation has been noted by Ekholm's sharp and practiced eye, and to eliminate the only explanation offered up to now, in the light of present knowledge, is hasty and premature. In his review of the Wauchope book in *American Antiquity* (April, 1963), William E. Bittle of the University of Oklahoma, after protesting the deprecation of Ekholm's resemblances and the Evanses' Jomonians, wrote, "It is by no means certain that the last word on trans-Pacific contacts has by now been said and regardless of the general opinion of American anthropologists it seems hardly warranted to dismiss casually a small group of people who work toward a solution to this problem in the context of a method to which Wauchope himself subscribes."

The last word has certainly not been said, nor is the group of those working on the problem as small as it was, nor is the attitude of the establishment, though dubious, any longer hostile. The Society for American Archaeology held its annual meeting in May, 1968, at Santa Fe, New Mexico; if it could be said to have had a theme, with 180 papers having been presented on all aspects of American prehistory, that theme was transoceanic contact. Three half-day sessions of 7 papers each were given over to the topic, and no other rated half so much. It must be admitted that nothing startling issued from the rostrum, no excavation reports of trading posts or villages of factors dealing in Asiatic merchandise for the American market, no concentrations of artifacts of foreign manufacture, no provocative pottery like Valdivia or structures, like those of Pattee's Caves, of exotic design. The impression left most indelibly is that more and more students are beginning to believe in the probable existence of seaworthy vessels at times millennia earlier than formerly thought. Three papers especially were addressed to that point, which is the center about which this chapter revolves, covering the Pacific, the North Atlantic, and the South Atlantic. (All quotations are the précis of delivered papers in "Abstracts of Papers, Thirty-third Annual Meeting, Society for American Archaeology.")

Edwin Doran, Jr., of Texas A & M University, sums up his "The Sailing Raft as a Great Tradition" as follows:

> Strong similarities between sailing rafts of Ecuador and of coastal Asia have been suggested as evidence of a single origin. Seaworthiness and sailing ability which are quite adequate for a Pacific crossing aid this argument. To assist in establishing a genetic connection between the two, another approach is essayed here. Several great boat traditions are examined to indicate their antiquity, conservative nature and continuous distribution. By analogy one can contend that Coromandel-Annam-Formosa-Korea rafts and Ecuadorian rafts are persistent relics of a single trans-Pacific tradition of great antiquity.

Is this the answer to Ekholm's resemblances?

Alice B. Kehoe of the University of Nebraska sums up her "Small Boats upon the North Atlantic" thus:

> The probability of prehistoric contacts between Atlantic Europe and the east coast of North America is argued on the following grounds: (1) the numerous successful small-boat crossings of the North Atlantic in recent times; (2) the evidence of trans-Atlantic crossings by Eskimos and European fishermen; (3) the presence of boats and seafishing in Europe since the Mesolithic; and (4) cultural similarities or trait parallels between Europe and America in certain periods.

This gives aid and comfort to Ridley and the dwellers on Mystery Hill.

Robert A. Kennedy of the Pembrokeshire Museum says in his "A Trans-Atlantic Stimulus Hypothesis for Meso-America and the Caribbean, c. 3500 to 2000 B.C.":

The "navigational problem" can be dismissed. Indeed, the conditions for a North Atlantic route are quite reasonable, while those for the South Atlantic route are such that *many* Eur-African voyagers must have found themselves following it and a high proportion must have survived to land in the Caribbean Zone, or the mainland of northeastern South America, Middle America and the Florida peninsula.

This is pure assertion, of course; no one would think of denying that if Pacific and North Atlantic crossings occurred, the South Atlantic too, being water, would float a well-caulked bottom or well-lashed raft just as easily. But prehistory is what did happen, not what then-existent circumstances would have allowed to happen. Kennedy cites pottery similarities as his surest evidence. Having already dealt twice with examples of pottery transfer, we are a little impatient to get beyond pottery resemblances and motif coincidences. We want a Megalithic bronze dagger, or European flint, or African wood, or a cult object from Southeast Asia. Our appetite is whetted by such historical evidence as that of M. D. W. Jeffreys of Witwatersrand University (Dart's old school), whose entry in the "Abstracts" of 1968 reads:

Maize, an American plant, was cultivated in Pre-Columbian times in Asia, e.g. in Assam. Vishnu Mittre presents archaeological evidence for maize in India before 1435 A.D. Boxer noted over twenty million bushels as tribute in Peking in 1575. Pigafetta in 1521 reported maize in the Philippines. A Chinese expedition reported grain with enormous ears at Melinde in 1414. Maize names, both of European contemporaries of Columbus and of people in Asia indicated Arabs as the disseminators of maize. Pre-Columbian trans-Atlantic Arab voyages have been reported.

We are listening intently. Now give us something to hold in our hands. Archaeology is the science of fact and artifact.

With the 1970's upon us, here is the direction in which we may look for the discoveries that will put America into the *orbis terrarum* earlier than we thought, not as the despoiled victim of Old World exploitation, but as a contributor in some measure to universal culture.

13

The Future of the Past

THE STANDARD MODEL of American prehistory, with the description of which this book was begun, has been steadily eroded away by the researches of the 1960's. What has emerged instead is a picture of American independence and uniqueness in cultural development, beginning at or near the time when the first men of modern aspect appear in Western Europe. It is a picture with bright spots of hard archaeological data, a chronology that contradicts the standard model of the big-game hunter as the primal population, or even as a migrant population, and a tradition in technology like none anywhere else in the world; but it is not as nearly whole a picture as we should like. Perhaps it can never be. Cynthia Irwin-Williams of Eastern New Mexico University, coexcavator with Juan Armanta Camacho of Puebla University, Mexico, of the cardinal Valsequillo sites of Puebla, which point the way to future Early Man archaeology, wrote in a report on the sites, "Whatever the ultimate solution, it is apparent by now that the earliest Americans were few in number and left relatively little imperishable material culture." The "ultimate solution" is therefore a matter of plain poker luck: are the earliest sites still in satisfactory contextual existence? and will we ever stumble on them?

Clearly, Americanists must look, and that will be the work of the next decade. And when it is reasonably complete, of one thing we may be sure: the model that emerges will not be as simple as the one outlined in these chapters. We shall probably have been made aware that there were both a Western and an Eastern tradition of pebble-tool chopper-flake workers; a tradition that preferred bone, antler, and ivory to stone, as glimpsed at the Marmes site and in the stratum under Clovis points at the Clovis site; a bifacial-stone-working industry, as in Lanning's Andean Biface tradition; and a uniface industry that may some day be called the Caulapan tradition, after the locus at Valsequillo where it had been found in lowest stratigraphic position. The complexity of American Early Lithic, or Paleolithic, or whatever name will catch on—that is, the span of time between the Clovis hunters of twelve thousand years ago and the beginning of American habitation—will parallel, in scheme at least, that of the Old World, without having been derived from it.

But where to look? Will it be just a matter of waiting until a backhoe rips through an ancient horizon while digging a foundation, or a power shovel bites forty feet deep into gravels, as at Lewisville? We would hope not. Leakey and Simpson set the example, with their prospecting in the Calico Mountains; a few more such strikes, one of them with a more firmly fixed geology, and the Western pebble-tool tradition will go into the textbooks. Yet, if money and time are to be spent in the search for the Earliest Americans, a search that it must now be obvious is worth the expenditure of money and time, one would choose Mexico, and in Mexico, the Valsequillo Reservoir in the state of Puebla. Readers will remember how MacNeish, pursuing the origin of corn through the caves of Tamaulipas and Tehuacán, tracked the ancestral grass to its lair. He looked where he looked because in that region corn had been a staple longer than anywhere else, because the oldest corn then known had been found in a cave, Bat Cave, and because the region was honeycombed with caves. The excavation of the Valsequillo Reservoir by Irwin-Williams and Camacho has provided much the same kind of circumstantial evidence: the right geology, a series of early sites, and a very early C14 date of 21,850 ± 850 years B.P. on an artifact found *in situ*.

The Valsequillo sites might well have been included in the discussion on Earliest Man sites, such as Lewisville and the Calico Mountains. But more than the Calico Mountain sites, which will remain disputable for some time, more than Lewisville, which is "dead," in that it cannot be dug further, and more than other single-manifestation sites which have been exhausted of information, they have the potential to fill in the Early Man story as MacNeish filled in the story of corn; and we have waited month by month for some new announcement from Irwin-Williams or one of the specialists who are doing analysis of the geology or chronology. Though the series of excavations that began in 1963 and was carried on under a National Science Foundation grant until 1966 has been concluded, some of the dating results were not in until recently. But we can, I think, be reasonably sure that what is reported here about Valsequillo will hold for the time being, since it has been affirmed within days of this writing by personal communication from Irwin-Williams.

Five localities were dug in the Valsequillo Reservoir vicinity: Hueyatlaco, Tecacaxco, El Mirador, El Horno, and Barranca Caulapan, all of them yielding stone artifacts and the bones of extinct animals, including mammoth, mastodon, horse, camel, dire wolf, and four-pronged antelope. Of the five, Hueyatlaco alone yielded occupation evidence in superimposed strata; there were three of these. In the uppermost was an assemblage of hunter's tools we might recognize immediately from the single projectile point. It is what Irwin-Williams calls "pseudo-fluted," a stemmed point with a pronounced basal thinning or grooving which must have served the same purpose as the flute and may have been only another way of producing the effect. It has been confirmed by William Mayer-Oakes, who made the first collection at El Inga, the Ecuadorian surface site, that this point accords typologically with the "fluted" stemmed points he found there, as bases only. These, it will be remembered, were compared typologically with the points found at Fell's Cave at the tip of South America; there they were on the order of ten to eleven thousand years old.

Under the pseudo-fluteds was an assemblage with another old friend, the bipoint of Lerma or Cascade pattern. As we already know, this simple but distinctive form has many relatives, including cousins at El Jobo, and it was probably made over a span of two to three millennia. It is certainly as old as any Clovis so far dated. Incidentally a pebble chopper was found with this age group of artifacts; it was embedded in the jawbone of a horse. Yes, there were flakes present; however, this time they were no longer random chips off the old block, but controlled "strip" blades, struck from prepared cores.

The upper two assemblages at Hueyatlaco are of mixed-blade and bifacially worked tools. The lowest assemblage is described thus by Irwin-Williams in her paper delivered at the Valsequillo field conference in Mexico City, November, 1968:

Artifacts of the older period at Hueyatlaco, which in places underlies an unconformity and more than a meter of archaeologically sterile deposits, lack bifacial tools. Like artifacts from the lower Valsequillo sites [Tecacaxco, El Mirador, El Horno, and Barranca Caulapan] they evidently express a different, less sophisticated method of working stone, which resulted in projectile points made on well executed blades and flakes. By applying percussion and pressure, these blades and flakes were shaped into useful tools by simple edge trimming. In short, these artifacts are significantly distinct from the bifacial tools found in the younger layers at Hueyatlaco.

The sites lower than Hueyatlaco yielded archaeological material technologically similar to the older part of Hueyatlaco material. Tecacaxco, in addition to some remains of the extinct fauna produced several flakes and blades, some retouched to make scrapers. A projectile point from El Mirador resembles those from the lower part of Hueyatlaco and was made on an edge-trimmed blade that retains a prepared striking platform. El Horno contained the remains of a butchered mastodon associated with scrapers, perforators and a possible projectile point, which together express the kind of technology represented by the other non-bifacial tool assemblages at Valsequillo, except that no blades were found.

The single find at Barranca Caulapan was an edge-trimmed flake scraper, but chronologically it is the pivotal find of the Valsequillo sequence. Conditions in the Valsequillo region are not favorable to the preservation of C14-datable material, but there were snail shells in association with the Caulapan scraper that tested 21,850 ± 850 years. "This association," Irwin-Williams says, "constitutes the only available *direct* evidence on the antiquity of man in the Valsequillo region."

But the indirect evidence is that the dated Barranca Caulapan deposit is of the same age as the gravels in which the El Horno complex was found; and this complex, typologically, correlates with the earliest Hueyatlaco, El Mirador, and Tecacaxco assemblages. Thus we have an horizon date for the Caulapan-El Horno flake-blade tradition of 21,000 B.P. And 21,000 B.P. was a time when Wisconsin III lay across Canada, absolutely interdicting any kind, even any thought, of intercontinental movement. People living in the Valsequillo region at that time must have had an ancestry reaching back for several thousand years. Irwin-Williams says, in summation of the exhaustive dating tests and geologic studies at Valsequillo, "Accordingly there is no archaeological reason why they [the flake-blade assemblages] should *not* be of considerably greater antiquity, quite possibly as early as the single 21,850 year old artifact from Caulapan, and possibly even as old as the 35,000 year date suggested from the sample [shells] at the base of the Caulapan section."

It is now incumbent on us to refer this data to the model we have set up of a stone-working basic industry of core and flake tools. Evolution of this industry could follow either of two directions of specialization: the refining of the core into more shapely tools, and self-training through experience in the production of blade-shaped flakes. Each specialization is a matter of emphasis and skills developed by practice: the former specialization resulted in the Andean Biface tradition, the latter in the El Horno tradition. By Lerma-Clovis times, in Mexico at least, the two traditions had learned something from each other, and bifacial projectile points were being made by the same hands that struck off unifacial blades for knives and other tools.

There is nothing surprising, nothing improbable, nothing pere-grine, in these natural developments—natural, that is, in the sense that they are in accord with the clastic characteristics of stone and the apprehending faculties of man. These are the lines along which stone work developed—and had to develop, wherever it did develop—and once we posit an early arrival in America of stone-working man, the rest follows: a primitive stone technology and the time to develop that technology to a high sophistication.

The future of American archaeology lies, therefore, in the exploration of those millennia, not so much lost as neglected, between the established projectile-point horizon of twelve thou-sand years ago and the thirty-five to forty thousand years ago of Valsequillo and Lewisville. If there is anything earlier in America that will substantiate the reality of the eighty-thou-sand-year-old pebbles and flakes of the Calico Mountains, it should turn up during this exploration. But it is of less urgent importance to find if man became American that early than if he became American early enough to have worked out the whole pattern of adjustment to America's multiplicity of envi-ronments for himself. And thirty-five thousand years is sufficient for that. An eighty-thousand-year-old American would present us with a quite different implication altogether: that man en-tered America not as *Homo sapiens sapiens* but as Neanderthal man. Only Leakey's unassailable reputation in human paleon-tology has prevented a storm from breaking out over the Calico Mountain report such as has battered George Carter for his Texas Street site, because an Amerind Neanderthal is more than either the archaeologists or the physical anthropologists can now find it in their hearts to accept.

Of all the loci of Early American finds we have discussed here, Valsequillo would seem to offer the likeliest field for sifting down into our pre-Clovisian past. The situations dis-covered by Irwin-Williams and Camacho are of kill and butch-ering incidents, camp sites only insofar as an Amerind band stayed by the kill to protect and eat from it until the carcass was stripped to the bone or the meat became too rank to con-sume. Even though the human population was very sparse, the few there were had to eat regularly, and over the millennia there were thousands of such incidents. One of Irwin-Williams's reports on Valsequillo was given at the seventh congress of the International Association for Quaternary Research (the conference that also produced the work on Beringia edited by Hopkins) before that section devoted to "Pleistocene Extinctions: The Search for a Cause." Several participants, Irwin-Williams being one, stressed the factor of hunting by man as one of the probable causes of big-game extinction, which is to say that man is considered to have done a great deal of hunting and that kill sites must be innumerable—if they can be found.

During the latter half of the Wisconsin, at least, the Valsequillo region abounded in big-game animals, the cynosure of carnivores of all kinds, the killers and the scavengers—and man was undoubtedly both. Not every site of man's dining would have been accompanied by imperishable artifacts, but one would think that most of them were: flake knives slip easily out of greasy fingers, and projectile points, deeply buried in the flesh of game, can be lost or forgotten. It is the attraction of Valsequillo that it provides the legible geologic contexts for the Wisconsin period, still in place, still holding *in situ* what was deposited in them, the bones of the slain game and anything else left at the scene. Where else would the probability be higher of finding what we most want to find?

A pint of artifacts for four seasons' digging hardly seems a fair return; but these artifacts are priceless and worth ten thousand arrowheads picked up from somebody's field after a plowing. The reader will not have failed to evaluate their rarity and meaning. Much earlier on, Gordon Willey's prescription for acceptance of pebble tools was quoted: "As things stand now, the 'pre-projectile point horizon' will not be demonstrated beyond reasonable doubt until a complex or assemblage of materials attributable to it are found stratigraphically beneath artifacts of the well-known 10,000 to 12,000 year old, bifacially-flaked lanceolate or leaf-shaped class. . . ." No, it was not a pebble-tool horizon beneath the leaf-shaped Lerma-like point in Hueyatlaco II; it was something completely unexpected: an industry of flake blades that are, Irwin-Williams says, "techno-

logically simple and typologically distinct from any other dated
archaeological materials in the New World." The prescription
now must read that pebble tools must be found stratigraphically
beneath *them*. Though the pebble-tool-making folk were very
probably not big-game hunters and there is no certainty that
they will be found where we find their occupational hunter
descendants, it is not improbable either: remember the pebble
chopper in the jawbone of a horse. If four more seasons of work
at Valsequillo produce only as much material, quantitatively
and qualitatively, as did those of 1962–66, our model will have
to be extensively revised by 1980, by which date the ancillary
studies will have been completed and we can see Valsequillo in
perspective as a whole environment.

In truth, whether, Valsequillo imposes the necessity or not,
there will have to be a new model or scheme of American prehistory for the 1980's and the 1990's and the 2000's. It has been
only one ten-thousandth dug; it is certainly, missing that much
data, less than half understood. It has provided surprises, even
rude shocks—partly because of the school of Hrdlicka, who
stood up so staunchly and held out so inflexibly for the wrong,
and partly because it is *sui generis*, and no arguments by
analogy from Old World prehistory serve to illuminate it. It
does not yield to easy interpretation by the naïve pouring of
Old World wine into New World bottles. Those who try to do
it do not seem to realize how near in attitude they are to
Ignatius Donnelly and the Mormon Joseph Smith, who made
an attempt to tie up some apparent loose ends in Europe with
what was at the time the inexplicable in America. We know
now that there were no such loose ends, but that example has
not prevented the similar assumption that there are loose ends
of cultural ties a little further back in time that even, as we
say in the navy, are bended together.

The major, and first, shock was the discovery of eleven-thou-
sand-year-old Folsom points in the ribs of extinct bison, rein-
forced soon after by the discovery of twelve-thousand-year-old
Clovis points in the backbone of a Columbian mammoth. Followed then Ritchie's recognition of the usufructian Archaic pattern, totally different from that of the big-game hunter, and

Coe's demonstration in the Carolina Piedmont, adumbrated by Broyles's work in West Virginia, that the Archaic begins at least as deep in time as the Clovis hunters. Meanwhile Hibben had found Sandia points, older than Clovis, and a half-dozen investigators have proved that the bipoint Cascade-Lerma-El Jobo tradition is the peer of Clovis in age. A bone-point tradition turned up with thirteen-thousand-year-old Marmes man; Irwin-Williams unearthed the twenty-one-thousand-year-old flake-blade tradition; and Lanning found a chopper-flake horizon beneath his Andean Biface. And beyond all this there hover in the background the pebble tools, of which at least two dozen occurrences are known and probably as many more await the day of professional amnesty to be published before the world. Our model has accounted for all these, but we have to face the fact that there will be more to come.

So it is not the end, by a long chalk; the last word has not been said, by several volumes. It has become standard to conclude reports that raise more questions than they answer with the trite and true "More work needs to be done." Decidedly more work needs to be done, both in the field and in the laboratory of the mind, with that invaluable but wholly imaginary tool the runcible spade, constructed on the design of the runcible spoon, half spoon and half fork, which, if properly used, uncovers the evidence and sifts it at the same time.

On Reading and
the Nature of Sources

INASMUCH AS THE references from which quotations have been excerpted or ideas and viewpoints adopted or otherwise used are noted in the text, the bibliography here appended is intended as a reader's guide. There are several approved scholarly methods of denoting references—none of which I have followed here, because I wanted to achieve the conversational tone of direct communication. When a speaker or lecturer quotes or brings into his talk material that requires attribution, he cannot do it by footnotes or parenthetical keys, but must introduce the momentary speaker by name and work viva voce, providing a relevant identification of him in the flow of discourse. The references in the present volume are detailed enough for the student to check or pursue in the furtherance of research, but their real purpose is to recognize originators or corroborators of ideas so that the reader may feel some confidence that what is argued has its basis in a fundament of respectable knowledge and opinion.

A complete and honest list of references for a book like this would include half a lifetime of reading, innumerable conferences attended, countless dialogues and debates engaged in, a great deal of correspondence, and a great many mentions that would appear to have no pertinence at all. I can do no better than to quote from the first chapter of Stuart Piggott's *Ancient Europe*, to show both the kind of influence that was at work in this book yet has no proper place in its bibliography, and the principle by which the reading list was drawn up:

It is perhaps worth reminding those who are not archaeologists that we are dealing with a discipline which is constantly and rapidly developing, which is dynamic and not static, and which constantly enforces on the research worker the necessity of keeping abreast of the new material or changed viewpoints circulating in conversation, correspondence or in publications, and of the assimiliation of these within the existing framework of knowledge. This is a situation familiar enough to those who work in scientific disciplines, but is perhaps less apparent to those in other fields of learning where the tempo of discovery is slower, and sources a generation or more old may still be valid documents. A recent review in a scientific journal stigmatized a new book as "middle-aged," on the grounds that certain chapters had been written two years previously: if we have not reached this alarming state of affairs in prehistory, a glance at the bibliography of this book will show how very few sources more than ten or fifteen years old have been included and will emphasize the dangers in wait for the non-specialist who inadvertently uses out-of-date material.

Yet this out-of-date material lies in the background of all of us over forty; and I do go back to the days of Ales Hrdlicka and his colleagues, from whose reign of error American prehistory is still trying to extricate itself. Because this book is an attempt to escape from Hrdlickanism and to cope with Neo-Hrdlickanism, its list of references should be full of Hrdlicka and the Neo-Hrdlickans to be full and precise. But that these would interest a reader, or even a student, I doubt sincerely. The bibliography is heuristic, encouraging the reader, as student, to do the reading and to inform himself from some of the sources I used. And he may very well come up with a quite different concept. For, while I have acknowledged the debts of which I am aware, even the most independent and self-willed declaration is based on some moment of second-sight reading or stopped-instant listening to someone wiser or better informed than oneself whom one has completely forgotten.

Because it is repeated all too often, one critical cliché of reviewers should be discussed: that a bibliography shows the book to have been written from secondary source material. It assumes a priori that all primary sources are good and secondary sources are bad, a proposition that hardly stands on its merit. Primary sources, which in archaeology would probably be defined as reports of site excavations and investigative field work by the immediate investigators, can be no better and are frequently worse than the capacities of the investigators. The material that falls fresh into an investigator's hands or within his observation can never be more than his idea of it, by reason of what he identifies and interprets it to be, despite the illusion, rife among archaeologists, that they are trained three-dimensional mirrors who reflect it exactly in its whole and unedited truth. Primary sources are actually first impressions as well as announcements of first discoveries; and, as time passes, knowledge increases, and the mind's eye begins to perceive perspectives, they begin to yellow around the edges and sometimes to soften in the middle. Their acceptance as immutable truth is only to perpetuate the errors of their inherent fallibility, and it is recommended that they be read alertly, with one eye searching for the dubious while the other absorbs the veritable. And damn me not as an iconoclast. I heard it from John Witthoft, already quoted in these pages, who at the time was Pennsylvania State Archaeologist. He wrote, in 1953, in an obscure review of an areal summary based on primary sources, "The original literature is unreliable, and one must go back to the relics and sites for reliable data."

At least one instance is known where an investigator suppressed important but awkward evidence in the compilation of a report on an early site, from no apparent motive of dishonesty but because he thought it did not signify. What signifies and what does not is exemplified by the initial report on the Modoc Rock Shelter, written at a time when excavation had reached levels of projectile-point types that were thought to be transitional from Paleo-hunter lanceolates to Archaic-period notched blades. Since the general trend of thought then was that the Paleo-hunter tradition did undergo transition both technologically and economically into the Archaic, the lesson of the Modoc Rock Shelter was seen to be a confirmation of that view. Any deeper excavation it was assumed could only bring to light an actual fluted point, if any type at all. But what deeper excavation revealed was a side-notched blade point, of what I have designated herein the Big Sandy pattern and far from Paleo-hunter.

Similarly, Paleo-hunter "transitional" types of points were found in lowest levels at Graham Cave and the Stanfield-Worley Rock Shelter: in the former, the "transitional" points were actually fluted lanceolates that appeared to be Clovises lapsing from the classic norm; in the latter the transitional types were the fluted but trianguloid Daltons. Yet, in the *same levels* were the Big Sandy-style side-notched Archaic-style blades. Readers of the reports of these two excavations would certainly come away with the impression that these notched blades are of trivial importance and that the site story is of a Paleo-Archaic transitional stage. It is a matter of emphasis, not data, and the emphasis is that of the excavator-reporter; but emphasis is bias, to which every investigator is entitled, as the man who did the dirty work. That is, he is entitled to full and respectful attention, since his emphasis or bias is the expression of his interpretation. What he is not entitled to is exemption from questioning and reinterpretation. If archaeological literature consisted of nothing more than a library of primary sources, the state of the art would have advanced very little in the past generation.

What the critics who use the term *secondary sources* so disdainfully actually mean by it, I am not at all sure from the way they use it. But secondary sources would have to include analyses and reevaluations, syntheses and reclassifications, summaries and surveys not done by prime investigators. Yet here is the heart of prehistory, which certifies it as a true member of the family of anthropology; here is where taxonomies are tested and hypotheses are advanced and those interpretations are made that give insight beyond the artifact into the lives of the people who made it. Such writing cannot be done, of course, without study of primary sources and the pertinent literature, but it is at one or several removes from the immediate apprehending experience of digging artifacts and handling them in the laboratory and of uncovering data and mapping or otherwise recording them on the spot. Except where I recount my own excavations, this book falls into the class of secondary treatment, and into its preparation went the examination of literally hundreds of primary sources and probably as many secondary sources.

Gordon Willey's *An Introduction to American Archaeology*, vol. 1, is a secondary source, as is most of Willey's work of the 1960's. He has written more than one survey and précis of American prehistory from several points of view—a very fine example is his "Historical Patterns and Evaluation in Native New World Cultures," from the symposium volume edited by Sol Tax, *The Evolution of Man: Mind, Culture and Society* (Chicago: University of Chicago Press, 1960), also appearing, slightly abridged, in *The North American Indians: A Sourcebook* (see Bibliography)—but I doubt that Willey, Bowditch Professor of Mexican and Central American Archaeology and Ethnology at Harvard University, would be on the "condemned list" of secondary sources. Nor would James B. Griffin, head of the Department of Anthropology, University of Michigan, who has been writing for the past twenty years on his specialities, the Hopewellian culture and the archaeology of the eastern United States—though the last primary source that I can find on which his name appears is *The Archaeological Survey of the Lower Mississippi Alluvial Valley 1940–1947* (1951), which is not about the eastern United States and only obliquely about Hopewell.

What makes a source secondary, as I have deduced it, is not its content or treatment, not its step-two synthesizing or summarizing or conceptualizing after step-one first-impression reporting, but the author—wherefore "secondary source" is actually to be understood as "second-rate" source, that is, work done by an unapproved author. And the unapproved author turns out to be, invariably, the "popular, non-academic writer by profession," to give him the dubbing administered by one recent reviewer. The right of the academic, profressional anthropologists to approve or disapprove the "popular, nonacademic writer

by profession" who turns to their researches for his material—
or the propriety of their doing so—will not be argued here
except to make this point: if the general objective of science
is to expand man's knowledge of himself and of his specific
and cosmic environment, then the popular, nonacademic writer
by profession has his function as an informer and educator. To
clarify by analogy, the actions and decisions that affect us all
are taken by heads of state and legislative bodies, but they
would not become public knowledge without newspapers and
the journalists who prepare the news so that the general reader
will understand not only what has happened but its impact.

Two books by nonacademic, professional writers in prehis-
tory-archaeology come to mind as performing this function so
well that they are actually original contributions: Macgowan's
Early Man in the New World and Silverberg's *Mound Builders
of Ancient America*. The late Kenneth Macgowan was a theater
critic, Broadway and Hollywood producer, and, for the last two
decades of his life, professor of theater arts at UCLA; yet his
Early Man, published by Macmillan in 1953 but written before
C14 dating began to affect the chronology of American prehistory, remains—in its original edition, rather than the post-C14,
slightly revised edition of 1962—a singular statement of the
field-theory problems in Early Man (American) research. Any
schedule of reading in American prehistory should begin with
it, as a kind of epistemological map of the area, with all landmarks clearly indicated. It is thoroughly documented but not
pedantic; it reads as easily for the beginner as Dick and Jane,
but by reason of clarity of style and organization, not coy con-
descension of language or expression to the assumed level of
the reader; and it is indispensable, for nobody had ever drawn
such a map before. And it need not be drawn again.

Silverberg's accomplishment is also unique. He has traced
with scholarly care the history of attitudes about America's
aboriginally constructed mounds among the science-oriented and
with the general public, for which they once held a romantic
fascination surprising to us today. These mounds are the single
instance where the prehistory of the present United States had
a patent effect on its cultural history. *Mound Builders of An-*

cient America is the only book on the shelf that deals with this effect fully. It belongs in any reasonably well stocked library on American prehistory.

But to continue thus is to strain the fragile wings of patience. A piece of writing is not justified by its author or by its species: it justifies itself by being honest, at the least, and beyond that, informative, contributory, provocative, or, best of all, illuminating. What I have compiled here is a list of books and pieces of writing of various lengths which the reader may consult to expand his knowledge of topics that he feels stimulated to examine in greater depth, to corroborate or to find evidence for rejecting my frank view—all of them with the first requisite of being earnest jobs of work, and several having something beyond to contribute. Some of the books are the published papers of symposia and miscellanies of essays, which have the merit of introducing the reader to more subjects than he bargained for when he resorted to the titles and of conciseness in presenting various aspects of archaeology and its problems. Delivered papers or essay-length pieces are invariably better statements of problems and positions than books or monographs: because of the necessity of compression imposed by the form itself, the writer has only a few minutes or a few pages to say what he has to say, convincingly and decisively.

Bibliography

A Note on Periodicals

THE OFFICIAL JOURNAL of the Society for American Archaeology, of which most professional scholars and most serious nonprofessionals in American prehistory are members, is *American Antiquity*, a quarterly journal printed by the University of Utah Press, Salt Lake City. The society has an open-membership policy, and the beginner need not hesitate to apply for membership to the secretary—who, unfortunately, changes biennially with the slate of officers. Fewer and fewer site reports have been appearing in the past few years, the editors now favoring specialized studies. It is unaccountably weak on the archaeology of the eastern United States—from the Mississippi to the Atlantic and from Florida to Maine—having missed most of what is important in that section for the past decade; but it has been increasing its coverage of work being done in South America for English-language readers. Its book reviews, while often up to two years late, will keep the reader abreast of the relevant literature, except for the mounting abundance now beginning to appear in the journals of regional state archaeological societies such as the New York State Archaeological Association *Bulletin* (of which I have been editor for ten years) and the highly regarded *Pennsylvania Archaeologist* of the Society for Pennsylvania Archaeology. Most of the reports of the dirt archaeologists are now to be found in these journals, usually edited by professionals, and in more ambitious site reports published as monographs by university presses.

Perhaps the best reports on current work in American archaeology are those that appear sporadically as main articles in *Science*, the weekly publication of the American Association for the Advancement of Science; since *Science* covers all fields, other articles of interest to American archaeologists, such as one on bristlecone pines, may turn up at any time. The department of "Reports" frequently includes short summaries of the results of specific investigation projects of immediate importance. The book reviews appear, as in *American Antiquity*, too long after publication and are of uneven quality, being not always reliable by reason of the bias of the reviewer, who is either too good a friend or too open an enemy of the author of the book or its school of thought. But the listing in *Science* of titles of books published is exhaustive and up to the minute.

The articles on American archaeology in *Scientific American* are excellent, always important, and, being pitched to the general reader in science, are free of those trade terms—unless they are explained—which are acceptable in *Science* writing. Articles on matters of high auxiliary interest to archaeologists—Fairbridge's best exposition of his sea-level-fluctuation hypothesis, for instance, appeared there—are published but on no predictable schedule.

The *National Geographic*, though the slant of the writing is for the doctor's-waiting-room reader, is an important source of archaeological material, because the National Geographic Society's sponsorship of important projects such as Leakey's excavations at Olduvai Gorge gives it exclusive rights to the American publication of those projects. The authorship is always authoritative, but the objective is to entertain rather than inform.

The titles under the following topics are listed in the suggested order of reading.

GENERAL

Kenneth Macgowan. *Early Man in the New World*. New York: Macmillan Co., 1953. Rev. ed., Macgowan and Joseph J. Hester, Jr. New York: Doubleday Anchor Book, 1962.

Gordon R. Willey. *An Introduction to American Archaeology*, vol. 1, *North and Middle America*. Englewood Cliffs, N.J.: Prentice-Hall, 1966. The map series is incomparable.

Harold E. Driver. *Indians of North America*. Chicago: University of Chicago Press, 1961.

Jesse D. Jennings and Edward Norbeck, eds. *Prehistoric Man in the New World*. Chicago: University of Chicago Press, 1964. A symposium, with each geographic-culture area covered by a different specialist.

Robert F. Spencer, et al. *The Native Americans: Prehistory and Ethnology of the North American Indians*. New York: Harper & Row, 1965. Prepared as a college textbook.

Roger C. Owen, James J. F. Deetz, and Anthony D. Fisher, eds. *The North American Indians: A Source Book*. New York: Macmillan Co., 1967. Also prepared as a college text, but in no way a duplication of the above.

Leo Deuel. *Conquistadores without Swords: Archaeologists in the Americas*. New York: St Martin's Press, 1968. Important or merely interesting discoveries told by the discoverers, with explanatory text placing the discoveries in their proper context of prehistory.

Gordon R. Willey and Philip Phillips. *Method and Theory in American Archaeology*. Chicago: University of Chicago Press, 1958.

Harold E. Driver and William C. Massey. *Comparative Studies of North American Indians. Transactions of the American Philosophical Society*, vol. 47, pt. 2, Philadelphia, 1957.

THE PALEO-HUNTERS

Frank C. Hibben. *The Lost Americans*. Rev. ed. New York: Thomas Y. Crowell Co., 1968. (Hibben discovered Sandia points.)

Chester A. Chard. "*New World Origins*. A Reappraisal." *Antiquity* 33 (1959).

H. M. Wormington. *Ancient Man in North America*. 4th ed. Denver: Denver Museum of Natural History, 1957.

Alan L. Bryan. *Paleo-Indian Prehistory*. Occasional Papers of the Idaho State University Museum. Pocatello, 1965.

Ronald J. Mason. "The Paleo-Indian Tradition in Eastern North America." *Current Anthropology* 3 (1962), no. 3.

Richard S. MacNeish. *Preliminary Archaeological Investigations in the Sierra de Tamaulipas. Transactions of the American Philosophical Society*, vol. 48. Philadelphia, 1958.
"Early Man in the Western American Arctic: A Symposium." *Anthropological Papers of the University of Alaska*, vol. 10, no. 2. College, Alaska, 1963.
B. Robert Butler. *The Old Cordilleran Culture in the Pacific Northwest*. Occasional Papers of the Idaho State College Museum. Pocatello, 1961.
Robert E. Funk, Thomas B. Weinman, and Paul L. Weinman. "The Kings Road Site: A Recently Discovered Paleo-Indian Manifestation in Greene Co., New York." *Bulletin of the New York State Archaeological Association* 45 (1969): 1–23.

PRIMORDIAL MAN

L. S. B. Leakey and Des Bartlett. "Finding the World's Earliest Man." *National Geographic*, September, 1960, pp. 420–35.
L. S. B. Leakey and Robert F. Sisson, "Exploring 1,750,000 Years into Man's Past." *National Geographic*, October, 1961, pp. 564–92.
Raymond A. Dart with Dennis Craig. *Adventures with the Missing Link*. New York: Harper & Bros., 1959.
Kenneth Oakley. *Frameworks for Dating Fossil Man*. Chicago: Aldine Publishing Co., 1964.
Carleton S. Coon. *The Origin of Races*. New York: Alfred A. Knopf, 1962.
F. Clark Howell. "The Villafranchian and Human Origins." In Joseph R. Caldwell, ed., *New Roads to Yesterday: Essays in Archaeology*. New York: Basic Books, 1966. The volume is a compilation of articles on Old and New World archaeology from *Science*.
L. S. B. Leakey. "The Origin of Genus Homo." In Sol Tax, ed., *The Evolution of Man: Mind, Culture and Society*. Chicago: University of Chicago Press, 1960.
Cesare Emiliani. "Dating Human Evolution." In Sol Tax, ed., *The Evolution of Man: Mind, Culture and Society*. Chicago: University of Chicago Press, 1960. This outlines Emiliani's "short count" of the Pleistocene.
Alan H. Brodrick. *Man and His Ancestry*. London: Hutchinson & Co., 1960; rev. ed., 1964. Reprint ed., New York: Fawcett World Library, 1964.
Marcellin Boule and Henri V. Vallois. *Fossil Men*. New York: Dryden Press, 1957.
Jacquetta Hawkes and Sir Leonard Woolley. *The History of Mankind*, vol. 1, *Prehistory and the Beginnings of Civilization*. New York: Harper & Row, 1963.

BERINGIA

D. M. Hopkins, ed. *The Bering Land Bridge*. Stanford: Stanford University Press, 1967.

THE PLEISTOCENE

(The chronology and glacial events of the Pleistocene are undergoing a restructuring with no consensus as yet on whether there were four major glacial episodes or more and whether the Pleistocene proper was two or three or four million years in duration.)

David B. Ericson and Goesta Wollin. "Pleistocene Climates and Chronology in Deep-Sea Sediments." *Science*, December 3, 1968, pp. 1227–1234. A four-glacier, two-million-year-long model is argued for, based on reversal of magnetism and other evidence in deep-sea cores.

F. Clark Howell. "The Villafranchian and Human Origins." (See Howell above under "Primordial Man.") A two-to-three-million-year Pleistocene of five glaciations is sketched.

(The study of the Late Wisconsin, on which so much of the theory of human migration into America depends, is also entering a new state of uncertainty. As it is now understood it is expressed in the following.)

Jack L. Hough. *Geology of the Great Lakes*. Urbana: University of Illinois Press, 1958.

Terah L. Smiley, ed. *Geochronology: With Special Reference to the Southwestern United States*. Tucson: University of Arizona Press, 1955. A symposium of eleven papers on climate, pollen analysis, and dating of nonglaciated areas.

THE PEBBLE-TOOL ERA

Alex D. Kreiger. "Early Man in the New World." In Jesse D. Jennings and Edward Norbeck, eds., *Prehistoric Man in the New World*. Chicago: University of Chicago Press, 1964.

Edward P. Lanning and Thomas C. Patterson. "Early Man in South America." *Scientific American*, November, 1967, pp. 44–50.

Mark R. Harrington and Ruth D. Simpson. *Tule Springs, Nevada, with Other Evidences of Pleistocene Man in North America*. Southwest Museum Papers, no. 18. Los Angeles, 1961.

George F. Carter. "On Pebble Tools and Their Relatives in North America." *Anthropological Journal of Canada*, Quarterly Bulletin of the Anthropological Association of Canada 4, no. 4 (1966): 10–19.

Matthew Lively. "The Lively Complex: Preliminary Report on a Pebble Tool Complex in Alabama." Privately printed. Birmingham, Ala., 1965. Formal publication planned by the American Philosophical Society.

Daniel W. Josselyn. "The Lively Complex: Discussion of Some of the ABC's of the Technology." Privately printed. Birmingham, Ala., 1965. Formal publication planned by the American Philosophical Society.

George F. Carter. "Man in America: A Criticism of Scientific Thought." *Scientific Monthly* (now combined with *Science*) 73 (1951), no. 5.

E. B. Sayles and Ernest Antevs. *The Cochise Culture.* Medallion Papers, no. 29, Gila Pueblo, Globe, Ariz., 1941.

Arthur J. Jelinek. "An Artifact of Possible Wisconsin Age." *American Antiquity*, January, 1966, pp. 434–35

Patrick C. Munson and John C. Frye. "Artifact from Deposits of Mid-Wisconsin Age in Illinois." *Science*, Dec. 24, 1965, pp. 1722–23.

THE ARCHAIC

Douglas S. Byers. "An Introduction to Five Papers on the Archaic Stage." *American Antiquity*, January, 1959, pp. 229–32.

———. "The Eastern Archaic: Some Problems and Hypotheses." *American Antiquity*, Jan., 1959, pp. 233–56

Melvin L. Fowler. *Summary Report of Modoc Rock Shelter, 1952, 1953, 1955, 1956.* Springfield: Illinois State Museum, 1959.

Joffre L. Coe. *Formative Cultures of the Carolina Piedmont. Transactions of the American Philosophical Society*, vol 54. Philadelphia, 1964.

Jesse D. Jennings. "Danger Cave." *Memoirs of the Society for American Archaeology.* Salt Lake City: University of Utah Press, 1957.

William S. Webb and David L. DeJarnette. "An Archaeological Survey of Pickwick Basin in the Adjacent Portions of the States of Alabama, Mississippi and Tennessee." Bureau of American Ethnology Bulletin no. 129. Washington, D. C.: Government Printing Office, 1940.

William A. Ritchie. "The Lamoka Lake Site, The Type Station of the Archaic Algonkin Period in New York." In *Researches and Transactions of the New York State Archaeological Association*, vol. 7, no. 4. Rochester, 1932.

PROJECTILE-POINT CATALOGUES

H. M. Wormington. *Ancient Man in North America.* 4th ed. Denver: Denver Museum of Natural History, 1957.

Dee Ann Suhm and Alex D. Krieger. *An Introductory Handbook of*

Texas Archaeology. Bulletin of the Texas Archaeological Society, vol. 25. Austin, 1954.

Robert E. Bell. *Guide to the Identification of Certain American Indian Projectile Points*. Norman: Oklahoma Anthropological Society, 1958.

James W. Cambron and David Hulse. *Handbook of Alabama Archaeology*, part 1, *Point Types*. University, Ala.: Archaeological Research Association of Alabama, 1964.

William A. Ritchie. *A Typology and Nomenclature for New York Projectile Points*. New York State Museum and Science Service Bulletin 384. Albany, 1961.

CORN

Paul C. Mangelsdorf, Richard S. MacNeish, and Walton C. Galinat. "Domestication of Corn." In Joseph R. Caldwell, ed., *New Roads to Yesterday*. New York: Basic Books, 1966.

Mary Elting and Michael Folsom. *The Mysterious Grain: Science in Search of the Origin of Corn*. Philadelphia and New York: J. B. Lippincott Co., 1967. Written for juveniles but meticulously researched.

Richard S. MacNeish. *The First Annual Report of the Tehuacán Archaeological-Botanical Project, 1961*. Andover, Mass.: Peabody Foundation for Archaeology, 1961.

———. *The Second Annual Report of the Tehuacán Archaeological-Botanical Project, 1962*. Andover, Mass.: Peabody Foundation for Archaeology, 1964.

Paul Weatherwax. *Indian Corn in Old America*. New York: Macmillan Co., 1954. The corn problem before the MacNeish-Mangelsdorf solution.

MOUNDS

Robert Silverberg. *Mound Builders of Ancient America, the Archaeology of a Myth*. Greenwich, Conn.: New York Graphic Society, 1968.

Charles R. Wicks. "Pyramids and Temple Mounds: Mesoamerican Ceremonial Architecture in Eastern North America." *American Antiquity*, April, 1965, pp. 409–20.

Don W. Dragoo. *Mounds for the Dead: An Analysis of the Adena Culture*. Carnegie Museum Annals. Pittsburgh, 1963.

James A. Ford. "The Puzzle of Poverty Point." *Natural History*, November, 1955, pp. 466–72.

Clarence H. Webb. "The Extent and Content of Poverty Point Culture." *American Antiquity*, July, 1968, pp. 297–321.

Henry C. Shetrone. *The Mound Builders*. Port Washington, N. Y.:

Kennikat Press, 1964. A reissue without revision of the original edition (New York: D. Appleton, 1930) on Ohio Hopewell.

William S. Webb and Charles E. Snow. *The Adena People*. Reports in Anthropology and Archaeology. Lexington: University of Kentucky Press, 1945.

William S. Webb and Raymond S. Baby. *The Adena People: No. 2*. Columbus: Ohio State Historical Society, Ohio State University Press, 1957.

Thorne Devel, ed. *Hopewellian Communities in Illinois*. Scientific Papers of Illinois State Museum. Springfield, 1952.

Joseph R. Caldwell and Russell L. Hall, eds. *Hopewellian Studies*. Scientific Papers of Illinois State Museum. Springfield, 1964.

James A. Ford, Philip Phillips, and William G. Haag. *The Jaketown Site in West-Central Mississippi*. Anthropological Papers of the American Museum of Natural History, vol. 45. New York, 1955.

MISCELLANEOUS TECHNOLOGY

Willard F. Libby. *Radiocarbon Dating*. 2d ed. Chicago: University of Chicago Press, 1955.

H. A. Polack and J. Golson. *Collection of Specimens for Radiocarbon Dating and Interpretation of Results*. Canberra: Australian Institute of Aboriginal Studies, 1966.

Minze Stuiver and Hans Suess. "On the Relationship Between Radiocarbon Dates and True Sample Ages." *Radiocarbon* 8 (1966).

Robert F. Heizer and Sherburne F. Cook, eds. *The Application of Quantitative Methods in Archaeology*. Chicago: Quadrangle Books, 1960.

Robert F. Heizer, ed. *A Guide to Archaeological Field Methods*. 3d ed. rev. Palo Alto: National Press, 1958.

Maurice Robbins with Mary B. Irving. *The Amateur Archaeologist's Handbook*. New York: Thomas Y. Crowell Co., 1965.

DISAGREEMENT AMONG AUTHORITIES

Marvin Harris. *The Rise of Anthropological Theory: A History of Theories of Culture*. New York: Thomas Y. Crowell Co., 1968.

Index